Jetzt mit barrierefreiem Farbkonzept
Mehr Informationen auf *cornelsen.de/bf*

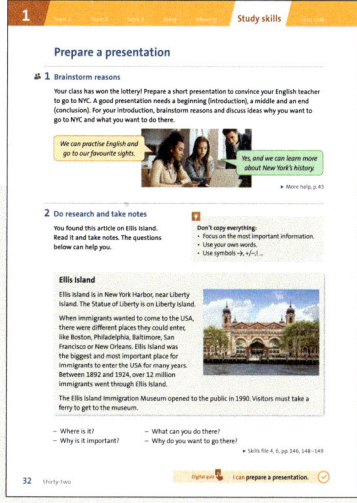

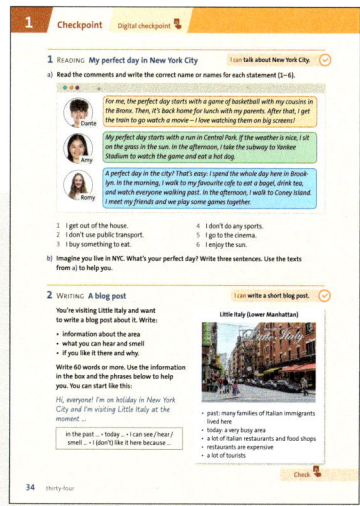

Lern- und Arbeitstechniken

Auf der *Study skills*-Seite übst du wichtige Lern- und Arbeitstechniken, z. B. wie du recherchierst und Notizen erstellen kannst.

Eine Aufgabe am Unit-Ende

In der *Unit task* erstellst du ein größeres Produkt, z. B. eine Präsentation. Dabei wendest du das Gelernte aus der Unit an.

Im *Checkpoint* wiederholst du

Hier überprüfst du, wie gut du die Lernziele der Unit schon erreicht hast.

Im Anschluss findest du ein *Text file* mit interessanten Texten zum Thema der Unit.

Diese Verweise führen dich in die *Diff bank* am Ende der Unit

► More help	► Parallel exercise	► More practice
Hilfen zu den Aufgaben	einfachere Variante einer Übung	weitere Übungen

Diese Lernangebote findest du im hinteren Teil des Buches

► Skills file	► Language file	► Wordbank
eine Übersicht über die Lern- und Arbeitstechniken	die wichtigsten Sprachregeln	zusätzliche Wörter zu bestimmten Themen

Let's talk	Vocabulary	Dictionary
Redewendungen nach wichtigen Themen und Situationen geordnet	eine Liste der neuen Vokabeln einer Unit mit hilfreichen Tipps	eine alphabetische Wörterliste zum Nachschlagen (Englisch – Deutsch)

lighthouse BASIC 4

Im Auftrag des Verlages herausgegeben von
Ulrike Rath, Aachen
sowie
Martin Bastkowski, Schellerten;
Sonja Mahne, Basel;
Berit Schaarschmidt, Aschaffenburg

Erarbeitet von
Olivia Wintgens, Würselen; Rebecca Robb Benne,
Kopenhagen; Zoe Thorne, Royston;
Jennifer O'Hagan, Bristol *(Checkpoints)*;
Ulrike Rath, Aachen *(Skills file)*;
Hartmut Tschepe *(Language file)*
und Ursula Fleischhauer, Hannover *(Vocabulary)*

In Zusammenarbeit mit der Englischredaktion
Klaus Unger (Projektleitung),
Kathrin Spiegelberg und Franziska Gräbe (koordinie-
rende Redakteurinnen), sowie Chiara Castellano,
Sandhya Gupta, Chelsea Ledvinka-Heß, Mara Leibowitz,
Elizabeth Pancake-Steeg, Julian Theo Wacker,
Karin Wedepohl
und Ingrid Raspe, Düsseldorf *(Vocabulary, Dictionary)*

Beratende Mitwirkung
Sabine Bay, Cloppenburg; Armin Düpmeier,
Warendorf; Lina Hein-Gehrmann, Wuppertal; Daniel
Henn, Frankfurt/Main; Tobias Pfeifer, Dossenheim
sowie
Prof. Dr. Christian Ludwig, Berlin;
Prof. Dr. Michaela Sambanis, Berlin

Illustrationen
Harald Ardeias, Schelklingen; Irina Zinner, Hamburg

Fotos
Chocolate Films, London
(Amy und Dante in Unit 1 und Tiana in Unit 4)

Umschlaggestaltung
Rosendahl, Berlin

Layoutkonzept
Klein & Halm, Berlin

Layout und technische Umsetzung
zweiband, Berlin

Druck
Mohn Media Mohndruck, Gütersloh

PEFC zertifiziert
Dieses Produkt stammt aus nachhaltig
bewirtschafteten Wäldern und kontrollierten
Quellen.
www.pefc.de
PEFC/04-31-1033

www.cornelsen.de

Soweit in diesem Lehrwerk Personen fotografisch abgebildet sind und ihnen von der Redaktion fiktive Namen, Berufe, Dialoge und Ähnliches zugeordnet oder diese Personen in bestimmte Kontexte gesetzt werden, dienen diese Zuordnungen und Darstellungen ausschließlich der Veranschaulichung und dem besseren Verständnis des Buchinhaltes.

Dieses Werk berücksichtigt die Regeln der reformierten Rechtschreibung und Zeichensetzung.

Die Webseiten Dritter, deren Internetadressen in diesem Lehrwerk angegeben sind, wurden vor Drucklegung sorgfältig geprüft. Der Verlag übernimmt keine Gewähr für die Aktualität und den Inhalt dieser Seiten oder solcher, die mit ihnen verlinkt sind.

Die *Cornelsen Lernen App* ist eine fakultative Ergänzung *zu Lighthouse*, die die inhaltliche Arbeit begleitet und unterstützt. Als solche unterliegt sie nicht der Genehmigungspflicht.

Alle Drucke dieser Auflage sind inhaltlich unverändert und können im Unterricht nebeneinander verwendet werden.

© 2025 Cornelsen Verlag GmbH,
Mecklenburgische Str. 53, 14197 Berlin,
E-Mail: service@cornelsen.de

1. Auflage, 1. Druck 2025
ISBN 9783060366958 broschiert

1. Auflage, 1. Druck 2025
ISBN 9783060366965 gebunden

Produktnummer 1100031746 E-Book

BASIC

lighthouse 4

Cornelsen

Unit 2
The South-East:
Changing times

L Listening · **R** Reading · **S** Speaking · **W** Writing · **M** Mediation · **V** Viewing · **IC** Intercultural competence · **MK** Medienkompetenz · **LS** Life skills · **GG** Global goals · **Voc** Vocabulary · **G** Grammar

Unit 5 OPTIONAL
Canada:
The northern neighbour

L Listening · R Reading · S Speaking · W Writing · M Mediation · V Viewing · IC Intercultural competence · MK Medienkompetenz · LS Life skills · GG Global goals · Voc Vocabulary · G Grammar

Anhang

Die Angebote des Schulbuchs sind nicht obligatorisch abzuarbeiten. Die Auswahl der Übungen und Übungsteile richtet sich nach den Schwerpunkten des schulinternen Curriculums.

Welcome to the USA

Alaska

Washington

Montana

Oregon

Idaho

Wyoming

Nevada

Utah

Colorado

California

Arizona

New Mexico

Hawaii

HOLLYWOOD

1 SPEAKING A beautiful country

a) **Look at the map and the photos and answer the questions.**

1 Where can you see alligators?
  – In Florida!
2 Where can you go surfing?
3 Which state has lots of snow?

4 Where are lots of tall skyscrapers?
5 Which state is important for films?
6 Where can you find cowboys?

b) **Choose one of the photos. Describe it to your partner.**

The photo of ... shows ...
In the foreground/middle/background you can see ...

▶ Skills file 7, p. 150

2 LISTENING & SPEAKING Which state?

a) Copy the table. Write the names of the six states in the photos. Listen and write one fact for each state.

b) Listen again. Can you add more facts?
Then compare with a partner.

c) Choose a state. Don't say the name! Describe it. You can use your facts from the table in a). Everyone else guesses which state it is.

A: My state has beaches   →   B: Is it California?   →   A: Yes, it is!
and really big cities.

States	Facts
Alaska	· isn't connected to the rest of country
New York	
__	...

▶ Workbook, pp. 6–7

A quiz about the USA

1 How many states are there in the USA?

A 40 B 50 C 60

2 What's the capital of the USA?

A Washington, DC
B New York City
C Los Angeles

3 Who is the leader of the USA?

A the prime minister   B the king
C the president

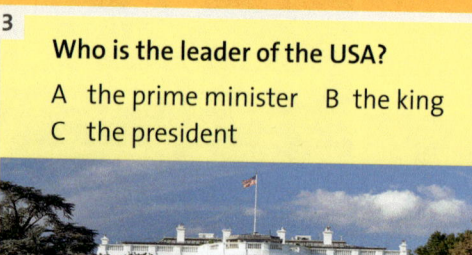

4 Which of these is NOT a type of American money?

A pound
B dollar
C cent

👥 **1** READING **What do you already know about the USA?**

a) Do the quiz and find out!

b) Check your answers at the bottom of the page.

1B · 2A · 3C · 4A · 5B · 6C · 7B · 8C · 9A · 10C

8–10 points: Great! You know a lot about the USA!
4–7 points: Well done! Are you ready to learn more?
0–3 points: Try again after you've finished this unit. You'll know much more 😊

5 The USA is how many times larger than Germany?

A 4 times
B 28 times
C 50 times

6 If it is 6 o'clock in New York, what time is it in Los Angeles? The map of the USA at the back of the book can help you.

A 5 o'clock
B 4 o'clock
C 3 o'clock

7 What are the stars on the American flag a symbol of?

A the stars of Hollywood
B the number of states
C the stars at night

8 How many people live in the USA?

A 100 million
B 200 million
C over 340 million

9 Which two states aren't connected to the rest of the USA? Look at the map on pages 10/11 for help.

A Alaska and Hawaii
B Rhode Island and Hawaii
C Alaska and Rhode Island

10 What are sweets called in the USA?

A chocolate
B dessert
C candy

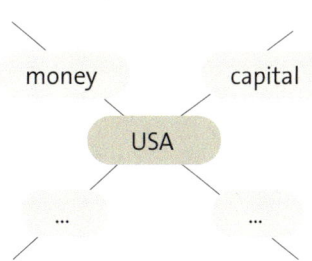

2 WORDS USA mind map

a) Start a mind map about the USA. Scan the quiz and write the information into your mind map.

b) What else do you know about the USA? Add more information, for example: American sports, famous people, famous sights, …

c) Compare your mind map with a partner.

money   capital

USA

…   …

▶ Workbook, pp. 7–8

At summer camp in the USA

Students from all over the USA spend their summer at the

Lakeview Adventure Camp!

Name	Amy Wu
Age	14
From	New York City, New York
Interests	sports, my blog, photography
Why I'm at the camp	I live in a city, but I love being outdoors and I want to try some new sports.

Name	Troy Freeman
Age	14
From	New Orleans, Louisiana
Interests	listening to music, band, reading
Why I'm at the camp	I'm here with my older sister. I want to learn new skills and spend more time in nature.

1 READING Meet the campers

a) BEFORE YOU READ **Read the box. Would you like to go to summer camp? Why or why not?**

b) **Read the profiles on pages 14–15. Find the places where the teenagers are from on the map of the USA at the back of the book.**

c) **Read the profiles again. Say what the teenagers are hoping to do at the camp.**

d) **Tell your partner which teenager you'd like to meet and why.**

I'd like to meet ... because we both like ...

Good to know

Lots of kids and teens go away to summer camp. There they can do different outdoor activities and arts and crafts. Young people can go to camp for one week, two weeks, ... – or even the whole summer (eight weeks). Camp counsellors look after the campers.

Name	Diego Perez
Age	14
From	Fredericksburg, Texas
Interests	robots, working for the school magazine, video games
Why I'm at the camp	I'm not a very good swimmer, but I want to do something outdoors. I also really like sitting around the fire at night.

Name	Tiana Moore
Age	15
From	Eureka, California
Interests	arts and crafts, music, dance
Why I'm at the camp	I can't wait to make some new friends from different parts of the USA. I'm interested in creative activities.

2 LISTENING & SPEAKING Camp activities

a) Copy the table. Listen to a camp counsellor. Write down as many different activities as you can for each column.

b) Listen again and add more to your table. Ask your partner: What activities do you have? Tell each other.

c) Decide on the best activities for you. Tell your partner.

Water sports	Other sports	Arts and crafts	Music
catch fish	...	...	...
...	...	...	
...	...		

> I'd like to do/go/play/try …

▶ Workbook, p. 9

Digital quiz **I can** talk about the USA. ✓

Unit 1
NYC: The world in a city

1 VIEWING Annalise's New York City

a) BEFORE YOU WATCH **What can you see in the pictures? Tell a partner.**   ▶ Skills file 7, p. 150

Picture A shows ... I can see ...

b) **Watch the video and match the pictures (A–F) to the places (1–6).**

> 1 Times Square • 2 the Statue of Liberty • 3 Union Square •
> 4 Washington Square Park • 5 the West Village • 6 Koreatown

c) **Watch again and check your answers from b). Which two places does Annalise think are for tourists?**

Nach dieser Unit kann ich ...

- über die Stadt New York sprechen
- einen kurzen Blogpost schreiben
- amerikanisches und britisches Englisch unterscheiden
- über Vielfalt in New York City sprechen
- um Hilfe bitten und Hilfe anbieten
- einen Text über Armut und Träume verstehen

Unit task

- eine kurze Präsentation über NYC vorbereiten und halten

2 Things to do in NYC

a) What does Annalise say that you can do in New York City? Tell a partner.

| You can | go to • watch • listen to • meet friends for • ... | a farmers' market • bakeries • restaurants • basketball games • movies • street musicians • pizza • ice cream • ... |

b) Agree on three things to do with your partner. Tell the class.

I'd like to ...

Well, I'd prefer to ...

OK, let's ...

► More practice 1, p. 40

► Workbook, p. 10

Digital quiz 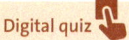   **I can** talk about New York City.

Out and about in NYC

1 LISTENING Amy, Dante and Romy

a) BEFORE YOU LISTEN Romy is an exchange student from Germany. Do you remember what an exchange is? What is good or bad about an exchange?

> different language • different food • fun • new friends • new places • scary • travel • …

b) Listen and answer the questions.

1 Who is Romy staying with?
2 Who has a cool accent?
3 Have Amy or Dante ever been on an exchange before?
4 What does Romy do when she is homesick?
5 What does Romy think of New York City?

Amy   Dante   Romy

c) Listen again. What are Amy, Dante and Romy going to do today? Why?

They're going to … because …

One World Trade Center and the 9/11 Memorial

Times Square

Central Park

The Staten Island Ferry and the Statue of Liberty

▶ English numbers, p. 253 ▶ More practice 2, p. 41

2 READING Amy's blog post

a) BEFORE YOU READ **Do you remember where Romy, Amy and Dante went? Read the title and look at the picture. From where did Amy take the photo?**

b) **Read and find out:**

1 Who gave the Statue of Liberty to the USA?
2 How long does the trip take?
3 Where do you need to stand for the best photo?

●●●   +   https://www.example.com/AmysNYCBlog

Secret tips from a New York City local: the Staten Island Ferry

NYC is awesome, but it can also be very expensive! Are you planning a visit? Keep reading for a secret tip.

The Statue of Liberty was a gift from France in 1886. For many years, millions of immigrants came to the USA by boat, and the statue was the first thing that they saw. It's an important symbol of freedom to many Americans.

Do you want the cheapest view of the Statue of Liberty? Take the Staten Island Ferry – it's free! The trip takes about 25 minutes. Make sure that you stand on the right side of the boat on your way there for the best photo. To return to Manhattan, just get on the ferry again for the free ferry ride back.

Did you like my post? Leave a comment below!

Spicy_Potato ~ Amazing photo, Amy!

RapFriend56 ~ Thanks for the info – I didn't know that the ferry is FREE 😊

My task

3 WRITING A blog post   ▶ Digital help ⤵

a) **First choose what you are going to write about in your blog post: your favourite place, sight or city? Make notes.**

the best food • the coolest building • the most interesting museum • the most beautiful view • the cheapest transport

b) **Now write your blog post. The blue phrases in Amy's post and the ideas in the boxes can help you.**
▶ Skills file 12, p. 155

• This city / sight / place is ...
• You should go to ... / ask for ...
• Take the ... / To return, just ...
• It costs ... euros / takes ... minutes

c) GALLERY WALK **Walk around and look at the posts. Write comments on sticky notes.**

▶ Workbook, pp. 11–12

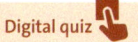 Digital quiz ⤵   **I can** write a short blog post.

NYC: A diverse city

1 LISTENING **After school**

a) BEFORE YOU LISTEN **What was the first thing that millions of immigrants to the USA saw?**

b) **Romy, Amy and Dante are talking after school. Listen and answer the questions.**

1   Who is Spicy_Potato?
2   Why is New York City so diverse?
3   What does Dante want to show Romy and Amy?
4   When did Dante's family come to the USA?
5   When did Amy's family come to the USA?
6   Who are they going to meet?

▶ Parallel exercise, p. 42

c) **Listen again and check.**

2 **Working with a chart**

Look at the chart and answer the questions.

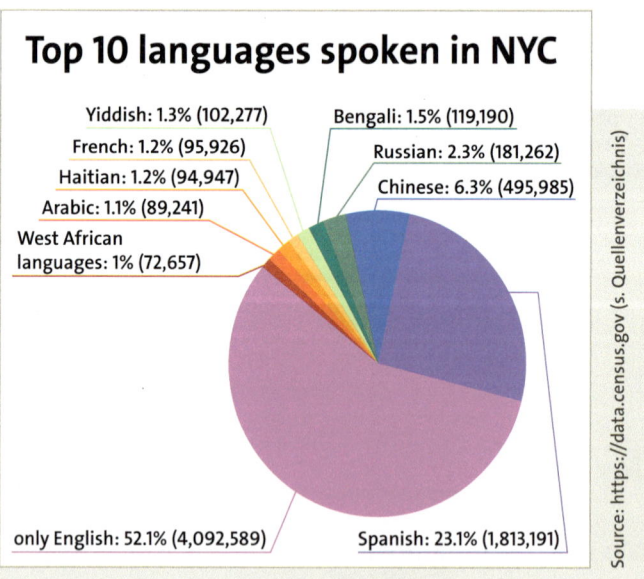

Top 10 languages spoken in NYC

Yiddish: 1.3% (102,277)
French: 1.2% (95,926)
Haitian: 1.2% (94,947)
Arabic: 1.1% (89,241)
West African languages: 1% (72,657)
Bengali: 1.5% (119,190)
Russian: 2.3% (181,262)
Chinese: 6.3% (495,985)
only English: 52.1% (4,092,589)
Spanish: 23.1% (1,813,191)

Source: https://data.census.gov (s. Quellenverzeichnis)

New York City is one of the most diverse places in the world. This chart shows the top 10 languages that New Yorkers speak.

1   What per cent of New Yorkers speak only English?
2   After English, what are the top three languages?
3   What per cent of New Yorkers speak these three languages? Say the per cent for each language separately.

▶ Wordbank 5, p. 184   ▶ Skills file 8, p. 151

Good to know

In English, we don't say:
56 ~~comma~~ 7%.
We say: 56 **point** 7%.

We write very large numbers:
fifty-six thousand = 56,000
(**not** ~~56.000~~).

▶ Workbook, p. 13

3 READING **Mr Wu's American Dream**

a) BEFORE YOU READ **What's the correct answer?**

*The American Dream is
the idea that, in the USA, ...*

A only certain people can dream.
B hard work will give you a better life.
C you don't have to work.

b) Now read the conversation. Were you right?

Dante   Thanks for having us, Mr Wu.

Mr Wu   You're welcome, I like meeting Amy's friends.

Romy   And thank you for the biscuits, they're great.

Dante   Biscuits? These are cookies, Romy.

Romy   We say biscuits in British English. Mr Wu, Amy
told us that you came to New York in the 1970s.
So you've lived here for a long time. You're a real
New Yorker.

Mr Wu   Yes, I am. My parents and I left China in 1972. We didn't have very much back then,
but that didn't stop us! It was difficult, but this country has been good to me.

Romy   I've read a lot about the American Dream. Do you believe in it?

Mr Wu   Hm, that's a good question. You know what? Yes, I do. I think that this is the land of
equal opportunity, and that all Americans can be successful if they work hard.

Romy   Is that really true for everyone?

Mr Wu   Oh, I don't know if I can answer for everyone! But for myself and many others, it's
true. I started with very little, and today I own a business, I own this apartment, and
my grandchildren can go to university. Of course, I've worked very hard, and I've had
lots of challenges. I've experienced racism. For example, once someone told me to go
back to where I came from. That made me so angry. I've been here for over fifty years!

Romy   I'm so sorry to hear that.

Mr Wu   Well, that man didn't think before he opened his mouth. I'm sure his family
immigrated to the USA too. This is my home, and I'm happy that we're Chinese
American.

Amy   Me too, Grandpa!

c) Are the sentences true, false, or not in the text?

1 Mr Wu is a real New Yorker.
2 His parents loved the USA.
3 He doesn't believe in the American Dream.

4 He is successful because he worked a lot.
5 No one has ever been racist to him.
6 Amy wants to visit China.

d) What do you think: Can everyone be successful if they work hard? Discuss with a partner.

| I think that ...
In my opinion / experience, ...
If you ask me, ... | everyone can be successful if they ...
the USA / Germany / ... is a great place to live.
it's easy / difficult / ... to have a good life.
lots of people experience racism / problems / ... |

Erklär-film

4 Mr Wu's experience

a) Complete Mr Wu's sentences from **3**.

1 My parents and I ... **(leave)** China in 1972.
2 We ... **(not have)** very much back then.
3 But that ... **(not stop)** us!
4 It ... **(be)** difficult.
5 Someone told me to go back to where I ... **(come)** from.
6 That man didn't think before he ... **(open)** his mouth.

> **Remember**
>
> Mit dem **simple past** sprichst du über Dinge, die in der Vergangenheit geschehen sind.
> Bei regelmäßigen Verben hängst du *-ed* an den Infinitiv des Verbs.
> Unregelmäßige Formen musst du lernen:
>
> *go → went*; *have → had*; *see → saw*.
>
> Lerne am besten immer gleich alle drei Formen der Verben! Du kannst sie auf S. 254–256 nachschlagen und dir dazu einen Chant anhören.

b) Now complete these sentences. Use the simple past.

It was difficult back then. We *didn't speak* (**1 not speak**) English, and we ... (**2 not know**) anyone in the city. It's hard to be an immigrant. But there were people who ... (**3 help**) us. There was one woman who ... (**4 live**) in our apartment building, Ms Rosenberg. She always ... (**5 ask**) us if we needed anything, and sometimes she ... (**6 give**) me English books. It ... (**7 be**) nice to talk to someone in English too. She always ... (**8 say**), 'Henry, tell me what you ... (**9 see**) today.' And then we ... (**10 sit**) together on the steps and ... (**11 share**) cookies. She ... (**12 make**) the best cookies! In fact, this is her recipe. Do you like them?

REVISION The simple past: ▶ Language file 5, p. 163   ▶ More practice 3, p. 42

5 WORDS British and American English

a) Some words are different in British and American English. Listen and match the American words in the box to the British words.

> cookies • French fries • pants • restroom • sneakers • subway

1 biscuits = cookies, 2 ...

 1 biscuits   2 underground    3 trainers    4 toilet    5 chips    6 trousers

b) Listen again and check. One word means 'underwear' in British English. Which one is it?

▶ More practice 4, p. 42   ▶ More practice 5, p. 43

c) Start a mind map for American English. Write the headings *town & city, food, clothes* and add new words as you find them in the unit.

▶ Skills file 1, p. 144

▶ Workbook, p. 14

6 READING **Famous New Yorkers**

On the subway on the way home, Romy is reading about famous New Yorkers.
Read the articles and answer the questions. Write LMM, JJ or both.

1 Who has followed their dreams since they were young?
2 Who can sing and act professionally?
3 Who was born outside the USA?
4 Who has spoken in public about problems with their job?
5 Who has been very successful?

Follow your dreams

Lin-Manuel Miranda is a famous writer, musician and actor. He has written successful musicals that take place in New York. He also performed in theaters and created music for movies like *Encanto* and *Star Wars*. Miranda was born in NYC and speaks Spanish as well as English, because his parents are from Puerto Rico. When he was little, Miranda knew that he wanted to become a writer. His father once wrote him a letter telling him to follow his dreams – and he did.

Proud to be herself

Jonquel Jones is one of the best players in the WNBA (the Women's National Basketball Association). She was born in the Bahamas (where people speak English) but moved to the USA when she was 14 to follow her dream of becoming a professional player. She has had a lot of success and played for lots of different teams, some in other countries, and joined the team New York Liberty in 2023. Jones has said women's basketball can be sexist. Male players just have to play well, but female players have to wear pretty clothes and be polite. That's not how Jones wants to do things! She wants to be herself, and she wants to play basketball.

▶ Language file 7, p. 165

My task

7 Hot seat   ▶ Digital help

a) **You're going to play hot seat. First decide who is going to play Lin-Manuel Miranda
and who is going to play Jonquel Jones. These students take notes on the articles.
Everyone else writes questions. The answers don't have to be in the articles.**

Why did you ...   How does it feel to ...   ▶ More help, p. 43

☒ b) **Now play hot seat. The people who are playing characters sit in the hot seat one at a time.
Everyone else asks questions.**

> *How does it feel to follow your dreams?*   *It feels great!*

▶ Workbook, p. 15

 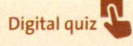

A city of sports

1 Reading Sports in New York City

a) Before you read Look at the pictures. Can you name the different kinds of sports? Do you know any American teams or any players?

b) Read Amy's newest blog post. What are Amy's two favourite teams?

https://www.example.com/AmysNYCBlog

Most Popular Sports in NYC

Are you interested in learning about the most popular sports in NYC? Then keep reading this post!

New Yorkers love the game of baseball. The two biggest teams in the city are the Yankees and the Mets. My team is the Yankees, because that's my family's tradition. Watching games together is the best!

Then we have football. It's probably the most popular sport in the country! Did you know that in the rest of the world, people call it 'American football'? But here we just say 'football'. And the game that they call 'football' is what we call 'soccer' in the USA.

Basketball is a very popular sport to play, and I like playing it too. There are a lot of outdoor basketball courts in our city, and they're free for everyone to use. If you like to watch basketball, New York Liberty is the best team!

If you're in the city in November, you'll see the New York City marathon. It's one of the biggest marathons in the world! Standing at the side and cheering for people as they run past is really fun. I'm good at running and I hope to run it one day.

c) There's one mistake in each sentence. Find and correct them.

1 Amy is a Mets fan because her family likes that team.
2 Baseball is the most popular sport in the country.
3 In the USA, people just say 'American football'.
4 Many outdoor basketball courts in NYC are expensive.
5 The New York City marathon takes place in December.

Erklär-
film

2 LOOKING AT LANGUAGE **Gerunds (*ing*-form)**

Read the examples. The words in blue are gerunds. Complete the last sentence and the rule in the box.

1 **Watching** games is the best!
2 I like **playing** baseball too.
3 **Cheering** for people is fun.
4 I am good at ... **(run)**.

> Ein **gerund** ist eine Verbform, die wie ein Nomen verwendet wird. Wir bilden es, indem wir ... an den Infinitiv des Verbs anhängen.
> ▶ Language file 8, p. 166

3 The Superbowl

Amy is talking to Romy. Complete the sentences. Use gerunds.

Celebrating **(1 celebrate)** the Superbowl (the biggest football game of the year) is an American tradition! My family always watches it together. The game is usually very exciting. ... **(2 enjoy)** the game is the main thing, of course, but the Superbowl is about more than football! We especially like ... **(3 watch)** the half-time show. There are often awesome singers who are great at ... **(4 dance)** too. I also recommend ... **(5 take)** a look at the TV commercials because they're

really funny. Everyone makes lots of snacks to eat during the game like chicken wings, pizza, and chips with different kinds of dips. I don't miss ... **(6 have)** those things because my dad makes dim sum – my favorite food. Weeks before the game, I dream about ... **(7 eat)** my dad's dim sum!

▶ More practice 6, p. 43

4 WRITING **A message**

Read this message from Romy. Write an answer. Use gerunds.

Hi, there! It was good to get your message and hear about you and your family.
Can you tell me some more about yourself?
What do you like doing?
What are you good at (and not so good at!) doing?
And what do you hate doing?

Hi, Romy! How's it going?
You wanted to know what I'm interested in. Well, ...
I love ...
... is really fun.
I'm good at ...
And I hate ...
What about you?
Have a good day!

▶ More help, p. 44

▶ Workbook, pp. 16–17

5 LISTENING On the subway

a) BEFORE YOU LISTEN **Read the box. Say what's
different to public transport in your area.**

In my area, we have / don't have …
The underground in … runs …   The buses run …

**b) Romy is taking the subway to meet Amy. Listen.
Match the announcements (1–3) to the sentences
(A–C).**

A   Please be careful when you get off the train.
B   A train is coming into the station.
C   The doors are closing.

**c) Listen to the announcements again and answer
the questions.**

1   Which train does Romy take?
2   At which street does Romy get off?
3   Which train do Romy and Amy need to take to Yankee Stadium?
4   Do Romy and Amy need to change on the way to the stadium?

Good to know

In the NYC subway, people refer
to the trains by their letter (the A
train) or number (the 2 train). The
subway runs 24 hours every day.

6 MEDIATION Using the subway

**Romy and Amy want to help a German tourist. In groups of three, complete the dialogue and
then act it out.**

Tourist Ach Mensch, warum gibt es zu den Fahrkarten
keine Information?
Romy Hallo, können wir Ihnen helfen?
Tourist Sehr gern, danke! Wenn ich einen Einzelfahr-
schein kaufe, kann ich damit umsteigen?
Romy He wants to know if **… (1)** with a single ticket.
Amy Yes, he can use the single ticket for two hours
and change trains once.
Romy Sie können die Fahrkarte für **… (2)**.
Tourist Na, prima! Und wissen Sie, welchen Zug ich
nach Chinatown nehmen muss?
Romy He wants to know which train **… (3)**.
Amy He needs to take the 4 or 5 train to Canal
Street. It's four stops.
Romy Fahren Sie vier Haltestellen mit **… (4)**.
Tourist Vielen Dank und einen schönen Tag noch!

7 SPEAKING Let's ask

a) Amy and Romy are at the subway and want to meet Dante at gate 4. Look at the map and read the dialogue. Which gate is 4?

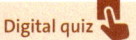

Amy	I don't understand which way we go to get to gate 4. The map on my phone isn't very clear.
Romy	Let's ask somebody. ... Excuse me, could you help us, please? Could you tell us how to get to gate 4 of Yankee Stadium?
Woman	Sure. Take the exit for East 161st Street over there. Then go straight on down the street. It's the second gate on the right.
Amy	Thanks for your help.
Woman	No problem!

b) Find four polite sentences in a) and write them in your exercise book.

c) Partner B: Look at p. 40.
Partner A: Be polite. Ask partner B:

- where you can buy a hot dog
- how much a hot dog costs
- where the nearest restroom is

- Yankees team store:
  Great Hall, gate 6 (near ticket office)
- Veggie burger:
  on the first level near gate 2
- Cost of veggie burger: $10.50

d) Look at the information on the right and answer partner B's questions. Be polite.

▶ Wordbank 1, p. 180   ▶ More practice 7, p. 44

My task

8 ROLE-PLAY At a sports event

a) You're at a sports event. Look at the situations and think what you can say. Make notes. Remember to be polite!

▶ Wordbank 1, p. 180
▶ More help, p. 44

▶ Digital help

b) Role-play the two situations.

Situation 1
Partner A: You are in the stadium, but somebody is in your seat. Start by saying excuse me.
Partner B: You're the person in the seat. At first you think that you're right, but then you check your ticket: You're in the wrong seat.

Situation 2
It's several hours later. The weather is really hot and sunny.
Partner A: There are two people next to you. One of them says they don't feel well. You know that inside the stadium it is cooler. Start by asking if everything is ok.
Partner B: Your friend doesn't feel well, and you didn't bring enough water.

▶ Workbook, p. 18

 Digital quiz   I can ask for and give help.

Hard times

1 What is going to happen?

a) BEFORE YOU READ **Read the title and look at the pictures. Say what you think the story is about.**

I think the story is about …

b) **Now read the story and find out if you were right.**

'Paul, this is the fourth time this month that you've fallen asleep in my class,' said Ms Acosta. She sighed and opened a book on her desk. 'What are we going to do
5 about this?'
Paul shrugged, but he was worried. Ms Acosta said *we*, but he knew that she meant *you*. *What are you going to do about this?*

10 'How are things at home?' Ms Acosta asked. 'Is your mom working right now?'
Paul took a deep breath. 'She lost her job again last month,' he answered. He watched Ms Acosta write something down
15 in the book.

'That's hard,' she said. 'Are you helping her?'
'Yes,' he said. 'I'm working at the mall, but it's not a lot of money.'
'So, it's not enough for the whole family,'
20 said Ms Acosta. 'You have … how many, two sisters?'

'And one brother,' he replied. Ms Acosta added something to her notes.

'Five people need a lot of food. With only
25 one person working part-time, that's hard to pay for. Do you ever skip meals?'
Paul shrugged again. 'Yeah, I guess. On some days I just fall asleep without dinner.'
Ms Acosta looked at him kindly. 'Now that's
30 really hard. I'm sorry, Paul.'

Suddenly he was annoyed with her. She didn't really understand, how could she? Everything was so expensive. Did she ever have to choose between food and rent?
35 Paul didn't think so. Ms Acosta wore nice clothes and jewelry. Her life was different. She probably had important goals and dreams, like traveling or buying a house. Paul's dream was to never worry about food
40 again. He didn't want to answer her stupid questions. It was frustrating, but he knew that he had to be polite because he didn't want to get into any more trouble.

Ms Acosta found a brochure in her desk and
45 gave it to him.

He read the title out loud: 'Information
for Food-Insecure Families.'

He thought about what it meant. He
knew what it meant to feel insecure.
50 He sometimes felt insecure. In class,
when a teacher asked him a question
and he didn't know the answer. Or when
Emily gave him one of her beautiful smiles.
In those moments he felt small, shy. The
55 opposite of confident. But what did it
mean for a family to be 'food-insecure'?
He didn't understand.

'There are organizations that can help you,
Paul,' said Ms Acosta. 'Will you give this
60 brochure to your mom, please?'
He put the brochure in his backpack.
'I will, Ms Acosta.'

That weekend he and his mom took the bus
to one of the places in the brochure. They
65 found the fire station and walked inside.
A volunteer wrote down their names and
address and told them where to go.

'Just follow those signs,' he said and smiled
at them.

70 It was busy in the big hall. People walked
around with bags of food and clothes. He
saw a woman with cat food, a man with a
box of diapers. Some people talked to each
other and laughed, others were quiet and
75 looked down at the floor as they waited.

'Paul, hello!' said a voice. It was Ms Acosta.
'Nice to see you, Mrs Henderson.' She
smiled at Paul's mom.
'Hi, Ms Acosta,' said Paul's mom. 'Thanks for
80 telling us about this place. That was really
nice of you.'
'Oh, no problem,' said Ms Acosta, 'We all
have hard times. In fact, I used to come here
too – and now I volunteer. You never know
85 when you'll need a little help.'

Paul was surprised. Ms Acosta? Hard times?
'That's so good of you to give back to your
community, Ms Acosta,' said Paul's mom.
'Being hungry is no joke,' said Ms Acosta.
90 She put her hand on Paul's shoulder. 'Paul is
a smart kid, and I would like to see him do
well at school.'
'Oh,' said Paul. 'Um ... Thanks, Ms Acosta.
I'm really grateful for your help.'
95 'You're welcome,' she replied. 'Now – shall
we find you a box?'

2 What happens

Read again and complete the sentences.

1 At first, Paul is in trouble because he …
2 Then Ms Acosta learns that his mom lost …
3 Paul is working at the mall, but it's not …
4 Sometimes in the evening, Paul just falls asleep …
5 Never being hungry again is …
6 On the weekend, Paul and his mom go to …
7 Inside the hall they meet …
8 She used to need help, but now she …

3 How Paul feels

How does Paul feel when …

1 … Ms Acosta asks, 'What are we going to do about this?' (ll. 4–6)
2 … Ms Acosta looks at him kindly. (ll. 29–31)
3 … Emily gives him one of her beautiful smiles. (ll. 52–54)
4 … he finds out that Ms Acosta used to need help. (ll. 83–86)
5 … he hears that Ms Acosta thinks he's clever. (ll. 90–94)

He feels …

▶ More practice 8, p. 45

4 GLOBAL GOALS No poverty

a) THINK **What do people need?
What is just nice to have?
Copy the table and make notes.**

What people need to have	What is nice to have or do
water	a really big TV
food	

b) PAIR **Compare your ideas.**

People need …

It's nice to have …

c) SHARE **Discuss your ideas with the class.**

▶ Workbook, p. 19

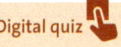 Digital quiz   **I can** understand a text about poverty and dreams.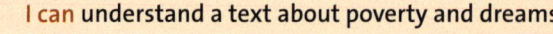

Chris the comic book writer

1 BEFORE YOU WATCH Comic books

YOU CHOOSE **Talk to your partner about comics. Do A or B.**

A   Which comics do you know?
What do you like about them?
Which characters do you like and why?

B   Have you ever created a comic?
What was it about?
If you haven't, why not?

2 VIEWING Chris's dream

a)   **Watch the video and complete the sentences.**

1   Chris is a ...
2   His dream is to make his own ...

CHRIS - THE COMIC CREATOR

b)   **Before you watch again, write 1–6 in your exercise book. Watch the video again and complete the profile.**

| 1 Name of superhero |
| 2 Costume |
| 3 Artist |
| 4 How many pages is it? |
| 5 What else does Chris make? |
| 6 What's the result? |

c)   **Answer the questions.**

1   What do you think of Chris's superhero?
2   How hard do you think it was for Chris to make his dream come true?

3 LIFE SKILLS Make your dreams come true

a)   **Think about your dream and how you can make it come true. Make notes.**

*My dream is to be ... / One day I hope to ... / I've always wanted to become ... / ...
I'll have to go to ... / move to ... / find someone who ... / save money for ... / ...*

▶ More help, p. 45

b)   **Tell a partner.**

Prepare a presentation

1 Brainstorm reasons

Your class has won the lottery! Prepare a short presentation to convince your English teacher to go to NYC. A good presentation needs a beginning (introduction), a middle and an end (conclusion). For your introduction, brainstorm reasons and discuss ideas why you want to go to NYC and what you want to do there.

> *We can practise English and go to our favourite sights.*

> *Yes, and we can learn more about New York's history.*

▶ More help, p. 45

2 Do research and take notes

You found this article on Ellis Island. Read it and take notes. The questions below can help you.

 Don't copy everything:
- Focus on the most important information.
- Use your own words.
- Use symbols →, +/−,! …

Ellis Island

Ellis Island is in New York Harbor, near Liberty Island. The Statue of Liberty is on Liberty Island.

When immigrants wanted to come to the USA, there were different places they could enter, like Boston, Philadelphia, Baltimore, San Francisco or New Orleans. Ellis Island was the biggest and most important place for immigrants to enter the USA for many years. Between 1892 and 1924, over 12 million immigrants went through Ellis Island.

The Ellis Island Immigration Museum opened to the public in 1990. Visitors must take a ferry to get to the museum.

- Where is it?
- Why is it important?
- What can you do there?
- Why do you want to go there?

▶ Skills file 4, 6, pp. 146, 148 – 149

Digital quiz 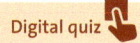   **I can prepare a presentation.**

Your trip to NYC – a short presentation

Step 1: Write your introduction and conclusion

▶ Digital help

Work in a group on your presentation. Write an introduction and a conclusion for the presentation. Use your ideas from p. 32, ex 1.

We should go to New York City because …
This trip is a good idea because …

So you see, there are many reasons why …
Now you know lots of good reasons for …

Step 2: Choose three or four sights and take notes

▶ Digital help

a) Next, collect sights or activities you want to see and do in NYC. You can find ideas on pages 16–17, 18–19, 32, 40–41.

b) Agree on three or four sights that you want to present and take notes. Look for pictures in books or online.

Use creative commons pictures.

Step 3: Write your part

a) Each group member takes one sight or activity and writes two or three sentences to explain why they chose it.

b) You can research more information online.

▶ More help, p. 45   ▶ Skills file 4, p. 146   ▶ Digital help

We chose … because …
We'd love to … because …

Check information on at least two websites.

Step 4: Practise your presentation

Put the parts of your presentation together and practise it. You can also record your presentation and present it in class.

▶ Skills file 6, p. 148–149

Check the camera, sound and light for your recording.

Step 5: Give feedback

Listen to or watch each group's presentation and give feedback. Did you convince your teacher?

▶ Feedback phrases, p. 191

You spoke very clearly. The most interesting part was about …

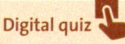

1 READING **My perfect day in New York City**

I can talk about New York City.

a) Read the comments and write the correct name or names for each statement (1–6).

Dante

For me, the perfect day starts with a game of basketball with my cousins in the Bronx. Then, it's back home for lunch with my parents. After that, I get the train to go watch a movie – I love watching them on big screens!

Amy

My perfect day starts with a run in Central Park. If the weather is nice, I sit on the grass in the sun. In the afternoon, I take the subway to Yankee Stadium to watch the game and eat a hot dog.

Romy

A perfect day in the city? That's easy: I spend the whole day here in Brooklyn. In the morning, I walk to my favourite cafe to eat a bagel, drink tea, and watch everyone walking past. In the afternoon, I walk to Coney Island. I meet my friends and we play some games together.

1 I get out of the house.
2 I don't use public transport.
3 I buy something to eat.

4 I don't do any sports.
5 I go to the cinema.
6 I enjoy the sun.

b) Imagine you live in NYC. What's your perfect day? Write three sentences. Use the texts from a) to help you.

2 WRITING **A blog post**

I can write a short blog post.

You're visiting Little Italy and want to write a blog post about it. Write:

- information about the area
- what you can hear and smell
- if you like it there and why

Write 60 words or more. Use the information in the box and the phrases below to help you. You can start like this:

Hi, everyone! I'm on holiday in New York City and I'm visiting Little Italy at the moment …

> in the past … • today … • I can see / hear / smell … • I (don't) like it here because …

Little Italy (Lower Manhattan)

- past: many families of Italian immigrants lived here
- today: a very busy area
- a lot of Italian restaurants and food shops
- restaurants are expensive
- a lot of tourists

Check

---

3 MEDIATION **At the cafe**

You and your grandma are in a cafe in Manhattan. Your grandma doesn't speak English very well, so you mediate for her. Complete the sentences (1–5).

Oma	Hmmm, das riecht aber lecker hier!
Juan	Guten Tag and, erm, willkommen!
Oma	Sie sprechen Deutsch, das ist ja toll!
Juan	Oh, I'm sorry, I only know a few words of German.
Du	Er kennt nur … **(1)**.
Oma	Ach so, OK. Hat er Deutsch in der Schule gelernt?
Du	My grandma would like to know if you … **(2)**.

Juan Oh no. But when you live in NYC, you meet a lot of people from a lot of places. Some are born here, some are on a trip, and others have lived here for years – like me!

Du Wenn man … **(3)**.

Oma Stimmt, man hört hier so viele verschiedene Sprachen. Menschen aus der ganzen Welt kommen nach New York, um den amerikanischen Traum zu leben.

Du You can hear lots of different languages here because people … **(4)**.

Juan Yes, and I'm so happy to live here.

Du Er ist sehr … **(5)**.

Oma Das kann ich gut verstehen!

---

4 WORDS **American words**

Complete the sentences with the correct words from the box.

awesome • backpack • candy • mall • mom • movie • restroom • sneakers • soccer • subway

1 Our walk is going to take over an hour. You should wear …
2 Can you wait here for a minute, please? I need to use the …
3 My … says that I can go on the trip! I'm so excited.
4 Don't eat … right before dinner. You won't be hungry.
5 I hope our … team wins the game tomorrow. I'll be so sad if they don't.
6 Do you want to take the …, or do you prefer walking?
7 Have you seen that …? I heard that it's really good.
8 I have some … news for you! Call me when you see this.
9 Let's go to the new …! There are many cool stores.
10 I have so many books in my … . I can't close it.

5 On the subway

I can **ask for and give help.** ✓

a) LANGUAGE **Read the conversation between Dante and a tourist.**
Complete the sentences (1–6) with the correct <u>gerunds</u> of the verbs in the box.

be • get • travel • understand • visit • walk

Tourist Excuse me, could you help me, please? Could you tell me if this is the right train for me? I want to go to the Natural History Museum.

Dante Well, you're on the right line, but you're going the wrong way. You need to get off at the next stop and look for the 'D' train that goes to Bedford Park Boulevard.

Tourist Right, thank you. I don't know how I made that mistake. I love … **(1)** big cities and I'm usually good at … **(2)** subway maps.

Dante Don't worry about it. … **(3)** by public transport can be hard! Is it your first time in New York?

Tourist It is, yeah. I already knew a lot about it from films, but I really enjoy … **(4)** here in real life!

Dante It sure is a great city. If you have time, I recommend … **(5)** off the subway at Columbus Circle and then … **(6)** to the museum. Then you can see some of Central Park too.

Tourist Great idea! Thanks so much for your help.

Dante No problem!

b) SPEAKING **You're travelling on subway line 7. Decide who is A (a tourist) and who is B (a New Yorker). Make a dialogue. Use the map and the purple phrases from a) to help you.**

Excuse me, …

This is a 7 train for Manhattan. The next station is 5th Avenue.

Manhattan — 34th Street – Hudson Yards — Times Square — 5th Avenue — Grand Central

Local 7

Partner A: You start. You're a tourist and you want to go to Times Square. You're worried you have missed your stop.

Partner B: You live in New York City, and you often travel on the subway. You help the tourist with their questions.

Check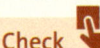

6 LISTENING **Mr Wu's dreams**

I can understand a text about poverty and dreams.

a) Mr Wu arrived in New York in the 1970s. What do you think his dreams were for his new life? Compare your ideas with a partner.

b) Now listen to Romy's conversation with Mr Wu. What were his dreams? Choose three of the pictures (A–E).

c) Listen again and choose the correct answer.

1 Mr Wu dreamed of wearing A **sneakers** B **a uniform** C **cool clothes** to school.
2 Now he feels A **unhappy**. B **rich**. C **lucky**.
3 Mr Wu met his wife in A **1971**. B **1981**. C **1991**.

d) Imagine you have just moved to New York City. What are your dreams? Tell your partner.

My dream is to … get an amazing job / become rich and famous / meet someone special …

7 STUDY SKILLS **The Empire State Building**

I can prepare a presentation.

a) Romy is preparing a presentation. Read her notes. Match them to the correct headings in the box.

> things to see and do • introduction and important facts • conclusion

1
- *great place to visit on holiday*
- *thanks, questions?*

2
- *see some great views on 86th and 102nd floors*
- *learn about the building's history*
- *buy a souvenir at the shop*

3
- *in Manhattan*
- *one of the tallest buildings in the city: 102 floors!*
- *opened in 1931*
- *has appeared in more than 250 TV shows and films*

b) SPEAKING **Give Romy's presentation. Use the notes from a) and the phrases below.**

> Hi, everyone! • Today I'd like to talk about … • First, I'd like to tell you … • Next, I'd like to talk about … • Finally, I think that … • Thanks for listening • Are there any questions?

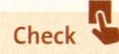
Check

What do you know about 9/11?

A magazine for young people across the USA

9/11: The day that changed New York City *by Dante Rossi*

On the morning of September 11, 2001, Helaina Hovitz was twelve years old and at her school near the World Trade Center (WTC). A group of terrorists took over four planes that were full of people travelling on holiday or for work. The terrorists flew two of the planes into the two towers of the WTC. They killed almost three thousand people, including many people who ran to help. When the first plane hit the tower, there was a really loud noise, and the ground moved. Helaina wrote about how she got home on that scary day.

Helaina's story

(from: *What the 20 years since 9/11 have been like for a survivor* by Helaina Hovitz)

[...] Now, of course, you know what happened next. The whole world knows what happened. But in real time, we – 11, 12, 13-year-olds – had no idea. When we went outside, it looked like we had walked onto the set of a disaster film. We were almost directly under the towers, which were yet to collapse[2], feeling the heat[3] on our faces. Rather than running uptown[4] like everyone else was, we ran further into the chaos. We were hoping to get home, which was just three blocks away from the towers on the other side of town. [...] We didn't make it home before the first tower fell, nearly an hour after being hit. Suddenly, voices shouted, 'Get inside! Quick!' and a group of people pulled Ann, Charles, and me inside a building with a giant[5] lobby, where we waited a few minutes [...]. Back outside people were running, falling over shoes, backpacks, and body parts, screaming and crying. Underneath[6] several inches of ash[7] were things that people wore that day and had now left on the street. For the next hour, we continued to try to get home, walking through the bleeding bodies of people covered in[8] soot[9] and ash [...].

In the days that followed, our neighborhood became a war zone [...]. We lived with unreliable electricity, little food, water, and medication[10], and the wreckage[11] from the towers was still on fire. [...] I was ducking[12] when I heard planes passing[13] above me, then crying, panicking, sometimes running back and forth[14] with nowhere to really go. Nightmares[15] and flashbacks[16] took over my days and nights. Lower Manhattan was destroyed[17], never to return as it was.

▶ Quellenverzeichnis, p. 263

---

[1] **united** *vereinigt, verbunden*   [2] **which were yet to collapse** *die noch einstürzen würden*   [3] **heat** *die Hitze*
[4] **uptown** *der nördliche Teil von Manhattan*   [5] **giant** *gigantisch*   [6] **underneath** *unter*   [7] **ash** *die Asche*
[8] **covered in** *bedeckt mit*

After 9/11: Bringing people together

After 9/11, events and festivals have brought people in NYC closer together and have helped them to remember the good things in life. People meet, dance, have fun and just enjoy being together. Here are my two favorite festivals!

River to River Festival

The first River To River Festival was in 2002, right after 9/11. The organizers wanted to use the power of art to make people in Manhattan feel happier. The amazing art and performances always make people smile! The festival takes place in June in Manhattan and all events are free.

Mermaid[18] Parade

The Mermaid Parade is one of NYC's greatest summer events! It takes place at Coney Island, Brooklyn, where there are cool beaches and two great theme parks. You can dress as a mermaid or a merman or just put on your favorite costume, walk

in the parade and party on the beach. If you don't like costumes, you can help as a volunteer and watch all the fun!

When you're **sad,** what **makes** you **feel** happy **?**

---

9 **soot** *der Ruß*   10 **medication** *die medizinische Behandlung*   11 **wreckage** *die Trümmer*   12 **to duck** *sich ducken*   13 **to pass** *hier: vorbeifliegen*   14 **back and forth** *hin und her*   15 **nightmare** *der Albtraum*   16 **flashback** *der Flashback, die Erinnerung*   17 **destroyed** *zerstört*   18 **mermaid/merman** *die Nixe (Meerfrau) / der Nix (Meermann)*

Partner page

▶Page 27

7 SPEAKING **Let's ask**

c) **Partner B: Look at the information on the right and answer partner A's questions.**

d) **Be polite. Ask partner A:**

- where the Yankees team store is
- where you can get a veggie burger
- how much a veggie burger costs

> - Nearest place to buy a hot dog: on the top level, between gates 4 and 6
> - Cost of hot dog: $ 6.75
> - Nearest restroom: on the main level

Diff bank

▶Page 17

More practice 1   READING **Food in New York City**

a) **Read this New York City food guide and answer the questions.**

1   How do New Yorkers eat pizza?   2   Can you only get vegetarian hot dogs in New York City?
3   What will a good cafe in New York City have?   4   What should you drink with this dessert?

1 Let's start with a classic NYC food: pizza! Pizza in New York City is amazing, and there are a lot of pizza places to choose from. Here's a tip: Eat it with your hands. Don't use a knife and fork – only tourists eat pizza that way.

2 You can find them everywhere in New York City: on the street, in parks and in restaurants. We're talking about hot dogs with ketchup, mustard, sauerkraut and onions – and there are often vegetarian options too. So good!

3 You have to try a bagel at least once because it's a New York tradition. A good cafe will have lots of different kinds of bagels, even sweet ones! Try a bagel with just cream cheese, or get one with different things like salad, hummus, cucumber, tomatoes, or meat.

4 Ready for dessert? It's time for New York cheesecake! It's different to German cheesecake because it's much creamier. It goes great with hot chocolate or tea.

b) **You're in New York City. What food would you like to try?** ✉ **Why?**

▶ Page 18

More practice 2 **The five boroughs of New York City**

a) BEFORE YOU READ Copy the table. Look at the map and write the names of the five boroughs.

Name	Sights	Things to do
Manhattan	...	...
_____ ...		

b) Read the texts and complete the table.

In **Manhattan** you can see all your favorite sights from American movies. Walk along the High Line, an old train track that is now a public park. Or if you want to get a great view of New York City, go up to the 86th floor of the Empire State Building!

The Bronx is the home of hip-hop – lots of artists were born or lived here. The Hip Hop Museum celebrates the music, dance and art of hip-hop. You can also find Yankee Stadium in the Bronx, one of the most famous baseball stadiums in the world.

Brooklyn is the borough with the most people. You can walk around and look at street art or check out the views from the Brooklyn Bridge. A lot of New Yorkers visit the beach and the piers at Coney Island and also go on the rides there.

Queens is the largest NYC borough by size. It has some great museums, like the New York Hall of Science and the Museum of the Moving Image (MoMI). Or go to Rockaway Beach. It's perfect for swimming, surfing or just relaxing by the water.

Staten Island is great for outdoor activities like hiking and picnics. There are also a many interesting museums, like a house where the New York writer, activist and teacher Audre Lorde lived with her partner and two children. She has won many prizes.

► Page 20

Parallel exercise **1 After school**

🔊 **b)** **Romy, Amy and Dante are talking after school. Listen and answer the questions.**

1 Who is Spicy_Potato?
   A Dante.   B Romy.
2 Why is New York City so diverse?
   A Because lots of people speak Spanish.   B Because almost everyone is an immigrant.
3 What does Dante want to show Romy and Amy?
   A An old photo.   B A chart.
4 When did Dante's family come to the USA?
   A In the early 1900s.   B In the early 1800s.
5 When did Amy's family come to the USA?
   A In the 1980s.   B In the 1970s.
6 Who are they going to meet?
   A Amy's grandma.   B Amy's grandpa.

► Page 22

More practice 3 **Dante's grandparents**

Read what Dante says about his grandparents. Write the verbs in the simple past.

My grandparents ... **(1 be)** born in New York, like me, but their parents ... **(2 come)** from Italy. Life ... **(3 not be)** always easy, but they ... **(4 love)** their new city. After a few years, they ... **(5 open)** an Italian restaurant. Their restaurant ... **(6 be)** very popular, so people often ... **(7 wait)** for hours to get a table! But they ... **(8 not care)** because the food was so good.

More practice 4 **American English**

Read Romy's message to her dad and change the blue words to American English.

New York City is amazing! I had the best hamburgers with **chips (1)** yesterday. And it's a great place to go shopping. I've already bought some new **trousers (2)**, sunglasses and **trainers (3)**. The **underground (4)** makes it so easy to get around the city.
Oh, and I'll make you **biscuits (5)** next time I see you. I have a great new recipe from Amy's grandpa!

▶Page 22

More practice 5 **The sound of American English**

a) Look at the picture.
What can you get at this hot dog cart?

🔊 b) Listen. Take notes.

   1 Who buys something?
   2 What do they get?
   3 What's Romy's problem?

🔊 c) Listen and repeat.

▶Page 23

More help **7** MY TASK **Hot seat**

Questions		Answers
Why did you …	choose to live in New York City?	Because it's a great place to live.
	decide to play basketball?	Well, I think it's the best sport.
	decide to write musicals?	I love music!
How does it feel to …	be so successful?	It feels great!
	win so many prizes?	I don't think about prizes that much.
	work really hard?	It's important to me to work hard.

▶Page 25

More practice 6 **About Romy and Dante**

Look at the notes. Choose one person and write about Romy OR Dante. Use gerunds.

Romy loves listening to music and … She's interested in … She doesn't like …

Romy Cook (14)	Dante Rossi (14)
What I love doing	What I love doing
What I'm interested in	What I'm interested in
What I don't like doing	What I don't like doing

▸ Page 25

More help **4** **A message**

Hi, Romy! How's it going? You wanted to know what I'm interested in. Well, ...

I love ... And I enjoy ... I'm good at ... I don't like ... And I hate ...!	playing football • running • going to school • cooking • being creative / online • seeing my friends / family • reading books / magazine / comics / ...
Practising basketball • Doing homework / chores / arts and crafts • Meeting new people • my friends • my family • Watching TV / films / videos online • ...	is the best / worst / ... is boring / really fun / ... is my favourite thing. is my least favourite thing.

What about you? Have a good day!

▸ Page 27

More practice 7 **At the hot dog cart**

a) **Complete the dialogue with polite phrases. There can be more than one correct answer.**

Customer	Hello, *can / could* **(1)** I have a hot dog with mustard and onions, please?
Assistant	Sure. ... **(2)** you like sauerkraut?
Customer	Yes, ... **(3)**. ... **(4)** I have some ketchup too?
Assistant	... **(5)**. Here you are. That's $6.75.
Customer	... **(6)**. Could you ... **(7)** me where the nearest restroom is?
Assistant	It's on the top level, just up those stairs.
Customer	... **(8)**.
Assistant	... **(9)**.

▸ Wordbank 1, p. 180

b) **Check with a partner. Then read your completed dialogues together.**

More help **8** **MY TASK** **At a sports event**

Situation 1

A	Excuse me, I think you're in my seat.
B	No, sorry, this is ...
A	Can you check ...?
B	OK ... Oh, sorry, I made a mistake. I'm ...
A	No problem! ...

Situation 2

A	Is everything OK?
B	No, my friend ...
A	Do you have ...
B	No, we didn't ...
A	Would you like ... Also, inside ...
B	Thank you ...

► Page 30

More practice 8 **Words**

Match the words 1–7 with the right definition A–H. You won't need one definition.

1	to sigh	A	how you feel when someone is kind to you
2	part-time	B	the money you pay to live in your flat
3	rent	C	a place that has food for people
4	a brochure	D	when you breathe out loudly
5	insecure	E	something that babies wear
6	a diaper	F	when you don't feel confident
7	grateful	G	a small magazine with information and pictures
		H	when you work for only part of the day or week

► Page 31

More help **3** LIFE SKILLS **Make your dreams come true**

a) **Think about your dream and how you can make it come true. Make notes.**

make	comics • music • films • amazing art • a difference in the world • lots of money • …
be	a scientist • an actor • a business owner • a professional football player • famous • …
go	to a different country • on an exchange • to New York City • …

► Page 32

More help **1 Brainstorm reasons**

> meet Americans • see places that we have learned about • eat real New York cheesecake • visit museums, for example … • do outdoor activities, for example … • travel by subway • …

► Page 33

More help UNIT TASK **Step 3: Write your part**

We want to go to We chose	Times Square • the West Village • Central Park • Yankee Stadium • …	because	it's so famous. we want to learn more.
We'd love to We want to	try pizza /… • go shopping • watch basketball • take the ferry • …		it's delicious. it looks fun.

Unit 2
The South-East: Changing times

Listen to country and rock in Nashville, Tennessee.

Ride the tram in New Orleans, Louisiana.

Visit malls and theme parks in Atlanta, Georgia.

Learn about slavery at the Whitney Plantation, Louisiana.

1 VIEWING Sights of the South-East

a) BEFORE YOU WATCH Look at the photos A–F and read the captions. Describe the photos.

b) Watch the video. Say which places in the photos (A–F) you see in the video.

c) Watch again and choose the correct answer: A or B.

1 K lives in   A Nashville   B New Orleans.
2 K is a   A drummer   B singer.
3 There's a man in a   A cowboy costume   B hockey uniform.
4 People are always waiting outside a famous   A stadium   B restaurant.
5 Abandoned buildings   A have people in them   B are empty.
6 K says that the view from the top is very   A cool   B boring.

▶ More practice 1, p. 71

▶ Workbook, p. 26

Nach dieser Unit kann ich ... ⊘

- ⊘ über den Südosten der USA sprechen
- ⊘ über Regeln sprechen
- ⊘ über Gerechtigkeit reden
- ⊘ Empfehlungen aussprechen
- ⊘ mich über Extremwetter austauschen

Unit task ⊘

- ⊘ eine Zusammenfassung schreiben

Take a boat trip on the Mississippi River, the most important river in the USA.

See the Batman Building in Nashville, Tennessee.

👥 2 SPEAKING Where should you visit?

Take turns to play roles from the box below. **Partner A:** Say what you're interested in. **Partner B:** Say which places in the South-East your partner should visit and why. Use the photos in 1 to help you.

> You love music. • You want to go shopping. • You're interested in skyscrapers. • You're interested in history. • You want to take cool photos for social media. • You're you!

I love music / want to go shopping / ... Where should I visit?

You should visit Nashville / ... one day because you can / it's / there's ...

▶ More help, p. 72
▶ Workbook, p. 27

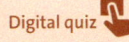 Digital quiz   I can **talk about the South-East of the USA.** ⊘

#EverydayRacism

1 LISTENING Shopping while Black

a) BEFORE YOU LISTEN Kisha is doing an interview on the news. She's talking about something that happened when she was shopping with her friend Maria. Guess what happened.

Kisha Freeman

Maria Davis

b) Listen and choose the correct answers.

1   The security guard wanted to ...
    A   look in Kisha's bag.
    B   look in Maria's bag.
    C   go to another store.

2   The security guard was ...
    A   polite.
    B   calm.
    C   racist.

3   Kisha's brother, Troy, had the idea to ...
    A   talk to their parents.
    B   email the store.
    C   post something online.

4   Kisha's post ...
    A   got racist comments online.
    B   wasn't that interesting to people.
    C   was very popular.

5   Lots of people came to ...
    A   get on the news.
    B   protest outside.
    C   go shopping.

6   After the protest, the ...
    A   store said sorry.
    B   store gave Kisha money.
    C   security guard lost her job.

c) Listen again. What do you think the title *Shopping while Black* means?

I think it means that ...

d) Why was the security guard's behaviour racist? What do you think about Kisha's post? Think for a minute and then tell a partner your opinion. Give reasons.

In my opinion, the security guard was ...
I think it's great that Kisha posted online because ...

▶ More help, p. 72
▶ Workbook, pp. 28–29

Erklär-film

2 LOOKING AT LANGUAGE Modal verbs

a) **Read the sentences from the interview with Kisha. Answer the questions in the box.**

A You **needn't** worry.
B You **must** do what I say.
C **Can** I go now?
D Yes, you **are allowed to** go.
E Many people **aren't able to** stay calm.
F You **mustn't** forget that.
G You **have to** be calm and very polite.

Welche der blauen Verben oder Wendungen bedeuten, dass jemand …

1 um Erlaubnis bittet?
2 Erlaubnis erteilt?
3 etwas tun muss?
4 etwas nicht tun muss?
5 etwas nicht tun kann?
6 etwas nicht tun darf?

b) **Kisha and Troy's parents have rules for them. What are they? Choose the correct answers.**

We know that it's unfair, but some people may treat you differently because you're Black. Racist people **can / can't (1)** be dangerous.
You **need to / needn't (2)** follow these rules: If you see the police, you **should / shouldn't (3)** put your hands in your pockets. Remember: You **have to / don't have to (4)** be calm and polite. When you buy something, you **must / mustn't (5)** always take the receipt and the bag from the store, so that people don't think you are stealing. Come home on time. You **are allowed to / aren't allowed to (6)** stay out too late. We love you and we want you to be safe.

Du weißt bereits, dass du *may* und *could* in höflichen Fragen verwenden kannst:
***May** I say something?* ***Could** you help me?*
Du kannst *may*, *could* und *might* außerdem benutzen, um auszudrücken, dass du etwas für möglich hältst: *Some people **may** treat you differently. You **might** feel better. They **could** do more.*

▶ Language file 10, pp. 167–168 ▶ More practice 2, p. 72

My task

3 Rules

a) **What rules do you know? Write down at least five.**

When I want to go out, I have to …
My friend isn't allowed to …

go out, do homework, spend money, surf the internet, do chores, buy clothes, …

b) **Which rules are fair? Talk with a partner.**   ▶ Digital help

I'm not allowed to … I don't think that's fair!

▶ Workbook, p. 29

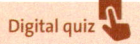Digital quiz   **I can talk about rules.**

Black lives

1 READING A fight for equal rights

a) BEFORE YOU READ Troy's history class is learning about Black people who have fought for equal rights. Look at the box. Have you heard of these rights? Talk with a partner.

I know one: the right to …
I've heard / haven't heard of that one.
I know another one: the right to …

> be free • believe in what you want •
> go to school • say what you think

b) Troy has to read an article for homework. Read the article. Why is January 15th important?

The history of Black people's fight for equal rights

Slave traders brought the first enslaved Africans here in the 1600s. Enslaved people didn't have any rights, and their owners were able to buy and sell them like animals. Many Black people fought against this horrible injustice.

One of those people was Harriet Tubman. She escaped from slavery, and later she bravely helped others to escape too.

Slavery officially ended in 1865, but most states made racist laws. Black people were not allowed to go to the same schools or hospitals as white people. They were not allowed to vote, buy houses, or have good jobs. They also had to sit at the back of the bus. This was called segregation and it continued for many years.

One of the most famous activists who fought against segregation and racism was Dr. Martin Luther King, Jr. He gave speeches and led peaceful protests.

The country started to make new laws to stop segregation in the 1960s. For example, in 1965, Black people were finally able to vote. Some white people were angry about these new laws and became violent. In 1968, Dr. King was killed.

These laws officially ended segregation, however, in the USA, racism is still a problem. January 15th is a public holiday to celebrate Dr. King, called MLK Day. He is a hero for many Black people who continue to fight for equal rights today.

c) Read the sentences. Which one summarizes the <u>whole</u> text best?

A Enslaved people didn't have any rights until 1865.

B In the 1960s, Dr. King stopped segregation.

C Black people have fought for their rights for hundreds of years.

▶ Workbook, pp. 30–31

2 WORDS **Definitions**

Match the definitions (A–F) to the words (1–6).

1	slave traders	A	when you get away from someone or something
2	enslaved people	B	when Black people weren't allowed to do the same things as white people
3	injustice		
4	to escape	C	when people choose something or someone (like a new president)
5	to vote	D	people who are not free
6	segregation	E	people who buy and sell enslaved people
		F	something that is unfair

3 **They had to fight for their rights**

Scan the text and complete these sentences.

1 In the 1600s, the owners of enslaved people **were able to ...**
2 During segregation, Black people **were not allowed to ...**
3 When they rode the bus, they **had to ...**
4 Later, the laws changed. In 1965, Black people **were able to ...**

Can, *must* und *must not* kannst du nur im Präsens verwenden. Deswegen verwenden wir diese Ersatzformen für Zukunft und Vergangenheit: *be able to, be allowed to* und *(not) have to*.

▶ Language file 10, pp. 167–168 ▶ More practice 3, p. 73

4 LISTENING **The Little Rock Nine**

a) BEFORE YOU LISTEN **What are the people in the photo doing?**

◀») b) **Listen to Kisha and Troy.**
What happened? Choose A, B or C.

A Black students weren't allowed to go shopping.
B Black students fought for their right to go to school.
C Black soldiers had to join the army.

◀») ⊠ c) **Listen again. Complete the sentences with one word.**

1 The Little Rock Nine were ...
2 They tried to go to a 'white' ...
3 But racist white parents were ...
4 To stop the students, the state sent ...
5 To help the students, the president sent the ...
6 Sometimes we have to fight for ...

▶ Parallel exercise, p. 73
▶ Workbook, p. 31

5 GLOBAL GOALS Peace and justice

a) **Partner B:** Look at p. 70.

Partner A: Scan the text about Serena Williams. Who is she a role model for?

Serena Williams

Serena Williams is most famous for being one of the greatest tennis players of all time – some people even say she is one of the greatest athletes ever. When Williams started playing tennis in the 1990s, there weren't many professional Black players and Williams has often experienced racist comments and behaviour, even today. However, she always speaks out and is a role model for all athletes. She also works as an activist who has always used her name and her money to support Black women and fight for justice. She says technology – for example the use of phones to film racist actions – has given Black people a voice.

b) **Read the text and answer these questions. Take notes.**

1 What sport did she play?
2 What is she most famous for?
3 What negative things has she experienced?
4 What other work does she do?
5 What does she use to fight for justice?
6 What has given Black people a voice?

c) **Ask partner B these questions about Colin Kaepernick.**

1 What sport did he play?
2 What is he most famous for?
3 What do Americans show when they stand during the national anthem?
4 What did he want to protest against?
5 What negative things did he experience?
6 What does his protest mean today?

d) **Answer partner B's questions about Serena Williams.**

e) **What do you think: Should players use their name to fight against racism and other problems? Should players protest at games? ✉ Why (not)?**

Yes, I think that players should …
No, I think that players shouldn't …

6 The history of Black Lives Matter (BLM)

group • justice • police • protests • video • violence

Complete the text with words from the box.

Racism and ... **(1)** from police are big problems in the USA. In 2020, the ... **(2)** killed George Floyd, a Black man. Black people were angry, but they were not surprised: They had seen this happen before. However, many white people were shocked, especially after they had watched the ... **(3)**. In it, Floyd says 'I can't breathe' more than 20 times before he dies. That summer many people joined ... **(4)** in the streets and shouted, 'Black Lives Matter!'
BLM didn't begin in 2020. In 2013, three Black women started the ... **(5)**. The year before, a man had killed a Black teenager called Trayvon Martin for no reason. Martin had only gone to the store to buy candy, but he never came home. Since 2013, BLM has become bigger and more famous around the world as people join the fight for ... **(6)**.

7 SONG *Black Lives Matter* by Dax

a) BEFORE YOU LISTEN **Look at the picture of Dax.
Do you know any of his songs? Which ones?**

b) **Find his music video *Black Lives Matter* on the internet.
After you have watched it, which words do you remember?**

c) **Choose the correct message of the song.**

  A   Protesting is a bad idea.
  B   The police in America aren't a problem.
  C   We should all do something about racism.

Dax is a Canadian-Nigerian rapper, singer and song-writer who lives in the USA.

My task

8 Fight for justice ▶ Digital help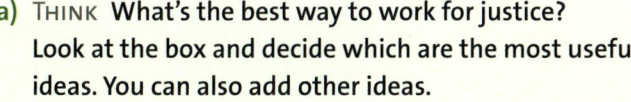

Ideas

a) THINK **What's the best way to work for justice?
Look at the box and decide which are the most useful ideas. You can also add other ideas.**

b) PAIR **Discuss your ideas with a partner and agree on your top three (1 = most useful).**

▶ More help, p. 73

c) SHARE **Discuss your ideas with the class.**

Our number 1 is ... because ...

A doing role-plays against racism at school
B having a protest in the street or in a school or shop
C signing an online petition
D telling people not to use a shop / brand
E writing a social media post
F uploading a video of discrimination

Digital quiz   **I can talk about justice.**   ✓

Let the good times roll!

1 MEDIATION Mardi Gras

a) Kisha has sent you an email about Mardi Gras. Read and find out: When does it take place?

From: kisha.free@example.com

Hey!
I want to tell you about Mardi Gras, which is what we call carnival celebrations here in New Orleans. To prepare for the festival, people first build colorful floats. I've never done it, and it looks **a little** difficult to me, but I'd like to try it one day.
Then in January, bakeries start selling King Cakes. Each cake has a toy baby inside, and if you find it, you have to buy the next cake. Once I almost ate the toy baby! I was **not very** happy about that.
The main Mardi Gras celebration is in February or March. The city is full of parades, music, costumes and **really** beautiful colors: purple, gold and green. Purple is my favorite color, so that always makes me happy! The parades travel through the city and people throw cups, toys and jewelry from the floats. Believe me – it's **extremely** fun!
Do you have something like this where you live?
Kisha

b) Write about five sentences for your school magazine to explain what Mardi Gras is. Write in German and don't include every detail.

2 WORDS Adverbs of degree

a) Adverbs of degree change how strong the adjective is. Match the **blue** adverbs of degree in **1a)** to the German words in the box.

ein wenig • extrem • nicht sehr • sehr

b) Complete the sentences for you.

1 Carnival is **extremely / not very** important in my area.
2 Big parties are **really / not very** fun for me.
3 I'm **a little / extremely** interested in trying King Cake.
4 In my opinion, Mardi Gras looks **a little / really** crazy!

c) WALK AROUND Find a partner and share your opinions for the first sentence. Then find a new partner for the next sentence.

▶ Language file 13, p. 170 ▶ More practice 4, p. 74

3 LISTENING **Grandma's food**

a) BEFORE YOU LISTEN **Match the descriptions (A–D) to the photos (1–4).**

A   A kind of sandwich.
B   A kind of donut that doesn't have a hole.

C   A bread that is made of corn.
D   A dish in a delicious sauce.

gumbo

cornbread

a po'boy

beignets

b) **Which dishes do you think are sweet? Which are spicy?
Listen to Troy, Kisha and Grandma and check.**

c) **Listen again and choose the correct answer, A or B.**

1   Where is Grandma selling her gumbo tomorrow?   A At the parade.   B At the store.
2   What isn't spicy enough for Kisha?   A Cornbread.   B Po'boys.
3   Which food is the best in the world for her?   A Cornbread.   B Beignets.
4   What does Troy give to Grandma?   A A spoon.   B A knife.
5   What does Kisha need to try again?   A Cornbread.   B Beignets.
6   What does Grandma ask Kisha and Troy to do?   A Get out of her kitchen.
      B Help her sell the food.

d) **Tell your partner which food in a) you would and wouldn't like to try and why.**

I'd like to try ... / ... sounds delicious ...
I'm not sure about ... because ... I don't like ...

▶ Workbook, pp. 32–33

4 READING The city of music

a) BEFORE YOU READ **Put up your hand high or low to show how much you agree or disagree with each sentence. Then tell your partner more information.** ▶ Wordbank 2, p. 181

1 Music is a big part of my life.
2 I play or would like to play a musical instrument.
3 I listen to music when I'm angry or sad.
4 I like lots of different kinds of music.

b) **Troy wrote a blog post about music in New Orleans. Which statements in a) are true for him?**

https://www.example.com/TroysBlogOnMusic

Music in New Orleans

Mardi Gras starts tomorrow and I'm so excited because I'm going to play in the parades for the first time! 🙌
I've played the trumpet in my school band for three years now, but this year, my teacher Mr Benoit says that I'm finally ready to join the older kids and play in the street. We've all
5 practiced really hard for months.

Of course, we play traditional New Orleans jazz in our band. It's not really my thing, but it's a big part of our culture and I enjoy playing with everyone else. And if you're a jazz fan, you'll love it! It's hard to get away from that kind of music in the city. Even when it's not Mardi Gras, we have small parades all year for weddings, funerals and all kinds of events.
10 Bands walk and play music in the street. You should check it out!

But don't forget all the other music we have here. There's country music, rock music, hip-hop and the only music that I really like: funk! I listen to it every day when I'm relaxing in my room or doing homework. If you're visiting New Orleans, I can recommend walking around the French Quarter to hear all the street musicians or going to one of the
15 hundreds of music clubs. Don't miss the parties on Bourbon Street where musicians create songs together – it's amazing!

Check out some of my New Orleans music clips and let me know in the comments what you think!

c) **Decide if the sentences 1–6 are true or false. Find the lines in the text that give you the information about each sentence.**

1 Troy plays in the Mardi Gras parades every year.
2 Troy's instrument is the trumpet.
3 Troy likes the music that his band plays.
4 The small parades are only for happy events.
5 Troy mostly listens to music at home.
6 Troy recommends visiting Bourbon Street to hear music.

▶ Workbook, p. 34

5 LISTENING & READING Troy's music clips

a) BEFORE YOU LISTEN AND READ Which styles of music does Troy mention in his blog post?

b) Listen to the music clips (1–5) and match them to Troy's descriptions (A–E).

A You'll hear a lot of hip-hop like this in music clubs.

B You get this kind of country music, bluegrass, a lot in the southern states. It always has lots of violins and guitars.

C This is metal, a kind of rock music. It has lots of electric guitars and drums in it, and it's really loud and fast, so it feels angry.

D This song is called *Down by the Riverside* and it's a famous jazz song. Every musician in the city can play it! It often has lots of trumpets.

E This is funk, my favourite kind of music. It often has electric guitars. It really makes you want to move to the music.

c) Tell a partner which of the five music clips you liked best and why.
What other musical styles do you know?   ▶ Wordbank 2, p. 181

I liked the … song because the rhythm is … / the instruments are … / it makes me feel …

My task

6 Local recommendations

a) Look at the phrases in blue in Troy's blog post. They are useful phrases to give recommendations. Make a list.

b) YOU CHOOSE Do task A or B.   ▶ Digital help

A Write a blog post like Troy's in 4. Give recommendations for things to do, see, listen to and eat in New Orleans. You can use information from this topic or do your own research.
▶ Skills file 12, p. 155

B Write a comment on Troy's blog with recommendations for things that he can do, see, listen to and eat if he visits your area. Is there a local festival you can recommend?

Use the phrases from a) to help you give recommendations.   ▶ More help, p. 74

c) Swap with a partner and check their work, then give feedback.
Which recommendations do you like best?

👍 *You gave interesting information about …*

👎 *Next time, you could use more recommendation phrases.*

▶ Feedback phrases, p. 191

 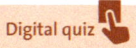

Hurricane!

Good to know

There are about 12 hurricanes every year in the USA, mostly in the South-East. In 2005 Hurricane Katrina hit New Orleans. Almost 2,000 people died in the storm and thousands lost their homes.

1 BEFORE YOU READ Extreme weather

a) Match the words in the box to the correct pictures.

flood • hail • hurricane • storm •
thunder and lightning • tornado

b) What extreme weather have you, your family, or people you know experienced?
You can also talk about extreme weather that you have seen online or on the news.
Tell a partner.   ▶ Wordbank 3, p. 182   ▶ More practice 5, p. 74

2 Where's Zahra?

Read the story about Hurricane Katrina. Say who Zahra is and why Tyler is looking for her.

A It was very quiet. The sky was a strange green color and black clouds were gathering. 'Are you ready, Tyler?'
5 his dad asked. 'We'll only be at your aunt and uncle's tonight,' he said.
'But what about our house, Dad? Will it be
10 OK?' asked Tyler.

Hurricane Katrina was on its way and people in their part of New Orleans had got a warning that they should stay with family out of town until the storm was over.
'Our house will be fine,' said his dad. 'Don't
worry, Tyler. While you're packing, I'm just going to see if Miss Elektra and Zahra want to come with us.'

Miss Elektra was their neighbor. Her daughter Zahra was fourteen like Tyler and they had grown up together. Last year he had tried to kiss her, but Zahra had just laughed. 'Tyler, you're my favorite person ever, but you're like my brother!'

'All OK,' said his dad when he came back. 'Miss Elektra's sister is on her way and she'll be here soon. Let's go!'

At his aunt and uncle's house, Tyler listened to the storm. The house was outside the path of the hurricane, but he could hear rain and wind blowing violently against the house. Sometimes he jumped when he heard thunder.

B In the early morning, Tyler and his dad drove home. As they got closer to New Orleans, the city looked terrible. Trees and parts of houses were everywhere and cars were on their sides. Many of the roads were full of water from the floods. Tyler didn't say anything.

In their street, some of the new houses were fine, some had no roofs, and some of the older ones were completely destroyed. Tyler saw his house and relaxed a little. It was OK. Then he saw Miss Elektra and Zahra's house. The roof wasn't there any more – and the door was open.

'Zahra!' shouted Tyler. He and his dad ran into the house. Miss Elektra was sitting on the kitchen floor. She looked tired but unhurt. 'I'm OK,' she said. 'My sister couldn't get through yesterday because of the floods but she's on her way now. Could you go and find Zahra, please? She ran out after Popcorn and I'm worried about her.'

Popcorn was a very big dog with sad eyes. Zahra had found him outside one day scared and hungry. Zahra had given him some food and they had been together since then.

C Tyler and his dad ran into the street and called Zahra's and Popcorn's names. Nothing. 'Please let her be OK,' thought Tyler. They walked to the next street. And there suddenly were Zahra and Popcorn. The dog barked happily when he saw his neighbors.

Tyler threw his arms around Zahra. He was laughing and crying at the same time. 'It's OK, Tyler,' said Zahra. 'I was really scared when the roof came off, but we're all fine.' 'Happy to hear it,' said Tyler's dad. 'But I'm sure a lot of other people weren't so lucky. Let's tell your mom that you're safe and then check on our other neighbors. We all need to help each other now.'

3 Tyler's story

Read the story again and put the events in the correct order.   *1A; 2 …*

A   Tyler's dad asks Miss Elektra if she and Zahra want to get in the car.
B   Tyler and his dad find Zahra and Popcorn.
C   Tyler and his dad leave their house to stay with family before the storm.
D   Tyler sees that the roof of Zahra's house is gone.
E   Tyler and his dad drive back home the next morning.
F   Miss Elektra is fine, but Zahra and Popcorn aren't at their house.

4 Feelings and reactions

Match Tyler's feelings and reactions (A–E) to the events in the story (1–5).

1   When he's packing to leave,
2   When they're in the car on the way back,
3   When he sees his house,
4   When he sees Zahra's house,
5   When they find Zahra and Popcorn,

A   Tyler is silent because the city looks terrible.
B   Tyler is worried about his house.
C   Tyler is shocked because the roof is gone.
D   Tyler laughs and cries.
E   Tyler relaxes a little because it is OK.

▶ More practice 6, p. 75

5 Freeze!

a)   **Choose a scene from the story. Describe what is happening or what has just happened and how the people feel. Look at 4 for help.**

Let's take the scene where Tyler is talking to …

I think we should choose the scene where …

b)   **Show your scene as a freeze-frame.**
Students from the other groups explain what is happening.   ▶ More help, p. 75

   Digital quiz 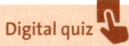   **I can talk about extreme weather experiences.**

Storm chasers

1 BEFORE YOU WATCH **What do you think?**

Look at the pictures and read the tip.
What is a storm chaser?

'To chase' means to follow
someone or something quickly.

2 Reed and his team

a) Watch the video.
Check your answers from **1** and say
what different kinds of weather you see
in the film.

b) Copy the sentences (1–8). Then watch
the video again and tick the things that
happen.

1   They follow a tornado.
2   They drive across Oklahoma.
3   They drive into the tornado.
4   Reed phones the local TV channel.
5   Reed live-streams the tornado.
6   Somebody in the team gets hurt.
7   The storm breaks part of the car.
8   They leave when it gets too dangerous.

c) Compare with a partner.

3 LIFE SKILLS Stay safe when you take risks

a) Talk about the questions (1–3).

1   Why do you think Reed and his team do this job?

   I think that they like ...

2   What risks do they take?

   They drive into ...

3   How do they stay safe?

   They use ...

   ▶ More help, p. 75

b) Would you like to be a storm chaser? Why (not)?

▶ Workbook, p. 35

How to write a summary

1 Get a main idea

What is the story on **pages 58–59** about?
If you can't remember, skim the story again.

▶ Skills file 11, p. 154

 When you skim a text, you read it quickly for the main ideas. Titles, photos and captions can also help you.

2 Take notes

a) What are the key events in the story?
Take two to three very short notes for each paragraph (A–C). For example, these could be your notes for paragraph A:

– Tyler + dad leave house before storm
– want to stay with aunt + uncle

b) Compare your notes with a partner. Do you have similar notes?

3 Tips for writing a summary

a) Read the summary of the story and compare it with your notes from 2a). Do you have the same or different information?

b) Answer the questions about the summary.

1 How long is the summary compared to the story: a bit shorter or a lot shorter?
2 What tense is the summary in: past or present?
3 Does the summary add information that is not in the story?
4 Does the writer of the summary give their opinion?
5 Does the summary include whole sentences from the story or only the writer's own words?

c) A summary needs an introduction. Which *wh*-questions does the introduction to the summary of *Hurricane!* answer? What **blue useful phrases** can you use?

What? Hurricane Katrina. Phrase: The story ... is about ...

A summary of *Hurricane!*

The story *Hurricane!* is about Hurricane Katrina. **It takes place** in New Orleans **in the year** 2005. **The main characters are** Tyler, his dad, Zahra and Miss Elektra.

Tyler and his dad leave their house before the storm. They want to stay with his aunt and uncle. Zahra and Miss Elektra want to stay with Zahra's aunt.

Tyler and his dad drive home the next morning. Houses and cars are broken, and everything looks terrible. Their house is fine, but their neighbour's house has no roof. Miss Elektra is OK, but Zahra and her dog Popcorn aren't there.

Tyler and his dad look for them and they find Zahra and Popcorn. Tyler is very happy and he cries. Then they go to help their other neighbours.

▶ More help, p. 75
▶ Skills file 14, p. 157

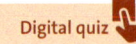 Digital quiz   I can prepare to write a summary.

Write a summary

Step 1: Think of a book or a film

You are going to write a summary of a book that you have read, or of a film that you have seen. First brainstorm ideas.

> *I like the book ..., so I might take that.*

> *I've just seen ..., so I could write about it. Or maybe ...*

Step 2: What is it about?

▶ Digital help

What's the book or film about? Answer the questions: *Who? When? Where? What?*
Write the introduction with your answers. Use the blue phrases from 3c) on page 62.

The film 'Wonka' is about a special man who loves chocolate. The film is from 2023 and takes place in England. The main characters are ...

Step 3: Take notes and write a summary

Write notes on the main events. Then use your notes to write the rest of your summary. Remember to use the present tense.

▶ Study skills, p. 62   ▶ Skills file 6, p. 149   ▶ Skills file 14, p. 157   ▶ Digital help

Step 4: Check your partner's summary

Read your partner's summary and check that:

- the summary has an introduction
- the summary isn't too long
- the summary is in the present tense

▶ Skills file 15, p. 158

Step 5: Give your partner feedback

List the good points of your partner's summary. Then make suggestions to make it better.

> *Your summary wasn't too long and the film sounded really exciting.*

> *You used the past tense in your summary.*

▶ Feedback phrases, p. 191   ▶ Digital help

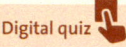 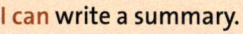

1 LISTENING A rainy day in New Orleans

I can talk about the South-East of the USA.

a) Look at pictures (A–E) and listen to the conversation between Kisha, Troy and their aunt Mae. Put the pictures in the correct order.

visit a church

visit a museum

try some beignets

ride a tram

enjoy some live music

b) Listen again and complete the sentences (1–6). Write the missing word.

1 It's ... in New Orleans today.
2 Kisha enjoys art from local and ... artists.
3 In the tram you get the best ... of the city.
4 The storm almost destroyed the whole ...
5 The French Quarter is always very ...
6 Mae doesn't usually eat in ...

c) SPEAKING Tell your partner which two activities from a) you would like to do and why.

2 Adam's email

I can talk about rules.

a) LANGUAGE Read Adam's email to Troy and choose the correct <u>modal verb</u>.

●●● ⌲ ▭

From: adam123@example.com

Hi Troy,

I'm so angry with my parents! I **needn't / am not allowed to (1)** go out late during the week. My parents say I **mustn't / don't have to (2)** come home later than 8 p.m. All my friends can stay out later than 8, so it's embarrassing when I **can / have to (3)** leave early. But my parents don't understand. They always say 'You **aren't able to / needn't (4)** worry about what other people think.' I know that I **should / am allowed to (5)** talk to my parents about this, but I don't know what to say. Do you have any ideas?

Adam

---

b) Write a short reply to Adam and give him some advice.

Hi, Adam, I think you should ... Tell them ... Ask them if you can ...

Check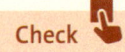

3 WORDS **Avery's text**

Avery is writing an introduction to the online school magazine, *Hear our voices*. **Complete the text with words from the box.**

In 2012, after a man had killed Trayvon Martin, people had different ... **(1)**. Some people were sad, others were angry – but many people felt that they needed to DO something. Students at our school decided to start this magazine to share their experiences of ... **(2)** and racism. Many years later, there are still too many injustices in this world. If you want to do something, too, we have ideas for you: You can collect names for our online ... **(3)**. You can ask for help if someone ... **(4)** you differently. You can speak out when you see something that is unfair. Now is not the time to be ... **(5)**. This is important, and what you decide to do ... **(6)**!

discrimination • matters • petition • reactions • silent • treats

4 READING **Beyoncé speaks out**

In 2020, singer-songwriter Beyoncé gave an online speech for university students. She thanked them for telling the world that Black lives matter, and told them that real change had already started with them. She also spoke out against sexism and racism and talked about the problems she has faced in her work. She said that there is discrimination against some people in the music business, including Black women, and that she had started her own music company to try and change this. She said that she is proud to give jobs to people from diverse backgrounds. Then she told the students to celebrate who they are and to keep working for change. Her speech has over one million views.

a) **Read the text about Beyoncé and decide if sentences 1–5 are true or false.**

1 Beyoncé gave her speech at a university.
2 She said that students need to start changing things.
3 She wants more diversity in the music business.
4 She said that students should celebrate their grades.
5 More than one million people have watched her speech.

b) SPEAKING **What do you think: Should singers use their name to fight injustice? You can use the ideas below or your own ideas.**

Yes, they should No, they shouldn't	because	they have a lot of fans/money. they are role models. they should just perform songs. they might do it for the wrong reasons. …

 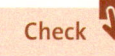

5 WRITING A winter holiday

Read the text message from your American friend Zoe. Write back with <u>three</u> recommendations. You can use the ideas and sentence beginnings on the right or your own ideas.

Christmas markets
ice rink
shopping (for presents)
skiing
for a walk in the snow
game / movie / show

Hey! I'm going to be in your area for a few days in December! Do you have any recommendations? Zoe 😊

Hi, Zoe! There are some great things to do in ... You should check out ... I can also recommend that you go ... If you're a fan of ..., you should watch ... I hope you enjoy ...

6 WORDS Extreme weather in the news

Read the news updates (1–6). Complete the sentences with the correct word from the box.

> blows • destroys • floods • live-stream • power • tornado

1 More than 3000 homes without ...
2 A ... is coming: Stay home!
3 ... turn city streets into rivers
4 Our channel will ... during the hurricane
5 Hail ... roofs and windows
6 Extreme wind ... during storm

7 MEDIATION A research project

Your friend Amir is doing a presentation about extreme weather events across the world. You found an article about the topic and want to tell him about it in your own words in German. You can start your email like this:

Hi, Amir, ich habe einen Artikel über die Auswirkungen des ... auf ... gelesen. Sanibel ist ...

Hurricane Ian destroys a lot of Sanibel Island

Sanibel is a small island off the coast of Florida. In September 2022, Hurricane Ian hit Sanibel. It was one of the worst hurricanes in Florida's history. It destroyed many things across the island – not only houses, businesses and buildings, but also trees and plants. Years later, people are still working hard to make life better on Sanibel Island.

Check

8 SKILLS **Tornado team**

'Leo, breakfast in two minutes!'
'OK,' called Leo, 'I'll be there after I've watched this video.'
'No, in two minutes!' called his mom, Tanya.
5 Leo sighed and stopped the new *Tornado team* video. It was an awesome video because the team was getting really close to the tornado!
'So Mom, I've been thinking,' said Leo, eating
10 his breakfast. 'Maybe I'll become a storm chaser. It looks like so much fun and I'd have enough work here in Oklahoma.'
'You want to take a lot of risks to do something that is really dangerous? I don't
15 think so. I thought you wanted to be a mechanic, like me?'
'Oh, come on, Mom! Those *Tornado team* videos are really cool!'
'Maybe a little,' said Tanya and smiled. 'Now,
20 hurry up, I need to be at work in half an hour.'

A few days later, Leo got a warning on his phone. 'Tornado warning for Oklahoma – stay home!' Then Leo checked the *Tornado team* and saw that they already had posted:
25 'Oklahoma: WE'RE COMING!'
That afternoon, Leo and Tanya started preparing the house for the storm. Leo was putting some food onto the shelves of the safe room when he saw another post from
30 the *Tornado team*: 'Everyone, we have car problems 😣. We can't close one of the windows! Sorry, Oklahoma, no tornado for us!'

Leo couldn't stop himself. He wrote a comment back to them: 'Hey guys, pretty 35 sure my mom can help with this. She can fix anything!'
'Why are you smiling so much?' asked Tanya.

A few hours later, a big car arrived in the street. 'Hey, Mom, they're here!' called Leo. 40
'Who is here?' asked Leo's mom, surprised.
'You'll see! Can you come help us, please?'

The next day, Tanya and Leo were feeling grateful. The worst weather was over, and their house was OK. Leo saw a message 45 from his friend Ally: 'Have you seen this?'

It was a link to a video of yesterday's storm. At the beginning of the video were the words 'Thanks to Leo and Tanya Diaz. We couldn't have done this without your help!' 'Mom!' 50 called Leo, 'I need to show you something really cool!'

a) **Read the story. Complete the sentences to write an introduction for a summary.**

The story 'Tornado team' is about a boy who … It takes place in …
The main characters are …

b) **What are the main events in the story? Take notes. Then discuss with a partner.**

United 🇺🇸

> *Find out about our national holiday – Juneteenth[1].*

A magazine for young people across the USA

Juneteenth *by Kisha Freeman*

'Juneteenth' became a national holiday[2] in the USA in 2021. I'd like to tell you more about it.

For hundreds of years, enslaved[3] people worked in the USA for no money and had no rights.

Slavery officially ended on different days in different states. In Texas, it ended on June 19th, 1865, and Black people have celebrated this date for many years. Some people call this day 'Freedom Day'.

Today people celebrate the day with music, parades, barbecues and other events. It's a day of happiness[4]. I asked my grandma what Juneteenth means to her and she said, 'Respect and equal rights for everybody. Black is beautiful and we are proud to be Black.'

Unfortunately[5], there is still a lot of racism in the USA, for example in neighborhoods, at work and in the police. That's why many Black activists use Juneteenth to protest for equal rights.

Black lives matter!

Imagine you **can** create **a** new **national** holiday.
What would **it** be **and** how **would** you **celebrate** it?

---

[1] **Juneteenth** (von *June* und *nineteenth*:) *der 19. Juni*   [2] **holiday** hier: *der Feiertag*   [3] **enslaved** *versklavt*
[4] **happiness** *die Freude, die Fröhlichkeit*   [5] **unfortunately** *leider, unglücklicherweise*

Black history *by Troy Freeman*

Every February, Black History Month celebrates the lives of Black Americans. I have just watched a film about an amazing Black woman, Harriet Tubman, and would like to share my review with you.

Celebrate Black History Month with us!

Harriet Tubman was born around 1820. Her family was enslaved on a farm in Maryland, so Harriet was born into slavery. We don't know her exact birthday, because white slaveholders[1] treated enslaved people like property. It wasn't important to remember their birthdays. Harriet had to work hard for the white family that owned[2] her, even as a small child. They hit her and treated her very badly, so in 1849, she decided to run away.

When Harriet was free, she helped other enslaved people to freedom. She fought for the rights of Black people until she died in 1913 (at about 91 years old). Today, most Americans would like to see Harriet Tubman on a new twenty-dollar bill[3]! She would be the first African American on a US dollar bill, and the second woman. How amazing is that?

Harriet film review

In this film we see Harriet Tubman's escape[4] from slavery and how her enslaver's son Gideon hunts[5] her. There's a scary scene where Harriet is on a bridge and Gideon and his men come from both sides of the bridge. Harriet climbs onto the top and says, 'I'm gonna be free or die.' Then she jumps into the river!

Luckily[6], Harriet is fine and she keeps walking. She walks 100 miles north to Philadelphia, where she can be free.

Harriet decides to help her family and other enslaved people. She joins a community of men and women called the Underground Railroad[7]. They guide enslaved people to freedom. It's very dangerous for Harriet, but she says, 'If I'm free, they should be too.'

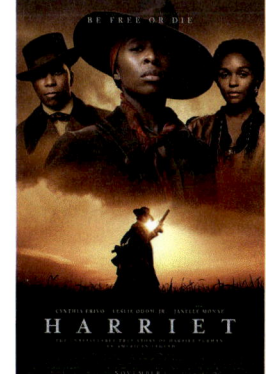

This is an awesome film and I think Harriet Tubman was a very brave woman. I learned a lot about her life and about Black history.

★ ★ ★ ★ ★ I give this film five stars because it's important to know our history and the actors are fantastic. Watch the movie (or the trailer on the internet)!

Who would *you* like to see on a *bill* ?

---

[1] **slaveholder** *der Sklavenhalter, die Sklavenhalterin* [2] (to) **own** *besitzen* [3] **bill** *der Geldschein* [4] **escape** *die Flucht*
[5] (to) **hunt** *jagen* [6] **luckily** *glücklicherweise* [7] **Underground Railroad** *die Untergrundbahn*, hier: *das Netzwerk aus geheimen Fluchtwegen*

Partner page

▶ Page 52

5 GLOBAL GOALS **Peace and justice**

a) **Partner B:** Scan the text about Colin Kaepernick. What has he won awards for?

Colin Kaepernick

In 2016, Colin Kaepernick played football for the NFL (National Football League). He is most famous for kneeling during the national anthem. In the USA, every game always starts with the national anthem. It's important for everyone to stand up to show respect. Kaepernick knelt to protest against police racism and violence.

Some people supported him, and other people didn't – they said that he shouldn't protest at a game. After he started to kneel, his team didn't want to keep him, and he couldn't get another job with the NFL.

Kaepernick has won many awards for his work as an activist, and he has given more than one million dollars to different charities. His protest has become an important symbol in the fight for justice.

b) Read the text and answer these questions. Take notes.

1 What sport did he play?
2 What is he most famous for?
3 What do Americans show when they stand during the national anthem?
4 What did he want to protest against?
5 What negative things did he experience?
6 What does his protest mean today?

c) Answer partner A's questions about Colin Kaepernick.

d) Ask partner A these questions about Serena Williams.

1 What sport did she play?
2 What is she most famous for?
3 What negative things has she experienced?
4 What other work does she do?
5 What does she use to fight for justice?
6 What has given Black people a voice?

e) What do you think: Should players use their name to fight against racism and other problems? Should players protest at games? ☒ Why (not)?

Yes, I think that players should ...
No, I think that players shouldn't ...

Diff bank

▶ Page 46

More practice 1   Atlanta, the place to be

Read the blog post and correct the sentences.

1   The blog writer doesn't think that Atlanta is a good city for teens.
2   Atlanta doesn't have many shops.
3   People go skiing in the Chattahoochee River.
4   *Dragon Con* is a big meeting for people who love nature.
5   You can drink 10 different kinds of cola at the museum.

---

https://www.example.com/AtlantaBlog

Atlanta, the place to be

Atlanta is the capital of the state of Georgia and I think there's no better place in the USA for teens. There's so much to do here. Check out my top 3 things for teens in the city:

▶   Atlanta is famous for its malls and busy streets, but if you prefer a more peaceful day in nature, go for a walk or enjoy a picnic near the beautiful **Chattahoochee** River. You can even go fishing or try paddleboarding.

▶   If sci-fi is more your thing, you can't miss **Dragon Con**. Every September, thousands of cosplayers, writers, comic fans and even movie actors come to this amazing event.

▶   One of the world's biggest and most famous **cola** brands comes from Atlanta: You can visit its museum to find out about the drink's history and its secret recipe. You can even try over 100 different kinds of cola from all over the world. How did this drink become so important? Get answers here.

▶Page 47

More help **2 Where should you visit?**

Take turns to play roles from the box. Say which places in the Southeast your partner should visit and why. Use the photos in 1 to help you.

I like … I love … I am interested in …	music. sport. history.		Where should I visit?
I want to…	go shopping. / take cool photos for social media. / take a boat trip. / watch a hockey game.		
You should go to … You'll be interested in … I think you'd like …	Nashville Atlanta New Orleans the Whitney Plantation the Mississippi River	because you can	listen to really good music. shop at the coolest malls. learn more about history. go to a hockey game. relax on the river.

▶Page 48

More help **1 Shopping while Black**

d) **Why was the security guard's behaviour racist? What do you think about Kisha's post? Think for a minute and then tell a partner your opinion. Give reasons.**

I think the security guard was racist because she only asked / she didn't ask …
In my opinion it's great that Kisha posted online because it's important to protest / people should know about these situations / …

▶Page 49

More practice 2 **May I?**

Read the sentences and choose the correct answer.

1 Jess asked her mom, 'May / Must I go to the movies tonight? It'll be so much fun!'
2 I'm going to have lunch at home, so you can't / needn't make it for me.
3 My brother is angry with me. He says that I am not allowed to / have to go into his room.
4 I'm so tired! Must / Can we have a break before we practise some more?
5 You haven't had anything to drink all day? You should / mustn't drink something now.
6 I want to see you! Must you / Are you able to come tonight?
7 We can / mustn't leave our bikes here. It's not safe.
8 I think Grandma wants to hear from us. We could / needn't try to call her later.

Zane's room
No sisters allowed!

▶ Page 51

More practice 3 **My parents are strict!**

Choose the correct form for each sentence.
The <u>time words</u> can help you.

1 My parents are strict. **I wasn't allowed to /
won't be allowed to** go to a party <u>last
weekend</u>.
2 If I don't do my homework, I **wasn't allowed
to / won't be allowed to** go to the cinema
<u>tomorrow</u>.
3 Before I played football <u>last Saturday</u>,
I **had to / will have to** tidy my room.
4 My parents want me to play the guitar. I **had to / will have to** practise <u>next summer</u>.
5 They took my phone <u>yesterday</u>, so I **will not be able to / wasn't able to** text my friends.

Parallel exercise **4** LISTENING **The Little Rock Nine**

c) **Listen again. Complete the sentences with the correct words: A, B or C.**

1 The Little Rock Nine were   A **states**   B **schools**   C **students**.
2 They tried to go to a 'white'   A **school**   B **state**   C **hospital**.
3 Racist white parents were   A **happy**   B **angry**   C **fine**.
4 To stop the students, the state sent   A **parents**   B **students**   C **soldiers**.
5 To help the students, the president sent the   A **US army**   B **state**   C **students**.
6 Sometimes we have to fight   A **to be happy**   B **for justice**   C **the army**.

▶ Page 53

More help **8** MY TASK **Fight for justice**

b) PAIR **Discuss your ideas with a partner and agree on your top three (1 = most useful).**

I think … is useful	because	it's an easy way to protest. people see it on social media. it hurts their business / name. it makes people see how terrible racism is. it shows clearly what happened. you can do it at home.

► Page 54

More practice 4 **Troy loves Mardi Gras**

Look at the smileys and choose the correct adverbs for each sentence.

extremely = 🤩
really = 🙂
a little = 😐
not very = ☹️

1 I always get 🤩 excited when it's time to celebrate Mardi Gras.
2 It's 🙂 important to my family, so we all take part in the festival.
3 Mardi Gras celebrations in smaller towns are different. If you ask me, they're 😐 boring.
4 My grandpa likes to celebrate Mardi Gras outside the city because he's ☹️ comfortable with loud noises.
5 But this year, he'll come to see me play the trumpet. I think that's 🙂 sweet of him!
6 I'm 😐 nervous, but I think it's going to be an 🤩 fun Mardi Gras this year!

► Page 57

More help **6** MY TASK **Local recommendations**

b)

You should / You can / Why not / You really have to	check out / eat / go to / listen to / see / taste / try / visit / ...
Don't forget / Don't miss / You should check out / You'll love	the beach / the castle / the festival / the street music / ...
I can recommend	going to / seeing / trying ...

► Page 58

✉ **More practice 5** LISTENING **Hurricane Katrina**

🔊 **a) Kisha did a presentation about Hurricane Katrina at school. Listen. Are the sentences 1–6 true or false?**

1 Katrina was a tornado.
2 Kisha was five years old when Katrina hit.
3 Some areas of the coast were OK.
4 One hundred people had to leave their homes.
5 Lots of people had to wait for help.
6 Most of these people were Black.

🔊 **b) What happened after Katrina? Choose the correct words to complete the sentence. Then listen again and check.**

Thousands of people never **came back to / visited** New Orleans because they didn't have **buses / homes** any more.

▶Page 60

More practice 6 WORDS **Phrases**

Match the words A–F to 1–6 to make phrases from the story *Hurricane!*.

1 the clouds   3 the wind   5 be
2 get   4 call   6 check on

A a warning   B lucky   C somebody's name   D blows   E people   F gather

More help **5 Freeze!**

b)

| Tyler and his dad are driving ... / looking for Zahra, and ... | In this scene, Tyler is packing because ... / at his aunt and uncle's house and ... | I think Tyler / his dad / Zahra feels ... |

▶Page 61

More help **3** LIFE SKILLS **Stay safe when you take risks**

a) **Talk about the questions (1–3). You can use the ideas in the boxes.**

1 Why do you think Reed and his team do this job?

> be exciting • like the danger • need the money • do something useful • ...

2 What risks do they take?

> drive into a dangerous situation • things flying around might hurt them • have an accident • ...

3 How do they stay safe?

> use special equipment • close doors and windows • leave when it gets too dangerous • ...

▶Page 62

More help **3 Tips for writing a summary**

c) A summary needs an introduction. Which *wh*-questions does the introduction to the summary of *Hurricane!* answer? What blue useful phrases can you use?

What?	Hurricane Katrina	The story ... is about ...
Where?	...	...
When?	...	
Who?		

Unit 3
Texas: Teen life

Texas is north of Mexico, so lots of people speak Spanish

The state capital: Austin

Space Center, Houston

Texas barbecue

Cowboy culture

1 SPEAKING **All about Texas**

a) Look at the photos (A–E) and read the captions. What do they tell you about Texas?

b) Copy this mind map and collect information on Texas in it. Add more facts as you work through the Unit.

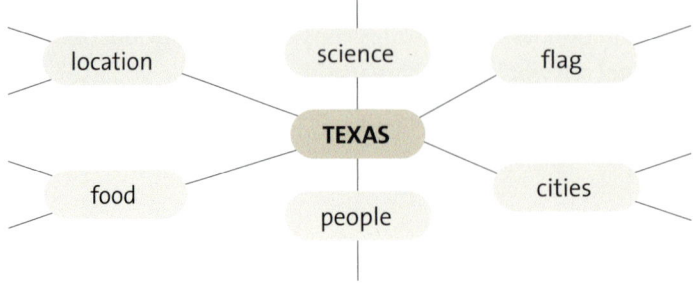

location science flag

TEXAS

food cities

people

▶ Map of the USA, inside back cover

Nach dieser Unit kann ich ...

- ⊘ über Texas reden
- ⊘ über das Leben in einer Kleinstadt sprechen
- ⊘ das Schulleben in den USA beschreiben
- ⊘ über Jobs und Zukunftspläne sprechen
- ⊘ über Kleidung in der Schule reden
- ⊘ Kommunikationsstrategien anwenden

Unit task ⊘

- ⊘ ein Interview führen

F Downtown in Lufkin, Texas

G A coffee shop

H A street mural

I Ruben on the family ranch

2 VIEWING With Ruben in Lufkin, Texas

 a) BEFORE YOU WATCH **Look at the pictures (F–I). What do you think this town is like? Use the words in the box.**

boring • busy • cool • cute • dangerous • exciting • pretty • quiet • rural • safe

b) **Watch the video and say if your ideas in a) were correct.**

c) **Watch again and answer the questions.**

1 What are Ruben's favourite indoor and outdoor activities in Lufkin?
2 What does Ruben think of his town?
3 What would you like to do in Lufkin?

▶ Workbook, p. 42

Digital quiz   **I can talk about Texas.** ⊘

Small-town life

1 LISTENING At home in Fredericksburg

Jacob Schmidt (15)   Diego Perez (14)

a) BEFORE YOU LISTEN Look at the pictures of the boys and of their hometown Fredericksburg, Texas. What's special about the town sign and Jacob's family name?

b) Listen to Diego and Jacob. Do they like their town?

c) Listen again. Who says it: Diego (D) or Jacob (J)?

1   I like the history of our city.
2   I think that people are really nice here.
3   It's a beautiful place to live.
4   The downtown area is great for tourists.

5   We want normal stores and places for teenagers.
6   We don't have a public transportation system.

▶ More practice 1, p. 103

2 SPEAKING Small towns: positive and negative

a) PLACEMAT What is positive (+) and what is negative (−) about small towns? Write your ideas in your part of the placemat. You can also use the ideas in the box or from exercise 1.

- places: movie theater, ...
- activities: football club, ...
- transport: buses, ...
- people: friendly, ...

b) Turn the paper and read each student's ideas.

c) Discuss the ideas with your group. Agree on the two most important positive and two most important negative things. Write them in the middle of your placemat.

- *I think no movie theater is really negative.*
- *I disagree, I think it's more fun to watch movies at home.*
- *OK, what about ...*

d) Tell the class your results. Do you have similar opinions about small towns?

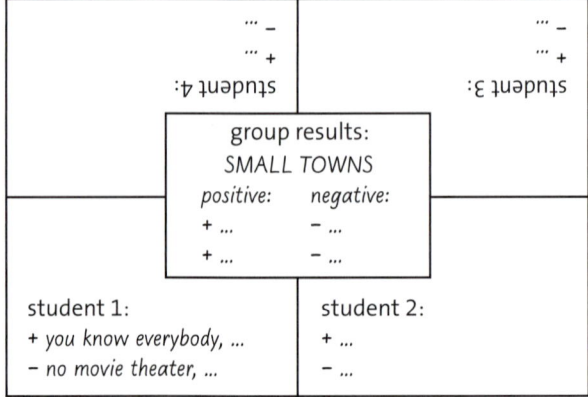

3 READING **A town for young people**

a) BEFORE YOU READ **How do you get around where you live? For example do you take the bus, does someone drive you, or do you travel another way? Tell your partner.**

Good to know

The USA is very big, and in most places, people need cars to get around. In Texas you can get a driver's license at 16.

b) **Read the letter to the editor. Are the sentences (1–6) true or false?**
☒ **Correct the false sentences.**

1 Melissa loves the people in Fredericksburg.
2 For her, the city is perfect.
3 She wants a public transportation system.
4 You can earn a lot with jobs for teens.
5 Melissa wants more places for tourists.
6 There aren't enough opportunities.

We want to hear from local teens

Fredericksburg

Are you a teenager in Fredericksburg? Do you have opinions about our city? Write a letter to the editor and send it to newspaper@example.com.

If we had more cool places for teenagers …

1 …
Dear editor,
I am writing to you because I am a teenager in Fredericksburg. Last week, you asked local teens to send you their opinions about our city.
2 …
First, I love the people in Fredericksburg because they are always ready to help others. If I moved to a different city, I would miss the friendly people here.
3 …
But our city isn't perfect. When you want to go somewhere, you need a car. If I ran the city, I'd create a public transportation system. And if there was a bus, my parents wouldn't need to drive me around. I hope I can buy a car one day, but you can't earn a lot of money with jobs for teens. If I won the lottery, I'd buy a car.
Also, I think there are too many expensive stores and restaurants for tourists. We need normal places for teens to go to. If our city wasn't so expensive, teenagers would be happier.
4 …
Finally, my friends and I will probably move to a bigger city after we finish school. If there were more opportunities here, I wouldn't leave Fredericksburg. Will things get better?
Yours faithfully,
Melissa S. (16)

c) **Match the labels A–D to the paragraphs 1–4.** *1D, 2 …*

A Things that should change   B Positive things   C Conclusion   D Introduction

▶ Skills file 13, p. 156
▶ Workbook, p. 43

Erklär-
film

4 LOOKING AT LANGUAGE **Conditional sentences type 2**

a) Match the two clauses in the sentences from the letter to the editor on **page 79.** *1C, 2 …*

1 If I **moved** to a different city,
2 If I **ran** the city,
3 If there **was** a bus,
4 If I **won** the lottery,
5 If our city **wasn't** so expensive,
6 If there **were** more opportunities here,

A teenagers **would be** happier.
B my parents **wouldn't need** to drive me around.
C I **would miss** the friendly people here.
D I **wouldn't leave** Fredericksburg.
E I**'d create** a public transportation system.
F I**'d buy** a car.

b) Choose the correct answer A or B to complete the rule.

Mit Bedingungssätzen Typ 2 sagst du, was unter bestimmten Bedingungen geschehen würde, also „Was wäre, wenn …".

Die Bedingung, die im *if*-Satz genannt wird, ist …
A sehr wahrscheinlich.
B möglich, aber unwahrscheinlich.

Bedingungssätze Typ 2 haben zwei Teile:

If-Satz (Bedingung)	Hauptsatz (mögliche Folge)
If I **moved** to a different city **simple past**	I **would miss** the friendly people here. **would** (oder Kurzform **'d**) + **infinitive** (Grundform)

c) What about you? Complete the sentence in three different ways. Then tell a partner.

If I won the lottery, I'd …	buy a car / a house / lots of clothes / video games / … give money to charity / a friend / my family / … start a restaurant / cafe / business / … travel around the world / to space / … move to the USA / …

► Language file 15, p. 171

5 **If I lived in …**

Complete the sentences with the correct form of the verb (*would* or *'d* and infinitive).

1 If I lived in Texas, I **…** **(buy)** a pair of cowboy boots.
2 If I visited New York, I **…** **(find)** a new baseball hat.
3 If I was in California, I **…** **(get)** some cool sunglasses.
4 If I went to Alaska, I **…** **(look for)** very warm clothes.
5 If I travelled to Hawaii, I **…** **(wear)** a colourful shirt.
6 If I was in Florida, I **…** **(run)** from hungry alligators!

► More practice 2, p. 104

6 What would you do?

a) Partner B: Look at page 102.
Partner A: Ask your partner these questions.

1   If you had a year to travel the world, where would you go?
2   If you bought your own house, what would it be like?
3   If you moved to a different country, what would you miss about where you live now?
4   If your town had no electricity for one week, what would you do?
5   If you were an architect, what would you build?

b) Partner A: Answer partner B's questions.

If I was an animal, I'd be a …

c) Tell the class one interesting thing about partner B.

If Ahaim had a year to travel the world, he'd go to …

My task

7 A letter to the editor   ▶ Digital help

a) You are going to write a letter to the editor about where you live. In a small group, brainstorm what is good and bad for teenagers in your area. Use your placemats from exercise 2, p. 78.

b) Use your notes as well as the ideas below and write your letter.

Dear editor,
I'm writing to you because I am a teenager in … *(place)*.

I love living here, because …	there's a lot to do / people are friendly / …
But we don't have …	a cinema / a swimming pool / …
I think that it's …	a bit boring for teenagers / too quiet / …
If I ran the town, I would create …	a youth centre / a disco / new places for teenagers to go / …
If I had a lot of money, I would buy …	more buses / a new skatepark / a nicer school building / …

Finally, I hope that our area will change a lot. / Finally, I love this place, and I don't want it to change too much.

Yours faithfully,
(name)

▶ Skills file 13, p. 156

c) Swap letters with a partner and give each other feedback.

> *I like what you wrote.*
> *I want a new skatepark too.*

> *Thanks. You've done a great job!*
> *Your ideas for our town are really creative.*

▶ Feedback phrases, p. 191

▶ Workbook, pp. 44–45

School life

1 READING A German exchange student

a) BEFORE YOU READ Alicja is a German exchange student in her freshman year. Look at the box: what grade is she in?

freshman = 9th grade
sophomore = 10th grade
junior = 11th grade
senior = 12th grade

b) Read the interview and find out if Alicja has made any friends.

Alicja thinks our school is awesome!

Diego Hi, Alicja, how do you like your exchange so far?

Alicja The school is awesome! Everyone is really nice.

Diego How do you get to school?

Alicja I take the school bus. If I had a driver's license, I would drive to school like juniors and seniors do.

Diego What's different to your school in Germany?

Alicja The cool events every week. For example, there are big parties before sports games – everyone wears school colors, the band plays music and we all cheer for our teams.

Diego They are fun, aren't they? Are there any other differences?

Alicja In Germany, we don't say the Pledge of Allegiance to the flag. You're very proud of this country, aren't you?

Diego Yes, we are! Is there anything that you don't like?

Alicja I think it's scary that there are security guards with guns at this school. We don't have that in Germany.

Diego OK, but I guess that in Germany, there aren't as many guns or school shootings as in the USA. However, let's finish with something positive. What do you like about the school day?

Alicja The electives – you know, the fun classes. I'm designing my own website in one class.

Diego Cool! What time does school end in Germany?

Alicja Well, it depends, but the school day at my German school is as long as the school day at your school.

Diego Do you do any after-school activities here?

Alicja I play on the softball team, and I'm in several clubs. I've made lots of new friends in clubs.

Diego That's great. Is there anything that you're looking forward to?

Alicja Yes, I think that prom sounds great. I've never been to a dance with a theme and really fancy clothes before. It looks amazing!

Diego It does, doesn't it? Thanks for doing this interview with me, Alicja.

c) Talk to a partner about American schools.

There are yellow school buses and …

Right. And there's …

▶ More practice 3, p. 104

▶ Workbook, p. 46

Erklär-
film

2 Comparing American and German schools

a) Create sentences and tell each other what you think about American schools versus German schools.

In American schools, there are more	events / electives / clubs / ...	than	in German schools.
American schools are	cooler / scarier / more fun / more interesting / ...		German schools.
German schools are	as cool as as interesting as ...		American schools.

b) Say what you like or don't like about American schools.

Remember

cool
cooler than
the coolest

interesting
more interesting than
the most interesting

Wenn du sagen willst, dass zwei Sachen ähnlich sind, verwendest du *as ... as*:
as cool as; as interesting as

REVISION Comparison of adjectives:
▶ Language file 16, p. 171

---

3 SONG *Fifteen* by Taylor Swift

a) BEFORE YOU LISTEN **Do you know what a 'Swiftie' is?**

It's someone who ...

A ... is fast, or 'swift'.   B ... is a very big fan of Taylor Swift.
C ... doesn't like Taylor Swift's music.

b) **Find the song 'Fifteen' by Taylor Swift online and listen. What is it about? Choose three correct topics.**

c) **Listen again. Choose the correct answers. Then check with the lyrics on page 102.**

1 On her first day at school, Taylor feels **nervous / confident**.
2 Taylor is in the **first / second** year of high school.
3 She is going to be in that town **forever / for the next four years**.
4 At 15, when somebody tells you they **love / hate** you, you believe them.
5 Taylor **doesn't like / is best friends with** Abigail.
6 She will do greater things than **dating this guy / being on the football team**.

d) **How would you describe the music of the song and how does it make you feel?**

It's country / metal / pop / rock / ...
It's happy / sad / slow / ...
It makes me feel happy / sad / that 15 is a great age / ...

boys • friends • homework • moving • mean teachers • part-time jobs • school

Country and pop musician **Taylor Swift** was born in 1989. She often writes songs about her own life. 'Fifteen' is about her high school experience.

▶ Wordbank 2, p. 181

4 MEDIATION A prom invitation

Alicja is writing an email in German.
Her friend Melissa is curious and asks questions.
Help Alicja to answer in English.

● ● ●   ✈   ▤

Betreff: Deine große Schwester geht zum Prom!

Liebe Marta,

ich muss dir unbedingt erzählen, was mir heute passiert ist! Oscar hat mich zum Prom eingeladen – also dem Abschlussball am Ende des Jahres. Er ist richtig nett und ich mag ihn – aber wir sind nur Freunde, wirklich! In den letzten Wochen gab es viel Diskussion über Einladungen, wer fragt wen und so. Prom ist eine große Sache hier, und alle tragen sehr schicke Kleidung – es kann auch richtig teuer werden. Ich werde mit meiner Freundin Melissa einkaufen gehen, um das richtige Outfit zu finden.

Liebe Grüße,

Alicja

Melissa	I can speak a little German! Who are you writing to?
Alicja	I'm writing to …
Melissa	What did you write to her about Oscar?
Alicja	Oscar's nice and I like him, but …
Melissa	OK, if you say so. What about this word, 'Einladung'? That means invitation, doesn't it?
Alicja	Yes, lots of people have been talking about who is …
Melissa	And here, isn't 'Kleidung' something like 'clothes' in English?
Alicja	That's right! It can get …
Melissa	Right. Hey, there's my name!
Alicja	Yes! We're going to go shopping, so that we can …
Melissa	We sure are.

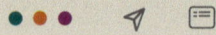

Erklär-film

5 Time for prom!

Your class is going to have an American-style prom at your school. With a partner, decide on the things below. Then discuss ideas with the class.

1 what the prom theme is going to be
2 what you are going to wear / what the dress code is going to be
3 what prom food there is going to be

The theme of our prom is going to be … /
We're going to wear … / We're going to eat …

Remember

Mit dem **going to-future** sagst du, was du in der Zukunft vorhast oder planst. Du bildest das **going to-future** mit *am / is / are + (not) going to + Verb (Infinitiv)*: *The theme of our prom **is going to be** James Bond. **We're going to wear** formal clothes.*

▶ More help, p. 105 ▶ More practice 4, p. 105
REVISION The going to-future: ▶ Language file 17, p. 172
▶ Workbook, p. 47

6 READING Yearbooks

a) BEFORE YOU READ
Look at the Good to know-box.

> **Good to know**
>
> Every year, most American students get a yearbook. It's a book with pictures of all the students from that year, as well as photos from special events. At the end of the school year, students pass around and sign each other's yearbooks.

Do you have something similar?
Do you think this is a good idea?
Say why or why not.

b) Read the messages on this yearbook page and answer the questions.

1 Whose yearbook is it?
2 Which student is leaving soon?
3 Where is that student going and why?

c) Find different words for saying 'thank you' in the messages.
In how many languages can your class say thank you?

> Hey, Diego!
> I had fun with you in a certain teacher's class – I won't write his name, but I can't believe we made him laugh! Let me know if you want to hang out this summer.
> Selena
>
> Mr. Diego C. Perez !!!
> Favorite event: Our class trip to San Antonio! Favorite school meal: pizza.
> Favorite French partner: You.
> Thanks for saving my life in French class! Never change, always stay the same.
> Merci! Jacob
>
> Diego,
> We didn't talk much this year, but there's always next year ☺
> HAGS (That means: Have A Great Summer!)
> Pete
>
> Dear Diego,
> Thank you for making me feel welcome here!
> I had an amazing time.
> My exchange year is almost over, so I'm going to fly back in a few weeks.
> I hope you will visit me in Germany one day.
> All the best,
> Danke! Alicja

My task

7 Sign a yearbook   ▶ Digital help

a) Make small groups. Brainstorm things that have happened during the school year so far. They can be special events or normal things that happened. They should be positive.

> Do you remember when we won the big match with our Handball-AG?

> Oh yeah! What about our Projektarbeit? That was fun.

b) Write your name on a piece of paper. That's your yearbook. Now swap papers and write short, kind messages to each other. You can look at the messages in 6 for ideas.

c) GALLERY WALK Put your yearbook pages on the wall. Walk around and put sticky notes on the pages with nice comments.

> This one is really funny ☺

> This message almost made me cry!

▶ Workbook, p. 48

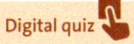

Thinking about the future

1 LISTENING When I leave school

a) BEFORE YOU LISTEN Stand on a 'line of agreement' about your future after you leave school. One end of the line means 'I don't know at all' and the other end means 'I know exactly what I want to do'. Talk to your neighbour about your position.

I don't know at all   I have some ideas but   I know exactly what
                                   I'm not sure yet   I want to do

b) Listen to the conversation. Where should Jacob and Diego stand on the line in a)?

c) Listen again and decide if each sentence is about Jacob or Diego or both.

1   He wants to study business.
2   He has a plan for how he'll pay for college.
3   He doesn't need to go to college for the job that he wants to do.
4   His mom says that he should go.
5   He wants to work so that they can go out this summer.
6   He wants to save some money to buy something special.

> ### Remember
> Du verwendest das **will-future** für spontane Entscheidungen und Voraussagen für die Zukunft.
> Du bildest das **will-future** mit *will/won't* + Verb (Infinitiv).
> *How **will he pay** for college?*
> *He's worried that he **won't have** enough money.*

REVISION The will-future: ▶ Language file 18, pp. 172–173   ▶ More practice 5, p. 106

2 SPEAKING My choices

a) Look at the different options in the box of things that you could do in the future and check that you know what they mean. Choose your top two and bottom two options.

b) Compare with a partner. What's the same? What's different?

We both want to … / I also want to …
You don't want to …   And that's the same for me.
I'd like to …, but you wouldn't like that.
You'd like to …, but I wouldn't like to …

A   do an apprenticeship
B   go to a vocational school
C   go to college
D   get a job
E   go travelling
F   live in another country
G   work as a volunteer
H   join the army

3 READING **Finding a job**

a) BEFORE YOU READ As a class, brainstorm weekend or summer jobs that young people in your area can do to earn money.

b) Jacob and Diego are looking at job adverts. Make groups of four.
Partner A: Read the advert. Tell the group about the main details: what, when, how much.
Partner B: Look at p. 103. **Partner C:** Look at p. 104. **Partner D:** Look at p. 105.

NEED FARM HELP
Are you strong and hard-working? We are looking for a reliable young person to help clean out the stables at our farm on Saturdays. We offer $15 an hour. Email us at …

c) Read what Jacob and Diego say and decide which job would be best for each one.

> *I'd like to work outside – I don't want to be inside all day! I need regular hours so I can save some money every week. I'm free most weekends.*

> *I don't mind working with kids because I look after my little sister a lot, but I don't like animals. I'm often busy, so I don't want to work every week. I'd like a flexible job.*

d) Tell the group which of the four jobs you would like best.

► More practice 6, p. 106

My task

4 Hello, future me!

► Digital help

a) Make notes about what you think you'll do in the future. You can choose to think about:

★ in one year   ★ in five years   ★ in ten years

► Wordbank 4, p. 183

b) Use your notes to record a video time capsule or write a letter to yourself. Talk to future you and say what your predictions are.

Hello, future me! I think that in the next five years, I'll …

I'll	be / become	famous / rich / a nurse / …
I hope I'll	have	a car / a new phone / lots of friends / …
Maybe I'll	learn	to drive / to speak other languages / …
I don't think I will	go	on holiday / to college / out with friends / …
I probably won't	live	in a different country / with my friends / with my parents / …

c) Save the video or the letter with the date in the future so that you can check if you were right!

► More practice 7, p. 106

► Workbook, pp. 49–50

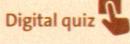 Digital quiz   **I can** talk about jobs and future plans.

Popular

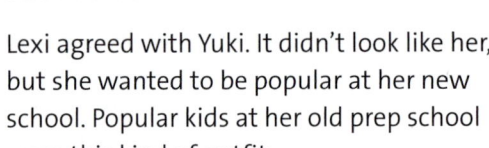

1 Dress codes

a) BEFORE YOU READ **Discuss the following questions with a partner.**

1   What is or isn't OK to wear to school? Are you allowed to wear caps, sweatpants, …?
2   How important is it at your school to wear trendy clothes? What happens if you don't?

b) Read the story and find out what it is like at Lexi's new school.

1   Lexi tried on another outfit: a blue and white sweater with smart trousers. She took a picture of herself in the mirror and sent it to her best friend in the whole world, Yuki.

> I can't believe that we're going to go to different schools tomorrow. 🥺 I don't know what to wear. What about this outfit?

> I don't know, it doesn't look like you. 🤔 It's very formal, isn't it? Do you want to look so preppy?

> 🙁 I don't know either.

Lexi agreed with Yuki. It didn't look like her, but she wanted to be popular at her new school. Popular kids at her old prep school wore this kind of outfit.   5

'Well then, it's perfect, I guess,' she said to her picture in the mirror. 'Tomorrow I'm going to have my first day as a freshman at high school in a new city. Nobody knows me, so I can decide who I want to be.'   10

2   The next day was stressful. Her new school was much bigger than her old one, and she got lost several times.   15

At 11:45 she went to the cafeteria and stood in line to get her lunch with everyone else. The line moved quickly, then suddenly, everyone stopped, and she bumped into the person in front of her.   20

'Hey! You don't know who I am, do you?' When Lexi saw who it was, she almost forgot to breathe. After only three hours at the school, Lexi did know who it was: Kelsea   25 Sherman, probably the coolest freshman there. She was wearing a pretty dress with white cowboy boots. Kelsea's sister was one of the most popular juniors.

Juniors were only one year away from being   30 seniors, which meant they were tall and really cool. Although she was only a freshman, Kelsea was already in the popular group.

'Sorry!' said Lexi, and picked up Kelsea's fork,   35 knife and spoon from the floor.

'Oh, it's Lexi the loser from geography class,' said Kelsea. 'Honestly, what are you wearing? Are you going to go fishing later in that outfit 40 or something?'

Lexi heard people laughing behind her and wished she could disappear. Kelsea kept going. 'You really are embarrassing, aren't you?'

45 'Oh, shut up, Kelsea,' said a voice behind them. 'It was an accident; I saw the whole thing from here.'
'Stay out of this, Sharon!' Kelsea shouted and turned around to choose her food.

50 Sharon rolled her eyes and smiled at Lexi, who was still holding Kelsea's things in her hands. 'Don't be upset, she's just a bully. I'm Sharon, and I'm a junior. You're a freshman, right?'

55 'Yeah, I am. I'm Lexi. I just moved here.'
'Well, that's fun!' laughed Sharon. 'So you don't know anybody, right? Do you want to eat together?'
'Yes!' replied Lexi excitedly.

60 **3** Over lunch, Sharon explained the school to Lexi. 'You have to ignore Kelsea. She can be annoying, just like her sister ... actually that whole group is really terrible. The only thing is ... well, I don't know if I should –'

65 Lexi interrupted her. 'What is it? Tell me.'
'OK, here's the thing about the popular group. They know when someone is trying too hard – for example, when you wear certain clothes to be cool.'

Lexi noticed that Sharon was wearing jeans 70 and a T-shirt. Normal clothes. She looked at her own outfit and laughed. 'I see what you mean,' she replied.
Sharon nodded and opened her yoghurt.
'You have to be *yourself*, you know?' she said. 75
'Nothing else matters.'

4 That night Yuki texted Lexi.

The first day is OVER! 🥳 Did you meet any nice people?
Of course, no one is as nice as me, I know ... 😇

😅 Yuki, you're the best!
There was one scary person from the popular group, Kelsea. She said something mean about my clothes ... but then I met a really nice junior, Sharon. She explained how to deal with Kelsea.

So I guess you're not going to wear the preppy outfit again?

No, I'm not – but not because of Kelsea. I'm just going to wear my normal clothes from now on. I just want to be myself, *you know? That's my new motto.*

Good for you!! 🤗

2 What's the story about?

Read the texts A–C. Which one summarizes the story best?

| **A** Lexi texts her best friend because she is nervous about her new school. Yuki says she should wear formal clothes to be popular. Later, Kelsea is mean to her, and Lexi is upset. | **B** Lexi is in a new city and starts high school there. At first there is a conflict with Kelsea, a very popular freshman. At the end Sharon, a junior, is kind and helps Lexi to be herself. | **C** Lexi loves wearing preppy clothes, but then she goes to high school and Kelsea bullies her. So Lexi decides to dress just like Kelsea because she wants to be cool. |

3 Headings

Match the headings (A–D) to the correct parts of the story (1–4).

A Advice from a new friend

B An unhappy accident

C Lexi's new motto

D The night before

☒ 4 Characters in the story

Who is each sentence about, Lexi (L), Yuki (Y), Kelsea (K) or Sharon (S)?

1 … tries on different outfits.

2 … thinks her best friend looks different.

3 … is mean in the cafeteria.

4 … says that it was an accident.

5 … wants to wear her normal clothes again.

6 … is happy for her friend at the end of the first day.   ▶ Parallel exercise, p. 107

5 LIFE SKILLS Be yourself

a) **What would you do if you were Lexi and it was your first day of high school?**

If I was Lexi, I'd wear / go / be / …

b) **Sharon says to Lexi, 'You just have to be yourself'. When and where do you feel most like yourself? Think of what you like to do, wear, or who you are with.**

I feel most like myself when I …   ▶ More help, p. 107

▶ Workbook, p. 51

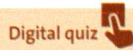 Digital quiz   **I can talk about clothes in school.**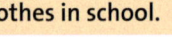

High Tech High School

1 What kind of school?

BEFORE YOU WATCH Look at the title of the video and the photos. What do you think could be different about this school? Discuss with your partner.

I think students at the school ...
Maybe this school has ...

2 A different kind of school

a) Watch the video and choose the best description of High Tech High (A–C). Did anyone guess correctly in 1?

A Students use lots of technology to help them learn.
B Students can choose what they learn at school.
C Students do all their exams online.

b) Watch the video again. Are these sentences true (T) or false (F)?

1 Students at this school use textbooks in their lessons.
2 The teachers are there to help, but not to lead the lessons.
3 Some students in the video are working on a science project.
4 The students are worried about being ready on time.
5 The students get good grades for their projects.

c) Make lists of what's the same and different at your school and High Tech High. Use the ideas in the box.

building • exams • grades • homework • lessons • subjects

d) Do you want to be an exchange student at High Tech High School? Why or why not?

I want / don't want to be an exchange student at High Tech High because ...

3 GLOBAL GOALS Quality education

a) Put these features of a good school in order of how important they are to you. Is anything missing?

b) In small groups, make notes about what your dream school is like, then present it to the class. Vote for the best dream school.

▶ More help, p. 107

A everyone is equal
B teachers care about students
C there is no bullying
D there are lots of clubs
E lessons are interesting
F students get good grades
G students can use the latest technology to help them learn

Communicate better

1 Listen and show respect

a) You're going to tell your partner about school, for example your school day, favourite subjects, homework, clothes at school, …

*My school day usually starts at …
and ends at … My favourite subjects are …*

b) Read the tips on how to listen.
Then talk about school in groups of three. One person talks and one person listens. The third person watches and uses the box as a checklist. Then swap roles.

> **When you listen …**
> - Look interested and make eye contact.
> - Use encouraging words:
>   *Go on. • Uh-huh. • Right.
>   Really? • That's interesting.*
> - Focus on what the speaker is saying.
> - Try not to think about what <u>you</u> want to say.
> - Be patient and don't interrupt.
>
> ▶ Skills File 5, p. 147

2 Ask questions to find out more

a) With your partner, think of a wh-question that you could ask after the yes/no questions in 2–5.

1 Do you like school?
   If yes: What do you like most?
   If no: Why don't you like school?
2 Do you walk to school?
3 Do you eat in the school canteen?
4 Do you usually go home after school?
5 Do you like PE / music / …?

b) Take turns to ask and answer the questions in a).

3 Check and show you understand

a) If you haven't understood, you can ask and check. Look at the phrases in the green speech bubble.

b) In pairs, imagine you are an American exchange student and a German student.

German student: Explain about the German school system, the types of school, the school day, …

American student: Use a phrase in the bubble and check.
Then swap roles.

> *In Germany there are different types of high school, for example I go to a "Sekundarschule".*

> *I'm not sure I understood / got that.
> Do you mean …?
> So you mean …?
> Tell me more about that. …*

Digital quiz 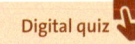   **I can use strategies to communicate better.**

Do an interview about school

Step 1: Choose roles

Work in groups of three. You have an American exchange student at your school and you're going to do an interview with them. You want to find out what's the better school system. First agree on your roles:

- **Partner A:** an American student
- **Partner B:** a German student
- **Partner C:** the interviewer

▶ Digital help

Step 2: Make role cards

a) Look at your role card.

Partner A: Look at p. 103.
Partner B: Look at p. 107.
Partner C: Look at this page.

b) All partners A, partners B and partners C meet together in a new group.
All As and Bs: Help each other with information about the topics on your role cards. All Cs: Help each other to think of questions.

Partner C: You are the interviewer. You start.
1) Say what the topic of the interview is and introduce the two students.
2) Ask both students questions about school life. For example, ask: *Does the school have a dress code? What do students wear? Is there a special school celebration? What happens?*
3) Ask what they think of the other school system. *What do you think of …?*
4) Sum up the interview and thank everybody.

▶ Study skills 2 + 3, p. 92

Step 3: Practise your role

a) Study your role alone and practise what you can say. Check how to say words and think of useful phrases.

b) Practise your interview with your group. Remember to listen to the others and ask questions to find out more.

Im Englischen hebst du nur am Ende von Ja/Nein-Fragen die Stimme, bei wh-Fragen senkst Du sie (wie nach Aussagesätzen).

Step 4: Do the interview

a) Present your interview to another group. ▶ Study skills 1 + 2, p. 92

b) Give feedback to the other group on their interview.
- Did the interviewer ask interesting questions?
- Did the speakers answer the questions well?
- Did the listeners listen carefully and in a friendly way?

▶ Feedback phrases, p. 191

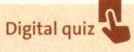 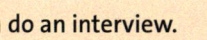

---

1 LISTENING **Tessa's Texas**

| I can talk about Texas. |

a) Listen to a new episode of Tessa's podcast about Texas. What is she doing in this episode? Choose the best answer.

    A   She is answering questions from different people.
    B   She is interviewing different people.
    C   She is talking about fast fashion and its problems.

b) Copy and complete the table. Write short answers.

Name	From:	Wants to know more about …	Tessa's answer (one fact):
Lucy	*Scotland*	…	*San Antonio: rent a bike and …*
Salim	…	*fashion in Texas*	*small towns: cowboy hats and boots bigger cities: …*
James	…	…	*lots of hard work to …*

c) Listen again. Check and complete your answers.

d) SPEAKING   What was new to you? What did you already know about Texas? What would you like to know more about? Tell your partner.

---

2 If we moved to Wimberley

| I can talk and write about small-town life. |

a) LANGUAGE   Read Aaron's blog. He lives in a big city. Complete the <u>conditional sentences type 2</u> with the correct form of the blue verb in brackets.

Hi, guys, I've just come home after a weekend visiting my cousins. They live in a small town called Wimberley. If we moved there, I'*d see* **(1 see)** my cousins more often. My life would be very different! If I lived in Wimberley, I… **(2 know)** most people there. And if I knew everyone, I… **(3 feel)** safe. If I wanted to spend time outside, I… **(4 go)** swimming and hiking. But it could also be boring. If I wanted to shop at cool stores, I… **(5 travel)** to the next city. And if I wanted to see a movie, I… **(6 watch)** it online, not in a movie theater.

b) WRITING   What would your life be like if you moved to a small town in Texas? Write a comment to Aaron. Use the ideas below or your own ideas.

If we moved to a small town in Texas, If my family had a house there, If I went to school there, If my friends from Germany came to visit,	I'd / I would	miss my town / school / … in Germany. have my own room / a big garden / … join the soccer team / take cool electives / … introduce them to my new friends / show them the town / …

Check

3 WORDS **Matteo's first day**

Complete the dialogue with the correct words from the box.

| cafeteria • elective • freshman • grade • responsible • stressful |

Alicja	Hi, are you Matteo?
Matteo	Yes, I'm new here. I'm from Italy.
Alicja	Great. I'm going to take you to Ms Garcia's office. She's ... **(1)** for the exchange students. You can ask her for help whenever you need it.
Matteo	I missed the school bus, so this morning has been a little ... **(2)**. Am I late?
Alicja	No, it's OK. Here's Ms Garcia's office.
Ms Garcia	Hello, Alicja. Ah, this is our new ... **(3)**, Matteo, right?
Matteo	Sorry, a new what?
Ms Garcia	Oh, that's just the word for a student in the first year of high school, in 9th ... **(4)**. Welcome to Westfield High, Matteo.

Matteo	Thank you, Ms Garcia.
Alicja	Right, it's almost 9. I'll take you to your first class, and then maybe we can meet for lunch in the ... **(5)**, OK?
Matteo	Yes, please.
Alicja	So here's your first class. Ah, good, you have a nice, easy start to the day with an ... **(6)**. You know, a subject that you can choose to do. Lucky you!
Matteo	Thanks for your help, Alicja! See you at lunch.

4 WRITING **Alicja's blog post**

Alicja is back in Germany, and she wants to write a blog post in English about her exchange year. Write her text. Use her notes below and your own ideas. Your text should have four parts:

1 Introduction	– felt nervous (at the start) + didn't understand new words – it was exciting → had lots of fun (later)
2 Challenges	– spent birthday away from family → lonely – long school days were stressful: lots of new topics (= difficult to follow in English!) → tired!
3 The best part	– the prom with Oscar – all the friendly people in Texas
4 Conclusion	– was sad to leave – am happy about my English → very good now!

You can start like this:

Hi, everyone!
I want to tell you about my exchange year at Westfield High. At the start, ...

Check

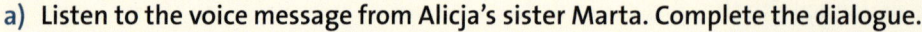

🔊 **5** MEDIATION **A voice message**

I can **talk about jobs and future plans.** ✓

a) **Listen to the voice message from Alicja's sister Marta. Complete the dialogue.**

Oscar	Hey, is everything OK? You look a bit worried.
Alicja	Well, I've just listened to a voice message from my sister. She's feeling stressed because she ... **(1)**.
Oscar	Oh, I'm sorry. Has something happened?
Alicja	Well, she has to decide really soon if she'll do an apprenticeship or ... **(2)**.
Oscar	Where does she want to travel to?
Alicja	She'd like to ... **(3)**.
Oscar	Oh! Like you.
Alicja	Yes, but the problem is that ... **(4)**.
Oscar	That sounds difficult. Maybe you should call her back now? I can come back later.
Alicja	Thanks, Oscar. I think that would ... **(5)** her.

b) **Listen again and check.**

---

6 STUDY SKILLS **Planning the prom**

I can **use strategies to communicate better.** ✓

a) **Oscar is planning next year's prom and Hazel would like to help. Choose the correct words or phrases.**

Oscar	Hey, Hazel. So, first of all, tell me why you want to be on the prom planning team.
Hazel	Well, I think it's a really important event for the school and I ... erm ...
Oscar	**Thanks! / Go on. (1)**
Hazel	Well, I've always enjoyed planning events.
Oscar	**Right. / Wrong. (2)**
Hazel	Yeah, and I have a pretty cool idea.
Oscar	**Why? / Really? (3)** So what were you thinking?
Hazel	Well, we're in Fredericksburg, so our theme could be Germany!
Oscar	So **do you mean / go on (4)** with German food and drinks?
Hazel	**I don't think so. / Sure! (5)** And maybe also German costumes.
Oscar	Hm, **that's interesting. / really? (6)**
Hazel	Thanks!
Oscar	You're welcome! So, Hazel, you'll hear from me next week, OK?

b) **Practise the interview with a partner. Remember to ...**

★ sit up straight ★ look interested and friendly ★ make eye contact.

Check

7 READING **A survey in the school magazine**

I can **talk about clothes in school.**

a) Read the article. Choose the correct heading (A–E) for each paragraph (1–5).

A What next?

B Clothes are part of students' personality

C No to uniforms!

D The rules are unfair

E A question from our exchange students

1 As many of you know, Leah from the UK is visiting our school this year. One topic that she finds really interesting is the freedom that we have here to wear
5 the clothes that we want at school. Last month, Leah asked me "Could you imagine introducing uniforms at this school?" I thought it was a good question, so we asked 100 students.
10 The results were very interesting!

2 Most of us aren't interested in having uniforms at school. In fact, only 9% of students thought it would be a good idea. However, one student in 9th grade
15 wrote that 'uniforms could help to stop bullying because we'd all look the same.'

3 But that doesn't mean that we like how we dress at school. When we asked if you feel good about what you can wear to school, only 38% of students said 'yes'. 20 The main reason for this was the dress code. Around 60% of students said that they agree with the sentence 'clothes are part of my personality and not something that the school should decide 25 for me.'

4 Students also told us that they think some teachers care more about the dress code than others. One student in 11th grade wrote 'It feels like the rules aren't 30 the same for everyone' and a student in 9th grade said "I always have to take off my cap, but there are some older students in our school who wear caps all the time. That's so unfair." 35

5 We shared our results with our teacher, Ms Bold. She told us that she's going to organize a meeting about the dress code to see how we can make it better. It's next Monday at lunchtime in room 16, 40 and all students are allowed to take part.

b) Complete the sentences with the correct word or number.

1 Leah thinks that we have more ... because we can wear what we want to school.
2 ... per cent of students would like to wear uniforms at school.
3 Some teachers care more about the ... than others.

4 ... per cent of students feel good about the clothes that they wear to school.
5 One student finds it ... when older students get away with wearing a cap.
6 Next week there will be a ... about the dress code.

c) Choose one of the sentences in red and discuss it for your school.
Do you agree or disagree with the statement? Give reasons.

Check

United

What type of books or magazines do you like reading?

A magazine for young people across the USA

My reading tip *by Diego Perez*

I love reading and I just finished *Hartford moves* by Marc Proulx. Iris Quinn is the main character, and she's in big trouble. The principal[1], Mr. Barnes, thinks that she sprayed the words 'All lives matter' on a wall, but she thinks that two other students at school did it, Kellyann and J.J. Iris talks to her friend Lalo, and the two of them create a plan. They walk into the cafeteria and see Kellyann and J.J.

What's wrong with 'All lives matter'?

This phrase began as a reaction to the 'Black lives matter' movement in the USA. It sounds like a good thing, but people who say 'All lives matter', often argue that racism against Black people isn't real. That's why experts say that this phrase is a problem, because for too long, white lives have mattered more than Black lives.

Hartford moves (by Marc Proulx)

[...] I took a deep breath. Let's play this cool, I thought. Kellyann and J.J. were sitting next to each other and didn't notice when we walked up to the table. [...]

5 'Hey, is that vegetarian lasagna[2]?' I said to Kellyann. 'That's my favorite too. Isn't that funny?'

We sat down opposite them. J.J. had his mouth[3] full of food. He looked at Lalo like he was from another planet. Lalo looked back at him. 10

'Hola,' he said. Neither[4] of them reacted.
'How was the bowling on Saturday?' I asked, not really interested in their answer.
'You missed it. It was awesome,[5]' J.J. said. 15

Lalo Mendez · Iris Quinn · Kellyann Moore · Mrs Gonzalez · J.J. Hannigan

---

[1] **principal** *der Schulleiter, die Schulleiterin*   [2] **lasagna** *die Lasagne*   [3] **mouth** *der Mund*   [4] **neither** *keiner, keine*
[5] **awesome** *großartig*

Kellyann gave me a cold look. 'I heard you got into trouble,' she said. 'Something about some graffiti?' I let her enjoy the moment.

20 'Yeah,' I said. 'The principal thinks I painted over the wall mural. They found a bag of mine with spray paint in it. I can't explain it.' I paused […], then looked straight at

25 both of them. 'You don't know anything about that, do you?' I asked. […] 'Me? I don't know anything about any graffiti. Or your gym bag,' Kellyann

30 said.

Lalo and I looked at each other. 'Sorry, did you just say "gym bag"?' I said. 'What makes you think I'm talking about my gym bag?'

35 'Did I say gym bag?' I turned to J.J. 'She did say gym bag, didn't she?' […] 'I definitely heard gym bag,' Lalo said. 'Who asked you, gay-boy?' J.J. said, his

40 voice hard. His words surprised me. I wondered[1] how Lalo felt. Was it the first time someone had said that to him? Lalo's reaction was beautiful. He smiled.

45 'I don't need your permission[2] to talk, white boy.'

I looked at Kellyann. 'I think you know more about that graffiti than you say you do,' I said calmly.

50 Kellyann looked surprised. […] 'Maybe,' she said. […]

Anyway, it's true what it says on the wall, so what's the problem?' J.J. smiled. 'Don't you like my handwriting?' he said. 55 I sat back. 'Wow. So you're both admitting[3] it.' 'We're not admitting anything,' Kellyann said. 'Nope[4],' J.J. said. 60 'I just heard you,' I said. 'And Lalo is my witness[5].' 'Yup[6],' Lalo said. Kellyann's cold blue eyes looked at me. 'Well, J.J. is my witness and I'm his. 65 You can't prove[7] it,' she said. 'So get your thin ugly butt[8] out of here and take fat[9]-boy with you.' […] 'At least I don't try to cover my face up with cheap make-up,' I said. 70 Her face went tomato red. […]

What do you think happens next?

Look at the picture and read the next part. Were you right?

'You little shit,' she said. 'Here's your freaking[1] vegetarian lasagna.' [...]
With one quick movement[2] she tried to
75 dump[3] her lunch on me. [...]
I blocked the tray[4] with both hands and everything on it flew back at her. [...]
The cafeteria went silent. All eyes were on Kellyann. [...] Tomato sauce and mozza-
80 rella cheese were on her face and all down her neat, expensive blouse[5]. [...] She looked shocked. [...]
The next voice I heard was Mrs. Gonzalez's.

85 Mr. Barnes's office had begun to feel familiar[6]. He was sitting at his desk. [...] Kellyann looked uncomfortable. [...] She was a mess[7], with red spots[8] on her blouse and skirt and cheese in her hair.
90 Lalo was standing next to me. He looked amazingly calm and relaxed, like he knew exactly why he was there.

Mrs. Gonzalez had already given her view of the events in the cafeteria. [...] I was
95 sure I was in trouble again. [...]
After hearing Mrs Gonzalez, Mr. Barnes got up, walked around his desk and stood between the four of us. He had his arms crossed and was holding his reading
100 glasses in one hand. He looked at Kellyann and J.J., then at Lalo and finally at me. He kept looking at me. He seemed tired. Then he turned again to Kellyann.
'Miss Moore, what's your side of the
105 story?' he asked.

Kellyann started slowly. She was choosing her words carefully. [...] She looked upset, like her feelings had been hurt. She was a good actor. J.J. nodded[9] the whole time, like[10] he would have told it exactly the 110 same way.
Mr. Barnes nodded too. He turned back to me.
'Why do I get the feeling that she's telling the truth, Miss Quinn?' he said. 115
'Because you don't know the full story, Mr. Barnes,' I said.

---

[1] **freaking** *verdammt*   [2] **movement** *die Bewegung*   [3] **(to) dump** *auskippen, wegwerfen*   [4] **tray** *das Tablett*
[5] **neat blouse** *die saubere, schicke Bluse*   [6] **familiar** *vertraut*   [7] **(to) be a mess** *völlig verdreckt sein*   [8] **spot** *der Fleck*
[9] **(to) nod** *nicken*   [10] **like** (adv) *als ob*

Mr. Barnes lifted his tired eyebrow[1].
'Tell me then. What part of the story
120 am I missing?'
'The part about my locker[2]. You see,
it doesn't work. Anyone can open it,'
I said. 'It's been like that for weeks. Only
three people know about it:
125 Jason Lee and these two.' [...]
'So what are you saying, Miss Quinn?'
he asked.
'One of them could have taken my gym
bag out of my locker and put the spray
130 cans[3] in it [...]' I said. 'It had to be
someone with racist views. Someone
who wasn't happy with me. Like
Kellyann. On Friday I disagreed with
her view of Black activism[4] [...].
135 Kellyann's mouth dropped[3] open.
'That's *so* not true.' [...]

'These guys have already admitted it,'
I said. 'That's what the scene in the
cafeteria was all about.' [...]
140 'That's a lie!' J.J. said. 'I was there.
Kellyann didn't say anything like that.'
'J.J. didn't either,' Kellyann said.
Mr. Barnes rubbed[5] his eyes and sighed.
'It sounds like it's your word against
145 theirs, Miss Quinn,' he said.

Lalo spoke for the first time. 'Not
exactly,' he said.
He reached[6] into the pocket of his jacket
and pulled out his cell phone. He held it
up and tapped the screen. A recording   150
started. There was cafeteria noise and
the sound of voices, including my own.
We heard the whole conversation.
Mr. Barnes listened, both of his
eyebrows slowly rising. Kellyann's face   155
was frozen. J.J. looked at the floor. [...]
Lalo stopped the recording. The room
was silent. [...] Finally, Mr. Barnes spoke.
'Miss Quinn, Mr. Mendez, you can go
now,' he said.   160

▶ Quellenverzeichnis, p. 263

How does **this** ending **make** you **feel**?
If you **liked** this **part,**
read **the** rest **of** the **book**!

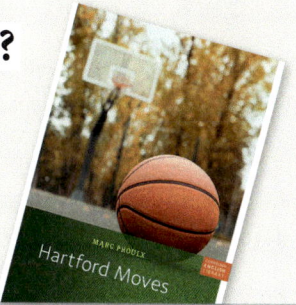

Hartford Moves

---

[1] (to) **lift an eyebrow** *eine Augenbraue hochziehen*   [2] **locker** *das Schließfach*   [3] **(spray) can** *die (Sprüh-)Dose*
[4] **activism** *der politische Aktivismus*   [5] (to) **rub** *reiben*   [6] (to) **reach** *reichen, greifen*

Partner page

▶ Page 81

6   What would you do?

a) **Partner B: Answer partner A's questions.**

If I had a year to travel the world, I'd go to …

b) **Partner B: Ask your partner these questions.**

1   If you were an animal, what would you be?
2   If you were a superhero, what would your superpower be?
3   If you met a famous person, what would you say?
4   If you spoke perfect English, what would you use it for?
5   If you were a politician, what would you change?

c) **Tell the class one interesting thing about partner A.**

If Kaja were an animal, she'd be a …

▶ Page 83

3   Song   *Fifteen* (by Taylor Swift)

You take a deep breath and you walk through
the doors.
It's the mornin' of your very first day.
You say 'hi' to your friends you ain't seen
in a while,
try and stay out of everybody's way.

It's your freshman year and you're gonna
be here
for the next four years in this town,
hopin' one of those senior boys will wink
at you and say,
'You know, I haven't seen you around before'.

'Cause when you're fifteen
and somebody tells you they love you,
you're gonna believe them.
And when you're fifteen,
feelin' like there's nothin' to figure out,
well, count to ten, take it in,
this is life before you know who you're gonna be
at fifteen.

You sit in class next to a redhead named Abigail.
And soon enough, you're best friends,
laughin' at the other girls who think they're
so cool.
We'll be outta here as soon as we can.

And then you're on your very first date and he's
got a car.
And you're feelin' like flyin'.
And your mama's waitin' up and you're thinkin'
he's the one.
And you're dancin' round your room when the
night ends, when the night ends.

'Cause when you're fifteen
and somebody tells you they love you,
you're gonna believe them.
And when you're fifteen and your first kiss
makes your head spin round, well,
in your life you'll do things greater than
dating the boy on the football team.
I didn't know it at fifteen.
[…]

▶Page 87

3 READING Finding a job

b) **Partner B:** Read the advert. Tell the group about the main details: what, when, how much.

WANTED: Someone to cut the grass

*My grandmother needs help taking care of her garden. Pay is
$15.50 an hour (hours will change, so the job is very flexible).
If you're interested, please call ...*

▶Page 93

UNIT TASK **Do an interview about school, Step 2: Role card A (American student)**

Partner A: You are the American student.

1) Say hello.
2) Answer the interviewer's questions about **school life in the USA**,
   for example about:
   • the school day (electives? Pledge of Allegiance? clubs and sports
     after school?)
   • how you get to school (school bus, older students drive)
   • special celebrations in the school year (prom, yearbook, ...)
3) React to what the **German** student says: *The school day sounds ...*
4) Thank the interviewer.

Diff bank

▶Page 78

 More practice 1 **Fredericksburg: A German-Texan town**

Read about Fredericksburg's German roots. Imagine your partner doesn't understand German.
Take turns to explain the German words in blue in English. Choose three words each.

Partner A: *Saengerfest: I see the words "Sänger" and "Fest", so maybe it's a kind of festival where
people sing.*

In 1846 Germans founded the town of Fredericksburg, and it still is very
German today. Some places have German names – for example, Markt-
platz. For German food, try the Altdorf Restaurant & Biergarten, Der
Lindenbaum or Otto's German Bistro. Every year for three days in October,
the town celebrates Oktoberfest with musicians in Lederhosen and Dirndl.
Another German festival is Saengerfest with the many German choirs in
the area. And of course every year there is Weihnachtszeit. Check out the
beautiful Weihnachtspyramide and enjoy the holiday!

► Page 87

3 READING Finding a job

b) **Partner C:** Read the advert.
Tell the group about the main details:
what, when, how much.

Babysitter wanted
We are looking for someone
who is friendly and responsible
to babysit our five-year-old son
once or twice a month in the
evenings. We can pay $16 an hour. Please call …

► Page 80

More practice 2 **If I had magic powers …**

Jacob and Diego are talking about a test. Complete the conversation with the correct form
of the verb.

Diego   Jacob, how did you do in the French test?

Jacob   Not great. It was really difficult.

Diego   Yeah, it was. But French and Spanish are similar, so I think I did OK. If you spoke
Spanish too, you *would be* **(1 be)** better at French.

Jacob   Yeah. The problem is that France is so far away. If people spoke French in Texas,
I … **(2 be)** more interested in the language.

Diego   What if you learned Spanish instead?

Jacob   I don't know, Spanish is hard too. If I had magic powers, I … **(3 speak)** 500 languages.
If I spoke 500 languages, I … **(4 travel)** around the world!

Diego   If you had magic powers, you … **(5 not have)** to go to school. Keep dreaming, Jacob!

Jacob   If I had magic powers, I … **(6 not worry)** about getting a good job or making money.
Life would be so easy.

Diego   I just had an idea. Why don't you learn German?

Jacob   I can speak a little German already. That's a great idea, Diego!

► Page 82

More practice 3 WORDS **School words and phrases**

Write the correct words from the box for explanations 1–6.

elective • freshman • grade •
Pledge of Allegiance •
prom • senior

1   a student in their last year of high school
2   a dance at the end of the school year
3   a poem that people say to show respect to the USA and its
flag
4   the number that says which year of school you are in (and
it also is another word for the mark that you get on a test)
5   a student in their first year of high school
6   a class that you can choose and that is usually more fun

▶ Page 87

3 READING **Finding a job**

b) **Partner D: Read the advert. Tell the group about the main details: what, when, how much.**

PART-TIME JOB
We are a family-run hairdresser's in Fredericksburg and we are looking for someone to clean and make coffee on Saturday afternoons. The pay is $16.50 an hour. If you are punctual and friendly, come and visit us to find out more.

▶ Page 84

More help **5 Time for prom!**

Themes	Outfits	Food and drinks
• British garden party • under the sea • magical forest 	• fancy / formal dresses • short dresses 	• drinks: cola, fruit punch, lemonade, juice • snacks: mini pizzas, mini burgers, sandwiches, chips, sushi, chicken wings 
• superheroes • fire and ice • disco dancing 	• formal suits 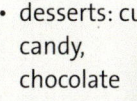 • skirts	• desserts: cupcakes, cookies, candy, chocolate fountain • ...
• royals • outer space • ...	• nice shirts • blazers and trousers • ... 	

More practice 4 **Plans**

a) **Diego is interviewing Oscar. Write the questions and answers. Use the going to-future.**

Diego So it's the weekend soon, Oscar. What *are you going to do?* **(1 you / do)**
Oscar Well, I'm ... **(2 volunteer)** at the hospital on Saturday as always.
On Sunday I'm ... **(3 work)** in my parents' cafe.
Diego Cool. Are you ... **(4 make)** coffee? Or how are you ... **(5 help)** them?
Oscar No, I'm ... **(6 not / make)** coffee. I'm going to learn about the business.
Diego Oh, that's cool.

b) **What are your weekend plans? Talk with your partner.**

What are you going to do at the weekend? – On Saturday / Sunday I'm going to ...

▶ Page 86

More practice 5 **What will they do?**

Complete Diego's sentences with the will-future.

1 My sister says maybe she *will be* (be) a mechanic when she's older.
2 I hope I ... (learn) to drive this summer. My parents can teach me.
3 I don't think it ... (rain) today. It looks like it ... (be) sunny all day.
4 We probably ... (not go) out this weekend because we ... (feel) tired after a long week.
5 I hope that Jacob ... (help) me with my homework. It's really hard!

▶ Page 87

More practice 6 LISTENING **A radio advert**

Listen to the advert and choose the correct answers.

1 The job is at a A **restaurant** B **shop** C **hairdresser's**.
2 Ted is looking for someone to A **take newspapers to customers** B **clean** C **make food**.
3 The working hours are A **weekends** B **evenings** C **weekday mornings**.
4 The pay A **is $25 an hour** B **is $2.50 an hour** C **can change**.
5 The person for this job should be A **reliable** B **on time** C **fast**.

More practice 7 LISTENING **Instructions**

a) BEFORE YOU LISTEN **Do you ever make and edit videos? Who or what do you film? Tell a partner.**

b) **Listen to the instructions on how to edit a video. Put the pictures (A–G) in the correct order.**

You can look at the yellow symbols for help.

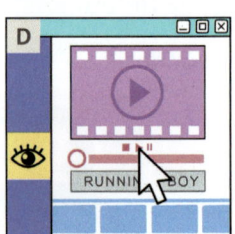
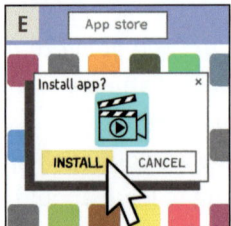
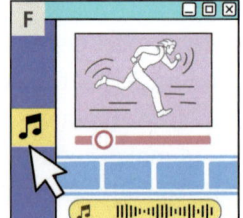
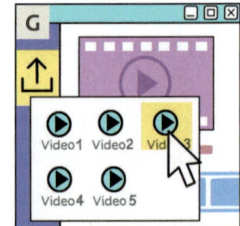

c) **Listen again and check. Then match the instructions in the box to the correct pictures.**
1 E: install an editing app, 2 ...

add captions • add music • watch the edited video • cut the parts that you don't need • install an editing app • save the video • upload the video to the app

▶Page 90

`Parallel exercise` **4** **Characters in the story**

Who is each sentence about? Choose the correct person.

1 **Lexi / Yuki** tries on different outfits.
2 **Kelsea / Yuki** thinks her best friend looks different.
3 **Kelsea / Yuki** is mean in the cafeteria.
4 **Lexi / Sharon** says that it was an accident.
5 **Kelsea / Lexi** wants to wear her normal clothes again.
6 **Lexi / Yuki** is happy for her friend at the end of the first day.

`More help` **5** LIFE SKILLS **Be yourself**

I feel most like myself when I'm …

riding my bike • playing football • swimming • …
outside in nature • at my best friend's house • travelling in a new place • …
putting on make-up • wearing comfortable clothes • …
dancing • listening to music • playing video games • …
alone • with friends or family • helping somebody • …

▶Page 91

`More help` **3** GLOBAL GOALS **Quality education**

In our dream school, we have / wear / learn …
The school building is …
The teachers / lessons are …
Students have to / are allowed to …
At our school, there is / are ….

▶Page 93

UNIT TASK **Do an interview about school, Step 2: Role card B (German student)**

Partner B: You are the German student

1) Say hello.
2) Answer the interviewer's questions about **school life in Germany**, for example about:
   • the school day (fun classes? clubs and sports after school?)
   • how you get to school (walk? by bus / car / tram / bike?)
   • special celebrations in the school year (parties?)
3) Give your opinion of **American** school life: React to what the **American** student says: *The school day sounds …*
4) Thank the interviewer.

Unit 4
California: State of contrasts

Hollywood, Los Angeles (LA)

San Francisco

Death Valley, a desert in Eastern California

Spanish market in LA

1 SPEAKING Californian contrasts

a) **Describe the photos (A–G) to a partner. Use the words in the box and your own ideas. Your partner says which photo it is.**

bridge • building • busy • celebrity • clouds • dry • empty • flat • hot • modern • mountains • ocean • peaceful • round • sky • skyscrapers • stalls • …

In the foreground of this photo there is/are … Maybe she/he/they …
In the background I can see mountains / …

▶ More practice 1, p. 135

b) **Choose two photos and compare them.**

Photo …	has more / fewer	buildings / clouds / mountains / people / trees / …	than photo …
	has as many		as photo …
	has lots of / some		but photo … has none.
	looks more / less	peaceful / stressful / interesting / boring / …	than photo …

Nach dieser Unit kann ich …

- über Kalifornien sprechen
- eine Diskussion über KI führen
- über die Geschichte der *Native Americans* sprechen
- die Natur in Kalifornien beschreiben
- Diagramme auswerten und präsentieren

Unit task

- eine Präsentation über Kalifornien erstellen und halten

E

Santa Monica Beach, LA

G

Silicon Valley

F

National parks with giant trees

2 VIEWING Welcome to Los Angeles (LA)

a) BEFORE YOU WATCH **You're going to watch a video about LA. What do you think you will see? Discuss with the class and take notes. You can start with the ideas in the box.**

> big houses • cool cars • farms • film stars • old castles • snow • …

b) **Watch the video and tick any ideas in a) that you see.**

c) **Watch again and say if each sentence is true or false.**

1 Julia moved to LA five years ago.
2 10 million people come to Griffith Park each year.
3 Julia rents a boat every morning at the lake.

4 Julia's neighbour Woody loves baseball.
5 There isn't a lot of traffic in LA.
6 Julia shows us a beach in the morning.

▶ More practice 2, p. 135
▶ Workbook, p. 58

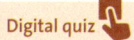 Digital quiz I can **talk about California.**

The future is now

1 LISTENING Riley's family

Riley's dad, Mike

Riley Walker, 14

Riley's mum, Nicole

a) BEFORE YOU LISTEN Look at the pictures of Riley's parents. What do you think they do in their jobs?

b) Listen to a phone conversation between Riley and her mum. Were your predictions in a) correct?

c) Listen again and answer the questions.

> **Good to know**
>
> **Silicon Valley** in California has thousands of technology companies. San Jose is one city in Silicon Valley.

1 Who lives in the town of Eureka?
2 Who lives in San Jose?
3 What is Riley's mum working on?
4 What does Riley want to do next weekend?

2 LOOKING AT LANGUAGE The passive: simple present

Erklär-film

a) Read the sentences 1–6. Which of them say who does the action? Which sentences don't say who does the action? Write the numbers.

1 Your dad **takes** amazing photos.
2 The game **is designed** to change for each player.
3 AI **makes** the next level easier or harder.
4 A game **isn't created** in a few days.
5 Our programmers **test** the game.
6 Then all the mistakes **are fixed**.

b) Complete the rule about the passive in the simple present.

> **Aktiv:** Our programmers **test** the game. **Passiv:** The game **is tested**.
>
> – Wir benutzen A **Aktivsätze** / B **Passivsätze**, um zu sagen, **wer etwas macht**.
> – Wir benutzen A **Aktivsätze** / B **Passivsätze**, wenn es vor allem darum geht, **was passiert**.
>   (Wer es macht, ist nicht so wichtig oder nicht bekannt.)
>
> Im **simple present** bildest du das Passiv mit *am, is* oder *are* und dem **past participle** (= dritte Form) des Verbs (regelmäßig auf *-ed*). Einige Verben haben unregelmäßige **past participle**-Formen (z. B. *taken, made*). ▶ Language file 19 a + b, pp. 173–174   ▶ Irregular verbs, pp. 254–256

▶ Workbook, p. 59

3 Artificial intelligence

Complete an online article about artificial intelligence.
Use the passive in the simple present with *is* or *are*.

Artificial intelligence (AI) is a popular topic
these days. But what is it really? These
programs *are given* **(1 given)** a lot of
information, called data. With this data,
they can write texts, create pictures and
make predictions.
This technology ... **(2 used)** in lots of
different ways. For example, AI technology
... **(3 added)** to fitness devices, video or
music streaming services, personal digital
assistants, chatbots and more. In fact,

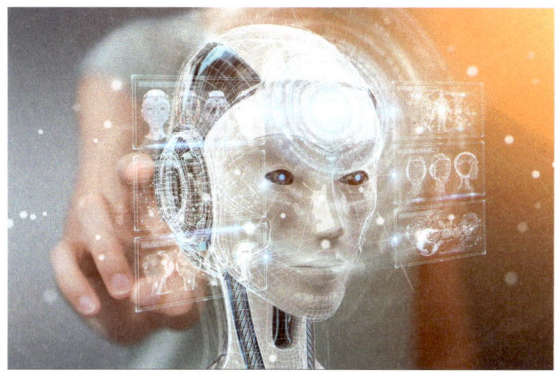

millions of AI pictures ... **(4 put)** online every day. All this can be very useful, but AI ... **(5 seen)**
as a problem too. Experts say that AI often copies discrimination (like racism or sexism) from
people. Others are worried about AI taking jobs away from people. Also, as more AI texts,
photos or videos ... **(6 created)** online, it gets harder to know when these are fake or real.

▸ Language file 19 a + b, pp. 173–174   ▸ More practice 3, p. 136

4 Building a game

a) **Partner B:** Look at p. 134.
   Partner A: Read the notes. Write steps 1,
   3, 5 and 7 in your exercise book. Add *is*
   or *are* to complete the sentences in the
   passive.

   Step 1: The idea for the game is chosen.

b) Read the first step for building a video
   game and check partner B's sentence.
   Now listen to partner B and write down
   step 2. Partner B checks your sentence.
   Take turns to complete all the steps.

   ▸ More practice 4, p. 136

Step 1:	the idea for the game – chosen
Step 2:	...
Step 3:	the characters and the levels in the game – designed
Step 4:	...
Step 5:	the music and the dialogue – recorded
Step 6:	...
Step 7:	any problems – fixed
Step 8:	...

▸ Workbook, p. 60

5 READING Riley's problem

a) BEFORE YOU READ Do you sometimes use AI to help with homework? Why (not)? Tell a partner.

I always / sometimes / never use AI to help me because ...

b) Read the chat between Riley and Tiana. Why did Riley get detention?

c) Decide if each sentence (1–5) is about Riley (R), Tiana (T) or both (B).

1 She had a problem at school today.
2 She uses AI to help her sometimes.
3 She agrees with the teacher.
4 She gives a reason for her opinion.
5 She changes her mind at the end.

d) What do you think about what Riley did and why? Tell your partner.

I think that it was OK / wrong / ... because ...

I'm so upset. I can't believe that I got detention today! 😠

Oh no, what happened? 😮 Did you talk in class again?

No, Mr Gomez said that I cheated on my history essay because I asked AI to write it! 🙄 Isn't that stupid?

I'm sorry that you got detention, but if you ask me, that IS kind of cheating. 😬

Are you serious? EVERYONE uses AI!

For research, sure, we all do – but not to write the whole thing! You didn't do your homework – a computer did! 🙆

I guess you have a point. 😔

6 LISTENING Can you believe your eyes?

a) BEFORE YOU LISTEN Look at the two pictures. Guess which one is real and which is made by AI. Give reasons.

I think picture A / B is real because the deer ...
The colours / legs / ... in picture A / B look ...
The background / light / ... looks strange / ...

b) Listen to the conversation between Riley and her dad. How does AI make him feel?

c) Listen again and choose the right options.

1 A company emailed Riley's dad to say that they **want to buy / don't need** his photos.
2 He thinks that the AI image of the deer is **not correct / better than his photos**.
3 He says that the company just wants to get **the best / free** pictures.
4 He's annoyed because AI companies use his photos to **sell magazines / train the AI**.
5 But when they do this, they don't **pay him / say thank you**.
6 He thinks that being a photographer is **difficult sometimes / the best job in the world**.

7 Opinions

a) Do you remember the jobs that Riley's parents have? Look at the speech bubbles and decide who might say them: Riley's mum or dad.

> 1 *The reason why I think that AI photos should be banned is that it takes people's jobs.*

> 3 *You have a point that AI can be useful in some ways.*

> 2 *But can't you see that AI is the answer to so many of our problems?*

> 4 *I hear what you're saying but I still don't think that AI is a bad thing for the world.*

b) Copy and complete the table with the phrases in blue. Add more examples.

Agreeing	Disagreeing	Giving reasons
...	...	...

My task

👥 8 Let's discuss

▶ Digital help 🔖

a) Read these statements. Work with a partner and decide if they describe something that is positive (+) or negative (−) about AI.

1 AI can do boring tasks so that people can work on more interesting things.
2 Some people might lose their jobs because of AI.
3 AI is often racist or sexist.
4 AI can work 24 hours a day, 7 days a week.
5 Scientists use AI to better predict when and where disasters will happen.
6 To train their technology, AI companies have stolen people's data.

b) Discuss the positives and negatives of AI with your partner.

Student A: You think AI is a **positive** thing.
Student B: You think AI is a **negative** thing.

Use the phrases in 7b and the statements in 8a. You can also use your own ideas.

AI is often racist. That's the reason why I think it should be banned.

c) After the discussion, decide which arguments were the best. Then tell each other how you feel about AI.

I liked your argument about ... AI makes me feel ...

▶ Feedback phrases, p. 191

▶ Workbook, p. 61

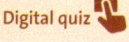 Digital quiz 🔖   **I can** have a discussion about AI.

My people

1 READING Tiana's essay

a) BEFORE YOU READ Tiana and Riley are learning about Native American history in school. Read the speech bubbles. Who wrote an essay and why is she nervous?

b) Read the essay. What is taught in Tiana's school?

Columbus discovered …
A North America
B a new medicine

> *Did you finish your essay on Native people in North America?*

> *Yes, and I'm nervous because I wrote something negative about our school.*

Native people in North America

In our history lessons at school, we are taught that North America was 'discovered' by Christopher Columbus in 1492. The truth is that Native people had
5 already been here for tens of thousands of years.
But Europeans didn't care about that when they arrived over 500 years ago. Native land was stolen by white people,
10 and millions of Native people were killed. They died in violent wars, and from illnesses that were brought by Europeans. Many Native children were taken from their families and forced to go to boarding
15 schools where they were treated terribly.

Thousands of Native children died in these schools.
This history is shocking and sad, but Native people survived. Today many Native people tell the world: 'We are still here'. 20
Native people are very diverse. In the USA there are 9.7 million Native Americans and 574 tribes.
My tribe is the Yurok, which is the largest tribe in California. 90% of Yurok land was 25
taken, but we bought back some land, and some land was given back by the government. This is a step in the right direction and shows how strong Native people are. 30

c) **Find the answers in the text.**

1 What does Tiana say is the truth?
2 What happened to Native land?
3 What do Native people tell the world?
4 Who are the Yurok?

▶ Parallel exercise, p. 136

d) **Find the missing numbers in the essay to complete the sentences.**

1 … is the year that Columbus 'discovered' America.
2 Europeans arrived in North America over … years ago.
3 There are … million Native Americans in the USA.
4 There are … tribes.
5 … of Yurok land was taken.

▶ English numbers, p. 253
▶ More practice 5, p. 137

Erklär-
film

2 LOOKING AT LANGUAGE The passive: simple past

**Look at these sentences from Tiana's essay on page 114 and complete them.
Then complete the rule in the box below.**

1   North America ... 'discovered' **by** Christopher Columbus. (lines 2–3)
2   Native land ... stolen **by** white people. (line 9)
3   They died from illnesses that ... brought **by** Europeans. (line 12)
4   Native children ... taken from their families. (line 13)
5   Some land ... given back **by** the government. (line 27)

> Im **simple past** bildest du das Passiv mit *was* oder *were* und dem **past participle** (= dritte
> Form) des Verbs.
> Wir verwenden *by* um zu sagen ...
> A   warum die Handlung passiert ist.
> B   wer die Handlung ausgeführt hat.
>
> You can use 'by' in the present tense too.

▶ Language file 19 a + b, pp. 173–174   ▶ Irregular verbs, pp. 254–256

3 The Yurok and the condors

**Complete the sentences. Use the passive in the simple
past with *was* or *were*.**

Californian condors are some of the largest birds in the
world. Condors play an important role in Yurok stories,
songs and traditions. In the past, this bird *was found*
(1 found) along the whole west coast of the USA.
When the Yurok's land ... **(2 taken)** by white people,
many condors ... **(3 killed)** or their eggs ... **(4 stolen)**. The
number of wild condors went down, and they almost
disappeared. The last condors ... **(5 caught)** by scientists
and put in zoos. In 2008, a new project ... **(6 created)** by

the Yurok with an important goal – to bring the condor back home. The good news? They have
been successful: in 2022, there were more than 300 wild condors in California.

4 WORDS What is it?

Read the definitions (1–5) and scan pages 114–115 to find the correct words. Take turns.

1   Something which was stolen by white people. – *Native land.*
2   A bird which was found along the west coast of the USA.
3   A terrible place where many Native children were forced to go.
4   Something that was brought by Europeans and killed a lot of Native Americans.
5   A type of text which was written by Tiana about Native people's history.

▶ More practice 6, p. 137
▶ Workbook, pp. 62–63

5 LISTENING Native Americans today

a) BEFORE YOU LISTEN Tiana is giving a presentation to her class about the Yurok people. Look at her slides and say what you can see.

Salmon fishing

At a powwow

b) **Listen and choose the right answers.**

1 Tiana **is / isn't** a member of the Yurok tribe.
2 People who aren't Native **have / haven't** taken care of the Klamath River.
3 Tiana **is going to / isn't going to** study law at university.
4 People who aren't Native **are allowed to / aren't allowed to** go to public powwows.
5 You **should / shouldn't** wear traditional clothes if you aren't Native.
6 You **should / shouldn't** ask for permission before you take pictures.

c) **Listen again and check.**
▶ More practice 7, p. 138

6 SONG *Run with the Wolves* (by Raye Zaragoza)

a) BEFORE YOU LISTEN Tiana plays a song to her class by Raye Zaragoza, who has multicultural roots. Look at the title of the song and the photo.
How do you feel when you run? How do you think animals feel when they run?

b) **Find the song on the internet. Listen. What do you think the song is about?**
Tell your partner. You can look at the lyrics for help.
▶ More help, p. 138

c) **Listen again. Do you have more ideas about the song? Take notes.**

nature, freedom, history, ...

d) **Do you like the song? Why (not)?**
▶ Wordbank 2, p. 181

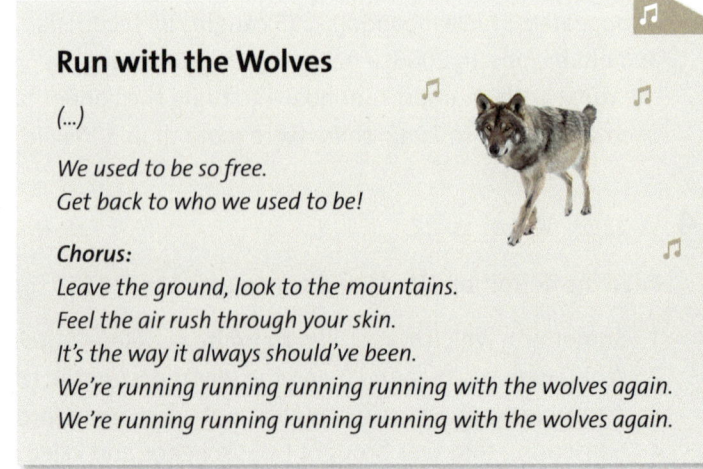

Run with the Wolves

(...)

We used to be so free.
Get back to who we used to be!

Chorus:
Leave the ground, look to the mountains.
Feel the air rush through your skin.
It's the way it always should've been.
We're running running running running with the wolves again.
We're running running running running with the wolves again.

7 MEDIATION **Respect other cultures**

Tiana met Max from Mainz at summer camp. He wants to tell her about a comment that he read on social media. Help Max mediate.

Hi, Tiana
Can I ask you something? A girl called Pia wrote that she saw someone who was dressed like ... She heard that Native Americans don't like ... They say that this shows too little ... At the end Pia asks how ... What do you think?
Max

Beim Karnevalsumzug in Mainz habe ich einen Typen gesehen, der als *Native American* verkleidet war. Ich habe allerdings gehört, dass *Native Americans* mit solchen Kostümen nicht einverstanden sind. Sie sagen, dass das wenig Respekt gegenüber ihrer Kultur zeigt. Vielleicht wollte dieser Junge niemandem wehtun, aber er hat es getan. Was meint ihr – wie sollte man in einer solchen Situation reagieren? *Pia (15), Mainz*

My task

8 A cartoon ▶ Digital help

Cartoons are often funny because they use a surprising or shocking subject for a serious message. Many use stereotypes – like the traditional look of the Native Americans in this cartoon.

OH, YEAH...THAT'S RIGHT...YOU DISCOVERED AMERICA!

a) **Look at the cartoon and describe it.**

In the foreground I can see two ... They are standing on ...
The man on the left is ... The man on the right is Columbus.
He's holding ... He's wearing ... In the background on the
left I can see two ... They are laughing at ... On the right ...

b) **Look at the speech bubble. What do you think it means?**
Think about what you have learned about Native American history.

The Native Americans are laughing because Columbus thinks that he ...
That's not true, because Native Americans have been there for ...

c) 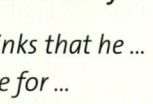 **Do you like this cartoon? Is it funny or does it make you think?**

In my opinion, this cartoon is / isn't funny because ... – It makes you think because ...

▶ Skills file 7, p. 150

▶ Workbook, p. 64

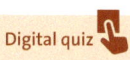

Our land

1 READING The Redwood National Park

a) BEFORE YOU READ Tiana, Riley and Riley's dad are going camping. Have you ever gone camping? What was it like? WALK AROUND Tell different partners.

I've often gone camping in the garden ... It's usually ... — Cool! I'd like to try that too!
I've stayed at a holiday campsite ... I really liked ... — That sounds fun!
I haven't gone camping before. And I wouldn't like to go camping because ... — I agree!

b) Riley read Tony's travel blog before the trip to Redwood National Park. Read it and look at the pictures: What do you find most interesting?

Tony's travel blog: The Redwood National Park

Redwood National Park is home to some of the oldest and tallest trees on earth: Redwoods can grow to over 300 feet (91 metres)! My family and I went on a forest walk and our guide told us about the tallest tree in the world which is in this park – it's 380 feet (nearly 116 metres) tall. That means that it's taller than the Statue of Liberty! The guide also told us that the Yurok live near here and they help to protect the trees and the condors in the forest.

We saw a lot of animals, but we didn't see any bears (although black bears live in the forests).

We stayed in a cabin in the park. We built a cool fire, told scary stories and made s'mores too. For those of you who aren't from the USA: you make s'mores with marshmallows, chocolate and cookies. They taste so good that you want 'some more' (s'more)! Unless, of course, you don't like chocolate! It was an amazing trip because I saw and learned so many new things.

c) Read Tony's blog again. True (T) or false (F)?
☒ Correct the false sentences.

1   Some trees in the national park are over ninety metres high.
2   The Statue of Liberty is smaller than the tallest tree in the park.
3   You can't see bears in the forest.
4   It's called a s'more because people always want to eat another one.
5   Tony enjoyed the trip because the weather was great.

2 LISTENING **Are you a bear expert?**

a) BEFORE YOU LISTEN Riley sees this sign. What do you think you should do in the forest? Copy the table.
Tick (✓) or cross (✗) the tips (1–6) in the second column.

	a)	b)
0 Go near bears.	✗	
1 Leave food outside.		
2 Run away.		
3 Wave your arms.		
4 Shout and make loud noises.		
5 Climb a tree.		
6 Use bear pepper spray.		

b) Listen and check your answers from a). Tick (✓) or cross (✗) the third column in your table. Did you get five or more answers correct? Then you're a bear expert!

c) Complete the sentences from the conversation in b) with the correct linking words.
Then listen again and check your answers.

1 They usually stay away from people, **so that / unless** they can smell food.
2 We'll talk, sing and clap **unless / so that** they know we're coming.
3 Hold up a jacket **so that / although** you look bigger.
4 It will probably go away, **because / although** if it doesn't, you have to get louder.
5 Don't climb a tree **because / although** bears can climb trees!

▶ Language file 20, p. 175   ▶ More practice 8, p. 139

My task

3 My travel blog post   ▶ Digital help

a) YOU CHOOSE You're going to write a short post for a travel blog. Do task A or B.
A Write about a trip to the Redwood National Park.
B Write about a trip to a place in nature (a mountain, a lake, …) that you have been to.

b) Think of ideas for your post. Collect them in a table or a mind map:

• Where did you sleep? (Or was it a day trip?)   • What did you see and do?
• Was it a good or bad trip and why?   ▶ More help, p. 139

c) Write your travel blog post. Tony's blog on p. 118 can help you. You can add photos.

d) PEER CONFERENCE In small groups, exchange your blog posts and give feedback. Which was the most interesting place to you? Why? Would you like to visit any of the places too?

▶ Feedback phrases, p. 191

▶ Workbook, pp. 65–66

Digital quiz   I can **talk about nature in California.**

Wildfire

1 Camping again

a) BEFORE YOU READ   **Look at the group chat and answer the questions.**

1 Who is Tiana writing to?
2 Where did Tiana meet them?

Do you need a tip? Look at pages 14–15.

b) Read the story. What happened and why did Amy write to Tiana in the end (p. 122)?

Lakeview campers

Amy, Troy, Diego, Tiana

> *Hi, everyone, I'm going camping again! This time with my friend Riley and her dad in a cabin in the Redwood National Park. Hope it's as good as Lakeview Adventure Camp last summer! Take care* ❤️

After their first day in the national park, Tiana, Riley and her dad made a fire next to their cabin.
'Remember,' said Riley's dad, 'when you make
5 a fire, you always stay near it when it's burning. The forests are very dry, so a bigger fire can start very easily.'

They cooked some food over the fire and talked about their day while they were
10 eating.
'I can't believe how tall these trees are,' said Riley. 'They make me feel so small! It's beautiful when you stand in the forest and look up.'
15 'I know, right?' said Tiana. 'For us Yurok, redwoods are very important, so we never hurt them. When we need wood, we find trees that have already fallen.'

When they had eaten, Tiana, Riley and her dad looked at some of the photos they had 20 taken that day. 'Look at this condor!' Riley said. 'What a great photo.'
'Yes, it is,' said Tiana. 'But I'm so tired that I'm falling asleep.'
'Let's put the fire out and go to bed,' said 25 Riley's dad. 'We have an early start tomorrow.'

Soon all three of them were asleep. Suddenly Tiana woke up – and smelled smoke. 'Something's burning,' she thought. 30 She looked out the cabin window. The forest was burning! Tiana shouted loudly to Riley and her dad. 'Fire! Wake up!'
'Maybe a fire at a campsite wasn't put out correctly. I'm sure it wasn't our fire – but 35 there are other people in the forest,' said Riley's dad. His voice was calm, but his eyes were worried. 'Let's go to the car quickly.'

In the car, Riley called 911 to tell them about
40 the fire. 'They know about it already, Dad.
There are firefighters in the forest.'
A few minutes later, they stopped. The road
was blocked by a tree.
'What do we do now?' asked Riley. She was
45 starting to get scared.
'I'll take a look,' said her dad. He got out of
the car and tried to move the tree, but it was
too heavy. He came back to the girls.
'I can see firefighters in the forest. I'm going
50 to ask them for help.'
'It's dangerous out there!' said Riley. 'You
could get hurt!'
'I'll be back in five minutes,' said her dad.
'Don't worry.'
55 Riley's dad
left, and
Tiana tried to
make her friend
feel better.
60 'Look up there. Can
you see the condor in the
sky? I think it's watching us.'
Riley gave a small smile. 'It's probably just
looking for food.'

'Where is he?' said Riley after five minutes. 65
'I'm going to find him.' She tried to get out
of the car, but Tiana stopped her.
'Just wait a little longer,' she said.
At that moment, Riley's dad came out of the
forest. With him were two firefighters. 70

'Cole and Ana are going to help us to move
the tree,' he said.
The firefighters and Riley's dad put a thick
rope around the tree and tied it to the back
of the car. Then slowly the car moved and 75
pulled the tree to the side of the road.
'Thanks for your help,' Riley's dad said to the
firefighters.
'You're welcome,' said Ana. 'Now it's time for
you all to get home.' 80

The next day, Amy wrote to Tiana.

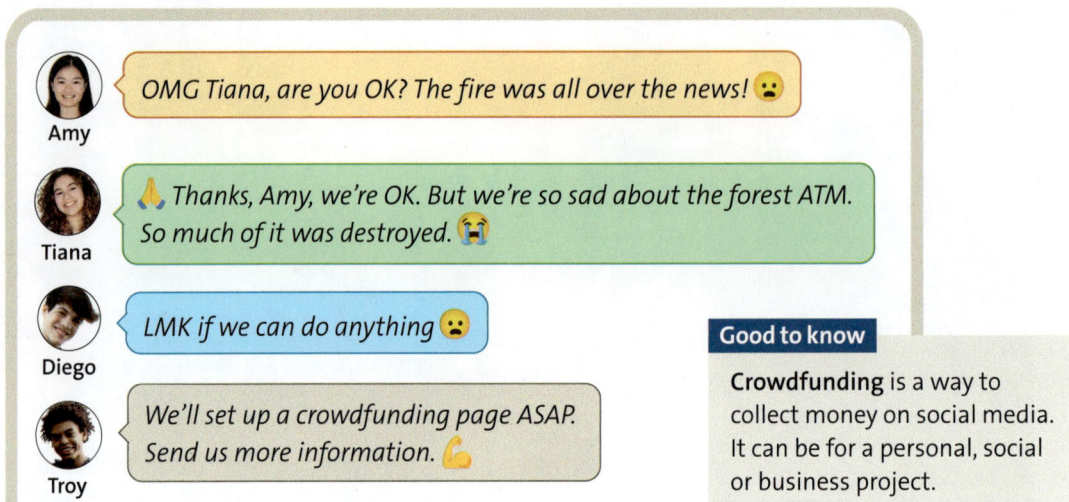

Amy: *OMG Tiana, are you OK? The fire was all over the news!* 😕

Tiana: 🙏 *Thanks, Amy, we're OK. But we're so sad about the forest ATM. So much of it was destroyed.* 😭

Diego: *LMK if we can do anything* 😕

Troy: *We'll set up a crowdfunding page ASAP. Send us more information.* 💪

Good to know

Crowdfunding is a way to collect money on social media. It can be for a personal, social or business project.

2 What was the result?

Read the story again. Write what happened as a result of each action or event (1–5).

1 A fire at a campsite wasn't put out correctly. ⟶ *A fire started in the forest.*
2 There was a tree on the road. ⟶ *The car ...*
3 Riley's dad got out of the car. ⟶ *He saw ...*
4 Two firefighters came to help. ⟶ *They ...*
5 Amy wrote to her friends. ⟶ *...*

3 Chat language

🔊 👥 **a)** The chat at the top of the page has four examples of chat language. Do you know what they mean? Tell a partner. Then listen and check.

b) Do you know others? You can look at the speech bubble for ideas. Exchange ideas with the class.

TTYL   IDK
BTW   NVM
CYA   NGL

4 LIFE SKILLS & LISTENING Think creatively

🔊 **a)** Tiana's three friends thought creatively to collect money for the forest. Listen to their group call. How much money did they collect?

🔊 **b)** Listen again and write what each friend did.

1 Amy, a photographer, organized an online exhibition of her ...
2 Diego, a robot builder, held a robot ...
3 Troy, a trumpet player, gave a concert with the church ...

👥 **c)** Now you want to crowdfund to help a friend. What are your ideas?

Digital quiz 👆   **I can** understand a story about problem-solving. ✓

Swimming in the desert

1 The title of the film

BEFORE YOU WATCH **Look at the title of the film.**
What is strange about it?
What do you think the film is about?

Good to know

California has three deserts. A desert gets less than 25 cm of rain in a year.

2 VIEWING **Making a river**

The film takes place in the town of Agua Dulce in California. Angie doesn't speak and uses sign language or writes things down, so a narrator tells her story:
Angie and her mother are going to move away, and Angie's grandfather is planning to leave too.

a) **Watch the first part of the film. Choose the best words.**

1 In the past, there was **more / less** water in the town.
2 A company decided to **give away / sell** the water from the river.
3 Now the area is very **green / dry**.

b) **Watch the second part of the film. Put the key events in the correct order.** *1 D, 2 …*

A Her mum comes back and picks Angie up.
B Her grandfather looks for her. When he finds her, they fight.
C Angie's grandfather helps to bring water back to the river.
D Angie's mum leaves Angie with her grandfather.
E A man wants to buy her grandfather's water. Angie runs out of the office.

c) **Why do you think Angie's grandfather changed his mind?**

I think he felt … / he realized that … / he wanted to …

3 GLOBAL GOALS **Save water**

How can we save water? Make a poster. You can use these ideas or your own ideas. You can add pictures if you like.

Take shorter …
Turn off the tap when you …
Only use dishwashers and washing machines when …

SAVE WATER –
TURN OFF THE TAP

▶ Workbook, p. 67

Talk about charts

1 How to explain a chart

A chart is a drawing that shows numbers. It's often easier to understand than just words and numbers. For example, charts about wildfires in California can help you to talk about the danger to nature there (landscapes, trees and wildlife). There are different kinds of charts, e.g. bar charts, column charts, line charts or pie charts.

a) **Introduce the chart: Say what kind of chart it is, what it's about and what the source is.**

This column chart shows the wildfire trends in …
The source of the data/numbers/statistics is …
The data/numbers/statistics are from the year …

Good to know

In the USA, the land is measured in acres. In Europe, we use square kilometres (km²).
1,000 acres = about 4 km²
1.86 acres = one football pitch

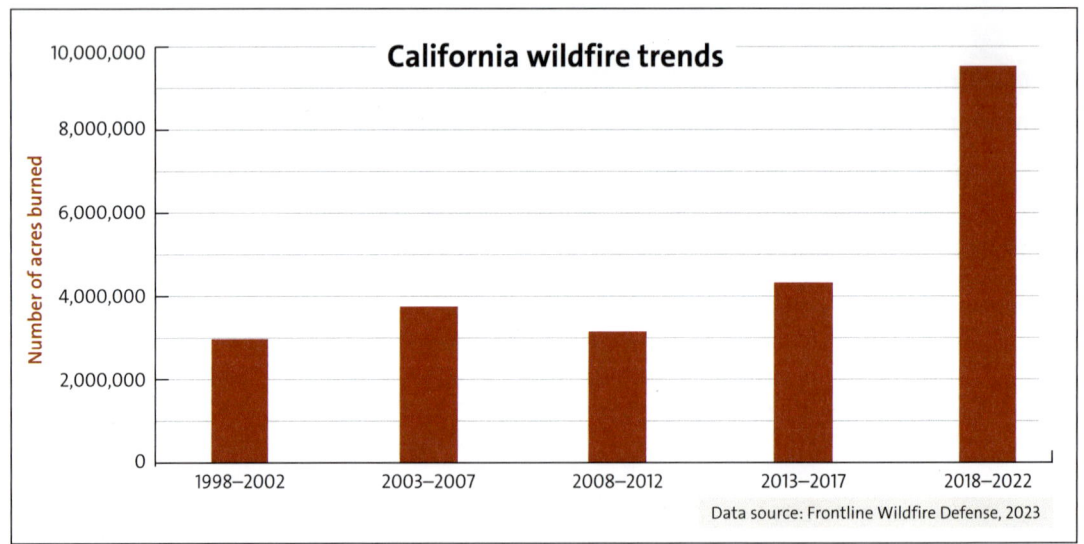

Data source: Frontline Wildfire Defense, 2023

b) **Talk about the numbers.**
In the years from … to …, about … million acres of land were burned.
This number went up / down in the years from … to …
More / Fewer acres of land were burned in the years … than …
The chart shows that the number of acres burned has gone up / gone down in the last 25 years.

▶ English numbers, p. 253   ▶ Wordbank 5, p. 184   ▶ Skills file 8, p. 151

2 Talk about other charts

Now talk about charts on artificial intelligence (AI) and Native Americans.

Partner B: Look at page 134. **Partner A:** Look at page 139.

Digital quiz 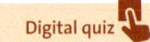   **I can talk about charts.**

Prepare and give a presentation

Step 1: Choose your topic

Choose a topic from this unit for your presentation:

Artificial intelligence

Native Americans

Californian nature

Step 2: Think of ideas

a) Make a group with students who have the same topic. Exchange ideas from the unit pages and make notes. You can also do some research.

▶ Skills file 4, p. 146

b) To support your ideas, choose a chart from p. 124, 134 or 139.

▶ Study skills, p. 124 ▶ Skills file 8, p. 151

c) Structure your ideas under headings, for example in a mind map. Decide who is going to present each part.

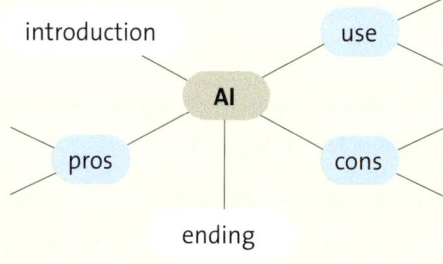

Step 3: Make notes, check and present

a) Prepare your part of the presentation. Make slides and cards with short notes and check everything.

▶ Skills file 6, pp. 148–149

b) Practise your presentation as a group.

c) Give your presentation to a group who chose a different topic. Use Touch – Turn – Talk.

Touch your slide or poster to show what you're talking about.
Turn to the group and look at them.
Talk using your short notes.

Step 4: Give feedback

Listen carefully to the other group's presentation. Then give the group feedback:

★ Were the ideas interesting?   ★ Did the presentation have a good structure?
★ Did the group explain the slides, pictures and chart well?   ★ What did you like most?

▶ Study skills, p. 92 ▶ Feedback phrases, p. 191

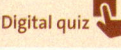
Digital quiz   I can prepare and give a presentation.

1 California in one picture

a) LISTENING **Listen to Riley's conversation with her dad.**
Put the pictures (A–D) in the correct order. *1 …*

b) **Listen again. True or false?**

1 The competition wants to find the most shocking photo of California.
2 Riley prefers pictures of buildings.
3 Mike thinks that people in California love nature.
4 Mike thinks that pictures should be beautiful.
5 To Riley it's important to show people of different ages.

c) SPEAKING **Which photo would you choose for the competition and why? Tell the class.**
Give reasons.

I would choose photo …   It shows …   I think this photo sums up California because …

2 SPEAKING Should we use AI?

a) **You and your partner have to write an essay for homework. Copy and complete the table with**
reasons for and against using AI (A–D) to write the essay. Add your own reasons.

for AI	against AI
…	…

A *we can save time*

B *sometimes big mistakes are made by AI*

C *we won't practise our writing skills*

D *we can focus more on research*

b) **Now have the discussion with your partner. Partner A: You want to write the essay using AI.**
Partner B: You disagree. Use the ideas from a) and the phrases below. Then swap roles.

> I think we should/shouldn't use AI because … • I hear what you're saying, but … •
> You have a point that … • But can't you see that … • That's the reason why I think that …

Check

3 The Hoopa tribe

I can **talk about Native American history.** ✓

a) LANGUAGE **For her essay about Native American history, Tiana is reading about the Hoopa. Complete the information with the correct form of the passive in the simple past.**

The Hoopa are a Native American tribe in northern California. While most Californian tribes *were forced* **(1 force)** to leave their land by white people, the Hoopa were able to stay. Their land **... (2 protect)** and white people couldn't take it from them. The photo on the right **... (3 take)** in 1923 and it shows a Hoopa man catching salmon in the Trinity River. The Trinity and the Klamath have been two important rivers for the Hoopa for many years. However, these rivers **... (4 not protect)**. One hundred years ago, big companies started to build dams on the Klamath River. The river is home to salmon and other kinds of fish, but so many fish **... (5 kill)** by these dams that they almost disappeared completely. Many protests **... (6 organize)** by the Hoopa and other Native American tribes to destroy the dams and save the river.

b) MEDIATION **Tiana shares an online article with her German friend Max from Mainz. Complete the dialogue with his little brother.**

Max	Ach, das ist ja toll!
Bruder	Was denn?
Max	Tiana hat mir einen Artikel geschickt. Einige Dämme im Klamath-Fluss ... **(1)**.
Bruder	Warum das denn?
Max	Um ... **(2)**, vor allem den Lachs.
Bruder	Aber wieso ist das besser für die Fische?
Max	Ohne die Dämme ... **(3)**.
Bruder	Was hat Tiana damit zu tun?
Max	Na, Tiana ist ein Mitglied der Yurok, und viele Yurok und Hoopa ... **(4)**. Jetzt können sie ... **(5)**.

Tiana   *today 12:05*

Hi, Max, how are you? How is life in Mainz? Check out this article, it's the news that we've been waiting for for so long!! 🎉 😊

Klamath River: four dams were destroyed
After many years of debate, the US government has finally destroyed four dams along California's Klamath River. This action was taken to save the river and protect the fish, especially salmon. Without the dams, the fish now can find cooler water more easily.

Many tribes, including the Hoopa and the Yurok, had protested against the dams for over twenty years. Now they can finally celebrate their success.

Check

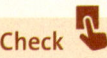

4 At Pinnacles National Park

I can **talk about nature in California.** ✓

a) WORDS **Read the definitions (1–6) and find the correct words in the text below.**

1 It's something that can protect you against bears.
2 It's used to say that something is not allowed.
3 It's used to describe something that has no water in it.

4 It's created when something burns.
5 It's a small house that you can sleep in.
6 It's a large, heavy animal that can be dangerous.

Welcome to our campsite! Please read our rules:
▶ **Don't burn anything. There's a ban on all fires because the ground is too dry.**
▶ **Call the campsite if you see smoke.**
▶ **Don't leave food in your cabin. Bears can smell any amount!**
▶ **You should always bring bear pepper spray with you**.

b) WRITING **Look at Matt's notes and write his blog post about his trip to Pinnacles National Park.**

Introduction	Last weekend, I visited Pinnacles National Park with …
Main part – Campsite – Animals – Area – Weather	slept in cabins, met friendly people, … saw deer, rabbits, no condors :-(there were mountains/cliffs, took photos of trees / … during the day – hot and dry, at night – very cool
Conclusion	I'd recommend … , I want to go back again, because …

5 STUDY SKILLS Condors in California

I can **talk about charts.** ✓

Riley has found a chart about condors for her geography homework. Copy and complete her text with the best word.

The **chart/drawing (1)** shows how the number of condors in California has changed over **32/42 (2)** years. The **source/writer (3)** for the statistics is the US Fish and Wildlife Service and the numbers are from 1980–2022. In 1985, there were **lots of / no (4)** condors in the wild. In 2000, there were nearly 200 condors, but **all/most (5)** of them were in zoos. In 2022, there were over 500 condors, and more than half of them were in the wild.

California's condor population

— Total population of condors
— Condor population in the wild
— Condors in zoos

Source: U.S. Fish and Wildlife Service, 2023

Datenquelle: https://www.fws.gov/media/california-condor-population-graph-1980–2022 (siehe Quellenverzeichnis)

Check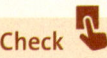

6 READING An interview with the firefighters

I can understand a story about problem-solving.

For her blog, Riley has interviewed the two firefighters at Redwood National Park.

Lots of you already know that I had a pretty scary experience when I was camping at Redwood. Well, today I finally spoke with Cole and Ana, the amazing firefighters who helped us.

Riley First of all I want to say thank you for agreeing to do this interview for my blog. And more importantly, thank you for helping us to move the tree that night.

Cole No problem, we were just doing our job and we're happy that you guys got home safely.

Ana And we're really excited to do this interview! We often visit high schools to talk about fire
5　safety, but this is our first interview!

Riley Oh great! So I would love to hear about your work. What's it like being a firefighter in California right now? And would you recommend it as a job?

Cole Yes, I would recommend it – it's a very important job and you can really make a difference. But it's very challenging, and it gets more challenging every year.

10　**Riley** That's because the number of fires keeps going up, right?

Ana Right. We're not getting enough rain, and the ground is very dry, so it burns easily. I'm sure you talk about climate change at school. It's a very big problem.

Riley Yes, of course we do. Are you ever upset or scared? The fires are getting worse.

Cole You're right, it can be scary sometimes. This job isn't getting easier, but we try to stay positive.
15　Did you know that around 95% of wildfires are started by people? If we want to change people's behaviour, we need to tell them about the dangers.

Ana And that's why we like going into high schools, doing tours of the fire station, and having conversations like this!

Riley That's great. Is there anything else that gives you hope?

20　**Ana** Well, AI is something that we're pretty excited about right now. We use it to understand what direction a fire will move in. This can help us stop fires more quickly.

a) The interview is about ...

A the day that Riley saved the firefighters.
B the job of firefighters in California.
C how AI can help students.

b) True, false or not in the text? Correct the false sentences.

1　Cole and Ana do a lot of interviews with high school students.
2　Cole recommends his job because the pay is very high.
3　Climate change is making the fires worse.
4　Cole and Ana often go into high schools to talk about how to make things better.
5　Most wildfires begin because of lightning.
6　Cole and Ana offer tours of the fire station every Tuesday.

Check

United

*Why would **you** like to visit California?*

A magazine for young people across the USA

California dreams *by Riley Walker*

Lots of people dream of seeing Hollywood, movie studios and famous movie stars. Others dream of California because of the sunny weather, the beautiful beaches and the awesome national parks. I love being outdoors and my dad and I often watch the surfers on the ocean. Did you know that surfing is the official state sport in California?

Californian surf culture

Caitlin Simmers is a young professional surfer who in 2024 became the youngest women's world champion in history. Caitlin is from the beach city of Oceanside in California and her parents and brother are all surfers. Caitlin began surfing with her family when she was very young and started surfing professionally in 2018, when she was only 13 years old.

When you watch surfers ride the waves, it looks easy, but it actually takes years of practice. The good news is that everyone can learn it!
Special surfboard equipment means that people with a disability can also surf. Some can stand on specially-made legs, others sit in a special chair on the board or lie down and paddle. Some even surf with the help of a surfing service dog!

Have you **ever** tried *surfing* or **would** you **like** **to** try **it?**

A special tour

In LA you can go on a lot of tours. I went on a very special tour with my mom where nothing was real – the streets, gardens, parks and events were all fake. That's because this was a movie studio tour and the places were movie sets[1]! All the buildings are made of thin wood and there is nothing behind the walls!

> What special tour have you been on?

Outside you can also see car stunts, for example scenes from the *Fast and Furious* movies and other movie sets.

But parts of films are also filmed inside, in large indoor studios. On the tour, you go into one of these studios in an electric tram, and are suddenly on the movie set of a subway! You experience the sights and sounds of an earthquake[2]: The subway shakes[3], the lights go out, a fire starts and lots of water comes in. The special effects are really good, and it all feels real!

Sometimes scenes are filmed in front of a green screen and then background photos and special effects are added later. This is often done for superhero and science-fiction movies. How cool is that?

Imagine you *can* go **to** the **set** of *your* favorite **movie** or *series*[4].

What **would** you **like** to *see* **and** why?

---

[1] **movie set** *die Filmkulisse*   [2] **earthquake** *das Erdbeben*   [3] **(to) shake** *schwanken, zittern*   [4] **series** *die Serie*

United

> What languages do you and people in your family speak?

A magazine for young people across the USA

I love languages! *by Tiana Moore*

Aiyekwee!

That's 'Hello' in the Yurok language – the language of the Yurok tribe in California. The last person who spoke Yurok as a first language died in 2013, but before he died he made lots of recordings and taught other people the language. At my school, the Eureka High School in California, there's a Yurok Language Program and I have also learned some Yurok phrases from my mom.

A lot of people all over the world speak English as a first or second language. If you go traveling, you'll always find someone who will speak at least a little bit of English! And what's best: On the internet you can connect with different people in English and talk about your favorite music, shows and games. It's really cool to find out how other kids live!

At school I have Spanish lessons because a lot of people speak Spanish in California and the USA. You can hear Spanish and see Spanish signs all over California.

> Hola![1]

Some of the kids in my class speak Spanish at home with their parents and with each other at break time. My friend Rosa and her two brothers were born here but their parents are from Mexico. Rosa and her brothers speak Spanish at home with their parents, but they speak English together. And Rosa says she feels more American than Mexican. I try and speak Spanish with Rosa although I feel a bit embarrassed about my accent! I probably also make a lot of mistakes but that's how you learn a language, right?

How many different languages are there in your class?

[1] **Hola!** (Spanisch) *Hallo!*   [2] **Se habla español.** (Spanisch) *Man spricht Spanisch.*

🌐 Making a language body map

We did an activity at school where we made a body map with the languages that we know or that we would like to learn.

- First you draw an outline[1] of a human body.
- You think about when you use each language or why you like it.
- Then you match each language to a part of the body.
- Choose a different color for each language and write a key.
- Finally, color in your body map.

Khalil's language body map

My friend Khalil speaks three languages: English, French and Arabic. All three languages are important to Khalil for different reasons. This is his map and what he told me about it:

"The heart[2] in my body map is pink – this is Arabic. My family's language is Arabic because my mom and dad come from Morocco. My mom has a big family and I love it when we all meet, have a meal together and speak Arabic.

I colored the legs in my body map pink too. That's because I speak Arabic with my dad when we play soccer together.

The head in my body map is yellow for English. This is because I speak English at school and learn things there. My hands are also yellow because English is the language that I write best.

I'm also learning French at school, and since my mom can speak French really well, she helps me with my homework. She sometimes cooks French dishes – I love that, so my stomach[3] is blue.

I feel very lucky to speak three languages! In the future, I'd also like to learn Korean because I like the sound of the language and I love K-pop![4] That's why I colored my ears green."

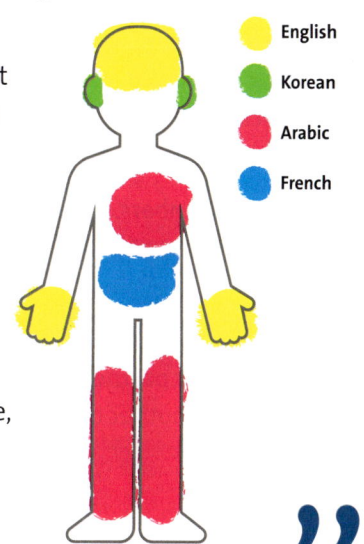

- English
- Korean
- Arabic
- French

Make a *language* body map for you and *explain* *it* to a friend!

---

[1] **outline** *der Umriss*   [2] **heart** *das Herz*   [3] **stomach** *der Bauch, der Magen*   [4] **K-pop** *die koreanische Popmusik*

Partner page

▶ Page 111

4 Building a game

a) **Partner B:** Read the notes. Write steps 2, 4, 6 and 8 in your exercise book. Add *is* or *are* to complete the sentences in the passive.

Step 2:
The main features of the game are decided.

b) Listen to partner A read the first step for building a video game and write it down. Partner A checks your sentence. Now read the second step and check partner A's sentence. Take turns to complete all the steps.

Step 1:	...
Step 2:	the main features of the game – decided
Step 3:	...
Step 4:	the game – programmed
Step 5:	...
Step 6:	the game – tested
Step 7:	...
Step 8:	the game – sold

▶ Page 124

2 Talk about other charts

a) **Partner B:** Explain this chart to partner A:

1 **Introduce the chart.**
   This chart shows ...
   The source is ...
   The chart is from the year ...

2 **Explain the numbers.**
   ... per cent have used ...
   ▶ English numbers, p. 253
   ▶ Wordbank 5, p. 184   ▶ Study skills, p. 124

b) **Partner B:** Listen to partner A who is going to explain another chart to you.

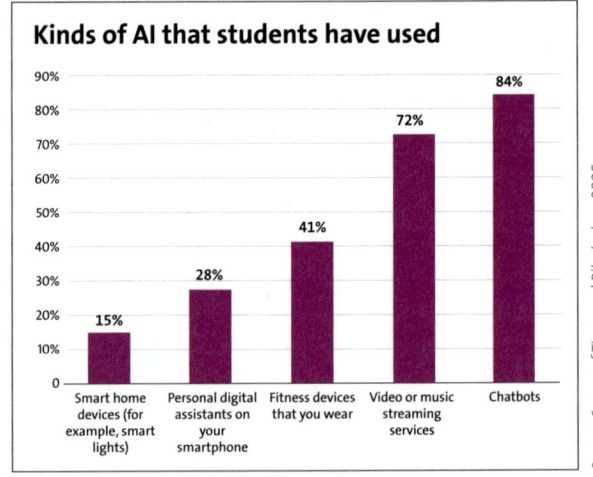

Kinds of AI that students have used

Smart home devices (for example, smart lights): 15%
Personal digital assistants on your smartphone: 28%
Fitness devices that you wear: 41%
Video or music streaming services: 72%
Chatbots: 84%

Source: Survey of Tiana and Riley's class, 2025

Diff Bank

▶ Page 108

More practice 1 WORDS **Antonyms**

a) Find pairs of antonyms in the word cloud.

> antonym = opposite (for example big – small)
> synonym = word that means the same (for example big – large)

empty · valley · mountain · full · modern · peaceful · tall · short · stressful · traditional

b) Write antonyms for these words.

1 boring   2 mean   3 cold   4 near   5 happy   6 stupid

▶ Page 109

More practice 2 **San Francisco**

Read the quotes from a tour of San Francisco (1–5) and match them to the photos (A–E). *1 C, 2 ..., ...*

1 'San Francisco is an easy city to walk around – if you like doing sport! It has more hills than any other city in the world except La Paz in Bolivia. That's why on this tour, we're going to take one of the famous San Francisco trams so that we don't have to walk everywhere!'

2 'On your left, you can see probably the most famous sight in San Francisco, the Golden Gate Bridge. It's 1.7 miles long and has been in many movies and TV shows. Isn't it beautiful?'

3 'San Francisco has always been an important city for LGBTQ people. We have the biggest Pride celebration in the USA! The parade takes place on Market Street. We were also home to the country's first openly gay politician, Harvey Milk, in 1977. Here's a photo of Harvey Milk; he is still very popular here.'

4 'If you look out at the water, you'll see a famous San Francisco sight: the old prison, Alcatraz, that is on an island in the water. It's been closed since 1963, but you can still take a ferry and visit it, because it's now a museum.'

5 'Our next stop is a San Francisco must-see: Pier 39. It's THE place to be, right by the water. You'll find shops, restaurants and an aquarium here and look – wild sea lions resting in the sun! There's no other city in the world like this one!'

4   Diff bank

▶ Page 111

More practice 3   **Riley's school day**

Complete the sentences. Use the passive form of the verb in brackets. Don't forget to use *is / are / isn't / aren't*.

Riley hates early mornings! That's why her dad helps her. First Riley *is woken* **(1 wake)** at 7 a.m. Then her dad makes breakfast. Later she ... **(2 drive)** to school. They always go by car. At school, students ... **(3 check)** before they can go inside. This is to make sure that guns ... **(4 not bring)** into the school. The national anthem ... **(5 play)** at the beginning of every school day. Next, homework and other projects ... **(6 collect)**. For lunch, she brings sandwiches because the meals in the cafeteria ... **(7 not cook)** very well. In the afternoons, there's an hour of free time, and Riley ... **(8 not tell)** what to do. She can decide which subject to work on.

More practice 4   WORDS   **Action verbs**

Choose the best verb from the box for the blue words or phrases in brackets.

> decide • design • fix • test • write

1   It's important to ... **(make right)** any problems before you start selling a product.
2   First, programmers ... **(choose)** what kind of game to build.
3   Today, artists often use computers to ... **(draw or plan)** video game characters.
4   Companies have special people to ... **(see if there's a problem with)** a new product.
5   I'd love to learn how to ... **(create)** code.

▶ Page 114

Parallel exercise   **1 Tiana's essay**

c)   **Complete the answers with one or two words.**

1   What does Tiana say is the truth?
    − ... had already been in North America for tens of thousands of years.
2   What happened to Native land?
    − It was ... by white people.
3   What do Native people tell the world?
    − 'We are ...'
4   Who are the Yurok?
    − The ... in California.

136   one hundred and thirty-six

▶ Page 114

More practice 5 **Thanksgiving**

a) Look at the pictures and read the article.
What do people do if they don't celebrate with family?

Each year, on the fourth Thursday of November, Americans celebrate Thanksgiving. The day is celebrated with big parades in cities like New York, Chicago, Philadelphia and Houston.

At home, families and friends come together for the special day. Before the Thanksgiving meal, each person says what they are thankful for that year. People often say that they are thankful for their friends, family, health, home, pets, and much more.

For the celebration meal, families traditionally eat turkey with lots of dishes, for example potatoes, corn and other vegetables, followed by pumpkin pie for dessert. Thanksgiving is one of the most important holidays of the year, and even if they don't celebrate with family, many people enjoy 'friendsgiving' with the people that they love.

b) What are you thankful for? Decide on at least two things and tell your partner. Use the ideas in the text or your own ideas.

▶ Page 115

More practice 6 **Lucky and unlucky**

Look at the pictures and write about Tiana's good luck and bad luck. What would she say? Use the passive in the simple past and the words under the pictures.

1 My bike was stolen at school.

my bike – steal – at school

I – choose – for the soccer team

my computer files – delete

it – give back – the next day

the game – win – by the other team

my computer files – save – by Mom

▶Page 116

More practice 7 | **Multicultural roots**

a) **Tiana has multicultural roots. Sometimes she is happy about this and sometimes it can be hard for her. Do you or your friends have multicultural roots? What's it like for you? Talk with a partner.**

It's a gift because ...	It's hard because ...
I / my friends speak two languages.	sometimes I am bullied / I am called names.
I / my friends experience different traditions.	I am criticized for my clothes and my behaviour.
I / my friends learn from different cultures.	My parents have different opinions to my friends'
I think I'm more open to different people.	parents.

b) **Discuss your ideas with the class.**

More help | **6** SONG *Run with the Wolves* (by Raye Zaragoza)

b) **Find the song on the internet. Listen and read along with the words here, then check your answers from a).**

Feel the earth beneath my feet,
it pulls me down.
I heard the sounds
echo softly in the breeze.
In the clouds
I hear them now.

We used to be so free.
Get back to who we used to be!

Chorus:
Leave the ground, look to the mountains,
feel the air rush through your skin.
It's the way it always should've been.
We're running running running running with the wolves again.
We're running running running running with the wolves again.

There was a time when we were wild,
moving fast.
You couldn't hold us back.
Then they came and stole our fire,
put us in a cage.
We could never change.

We used to be so free.
Get back to who we used to be!

▶ Page 119

More practice 8 **Fire safety**

Complete the fire safety tips with a word from the box.

| although • because • so that (2x) • unless |

1   Go online before your trip and get permission to make a fire ... you need that in California.
2   ... you can find an area away from trees, don't make a fire.
3   Put a circle of rocks around your fire ... it doesn't get bigger.
4   ... the fire may be out, put water on it to make sure.
5   Add earth to the fire area ... it isn't hot.

More help **3** MY TASK **My travel blog post**

b) **Think of ideas for your post:**

Where did you sleep?	I slept in a cabin / a tent / a hostel / ... It was a day trip, so I slept at home.
What did you see and do?	I saw a beautiful beach / forest / lake / ... I saw lots of animals / a bear / a deer / ... I went climbing / hiking / kayaking / swimming / rafting / ... I climbed a mountain / took lots of photos / made a fire / ...
Was it a good or bad trip? Why?	It was an awesome / a fantastic / ... trip because ... It was a boring / dangerous / terrible / ... trip because ...

▶ Page 124

2 Talk about other charts

a) **Partner A:** Listen to partner B who is going to explain a chart to you.

b) **Partner A:** Now look at the chart on this page and explain it to Partner B:

1   **Introduce the chart.**
    This chart shows how many Native Americans live in different ...
    The source is ...
    The chart is from the year ...

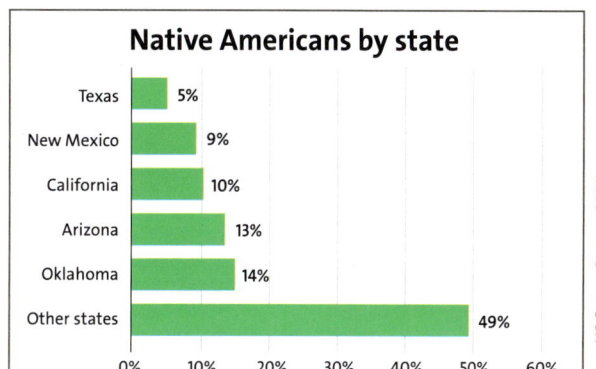

Native Americans by state

Texas	5%
New Mexico	9%
California	10%
Arizona	13%
Oklahoma	14%
Other states	49%

Source: US Census Bureau, 2020

2   **Explain the numbers.**
    Over half of all Native Americans live in these five states:
    ... per cent live in Texas, ...

▶ English numbers, p. 253   ▶ Wordbank 5, p. 184   ▶ Study skills, p. 124

Unit 5
Canada: The northern neighbour

Canada fact file

Size: It's the second largest country in the world (Russia is the largest).
Capital: Ottawa
Official languages: English, French
Population: 41 million
Native people: First Nations, Metis, Inuit
Name: 'Canada' comes from the word 'kanata' and means 'village' in the native language Laurentian.
Leader: the prime minister
Other facts: Canada is famous for being multicultural and welcoming to immigrants.

Statistics Canada (s. Quellenverzeichnis)

Montreal, a city where most people speak French

Niagara Falls, a famous waterfall in eastern Canada

1 A beautiful country

Copy the table. Look at the photos, read the Canada fact file and complete the table.

People	Languages	Sports	Nature & wildlife
native people: First Nations, ...	...	...	...

🔊 2 LISTENING A quick guide to Canada

a) Listen to the podcast. What fact makes you want to visit Canada?

I'd like to see / try / watch ...

b) Listen again. Add one more fact to each part of your table in 1. Then compare with a partner. Can you add more information?

Nach dieser Unit kann ich ...

- ⊘ über Kanada reden
- ⊘ Texte über Kanada verstehen

E
A moose

D
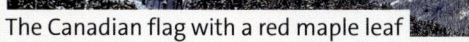
The Canadian flag with a red maple leaf

G
Orcas (whales)

F
Lacrosse

H
Vancouver, a city on the west coast of Canada

3 VIEWING **Vancouver**

a) BEFORE YOU WATCH **Find Vancouver on the map of Canada at the back of the book. Where is it?**

b) **Watch the video. What does Flora think of Vancouver?**

c) **Watch again. What can you do or eat in Vancouver?**

d) **What activities and foods can you remember? Tell a partner.**

You can go to the beach and you can watch whales. – Yes, and you can eat frozen yoghurt and ...

e) **What do you think of the city?**

Digital quiz **I can talk about Canada.** ⊘

► Workbook, p. 74

That's so Canadian, eh?

1 JIGSAW A travel guide

a) BEFORE YOU READ What makes a country different from other countries? Brainstorm ideas with the class.

I think that traditions make …

b) Make groups of four. Each student reads one of the texts (A–D). Take notes on anything in your text that makes Canada sound unique.

c) Find someone from another group who has read the same text and compare notes.

d) Go back to your group and share what you have learned. Listen to the other group members.

My text is called … I have learned that Canada / Canadians …

e) With your group, choose the top four things that you think make Canada unique.

A

Banff National Park

Proud to be Canadian

Canadians are very proud of their beautiful country. They enjoy spending time outside in nature, for example, swimming in lakes, skiing down mountains or camping under the stars. Canada is home to people from many different cultures. You can see this in festivals, foods, and traditions from around the world. Although Canada is part of North America, you should never call a Canadian person 'American'. Most Canadians don't like it because Canada is a different, independent country! If you make this mistake, you'll probably be corrected politely: Canadians are famous for being nice.

B

Two important national holidays

Every year on July 1st, people celebrate **Canada Day**, the day that the country was born: Canada became independent on July 1st, 1867. People watch parades and fireworks, wear red and white clothes, wave flags and have fun!

Orange Shirt Day, on September 30th, is a day to remember terrible parts of Canada's history. For over 150 years, native children were taken from their families and sent to boarding schools where they were treated terribly. Thousands of children died there. The last school finally closed in 1996. **Orange Shirt Day** was created to remember these children. People go to protests, learn more about this part of Canada's history, listen to survivors and wear orange T-shirts to show respect.

Canada Day in Ottawa, 2022

A survivor speaks on Orange Shirt Day, 2023

C Language

Many people in Canada speak more than one language. After the official languages French and English, some of the most common languages are Chinese, Punjabi, Spanish and Arabic. Cree and Ojibwe are two native languages that are spoken by many native people.

Canadian English can sound like American English, but there are certain words that you'll only hear in Canada. A 'Canuck' is a Canadian person, a 'Mountie' is a member of the Royal Canadian Mounted Police (the RCMP), a 'loonie' is the one-dollar coin (because it shows a loon, a kind of bird) and a 'toonie' is the two-dollar coin (because it joins 'two' and 'loonie').

You'll often hear Canadians say 'eh?' at the end of a sentence. This most often means: 'right?'.

Royal Canadian Mounted Police

A loon

D Hockey

Playing hockey in the winter

The Stanley Cup

Hockey is a big part of Canadian culture, but it's more than just a sport – it's a way of life for many Canadians. People of all ages play games on the street, on frozen ponds or inside at local ice rinks, which are open all year. Canadian children usually learn to skate before they're ten. Watching the game together is a tradition for many friends and families. Fans cheer on their favourite teams hoping that they'll win the Stanley Cup. Teams in the National Hockey League (NHL) dream that one day they'll lift this famous trophy over their heads after winning it.

▶ Workbook, p. 75

Digital quiz

I can understand texts about Canada.

Inhalt

Die mit diesem Symbol gekennzeichneten Abschnitte enthalten Hinweise und Tipps, die dir dabei helfen, elektronische Medien beim Englischlernen einzusetzen.

Dieses Symbol zeigt dir, dass du einen Erklärfilm zu diesem Thema in der App findest.

SF 1

Vokabeln lernen und strukturieren

▶ Unit 1 | pp. 22, 41   ▶ Unit 2 | pp. 51, 75
▶ Unit 3 | pp. 95, 104   ▶ Unit 4 | pp. 115, 135

Führe dein VOCAB FILE aus Klasse 7 weiter.

Neue Vokabeln lernst du am besten an einem ruhigen Ort. Je öfter du sie übst, desto besser kannst du sie dir merken.

Wie merke ich mir neue Wörter besser?

Einzelne Wörter merkst du dir leichter in sinnvollen Zusammenhängen. Hierfür gibt es mehrere Wege:

- Notiere zu einer neuen Vokabel einen Beispielsatz oder passenden Ausdruck (phrase): bottle → a bottle of water

- Erstelle Wortfelder zu einem Oberbegriff:
  nature → wild animals: bear, ... → pets: dog, ... → plants: tree, ... Nutze dafür Mindmaps oder Tabellen, die du immer weiter ergänzt.

- Erstelle Wortfamilien: friend, friendly, friendship, ...

- Sammle Gegensätze (antonyms: warm → cold) und Wörter mit der gleichen Bedeutung (synonyms: big → large).

- Stelle britische und amerikanische Wörter gegenüber.

- Nutze weitere Sprachen: biscuit (English) → bisküvi (Türkçe)

Checkliste Vokabeln lernen
- ✓ Lerne nur fünf bis zehn Vokabeln auf einmal.
- ✓ Lerne jeden Tag zehn Minuten.
- ✓ Lerne mit Freunden.
- ✓ Lerne in sinnvollen Zusammenhängen.
- ✓ Lerne unterwegs mit einer Vokabeltrainer-App oder mit Karteikarten.
- ✓ Schreibe schwierige Wörter mehrmals auf.
- ✓ Sprich die Wörter und nimm dich mit dem Handy auf.
- ✓ Wiederhole die Wörter, bis du sie kannst.

British and American English

food
chips (BE) ▶ French fries (AE)

clothes
trousers (BE) ▶ pants (AE)

Unbekannte Wörter erschließen

► Vocabulary | pp. 204, 214, 218

Du kannst englische Texte verstehen, auch wenn du nicht alle Wörter kennst. Diese Tipps helfen dir, die Bedeutung von Wörtern auch ohne Wörterbuch herauszufinden:

Wortfamilien und Wortbildungsregeln

Ein Wort gehört immer zu einer Wortfamilie. Wenn du ein Wort aus der Wortfamilie und ein paar Regeln zur Wortbildung kennst, kannst du die Bedeutung ableiten:

Checkliste Wörter erschließen

✓ Kennst du ähnliche Wörter in anderen Sprachen?
✓ Kennst du ähnliche Wörter aus derselben Wortfamilie?
✓ Gibt es Vor- oder Nachsilben, aus denen du die Bedeutung ableiten kannst?
✓ Können dir der Kontext, Bilder oder Bildunterschriften beim Verstehen helfen?

Vorsilben		
un-	Aus einem positiven Adjektiv wird ein negatives.	*happy → unhappy*
Nachsilben		
-er	Aus einem Tätigkeitsverb wird eine Person.	*(to) support → supporter*
-ful, -less, -y, -al	Aus einem Nomen wird ein Adjektiv.	*care → careful, help → helpless, risk → risky, magic → magical*
-ness	Aus einem Adjektiv wird ein Nomen.	*fit → fitness*
-tion, -ation, -ment	Aus einem Verb wird ein Nomen.	*(to) collect → collection (to) explain → explanation (to) argue → argument*

Erklär-film

Im Wörterbuch nachschlagen

Die Wörter im Dictionary (ab S. 226) sind alphabetisch aufgelistet. Neben oder unter dem Haupteintrag (z. B. **name**) findest du oft auch noch zusammengesetzte Wörter (z. B. **first name**) oder Redewendungen (z. B. **call sb. names**).

name [neɪm]:
1. (be)nennen 3
2. der Name 1
   call sb. names jn. beschimpfen 3 **family name** der Familienname, der Nachname 1 **first name** der Vorname 1 **What's your name?** Wie heißt du? 1

Die Ziffern 1, 2 usw. zeigen, dass ein Wort mehrere Bedeutungen hat (z. B. **free**: 1. frei, 2. kostenlos) oder als unterschiedliche Wortarten vorkommt (z. B. **act**: 1. die Tat, 2. handeln). Lies also immer den ganzen Eintrag und entscheide dann, welche Bedeutung die richtige ist.

In Online-Wörterbüchern stellst du nur die Suchrichtung (E−D oder D−E) ein und tippst dann das Wort ein. Auch hier werden dir oft mehrere Bedeutungen angeboten, aus denen du auswählen musst.

Durch einen Klick auf das Lautsprechersymbol kannst du dir ein Wort anhören.

SF 4

Im Internet recherchieren

▶ Unit 1 | pp. 32, 33   ▶ Unit 2 | p. 57   ▶ Unit 4 | p. 125

Suchen

Überlege dir Suchbegriffe, die zu deinem Thema passen. Je mehr Suchbegriffe du eingibst, desto passender sind deine Ergebnisse (z. B. *New York + activities + teens*).

Auswählen

Nicht alle Informationen, die du findest, sind richtig. Prüfe:

Von wem stammt die Seite? Wie verlässlich ist die Information? Ein Online-Lexikon ist vermutlich sachlicher als ein Chat-Forum. Achte auf die Endung der Internetadresse (http://www...). Sie kann dir wichtige Hinweise geben:

- **.com** bedeutet, es ist eine kommerzielle Webseite, die auch (versteckte) Werbung enthalten kann.

- **.gov** weist auf eine offizielle Webseite der US-Regierung hin.

- **.uk** bedeutet, es ist eine britische Seite.

Prüfe auch, ob die Informationen zu deinem Thema passen. Überfliege die Seite und achte auf Überschriften und Bilder.

Verlasse dich nicht auf nur eine einzige Internetseite, sondern ziehe zwei oder drei heran.

Vorsicht bei Wikipedia. Das Online-Lexikon wird von Freiwilligen geschrieben und kann Fehler enthalten.

▶ Skills file 11, p. 154

Sichern

- Mache dir Notizen oder drucke wichtige Seiten aus und markiere wichtige Textstellen. Schreibe die Texte nicht wörtlich ab – gib die Inhalte in deinen eigenen Worten wieder. Ordne deine Ergebnisse mit Überschriften oder sortiere sie in einer Mindmap.

- Wenn du Texte oder Bilder einer Webseite verwenden möchtest, nenne immer den Urheber oder die Urheberin und die Internetadresse. Kopiere sie direkt in dein digitales Dokument. Schreibe auch das Datum dazu, wann du die Webseite zuletzt aufgerufen hast.

- Wenn du Sätze oder Satzteile wörtlich übernehmen möchtest, kennzeichne sie als Zitat durch Anführungsstriche und nenne die Quelle.

'New York City is the best place in the world for teens.' (Quelle: *My New York* by Amy Wu, http://united.example.com (aufgerufen am 16.10.2024)

Kommunikationsstrategien anwenden

▶ Unit 3 | p. 92   ▶ Unit 4 | p. 113

Wie drücke ich aus, was ich denke?

In einem Gespräch oder einer Diskussion sagst du, was du über ein Thema denkst, und nennst Gründe oder Beispiele, die deine Aussagen unterstützen.

> *I believe / think that …*
> *In my opinion, …*
> *If you ask me, … because …*
> *For example, …*

Wie reagiere ich angemessen?

Frage die anderen auch nach ihrer Meinung und gehe höflich und respektvoll auf das ein, was sie sagen.

Frage nach, wenn du nicht sicher bist, ob du etwas richtig verstanden hast, oder wenn du noch mehr über das Thema erfahren möchtest. Nutze dafür die *wh*-Fragen.

Zeige durch deine Körpersprache Interesse am Thema: Sitze aufrecht, halte Blickkontakt und höre aufmerksam zu. Unterbrich andere nicht.

> *What do you think?*
> *That's interesting. / Go on.*
> *I agree. / That's a good point.*
> *I see it a bit differently.*
> *I'm not sure here.*

> *I'm not sure I got that.*
> *Do you mean …?*
> *When / Where / Why / …?*

▶ Let's talk 8, p. 189

Wie gebe ich Feedback?

Gegenseitige Rückmeldungen z. B. zu einem Vortrag, einem Text oder einer anderen Arbeit helfen dir und deinen Partnern oder Partnerinnen, Leistungen besser einzuschätzen und zu verbessern.

Feedback-Kriterien werden im Vorfeld in der Klasse besprochen, damit alle wissen, worauf sie bei der Erarbeitung achten müssen. Für eine gelungene Rückmeldung halte dich an folgende Tipps:

- Steige positiv ein und beschreibe, was gut war.

- Nenne Kritikpunkte: Was genau ist wie zu verbessern?

- Steige positiv aus: Worauf kann man aufbauen?

Lob
Kritik
Lob

Feedback-Burger

Wie reagiere ich auf Feedback?

Bleibe gelassen! Höre aufmerksam zu und prüfe in Gedanken, was du nachvollziehen und annehmen kannst. Frage nach, wenn du etwas nicht verstehst. Bleibe offen und lass das Gehörte auf dich wirken. Du brauchst dich nicht zu verteidigen oder zu rechtfertigen.

SF 6

Einen Vortrag vorbereiten und halten

▶ Unit 1 | pp. 32, 33   ▶ Unit 4 | p. 125

Um einen guten Vortrag vor der Klasse halten zu können, musst du ihn sorgfältig vorbereiten und üben.

Informationen suchen, auswählen, sichern

Nutze verschiedene Medien, um Informationen zu sammeln: das Internet, Bücher, Zeitschriften, Zeitungen. Prüfe deine Informationen und Quellen sorgfältig. Kopiere wichtige Seiten und Quellenangaben oder drucke sie aus.

▶ Skills file 4, p. 146

Checkliste Text markieren
Du kannst die wichtigen Stellen
✓ mit Textmarker markieren.
✓ unterstreichen oder umkreisen.
✓ mit Symbolen und Abkürzungen markieren. (? !, →, 😊, 🙁).
✓ durch Notizen am Rand hervorheben.

Textstellen markieren

Auf Kopien von Texten kannst du Informationen markieren, um sie hervorzuheben und einfacher wiederzufinden. Konzentriere dich dabei auf dein Thema und markiere nur die wichtigsten Informationen. Zusätzlich kannst du dir auch am Rand Notizen machen.

Informationen ordnen

Ordne deine Informationen, z. B. in einer Mindmap, unter Überschriften, in Tabellen oder auf Karteikarten. Überlege, was und wie viel du zu jedem Punkt sagen möchtest.

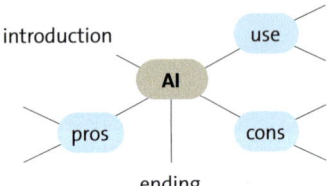

Strukturiere deinen Vortrag

Überlege dir, wie du deinen Vortrag strukturieren möchtest, und sammle nützliche Redewendungen für jeden Teil.

I'd like to talk about …
The question is: …

- **Einleitung:** Hier nennst du dein Thema. Überlege, wie du das Interesse deines Publikums wecken kannst, z. B. mit einer Frage, die zum Nachdenken anregt. Gib deinem Publikum zu Beginn deines Vortrags einen Überblick über das, was dein Vortrag beinhaltet.

To begin with, I'd like to tell you about …
Secondly, …
Finally, …

- **Hauptteil:** Nun nennst du nach und nach deine Hauptpunkte. Leite jeden neuen Punkt ein und sage mehr dazu.

- **Schluss:** Du fasst deine Hauptpunkte zusammen und bedankst dich fürs Zuhören. Erkundige dich, ob jemand Fragen hat.

To sum up, …
Thank you for listening.
Do you have any questions?

Die Inhalte veranschaulichen

 Gestalte nun dein Poster oder deine Folien gemäß deiner Struktur. Veranschauliche deine wichtigsten Punkte durch Bilder oder Diagramme. Beschreibe und erkläre sie. Nenne auch Beispiele, die deine Aussagen verdeutlichen.

Notizen erstellen

Bereite nun Karteikarten mit kurzen Notizen vor, um während deines Vortrags möglichst frei zu sprechen.

* Strukturiere deine Karteikarten genauso wie deine Präsentation.

* Schreibe keine ganzen Sätze, sondern das, was für dich wichtig ist, in Stichpunkten auf *(keywords)*.

* Hebe die wichtigsten Begriffe optisch hervor, z. B. durch Überschriften, Absätze und Farben. Du kannst auch kleine Erinnerungen zum Ablauf deines Vortrags notieren, z. B. wann du welches Medium einsetzt.

* Schreibe Ziffern anstelle von Zahlen, z. B. „15" statt „fifteen", und verwende gängige Abkürzungen.

* Nutze auch Symbole, z. B. Smileys für Gefühle, Flaggen für Länder, Strichzeichnungen für Personen.

Deinen Vortrag üben

Übe deinen Vortrag vor dem Spiegel oder nimm dich mit dem Smartphone auf. Oder ihr übt zu zweit und gebt euch gegenseitig Tipps, wie ihr euch verbessern könnt. Gib die Inhalte mit deinen eigenen Worten wieder. Verwende kurze, verständliche Sätze und vermeide schwierige oder unbekannte Begriffe. Erkläre diese, wenn es notwendig ist. Achte auf die Zeit.

Deinen Vortrag halten

Überprüfe zu Beginn, ob alles vorbereitet ist. Dann schaue dein Publikum an und warte, bis es ruhig ist. Sprich langsam, laut und deutlich.
Zeige während deines Vortrags auf deine Folien oder dein Poster. Lies den Text darauf nicht einfach ab.
Gib deinem Publikum Zeit zum Lesen oder erläutere deine Inhalte mit eigenen Worten oder Beispielen.

Checkliste Computerpräsentation
- ✓ Wähle ein einfaches Folienlayout.
- ✓ Verwende eine Schriftgröße von mindestens 16 Punkt.
- ✓ Beschränke dich auf wenig Text.
- ✓ Wähle nur ein Bild oder Diagramm pro Folie.
- ✓ Schreibe die Adresse der Internetseite dazu, von der du das Bild oder Diagramm hast.
- ✓ Gib alle Quellen, die du verwendet hast, am Ende der Präsentation an.

▶ Skills file 7, p. 150
▶ Skills file 8, p. 151

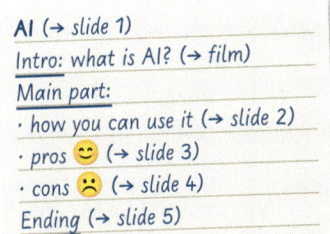

Es gibt auch Apps, mit denen du deine Notizen anfertigen kannst, wenn es deine Eltern erlauben.

Let me explain this word. It's somebody who … It's something that …

This chart shows … In this chart you can see …

A good example of this is …

SF 7

Bilder beschreiben

▶ Intro | pp. 10–11   ▶ Unit 1 | p. 16   ▶ Unit 2 | p. 46
▶ Unit 3 | pp. 76, 77   ▶ Unit 4 | pp. 108–109, 117

Wie gehe ich vor?

Erwähne zuerst, was du beschreibst, z. B. ein Foto oder einen Cartoon, und die dargestellte Situation.

> *I want to talk about this cartoon. I can see four people. They're on the beach.*

Was ist wo abgebildet?

Danach kümmerst du dich um die Details. Sage, wo sich was im Bild befindet. Wichtige Personen und Dinge befinden sich meist im Vordergrund:

in the background · at the top · on the left · in the middle · on the right · at the bottom · in the foreground

In the foreground I can see two people. The man *on the left* is a Native American. The man *on the right* is Christopher Columbus. *In the background* on the left, I can see two other Native Americans. On the right I can see a big boat on the sea.

Wer macht was? Was geschieht?

Beschreibe die Personen und ihre Handlungen genauer:

Columbus is wearing a black suit and a big black hat. He's holding a flag. *The Native Americans* are wearing traditional clothes. They're laughing at Columbus.

Was bedeutet es? Was denkst du?

Bei einem Cartoon findest du häufig auch eine Bildunterschrift *(caption)*, Sprech- oder Gedankenblasen *(speech bubble, thought bubble)*. Beschreibe auch diese und erkläre, was sie in diesem Zusammenhang bedeuten:

In the speech bubble the Native American is saying 'Oh yeah ... That's right. ... You discovered America!' He's saying that because ...

Am Ende deiner Beschreibung kannst du noch sagen, was du von der Abbildung hältst und warum:

I think this cartoon is / isn't funny because ...

Denke daran: Benutze immer das *present progressive*, wenn du beschreibst, was jemand in einem Bild macht. Andere Dinge im Bild kannst du mit *You can see ...* oder *There is / are ...* beschreiben.

Wenn du die Positionen von Dingen oder Menschen näher beschreiben willst, kannst du folgende Präpositionen nutzen: *behind · between · in front of · next to · over · under* *The flag is behind Columbus's head.*

Um zu zeigen, wo direkte Rede beginnt und endet, verwendest du Anführungszeichen. Sie stehen im Englischen auch am Satzanfang oben.

Diagramme beschreiben und erklären

► Unit 1 | p. 20
► Unit 4 | pp. 124, 128, 134, 139

Mit Diagrammen kannst du Informationen sehr gut veranschaulichen und vergleichen. Sie helfen dir, einen Überblick zu geben oder Entwicklungen aufzuzeigen, z.B. in einem Vortrag.

Ordne das Diagramm ein

Sieh dir zunächst die Überschrift und die Beschriftungen des Diagramms an. Sie geben dir Hinweise auf den Inhalt.
Sage, um was für eine Art Diagramm es sich handelt, was es aussagt (Thema), nenne die Quelle und das Jahr der Veröffentlichung:

This bar / column / line / pie chart shows ...
The source of the data / numbers / statistics is ...
The data / numbers / statistics are from the year ...

Beschreibe und erkläre das Diagramm

Schau dann auf die Einheiten der Angaben: Größen- oder Mengenangaben, Jahreszahlen oder Prozentsätze.
Beschreibe die Zahlen im Diagramm, vergleiche sie miteinander und erkläre, was du daran ablesen kannst:

In the years from ... to ..., ...
The x-axis / y-axis shows ...
This bar / column / line / section is for ...
The line shows an increase / decrease by ...
This number went up / down in the years from ... to ...
The number of ... has increased / decreased.
The number of ... fell / grew from ... in the year 2000 to ...
in 2024.
25 per cent / One quarter of ...
Nearly nine out of ten people ...
... is greater / less than ...
More / fewer ... of ...

Fasse die Aussagen zusammen

Fasse am Ende die wichtigsten Aussagen zusammen:
To sum up, we can see that ... / the chart shows that ...
The numbers show that ...
As you can see, ...

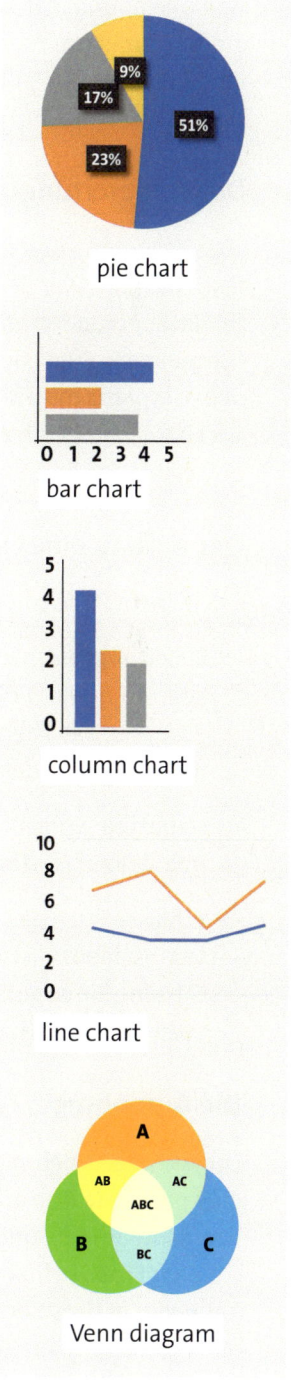

pie chart

bar chart

column chart

line chart

Venn diagram

► Wordbank 5, p. 184
► English numbers, p. 253

SF 9

Einen Podcast erstellen

Ein Podcast ist eine regelmäßig im Internet erscheinende Audio-Sendung, z. B. auf der Schulhomepage. Sie ist einem großen Publikum zugänglich, das sie nur anhört, wenn der Inhalt interessant, gut recherchiert und unterhaltsam ist. Zudem muss die Aufnahmequalität gut sein.

Die Vorbereitung

Lege das Thema und die Form (Interview, Gespräch, Vortrag, …) fest. Überlege, wer dein Publikum sein soll. Was könnte für die Zuhörenden interessant und unterhaltsam sein? Formuliere Fragen oder Themen, die du in einem Interview oder Gespräch mit einem Gast besprechen möchtest. Suche für einen Vortrag zu deinem Thema Informationen und wähle das Interessanteste aus.

Der Aufbau eines Podcasts

Gib deinem Podcast eine Struktur:

- **Einleitung:** Nach einem kurzen **Intro** (passende Musik) begrüßt du das Publikum, nennst den Titel deines Podcasts, das Thema der Sendung und deinen Namen. (Begrüße auch deine Gäste.)

- **Hauptteil:** Sprich über das Thema der aktuellen Sendung (mit deinen Gästen).

- **Schluss:** Fasse das Gesagte kurz zusammen. Verabschiede dich (und danke deinen Gästen). Gib eine kurze Vorschau auf die nächste Sendung. Spiel ein **Outro** (passende Musik) ab.

Die Aufnahme

Um dich aufzunehmen, reicht in der Regel dein Handy und eine passende App aus. Suche dir einen ruhigen Raum. Teste den richtigen Abstand zum Mikrofon oder Headset. Mache ein paar Probeaufnahmen. Wenn du Gäste hast, könnt ihr entweder in dasselbe Handy sprechen oder euch getrennt aufnehmen und die Teile später zusammenschneiden. Wenn du beim Sprechen Fehler machst, lege einfach eine kurze Pause ein und wiederhole dann deinen Satz. Schneide anschließend die fehlerhafte Stelle heraus.

Sind mehrere Personen an der Erstellung eines Podcasts beteiligt, so müssen alle einer Veröffentlichung im Internet zustimmen. Dies ist im Urheberrecht geregelt.

▶ Skills file 4, p. 146

Je nachdem, wie sicher du dich fühlst, kannst du ein Skript erstellen oder frei sprechen.

Musikaufnahmen sind urheberrechtlich geschützt. Suche im Internet nach kostenlosen und lizenzfreien Musikstücken bzw. Sounds oder komponiere sie selbst.

Hello and welcome to my podcast, Walid's World. *Today …*

*Well, that's all for now!
Thanks for …
I hope …
See you next week …*

Hörtexte und Filme verstehen

▶ Unit 1 | pp. 16, 17, 31   ▶ Unit 2 | pp. 46, 48, 61
▶ Unit 3 | pp. 77, 78, 91   ▶ Unit 4 | pp. 109, 110, 123

Vor dem Hören / Sehen

Lies dir die Aufgabenstellung genau durch und überlege, was du tun sollst. Finde die Schlüsselwörter in der Aufgabenstellung. Diese zeigen dir, worauf du beim Hören oder Sehen achten musst. Geht es um das allgemeine Thema *(gist)* oder um spezifische Dinge *(details)*?

Stelle dir die Situation bzw. das Thema vor – was erwartest du, dazu zu hören oder zu sehen? Welche Leute sind beteiligt und worum geht es? Was weißt du schon über das Thema und welche Wörter wären wohl typisch?

Beim Hören / Sehen

Versuche, zunächst grob zu verstehen, worum es geht. Konzentriere dich auf die Schlüsselwörter aus der Aufgabenstellung. Oft werden in den Aufgaben Synonyme der Wörter aus dem Hörtext oder Film verwendet.

Achte bei einem Hörtext auch auf die Hintergrundgeräusche. Wenn du ein wichtiges Wort nicht verstehst, dann denke an die Situation, um die es geht.

Bei einem Film helfen dir Bilder, Gesichtsausdrücke und Körpersprache, den gesprochenen Text zu verstehen. Achte daher beim ersten Sehen besonders darauf, wo und wann der Film spielt, welche Personen darin vorkommen und wie sie handeln. Konzentriere dich beim zweiten Sehen mehr auf den gesprochenen Text oder auf Details.

Mache dir Notizen und bleibe ruhig, wenn du beim ersten Mal nicht alles verstehst. Hörtexte oder Filme werden im Unterricht meist zweimal präsentiert. Vervollständige deine Notizen beim zweiten Hören bzw. Sehen.

Nach dem Hören / Sehen

Lies noch einmal genau durch, was du geschrieben hast. Passen deine Antworten zu den Fragen? Ergänze fehlende Antworten aus dem Gedächtnis.

Nutze verschiedene Möglichkeiten, um englische Texte zu hören. Wähle etwas aus, das dir gefällt, z. B. dein Lieblingslied oder dein Lieblingsbuch als Hörbuch auf Englisch.

Schaue Filme und Serien auf Englisch. Blende englische Untertitel ein, falls du Probleme beim Verstehen hast. Blende sie aus, wenn du dich sicherer fühlst oder eine Episode schon mehrfach gesehen hast.

Wo?   Wann?

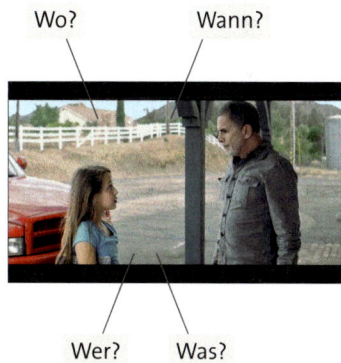

Wer?   Was?

Checkliste Notizen machen
✓ Notiere nur wichtige Wörter (Schlüsselwörter).
✓ Schreibe Ziffern statt Zahlwörter, z. B. „7" statt „seven".
✓ Verwende Symbole und Abkürzungen, z. B. „X" für falsch, „✓" für richtig und „...." für Lücken beim Hörverstehen.

SF 11

Lesetexte verstehen

▶ Intro | p. 14   ▶ Unit 1 | pp. 28–30   ▶ Unit 2 | pp. 58–60
▶ Unit 3 | pp. 88–90   ▶ Unit 4 | pp. 120–122

In diesem Buch findest du viele verschiedene Texte,
z. B. Artikel, Dialoge, Geschichten. Die folgenden Tipps helfen
dir beim Verstehen der Texte und Lösen der Aufgaben.

Vor dem Lesen

Schaue dir die Aufgaben zum Text an und achte auf
Schlüsselwörter. Überlege dir, was du tun sollst und welche
Lesestrategie *(skimming, scanning* oder *reading for detail)*
gefordert ist.

Skimming (reading for gist) hilft dir, schnell einen Überblick
über den Inhalt eines Textes zu bekommen. Dafür siehst du
dir diese Dinge an:

- die Überschrift und Zwischenüberschriften sowie Bilder
  und Bildunterschriften,

- hervorgehobene Wörter (z. B. durch **Fettdruck**),

- den ersten Satz jedes Absatzes, der oft die Hauptidee des
  Absatzes enthält,

- den letzten Absatz des Textes, der oft eine Zusammenfassung des Textes enthält.

Scanning (reading for specific information) hilft dir, schnell
nach bestimmten Informationen zu suchen:

- Überlege dir Stichwörter. Suchst du z. B. Öffnungszeiten,
  könnten das Wörter sein wie *open, hours* oder *days.*

- Überfliege den Text und suche nach den Stichwörtern.

- Du kannst dabei mit dem Finger in einer „S-Form" über
  den Text gehen.

- Lies die Textstelle, die dein Stichwort enthält, um zu
  sehen, ob du dort die gesuchten Informationen findest.
  Wenn nicht, scanne weiter.

Reading for detail hilft dir, jedes Detail eines Textes im
Zusammenhang zu verstehen, z. B. bei Gedichten, Rezepten,
Gebrauchsanweisungen oder Sachtexten mit Diagrammen
und Tabellen. Lies jedes Wort und jede Zahl sehr genau.
Benutze ein Wörterbuch für unbekannte Wörter, wenn du
dir nicht ganz sicher bist.

Je mehr englische Texte du
liest, desto größer wird
dein Wortschatz und desto
schneller und besser
verstehst du Texte.

Du musst nicht jedes Wort in
einem Text verstehen, um
den Inhalt zu verstehen. Um
einen schnellen Überblick
über den Inhalt zu bekommen,
überfliegst du den Text.

Wenn du mit Texten im
Internet arbeitest, kann
dein Browser dir viel Arbeit
abnehmen: Mit Strg+F
(Cmd+F am Mac) kannst du
nach deinen Stichworten
suchen und nur die Textstellen
lesen, in denen ein Stichwort
markiert ist.

Einen Artikel verfassen

▶ Unit 1 | p. 19 ▶ Unit 2 | p. 57 ▶ Unit 3 | p. 95 ▶ Unit 4 | p. 119

Mit einem (Zeitungs-)Artikel informierst du deine Leserschaft über ein interessantes Thema oder ein Ereignis, z. B. *Diversity in NYC* oder *My hometown – a good place for teens?* Der Stil sollte sachlich, knapp und verständlich sein.

Sammle Informationen

Nutze verschiedene Medien, z. B. das Internet, Zeitschriften und Bücher, und bemühe dich um Objektivität. Du kannst auch Interviews oder Umfragen durchführen. Überlege dir Beispiele und suche Bilder, Fotos, Zahlen und Statistiken, die den Inhalt ergänzen und unterstützen.

Strukturiere deine Informationen

*   **Einleitung:** Stelle anhand der wichtigsten *wh*-Fragen kurz dein Thema vor. Mit einer neugierig machenden Frage oder interessanten Aussage kannst du Interesse für dein Thema wecken: *What do teenagers think about ...?, Can you imagine that ...?, Lots of people think ...*

*   **Hauptteil:** Hier gehst du auf die Einzelheiten ein und präsentierst Fakten und Hintergründe zu deinem Thema oder nennst Argumente für und gegen eine Position. Ergänze deinen Text um Beispiele, Statistiken und Zitate.
    There are two sides to this question.
    One good thing about ...
    Felix S. (14) says: '...'
    On the other hand, ...

*   **Schluss:** Fasse das Wichtigste zusammen und gib einen Ausblick. Wäge das Für und Wider zu einer Fragestellung ab, ohne neue Aspekte oder Argumente zu nennen:
    To sum up, ... / All in all, ...
    In the future, he / she will ...
    The most important thing to remember is ...

Überlege dir auch eine Überschrift für deinen Artikel – sie sollte kurz sein und Interesse wecken. Bei längeren Artikeln kannst du auch Absätze mit Zwischenüberschriften versehen.

Zum Schluss überprüfst du deinen Text inhaltlich und sprachlich.

Beim Verfassen von **Blog-Beiträgen** kannst du ähnlich vorgehen wie bei Artikeln. Sie können aber weniger sachlich und förmlich sein.

▶ Skills file 4, p. 146

Bei Interviews und Umfragen ist es wichtig, dass du von deinen Interviewpartnern das ausdrückliche Einverständnis zur Veröffentlichung einholst. Am besten lässt du dir das schriftlich geben.

Achte darauf, dass du die Äußerungen korrekt und nicht sinnverändert wiedergibst! Nutze wörtliche Zitate.

Fotos wecken Interesse und lockern deinen Artikel auf und die Bildunterschrift kann neugierig machen. Aber nicht alles, was du fotografierst, darfst du auch veröffentlichen. Es gibt Persönlichkeitsrechte bei Fotos von Personen, Eigentumsrechte bei Aufnahmen auf Privatgelände und Urheberrechte bei Aufnahmen von Kunstwerken oder Designobjekten.
Kläre immer die Rechte, bevor du deine Fotos veröffentlichst.

How to explore NYC in one day

The Knicks – what's their secret to winning?

Killer Katrina

▶ Skills file 15, p. 158

E-Mails und Briefe schreiben

▶ Unit 2 | pp. 64, 66   ▶ Unit 3 | pp. 81, 87

Adresse und Datum

Hier steht die E-Mail-Adresse des Empfängers.
Hier kannst du weitere Empfänger eintragen.
Hier schreibst du ganz knapp, worum es geht.
Hier schreibst du deinen Text.

In englischen Briefen schreibst du deine Adresse
rechts oben. Darunter schreibst du das Datum.

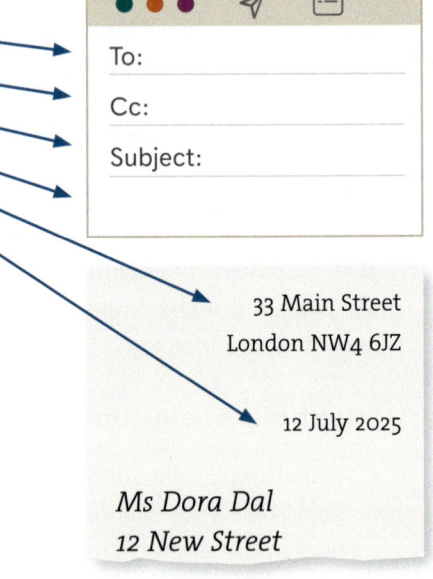

To:

Cc:

Subject:

33 Main Street
London NW4 6JZ

12 July 2025

Ms Dora Dal
12 New Street

Aufbau einer E-Mail oder eines Briefs

- **Einleitung:** Beginne mit einer Anrede:
  Bei Freunden reicht ein informelles *Hi, / Hello, Jim.*
  Ansonsten schreibst du: *Dear Jane / Mr Jones / ...*
  Wenn du den Namen nicht kennst, schreibst du:
  Dear Sir or Madam
  Sage im ersten Satz, warum du schreibst:
  I'm writing this e-mail / letter to ... oder *This is to ...*
  In einem persönlichen Schreiben frage nach, wie es der
  Person geht: *How are you?*
  Du kannst dich auch für die letzte Nachricht bedanken
  oder dich entschuldigen, falls du länger nicht geschrieben
  hast: *Thank you for your e-mail / letter. Sorry that I
  haven't written for so long.*

- **Hauptteil:** Hier schreibst du dem Empfänger Wichtiges,
  nimmst Stellung oder beantwortest Fragen. Für jedes
  Thema startest du einen neuen Absatz.

- **Schluss:** Beende deine E-Mail oder deinen Brief mit einem
  Schlusssatz oder einer Frage sowie einem freundlichen
  Gruß und deinem Namen.
  Bei Freunden kannst du informell sein: *Best wishes, Paul*
  oder *Love / Lots of love / All the best, Mia*
  Schreibst du an eine Organisation oder Firma, beendest
  du die E-Mail oder den Brief mit *Best regards, Lina Lee*
  oder förmlicher mit *Yours sincerely (BE) / Sincerely (AE).*
  Zwischen Schlussformel und Name ist ein Komma
  möglich, aber nicht nötig. Das gilt auch für die Anrede.

Zum Schluss überprüfst du deinen Text inhaltlich und
sprachlich.

 Das erste Wort nach der
Anrede wird im Englischen
großgeschrieben.

Subject: Thank you!

*Dear Oscar
This is to say thank you
for an amazing prom
night!
Thank you for asking me
to go with you and for ...*

That's all for now.
I hope to hear from
you soon.
Lots of love
Elif

▶ Skills file 15, p. 158

Eine Zusammenfassung schreiben

▶ Unit 2 | pp. 62–63, 67

Wenn du einen Text zusammenfasst, gibst du die wichtigsten Informationen und Ereignisse in kürzerer Form wieder. Eine Zusammenfassung nennt man im Englischen *summary*.

Lies den Text genau

Beginne mit dem *Skimming* des Textes, um dir einen Überblick über den Inhalt zu verschaffen: Überschriften, Bilder und Bildunterschriften sowie der erste Satz jedes Absatzes können dir dabei helfen.

▶ Skills file 11, p. 154

Lies den Text danach erneut durch, Satz für Satz *(Reading for detail)*. Mache dir Notizen zu den *wh*-Fragen oder markiere diese Informationen auf einer Kopie des Textes *(Who? When? Where? What? Why? How?)*.

Who *is the text about?*
When *does it happen?*
Where *does it happen?*
What *happens?*
Why/How *does it happen?*

Strukturiere deine Zusammenfassung

In der **Einleitung** beschreibst du kurz, worum es geht:
The story / article / … by … is about …   It takes place in …
The main characters are …

Checkliste *Summary*
- ✓ Nenne das Thema und die wesentlichen Inhalte (*wh*-Fragen).
- ✓ Fasse dich kurz!
- ✓ Schreibe im *simple present*.
- ✓ Verwende deine eigenen Worte, schreibe den Text nicht ab.
- ✓ Verwende keine direkte Rede.
- ✓ Verzichte auf Details, Beispiele oder deine eigene Meinung.

Im **Hauptteil** gibst du die wichtigsten Ereignisse (z. B. einer Geschichte) oder die Hauptpunkte (z. B. eines Zeitungsartikels) in deinen eigenen Worten wieder. Fasse dich kurz und schreibe im *simple present*, auch wenn der Originaltext andere Zeitformen verwendet. Verwende *linking words (and, but, because, …)*. Verzichte auf Ausschmückungen.

Überprüfe deinen Text am Ende inhaltlich und sprachlich.

▶ Skills file 15, p. 158

Eine Rezension schreiben

Möchtest du ein Buch, einen Film oder eine Serie empfehlen oder kritisch bewerten, schreibst du eine Rezension. Dafür fasst du zunächst den Inhalt zusammen (s.o.) und schreibst danach einen Absatz mit deiner Meinung. Sage, ob du das Buch, den Film oder die Serie empfehlen kannst oder nicht und warum:
This is a really cool / exciting / funny / … book / film / series.
If you're a … fan like me, you'll love it!
I can recommend reading / watching …
It's a must-read! / must-see!

Deine Meinung über ein Buch, einen Film oder eine Serie darf enthusiastisch sein. Wenn du magst, kannst du „Sterne" vergeben oder Emojis verwenden, um deine Meinung zu verdeutlichen.

SF 15

Texte überprüfen und verbessern

▶ Unit 1 | p. 33   ▶ Unit 2 | pp. 57, 63
▶ Unit 4 | pp. 111, 125

Ein Text ist noch nicht fertig, wenn du ihn zu Ende geschrieben hast. Du solltest ihn mehrmals durchlesen und auch in Partnerkorrektur durchlesen lassen.

Überprüfe und korrigiere deinen Text

Beim Korrekturlesen empfehlen sich mehrere Durchgänge, in denen du nacheinander auf folgende Dinge achtest:

Inhalt:

- Vollständigkeit: Hast du alle Aspekte der Aufgabenstellung beachtet? Sind alle Sätze vollständig?
- Gestaltung: Enthält dein Text alle typischen Merkmale, die du beim Verfassen eines Zeitungsartikels, einer E-Mail oder einer Zusammenfassung beachten musst? Benötigst du z. B. eine Überschrift oder hast du an eine Anrede- oder Schlussformel gedacht?
- Aufbau: Hat dein Text eine logische Struktur mit Einleitung, Hauptteil und Schluss? Hast du Absätze gemacht?
- Lesbarkeit: Ist dein Text verständlich und liest sich flüssig?

▶ Skills file 12, p. 155
▶ Skills file 13, p. 156
▶ Skills file 14, p. 157

Checkliste typische Fehlerquellen
- ✓ Groß- und Kleinschreibung
- ✓ unregelmäßige Pluralformen *(child – children, man – men)*
- ✓ gleicher Klang, aber unterschiedliche Schreibweisen und Bedeutungen *(to – too – two, their – there – they're)*
- ✓ Präpositionen *(by train, in the picture, on the bus)*
- ✓ unregelmäßige Verben
- ✓ Wörter mit stummen Buchstaben *(climb, know, walk)*

Sprache:

- Verwendest du eine abwechslungsreiche und lebendige Sprache und vermeidest Wiederholungen? Beschreibst du Personen, Orte oder Dinge mithilfe von Adjektiven?
- Hast du *linking words* (Bindewörter) benutzt?
- Stimmen Rechtschreibung, Zeichensetzung, Grammatik? Prüfe deinen Text anhand der Checkliste.
- Hast du die richtige Zeitform gewählt? Eine *summary* wird z. B. im *simple present* geschrieben. Bei anderen Textsorten, wie z. B. bei einer E-Mail oder einem Zeitungsartikel, musst du in jedem Satz überlegen, welches die passende Zeitform ist.

▶ Irregular verbs, p. 254 f.
▶ Wichtige Schreibregeln im Englischen, p. 178

Partnerkorrektur

Lasse deinen Text auch von anderen Korrektur lesen und hilf anderen, ihren Text zu überprüfen und zu verbessern. Gehe dabei wie oben beschrieben in mehreren Durchgängen vor – erst achtest du auf den Inhalt, dann auf die Sprache. Sprich danach mit deinem Partner oder deiner Partnerin über deine Korrekturvorschläge und gib konstruktives Feedback.

Markiere in fremden Texten mit einem Bleistift:
- was dir gefällt: + +
- was unverständlich ist: ?
- was verbessert werden muss:
  He lost his Handy.
- was ergänzt werden könnte.

▶ Skills file 5, p. 147
▶ Feedback phrases, p. 191

Mediation

▶ Unit 1 | p. 26   ▶ Unit 2 | p. 54   ▶ Unit 3 | p. 84   ▶ Unit 4 | p. 117

In manchen Situationen musst du zwischen zwei Sprachen vermitteln, um Personen zu helfen, die wenig oder kein Englisch oder Deutsch können. Dies nennt man Mediation. Du überträgst die wichtigsten Informationen von der einen Sprache in die andere, entweder mündlich oder schriftlich.

 Normalerweise gibst du bei einer Mediation nur das Wesentliche wieder. Nur bei Gebrauchsanweisungen ist es wichtig, genau zu sein.

Worauf muss ich achten?

Keine Panik vor unbekannten Wörtern
Wenn du für jemandem z. B. bei einer Wegbeschreibung vermitteln oder einen englischen Artikel auf Deutsch erläutern möchtest, musst du nicht alle Details übersetzen. Deshalb ist es auch in Ordnung, wenn du nicht jedes Wort verstehst. Es reicht aus, dass du die zentralen Aussagen verstehst.

Gib nur die wichtigsten Informationen weiter
Lasse unwichtige Wörter und Satzteile weg und bilde kurze und einfache Sätze. Ihr besucht britische Freunde und die Tochter spricht über ihren Hund: *I love **my** dog Teddy. He's the best. Teddy is **my** best friend. He's really great.* Du erklärst deinem kleinen Bruder: „Emma liebt ihren Hund Teddy, er ist ihr bester Freund."

Achte in Gesprächen auf den Perspektivwechsel
Überlege immer, an wen du dich gerade wendest, und passe die Pronomen entsprechend an. Im Beispiel oben wird aus „I" → „Emma" (oder „sie") und aus „my" → „ihren/ihr".

Oft benutzt man auch einen Einleitungssatz:
„Sie sagt, dass sie ihren Hund liebt."

Sage es anders
Wenn du ein Wort nicht kennst, versuche es mit anderen Wörtern zu umschreiben. Wenn dir zum Beispiel das englische Wort für „Onkel" nicht einfällt, kannst du auch sagen *my mum's / dad's brother.*

Achte auf kulturelle Unterschiede
Überlege, was für dein Gegenüber wichtig ist, um die Situation und die Inhalte verstehen zu können. Erkläre kulturelle Besonderheiten.

 Checkliste Mediation
- ✓ Gib nur die wichtigen Infos weiter.
- ✓ Umschreibe unbekannte Wörter.
- ✓ Verwende kurze, einfache Sätze.
- ✓ Achte auf Pronomen: An wen wendest du dich?
- ✓ Bedenke und erkläre kulturelle Unterschiede.

*Frage Sam doch mal, wie **ihm sein** Tag gefallen hat.*

*Did **you** enjoy **your** day?*

He / She says / thinks that …
He / She would like to know …
He / She asks if …
Here it says (that) we should …

Restroom?

Oh, right. That's the American word for public toilets.

Inhalt

Erklär-film ▶ Dieses Symbol zeigt dir, dass du einen Erklärfilm zu diesem Thema in der App findest.

LF 1 **Revision**

Die Wortstellung *(Word order)*

a) Aussagesätze *(Statements)*

subject	verb	
Jonquel	plays	basketball.
The Diaz	have moved	to NYC.
You	shouldn't ask	Hana.

Last year **the Diaz moved** to NYC.
Letztes Jahr sind die Diaz nach NYC gezogen.

If you need help, **you should ask** Lu.
Wenn du Hilfe brauchst, solltest du Lu fragen.

Jonqel **often plays** basketball.
Jonqel spielt oft Basketball.

Englische Aussagesätze haben folgende Wortstellung:
subject (Subjekt) – *verb* (Prädikat) – Ergänzung.
Auch wenn der Satz mit einer adverbialen Bestimmung beginnt (z. B. *Last year*; *If you need help*), bleibt die Wortstellung *subject – verb – ...* unverändert.
Häufigkeitsadverbien (z. B. *often*) stehen im Englischen meist direkt vor dem Hauptverb (z. B. *play*). Sie können nicht zwischen Verb und Objekt stehen.

b) Nebensätze *(Subordinate clauses)*

If **they ask** me, I'll help them.
Wenn sie mich bitten, helfe ich ihnen.

Maria says that **Jonquel is** her hero.
Maria sagt, dass Jonquel ihre Heldin ist.

Auch für Nebensätze gilt die Wortstellung *subject – verb*.

Erklär-
film

Die einfache Gegenwart *(The simple present)*

I always **get up** at 7 o'clock.
Ich stehe immer um 7 Uhr auf.

We all **love** Indian food.
Wir alle lieben indisches Essen.

Where **do** you **live**?
Wo wohnen Sie?

Mit dem *simple present* sagst du, was oft, regelmäßig, jeden Tag oder auch selten oder nie geschieht oder was immer so ist (Dauer-zustände). Oft findest du diese <u>Signalwörter</u> in Sätzen im *simple present*: always, never, often, sometimes, usually, every day.	

a) Bejahte Aussagesätze *(Positive statements)*

I / You / We / They	start.
He / She / It / Jo / School	starts.

hurry → **hurries**
miss → **misses**
wash → **washes**
catch → **catches**

💡 **He, she, it –** ein -**s** muss mit!

Das *simple present* hat dieselbe Form wie der Infinitiv, also die Grundform des Verbs.

❗ Bei der 3. Person Singular musst du aber immer ein -**s** an das Verb hängen. Beachte:
- Konsonant (z. B. -*r*) + *y* wird zu -***ies***.
- An -*s*, -*sh*, -*ch*, -*x* hängst du -***es***.
- Sonderformen: ***does, goes, has***

b) Verneinte Aussagesätze *(Negative statements)*

I / You / We / The	don't start.
He / She / It	doesn't start.

Aussagen im *simple present* verneinst du mit ***don't*** oder ***doesn't*** (für die 3. Person Singular). Das Verb nach ***don't / doesn't*** steht immer im Infinitiv: *She doesn't **start**.*

c) Fragen und Antworten *(Questions and answers)*

Do I / you / we / they **start**?
Does he / she / it **start**?
When **does** he / she / it **start**? – At ten.

Do they **start**? – Yes, they **do**.
Do you **like** musicals? – No, I **don't**.
Does he **do** a lot of sport? – No, he **doesn't**.

Who **loves** Amy? – Tim.
Wer liebt Amy? – Tim.

What **makes** you happy? – Chocolate.
Was macht dich glücklich? – Schokolade.

Fragen im *simple present* musst du mit ***do*** oder ***does*** bilden. Das Verb steht auch hier im Infinitiv: *Does he **start**?*

Auf Ja-/Nein-Fragen antwortet man nicht einfach *yes* oder *no*, sondern verwendet eine Kurzantwort mit *do* oder *does* (+ *not*): *Yes, they do. / No, he doesn't.*

❗ Wenn du mit *Who* oder *What* nach dem Subjekt des Satzes fragst, bildest du die Frage <u>ohne</u> *do / does*.

Erklär-
film

Die Verlaufsform der Gegenwart *(The present progressive)*

Dad **is making** dim sum.
What **are** you **doing** at the moment?
– **I'm working**.
Was machst du jetzt gerade?
– Ich bin gerade am Arbeiten. / Ich arbeite gerade.

Mit dem *present progressive* sagst du, was jemand jetzt gerade tut. Damit beschreibst du auch, was auf Bildern passiert. Folgende Zeitangaben findest du oft in Sätzen im *present progressive*: *at the moment, now, today*.

a) Bejahte Aussagesätze *(Positive statements)*

I'm You're He's / She's / It's We're They're	**working**.

Das *present progressive* besteht aus zwei Teilen: Form von *be* + *ing*-Form des Verbs.

am ('m) / *are* ('re) / *is* ('s)	+ *ing*-Form

❗ Beachte: *take → taking; putting, running*

b) Verneinte Aussagesätze *(Negative statements)*

I'm not You **aren't** He / She / It **isn't** We / They **aren't**	**playing**.

In verneinten Sätzen stehen *am / are / is* mit *not*:

am not / are not / is not	+ *ing*-Form

c) Fragen und Antworten *(Questions and answers)*

Am I **working**? – No, you **aren't**.
Are you **working**? – Yes, I **am**.
Where **is** he **going**? – Home.

In Fragen vertauscht man das Subjekt und *am / are / is*: *I am → **am I**?, you are → **are you**?, he is → **is he**?*

Erklär-
film

Simple present oder *present progressive?*

simple present	present progressive
Tiana **often makes** jewelry.	Look. Tiana **is** just **making** a ring.
💡 Signalwörter: ***always, often, never, every day, sometimes***	💡 Signalwörter: ***at the moment, just, (right) now, today***

- Mit ***makes** (simple present)* drückst du aus, dass Tiana regelmäßig Schmuck herstellt.
- Mit ***is making** (present progressive)* sagst du, dass Tiana jetzt gerade Schmuck herstellt.

❗ Verben, die einen Zustand bezeichnen (z. B. *have, hate, know, like, love, prefer, want, remember*) stehen nicht in der Verlaufsform.

Die einfache Vergangenheit *(The simple past)*

► Unit 1 | p. 22

Last week I **didn't have** any homework.
Letzte Woche hatte ich keine Hausaufgaben auf.

Did you **watch** the Yankees yesterday?
Hast du gestern die Yankees gesehen?

Mit dem *simple past* sprichst du über Dinge, die in der Vergangenheit geschehen sind. Du verwendest es oft mit Zeitangaben wie *yesterday, last week / last year / last summer, two weeks ago, in 2023.*

a) Bejahte Aussagesätze *(Positive statements)*

I / You	
He / She / It	**helped**.
We / They	**went**.

*Last year the rats **started** their own jazz band.*

Die Vergangenheitsform der Verben ist für alle Personen gleich:
- Bei regelmäßigen Verben hängst du **-ed** an das Verb: *walk → walk**ed**.*
- Bei Verben, die auf *-e* enden, wird nur **-d** angehängt: *arrive → arrive**d**.*
- Einige Konsonanten werden verdoppelt: *plan → plan**ned**; stop → stop**ped**.*

❗ Unregelmäßige Formen musst du lernen: *go → **went**; have → **had**; see → **saw**.* Du kannst sie auf S. 254–256 nachschlagen.

b) Verneinte Aussagesätze *(Negative statements)*

I / You	
He / She / It	**didn't help**.
We / They	**didn't go**.

Wenn du sagen willst, dass etwas nicht geschah, setzt du ***didn't*** vor das Verb. Das Verb steht dann immer im Infinitiv (der Grundform).

c) Fragen und Antworten *(Questions and answers)*

Did they **help**?
Did she **go**?
Why **did** he **help**? – Because he cared.

Did you **help**? – Yes, I **did**.
Did she **do** a lot of sport? – No, she **didn't**.

Who **helped** you? – My sister.
Wer hat dir geholfen? – Meine Schwester.

What **happened**? – I had an accident.
Was ist passiert? – Ich hatte einen Unfall.

Fragen im *simple past* bildest du mit ***did***. Das Verb steht auch hier im Infinitiv: *Did they help?, Did he go?*

Auch in Kurzantworten auf Ja-/Nein-Fragen verwendest du ***did*** (+ *not*): *Yes, I did. / No, she didn't.*

❗ Wenn du mit *Who* oder *What* nach dem Subjekt des Satzes fragst, bildest du die Frage ohne *did*.

Erklär-
film

LF 6 Revision

Das *present perfect* (*The present perfect*)

I **have** never **eaten** dim sum.
Ich habe noch nie Dim Sum gegessen.

Has Leo ever **been** to Rome?
Ist Leo schon mal in Rom gewesen? /
War Leo schon mal in Rom?

The train **hasn't arrived** yet.
Der Zug ist noch nicht angekommen.

> Mit dem *present perfect* sagst du, dass jemand etwas – irgendwann – in der Zeit bis jetzt gemacht oder nicht gemacht hat. Der genaue Zeitpunkt ist unwichtig oder unbekannt und wird nicht genannt. Oft hat die Handlung Folgen in der Gegenwart. Signalwörter: *already, just, ever, never, (not) yet, once, twice, lots of times*

a) Bejahte Aussagesätze (*Positive statements*)

I / You / We / They	have finished.
He / She / It	has finished.

Kurzformen:

I've / You've / We've / They've He's / She's / It's	finished.

> Das *present perfect* besteht aus **have / has** und der dritten Form des Verbs (*past participle*).
> - Das *past participle* regelmäßiger Verben bildest du aus Verb + **ed**: *walk → walk**ed***.
> - Bei Verben, die auf *-e* enden, wird nur *-d* angehängt: *arrive → arrive**d***.
> - Einige Konsonanten werden verdoppelt: *plan → pla**nn**ed; stop → sto**pp**ed*.
>
> **!** Unregelmäßige *past participle*-Formen musst du lernen: *go → **gone**; have → **had***. Du kannst sie auf S. 254–256 nachschlagen.

Have you *seen*? *They've started* a new sports club.

b) Verneinte Aussagesätze (*Negative statements*)

I / You / We / They	haven't finished.
He / She / It	hasn't finished.

> In verneinten Sätzen stehen *have / has* mit *not*:
>
> | have not (haven't) has not (hasn't) | + past participle |
> |---|---|

c) Fragen und Antworten (*Questions and answers*)

Where **have** you **been**? – At school.
Has he **booked** the trip? – Yes, he **has**. /
No, he **hasn't**.

> In Fragen vertauscht man das Subjekt und *have / has*:
> *you have → **have you**?, he has → **has he**?*

d) Das *present perfect* mit *since* oder *for* (*The present perfect with* since *or* for)

We **have lived** in Queens <u>since 2023</u>.
Wir wohnen seit 2023 in Queens.

Ella **has been** in our class <u>for two weeks</u>.
Ella ist seit zwei Wochen in unserer Klasse.

> Mit dem *present perfect* sagst du auch, wie lange etwas schon andauert. Du verwendest …
> - *since* zur Angabe eines Zeitpunkts:
>   *since three o'clock, **since** May*.
> - *for* zur Angabe eines Zeitraums:
>   *for two weeks, **for** ten days*.

LF 7

Erklär-
film

Present perfect oder *simple past?*

▶ Unit 1 | p. 23

present perfect	simple past
A: I **have been** to the USA. **Have** you <u>ever</u> **been** to the USA? **B:** Yes, I **have**.	**A:** <u>When / Where</u> **did** you **go**? **B:** I **went** there <u>in 2021</u>.
💡 Signalwörter: *ever, never, already, (not) yet*	💡 Signalwörter: *yesterday, last week, ten years ago, in 2000, when?*
A: <u>How long</u> **has** Alice **lived** in Texas? **B:** <u>Since 2022</u>.	**A:** <u>When</u> **did** she **move** to Texas? **B:** <u>In 2022</u>.
💡 Signalwörter: *how long?, since two o' clock, for three hours*	💡 Signalwörter: *siehe oben*

In zusammenhängenden Texten folgen *present perfect* und *simple past* oft aufeinander:
- Mit dem *present perfect* sagst du, dass etwas geschehen ist, aber du nennst keine näheren Umstände, sagst also nicht, wann / wo / wie es geschehen ist.
- Mit dem *simple past* sagst oder fragst du, wann / wo / wie etwas geschehen ist.

- Mit dem *present perfect* sagst oder fragst du, seit wann / wie lange etwas schon andauert.
- Mit dem *simple past* sagst oder fragst du, wann / wo / warum etwas geschehen ist.

*How long **have** you **lived** in the big city?*

*Why **did** you **move** here?*

*Have you **made** any new friends?*

For two years.

*Because I **didn't like** it in the country.*

*Yes, I **have**. I **joined** a rat dance group last year.*

Erklär-
film

LF 8

Das Gerundium *(The gerund)*

▶ Unit 1 | pp. 25, 44

Reading can open up new worlds.
Lesen kann neue Welten erschließen.
Vergleiche:
Books can open up new worlds.

> Die *ing*-Form eines Verbs kann als Gerundium, d.h. wie ein Nomen verwendet werden.

a) **Das Gerundium als Subjekt** *(The gerund as a subject)*

Dancing is fun.
Tanzen macht Spaß.

> Wie andere Nomen kann das Gerundium als Subjekt im Satz stehen.

b) **Das Gerundium als Objekt nach Verben** *(The gerund as an object after verbs)*

I **enjoy / like cooking**.
Ich koche gern.

Have you **finished cleaning**?
Bist du mit dem Putzen fertig?

I **don't mind helping**.
Es macht mir nichts aus zu helfen.

Stop talking.
Hör auf zu reden!

Start moving.
Fang an, dich zu bewegen!

They **continued talking**.
Sie redeten weiter.

> Wie andere Nomen kann das Gerundium nach bestimmten Verben stehen, z. B. nach:

enjoy	*begin / start*
finish	*continue*
keep	*hate*
mind / not mind	*like*
miss	*love*
practise	*prefer*
recommend	Nur nach den Verben
stop	in dieser rechten
	Spalte kann entweder
	die *ing*-Form oder der
	to-Infinitiv stehen:
	Start to move.

c) **Das Gerundium nach Präpositionen** *(The gerund after prepositions)*

Chris is **good at dancing**.
Chris kann gut tanzen.

I **look forward to meeting** you.
Ich freue mich darauf, Sie kennenzulernen.

I like the **idea of living** in NYC.
Mir gefällt die Idee, in NYC zu leben.

> Wie andere Nomen kann das Gerundium nach bestimmten Wendungen mit Präpositionen stehen, z. B.:

be against	*be sorry for*
be good / bad at	*look forward to*
be crazy about	*worry about*
be interested in	*the idea of*
be scared of	*the risk of*

Erklär-film

Die Verlaufsform der Vergangenheit *(The past progressive)* ▶ Unit 2 | pp. 58–59

What **were** you **doing** at midnight last night? – We **were celebrating**.
Was habt ihr gestern um Mitternacht gemacht? – Wir haben gefeiert.

Troy called while I **was doing** my homework.
Troy rief an, als ich gerade meine Hausaufgaben machte.

Das *past progressive* wird verwendet, um auszudrücken, dass zu einer bestimmten Zeit in der Vergangenheit eine Handlung oder ein Vorgang gerade im Gange und noch nicht abgeschlossen war. Du kannst mit dem *past progressive* auch sagen, was gerade vor sich ging, als etwas anderes passierte. Das neu eintretende Geschehen steht im *simple past*.

a) Aussagesätze *(Statements)*

I / He / She / It **was**	
I / He / She / It **wasn't**	**working.**
We / You / They **were**	**playing.**
We / You / They **weren't**	

Das *past progressive* besteht aus zwei Teilen: **was / were** + **ing**-Form des Verbs.
In verneinten Sätzen steht **wasn't / weren't**.
❗ Beachte: *take → tak**ing**; putt**ing**, runn**ing***

b) Fragen und Antworten *(Questions and answers)*

Where **was** she **going**? – Home.
Were you **working**? – No, I **wasn't**.

In Fragen vertauscht man das Subjekt und *was / were*:
she was → **was she?**, you were → **were you?**

Erklär-film

Modale Hilfsverben *(Modal verbs)* ▶ Unit 2 | pp. 49, 51

Can you **help** me, please? – Yes, I **can**.
We **must ask** how much it will all cost.
He's ill and **shouldn't go** to school.

Can, could, must, needn't, may, might und *should* sind modale Hilfsverben. Sie haben nur eine Form und stehen mit dem Infinitiv (der Grundform) eines Verbs.

a) Erlaubnis, Verbot *(Permission, prohibition)*

Can I open the window?
May / Could I ask you something?
Dad says I **can't / mustn't** go to the party.

Mit *can* sagst du, was jemand tun darf. Wenn du sehr höflich fragen möchtest, ob du etwas tun darfst, verwendest du *may* oder *could*. Um zu sagen, dass jemand etwas nicht tun darf, verwendest du *can't* oder *mustn't*.

You **aren't allowed to** take photos here.
I **was allowed to** stay up late last night.
You**'ll be allowed to** bring your own drinks to the concert tomorrow.

> ❗ Bei Erlaubnissen und Verboten kannst du *be (not) allowed to* verwenden. Es hat auch Vergangenheitsformen *(was / were allowed to)* und eine Zukunftsform *(will be allowed to)*.

b) Notwendigkeit, Zwang *(Necessity, compulsion)*

We **must** stop injustice.
I **have** to go now, but I **don't have to** run.
She **needn't** worry. Everything is OK.

We **had to** call the doctor.
You **won't have to** wait.

> Mit *must* oder *have to* sagst du, was jemand tun muss.
> Mit *needn't* oder *don't / doesn't have to* sagst du, was jemand nicht zu tun braucht.
> ❗ *Have to* hat eine Vergangenheitsform *(had to)* und eine Zukunftsform *(will have to)*.

c) Fähigkeit *(Ability)*

I **can** bake, but I **can't** cook.

Is Lu **able to** speak English?
I **was able to** dance well when I was young.
We**'ll** soon **be able to** speak Spanish.

> Mit *can / can't* (Langform: *cannot*) sagst du oft, was jemand tun oder nicht tun kann.
> ❗ Mit *be (not) able to* kannst du ebenfalls über eine Fähigkeit sprechen. Es hat auch Vergangenheitsformen *(was / were able to)* und eine Zukunftsform *(will be able to)*.

d) Möglichkeit *(Possibility)*

It **may** rain.
You **might / could** be right.

> Du kannst *may, might* und *could* auch verwenden, um zu sagen, was möglich ist oder sein könnte.

e) Empfehlung, Rat *(Advice)*

We **should** do something about racism.
You **shouldn't** eat so much sugar.

> Mit *should / shouldn't* rätst du jemandem, etwas zu tun oder nicht zu tun.

LF 11

Erklär-
film

Das *past perfect* (The past perfect)

▶ Unit 2 | pp. 53, 59

The match **had** already **started** when we finally got to the stadium.
Das Spiel hatte bereits begonnen, ...

I **had been** ill before the match.
Ich war vor dem Spiel krank gewesen.

> Das *past perfect* wird verwendet, um auszudrücken, dass ein Ereignis vor einem anderen Ereignis in der Vergangenheit stattgefunden hatte oder dass ein Zustand vor einem Zeitpunkt in der Vergangenheit begonnen hatte.

a) Aussagesätze *(Statements)*

I / He / She / It We / You / They	had started late. hadn't started early. had left late. hadn't left early.

*The rats **had left** when the cat arrived.*

Das *past perfect* besteht aus **had** und der dritten Form des Verbs *(past participle)*. In verneinten Sätzen steht **hadn't**.

❗ Unregelmäßige *past participle*-Formen musst du lernen: *go →* **gone***; leave →* **left**. Du kannst sie auf S. 254–256 nachschlagen.
❗ Für die deutsche Zeitform Plusquamperfekt (Vorvergangenheit) verwendest du „hatte" oder „war". Im Englischen steht immer *had*.

b) Fragen und Antworten *(Questions and answers)*

There was a broken window at the back of the house. **Had** someone **broken in**?

Julia showed me her new phone. What **had** it **cost**? A lot, I think.

In Fragen vertauscht man das Subjekt und *had*:
you had → **had you***?, it had →* **had it**?

Erklär-film

Adverbien der Art und Weise *(Adverbs of manner)*

A careful driver <u>drives</u> **carefully**.
Ein vorsichtiger Fahrer fährt vorsichtig.
Please <u>speak</u> **clearly**.
Bitte sprechen Sie deutlich!

Adjektiv	Adverb
clear	clear**ly**
quick	quick**ly**
nervous	nervous**ly**
careful	careful**ly**

You speak English very **well**.
A hard worker works **hard**.
A fast runner can run **fast**.

Adverbien der Art und Weise beschreiben, wie jemand etwas tut oder wie etwas geschieht. Sie beschreiben also ein <u>Verb</u>. Die meisten Adverbien bildet man, indem man die Endung *-ly* an das Adjektiv anhängt.

❗ Beachte die Schreibung:
angry → angrily, happy → happily, full → fully

❗ Beachte diese Ausnahmen:
• Das Adverb zu *good* ist **well**.
• Bei **hard** und **fast** sind Adjektiv und Adverb gleich.

LF 13

Gradadverbien *(Adverbs of degree)*

▶ Unit 2 | p. 54

My exchange family is **really** <u>nice</u> / **very** <u>nice</u>.
The room is **a little too** <u>small</u>.
That woman is **extremely** <u>rich</u>.
Do you **really** <u>think</u> that?

I **don't** <u>know</u> **at all**.
Ich weiß es gar nicht.

Gradadverbien – z. B. *a bit, a little, very, really, extremely, too* („zu"), *not at all* („überhaupt nicht") – verstärken oder schwächen die Bedeutung eines Wortes. Zum Beispiel verstärkt *extremely* in *extremely rich* das Adjektiv *rich*. Gradadverbien stehen meist direkt vor dem Wort, auf das sie sich beziehen.

LF 14 Revision

Erklär-film

Bedingungssätze Typ 1 *(Conditional sentences type 1)*

a) *if*-Satz und Hauptsatz (if-*clause and main clause*)

If it **rains** tomorrow, **I'll stay** at home.
Wenn es morgen regnet, bleibe ich zu Hause.

*If I **eat** too much in the evening, I **can't** sleep at night.*

I'll stay at home **if** it **rains** tomorrow.

Bedingungssätze bestehen aus zwei Teilen:
- Der Nebensatz mit *if (if-clause)* nennt eine Bedingung oder Voraussetzung.
- Der Hauptsatz *(main clause)* nennt die Folge, also was geschehen wird oder kann.

Zwischen *if*-Satz und Hauptsatz steht ein Komma.

⚠ Im Englischen setzt man kein Komma, wenn der Hauptsatz <u>vor</u> dem *if*-Satz steht.

b) Zeitformen im Bedingungssatz Typ 1 *(Tenses in conditional sentences type 1)*

If this **happens** again,	you**'ll be** in trouble.
	you **should call** the police.
	take action as soon as possible.

- Im *if*-Satz verwendest du das *simple present* (z. B. *happens*).
- Im Hauptsatz steht meist das *will-future*. Du kannst auch Modalverben (*should, can* usw.) oder den Imperativ (*take*) verwenden.

Erklär-
film

LF 15

Bedingungssätze Typ 2 *(Conditional sentences type 2)* ▶ Unit 3 | pp. 80, 104, 105

If I **lived** in NYC, I **would go** (= I**'d go**) to Broadway shows as often as possible.
Wenn ich in NYC leben würde, würde ich so oft wie möglich zu Broadway-Shows gehen.

If the traffic **wasn't** so bad, we **could drive** to a concert in Brooklyn.
Wenn der Verkehr nicht so schlimm wäre, könnten wir zu einem Konzert … fahren.

Neben Bedingungssätzen des Typs 1 gibt es auch Bedingungssätze des Typs 2:
- Im *if*-Satz des Typs 2 verwendest du das *simple past* (z. B. *lived, wasn't*). Mit dem *simple past* drückst du aus, dass du es für unwahrscheinlich hältst, dass die Bedingung eintritt.
- Im Hauptsatz steht *would* (Kurzform *'d*) + Infinitiv oder *could* + Infinitiv.

Erklär-
film

LF 16 `Revision`

Die Steigerung der Adjektive *(Comparison of adjectives)* ▶ Unit 3 | p. 83

a) Steigerung mit *-er / -est (Comparison with* -er / -est)

Komparativ (erste Steigerungsform)	Superlativ (Höchstform)
Troy's smile was **bigger** than Kisha's.	The **biggest** tree in the park is very old.
The airport is **busier** during the holidays.	The **busiest** time is the early evening.
The weather today is **better** than yesterday.	The **worst** part of the film was the ending.

Adjektive kann man steigern und in Vergleichen benutzen. Bei einsilbigen Adjektiven und bei zweisilbigen Adjektiven, die auf -*y* enden, hängst du **-er/-est** an das Adjektiv:
tall → taller / (the) tallest
❗ Beachte die Schreibung:
  - *big → bigger / (the) biggest*
  - *busy → busier / (the) busiest*
❗ Beachte diese Ausnahmen:
  - *good → better → (the) best*
  - *bad → worse → (the) worst*

b) Steigerung mit *more / most (Comparison with* more / most)

Komparativ	Superlativ
Lin-Manuel's music is **more creative** than Leo's.	The **most expensive** part of NYC is Manhattan.

Bei längeren (vor allem dreisilbigen) Adjektiven setzt man *more / most* vor das Adjektiv:
creative → more creative
expensive → (the) most expensive

c) *as … as*

I am **as tall as** my sister.	Wenn du sagen willst, dass zwei Sachen oder Personen gleich oder ähnlich sind, verwendest du *as … as: as tall as* („so groß wie").

LF 17 | Revision

Erklär-film

Die Zukunft mit *going to* (The going to-future)

▶ Unit 3 | pp. 84, 105

We**'re going to have** a barbecue tonight.
Wir wollen heute Abend grillen.

Are you **going to be** at the party?
Wirst du auf der Party sein?

> Mit *going to* ... sagst du, was jemand vorhat oder plant. *Going to* hat hier nichts mit dem deutschen „gehen" zu tun, sondern bedeutet „werden" oder „wollen".

a) Bejahte Aussagesätze *(Positive statements)*

I'm He**'s** / She**'s** / It**'s** We**'re** / You**'re** / They**'re**	going to leave.

> Das *going to-future* besteht aus einer Form von *be* + *going to* (*am* / *is* / *are going to*) und dem Infinitiv des Verbs.

b) Verneinte Aussagesätze *(Negative statements)*

I**'m not** He / She / It **isn't** We / You / They **aren't**	going to stay.

> In verneinten Sätzen stehen *am* / *is* / *are* mit *not*. (Kurzformen: *'m not, isn't, aren't*)

c) Fragen und Antworten *(Questions and answers)*

Are you **going to ask**? – No, **I'm not**.
Where **is** she **going to live**? – In NYC.

> In Fragen vertauscht man das Subjekt und *am* / *is* / *are*: *you are* → *are you?*, *she is* → *is she?*

d) Vorhersagen mit *going to* (Predictions with going to)

You're late. We**'re going to miss** the bus.
One day there**'s going to be** an accident if they don't do something about this road.

> Mit *going to* ... kannst du auch sagen, was wahrscheinlich (aufgrund bestehender Vorzeichen) bald passieren wird.

LF 18 | Revision

Erklär-film

Die Zukunft mit *will* (The will-future)

▶ Unit 3 | pp. 86, 106

I think you**'ll have** a great time in the USA.
Ich glaube, du wirst eine tolle Zeit in den USA haben.

Wait – I**'ll help** you.
Warte – ich helfe dir.

> Du verwendest das *will-future*
> • für Vorhersagen, also um zu sagen, was in der Zukunft passieren wird. Die Sätze beginnen oft mit *I think, Maybe, I'm sure*.
> • für spontane Entscheidungen und Hilfsangebote.

I'**ll call** you later.
Ich rufe dich später an.

I **want to go** home.
Ich will nach Hause gehen.

> **!** Im Deutschen steht oft das Präsens, wo im Englischen *will* stehen muss.
>
> **!** „will / wollen" zum Ausdruck eines Wunsches = *want to / would like to*

a) Bejahte Aussagesätze *(Positive statements)*

It **will**	
It'**ll**	**be** sunny tomorrow.

> Du bildest das *will-future* mit **will** (Kurzform *'ll*) und dem Infinitiv des Verbs. Alle Personen haben dieselbe Form: *I'll, you'll, he'll* usw.

b) Verneinte Aussagesätze *(Negative statements)*

It **will not**	
It **won't**	**be** sunny on Monday.

> In verneinten Sätzen steht *will* mit *not*. Die Kurzform von *will not* ist *won't*.

c) Fragen und Antworten *(Questions and answers)*

Will it **be** hot? – Yes, it **will**. / No, it **won't**.
Won't you **join** us for dinner? – I'd love to.
When **will** you **start** the new job? – Soon.

> In Fragen vertauscht man das Subjekt und *will / won't*:
> *it will → will it?, you won't → won't you?*

LF 19

Erklär-film

Das Passiv *(The passive)*

Aktiv	Passiv
Mike **plays** baseball.	Baseball **is played** all over the USA. Baseball wird überall in den USA gespielt.
Companies **develop** new products in Silicon Valley every day.	New products **are developed** in Silicon Valley every day. Im Silicon Valley werden jeden Tag neue Produkte entwickelt.

Man kann einen Vorgang aus zwei verschiedenen Perspektiven beschreiben:
- Ein Aktivsatz drückt aus, wer oder was etwas tut. Das Subjekt des Aktivsatzes *(Mike, companies)* führt eine Handlung aus.
- Ein Passivsatz hebt hervor, mit wem oder womit etwas geschieht. Im Passivsatz wird etwas mit dem Subjekt *(baseball, new products)* getan. Mit einem Passivsatz kann man Handlungen beschreiben, ohne zu sagen, wer die Handlung ausführt.

a) Das Passiv der Gegenwart *(The passive: simple present)*

▶ Unit 4 | pp. 110, 111, 136

Bejahte Aussagesätze	
I **am**	
He / She / It **is**	**respected.**
You / We / They **are**	

Verneinte Aussagesätze	
I'm	
He / She / It **is**	**not respected.**
You / We / They **are**	

Man bildet das Passiv mit einer Form von *be* und der dritten Form des Verbs *(past participle).*
Im *simple present* verwendest du also:

am ('m)	
is ('s)	
are ('re)	+ *past participle*
Verneint:	(z. B. respect**ed**,
am not ('m not)	ask**ed**, play**ed**,
is not (isn't)	open**ed**)
are not (aren't)	

Coffee **is drunk** more than tea.
Posters **are hung** all over town.

❗ Unregelmäßige *past participle*-Formen musst du lernen, s. S. 254–256.

b) Das Passiv der Vergangenheit *(The passive: simple past)*

▶ Unit 4 | pp. 115, 137, 138

Alcatraz **was closed** in 1963.
Alcatraz wurde 1963 geschlossen.

The articles **were written** by a team of six.
Die Artikel wurden von einem sechs-
köpfigen Team verfasst.

Im *simple past* bildet man das Passiv mit **was / were** + dritte Form des Verbs *(past participle).*

c) Das Passiv mit *by* *(The passive with* by*)*

My sister **is taken** to school **by** my dad.
Meine Schwester wird von meinem Vater
zur Schule gebracht.

The houses **were destroyed by** fire.
Die Häuser wurden durch ein Feuer zerstört.

Wenn du in einem Passivsatz sagen willst, von wem etwas getan wird/wurde oder wodurch etwas geschieht/geschah, verwendest du die Präposition **by** („von", „durch"). Die meisten Passivsätze stehen jedoch ohne *by*, weil unbekannt oder unwichtig ist, wer die Handlung ausführt.

*The cat's food **is** often **stolen by** the clever rats.*

Adverbialsätze *(Adverbial clauses)*

▶ Unit 4 | pp. 119, 138

Julie sings	when she is happy.
	because she loves music.
	beautifully.

As we got near the airport, we saw a plane come in to land.
Als wir uns dem Flughafen näherten, …

The phone rang **while I was having a shower**.
…, während / als ich gerade duschte.

I won't go **unless you come with me**.
…, du kommst mit.

They are going to have the barbecue **even if it rains.**
…, auch wenn / selbst wenn es regnet.

You must speak loudly and clearly **so that everyone can hear you**.
…, sodass / damit alle dich hören können.

That man talks **as if he knows everything**.
…, als ob er alles wüsste.

Everywhere I went, there were tourists.
Überall, wo ich hinging, waren Touristen.

Nebensatz			Hauptsatz		
S	V	O	S	V	O
If I	help	him,	he	'll help	me.
Wenn ich ihm helfe,			hilft er mir.		

Adverbialsätze sind Nebensätze, die – ähnlich wie ein Adverb *(z. B. beautifully)* – nähere Informationen zu einer Handlung oder einem Geschehen im Hauptsatz geben. Sie machen einen Text besser lesbar und interessanter.

Adverbialsätze werden durch Konjunktionen eingeleitet, z. B.:
- Adverbialsätze der Zeit mit *after*, *before*, *as* („als", „während"), *as soon a*s, *until / till*, *when*, *while*
- Adverbialsätze des Grundes oder der Ursache mit *because*
- Adverbialsätze der Bedingung mit *if, unless*
- Adverbialsätze des Gegensatzes mit *although, even if, though*
- Adverbialsätze der Folge oder des Zwecks mit *so (that)*
- Adverbialsätze der Art und Weise mit *as if*
- Adverbialsätze des Ortes mit *everywhere, where, wherever*

! Beachte:
- Wenn der Adverbialsatz am Anfang steht, setzt du ein Komma zwischen Adverbialsatz und Hauptsatz.
- Wenn der Adverbialsatz hinter dem Hauptsatz steht, brauchst du kein Komma.

! Im Englischen haben sowohl Hauptsätze als auch Nebensätze die Wortstellung S-V-O.

When the cat is away, the rats will play.

Erklär-
film

LF 21 **Revision**

Relativsätze *(Relative clauses)*

Are you the guy **who / that** developed this computer game?
Bist du der Typ, der dieses Computerspiel entwickelt hat?

This is the girl **who / that** we met yesterday.
Das ist das Mädchen, das wir gestern getroffen haben.

I know a shop **which / that** sells really cool trainers.
Ich kenne einen Laden, der richtig coole Sportschuhe verkauft.

Yesterday I saw a bird **which / that** sang beautifully.
Gestern habe ich einen Vogel gesehen, der wunderschön gesungen hat.

Jin is the girl **whose** parents have opened that new Korean restaurant.
Jin ist das Mädchen, dessen Eltern das neue koreanische Restaurant eröffnet haben.

Mit Relativsätzen kannst du zusätzliche Informationen über eine Person oder eine Sache geben. Man nennt diese Relativsätze *defining relative clauses* (bestimmende Relativsätze).
Solche Relativsätze werden im Englischen in der Regel nicht durch ein Komma vom Hauptsatz abgetrennt.

Relativsätze werden durch unterschiedliche Relativpronomen eingeleitet:
• *who* für Personen (und Haustiere mit Namen)
• *which* für Sachen (und Tiere ohne Namen)
• *that* für Sachen und Personen (für Personen ist *who* gebräuchlicher)
• *whose* („dessen“, „deren“) für Personen, aber auch für Sachen und Tiere. Auf *whose* folgt immer ein Nomen (z. B. *parents*).

*This is the rat **that ate the cheese that lay in the house that Jack built**.*

This is the boy **I met yesterday**.
= This is the boy **who I met yesterday**.
Das ist der Junge, den ich gestern getroffen habe.

In englischen Relativsätzen kann das Relativpronomen manchmal weggelassen werden. Das ist im Deutschen nicht möglich.

Grammatical terms *(Grammatische Fachbegriffe in diesem Buch)*

adjective	das Adjektiv	*old, good, popular*
adverb of degree	das Gradadverb	*extremely, very, really*
adverb of frequency	das Häufigkeitsadverb	*often, always, sometimes, rarely, never*
adverb of manner	das Adverb der Art und Weise	*well, carefully, quietly, angrily*
adverbial clause	der Adverbialsatz	*She left the room **because she was angry**.*
article	der Artikel	***a / the** book, **an / the** apple*
comparative	der Komparativ (erste Steigerungsform)	*older, better, more popular*
comparison	die Steigerung	*old – older – (the) oldest*
conditional sentence	der Bedingungssatz	*If I had a lot of money, I'd buy a house.*
conjunction	die Konjunktion, das Bindewort	*although, because, but*
gerund	das Gerundium, *ing*-Form	*I like **keeping** fit. **Dancing** is fun.*
going to-future	das Futur mit *going to*	*I'm going to eat ...; We're going to watch ...*
if-clause	der Nebensatz mit *if*	*If it rains, ...*
infinitive	der Infinitiv (Grundform)	*(to) do, (to) go, (to) love*
irregular adjective / adverb / verb	das unregelmäßige Adjektiv / Adverb / Verb	adjective: *bad – **worse** – **worst***; adverb: *good – **well***; verb: *(to) do – did – **done***
main clause	der Hauptsatz	*If it rains, **I won't go out**.*
modal verb	das modale Hilfsverb	*can, must, shouldn't*
negative	die verneinte Form	***don't** go, **can't** go, **aren't** going, **hasn't** gone*
noun	das Nomen / Substantiv	*friend, car, competition*
object	das Objekt	*I like **cats**.*
passive	das Passiv	*Lots of photos **were taken**. They **are developed**.*
past participle	das Partizip Perfekt (3. Form)	*loved, eaten, seen, done, gone*
past perfect	das Plusquamperfekt, die Vorvergangenheit	*After we **had got up**, we had breakfast.*
past progressive	die Verlaufsform der Vergangenheit	*We **were having** breakfast.*
personal pronoun	das Personalpronomen	*I, you, he, she, it, we, they*
plural	der Plural, die Mehrzahl	*books, children, potatoes, stories*
possessive determiner	der Possessivbegleiter	*my, your, his, her, its, our, their*
possessive pronoun	das Possessivpronomen	*mine, yours, his, hers, ours, theirs*
preposition	die Präposition	***in** the house, **on** the desk, **near** the river*
present perfect	das Perfekt	*He **has gone**.; **Have** you seen?*
present progressive	die Verlaufsform der Gegenwart	*I'm speaking, she's looking, we're talking, they **aren't** listening*
question tag	das Frageanhängsel	*... isn't she?; ... don't you?*
reflexive pronoun	das Reflexivpronomen	*myself, yourself, ourselves*
relative clause	der Relativsatz	*someone **who loves**, a shop **which sells***
relative pronoun	das Relativpronomen	*who, which, that, whose*
short answer	die Kurzantwort	*Yes, I do. / No, I'm not. / Yes, she does.*

simple past	die einfache Vergangenheit	it **was**; I **went**; he **talked**
simple present	die einfache Gegenwart	I **go**; he **talks**
singular	der Singular, die Einzahl	book, child, potato, story
statement	der Aussage(satz)	I like oranges. I don't like bananas.
subject	das Subjekt	**They** eat dinner.; **The cat** is cute.
superlative	der Superlativ (höchste Steigerungsform)	(the) oldest, (the) best, (the) most popular
tense	die Zeitform	present progressive, simple past, future
verb	das Verb; das Prädikat	(to) go, (to) do, (to) have, (to) think, (to) love
wh-question	die Frage mit Fragewort	What's this? Who are you?
will-future	das Futur mit *will*	Noah **will** phone, you'll see, he **won't** buy
word order	die Wortstellung	subject – verb – object: We know them.
yes/no-question	die Entscheidungsfrage	Are you OK?; Will she go?; Did it go well?

Wichtige Schreibregeln im Englischen

Groß- und Kleinschreibung

Im Englischen wird fast alles kleingeschrieben. Merke dir nur diese Ausnahmen:

- das Wort *I* (ich)
- Monatsnamen und Wochentage
- Eigennamen und geografische Namen
- Länder, deren Bewohner und Bewohnerinnen, Sprachen und Nationalitäten (*Germany, the Germans, German*)
- das erste Wort am Satzanfang und in Überschriften

Stumme Buchstaben

Manche Wörter enthalten Buchstaben, die du zwar schreibst, aber nicht sprichst:

b	lam**b**	k	(to) **k**now, **k**nife
c	s**c**ience	l	(to) wa**l**k, (to) ta**l**k
d	san**d**wich	u	g**u**itar, b**u**ilding
g	desi**g**n	t	(to) lis**t**en
h	tec**h**nology	w	(to) ans**w**er, **w**rong
i	fru**i**t		

Anführungszeichen bei direkter Rede

Wir verwenden Anführungszeichen, um zu zeigen, was gesprochen wird. Die Anführungszeichen stehen im Englischen am Satzanfang und am Satzende oben:
'I love my dog,' Lou said.

Verdoppelung der Endkonsonanten

(to) sto**p** – sto**pp**ing, sto**pp**ed
(to) wi**n** – wi**nn**ing, wi**nn**er

-y wird zu -ie

- im Plural: a pon**y** – three poni**es**
- in der 3. Person Singular:
  (to) tid**y** – he tid**ies**
- bei der Steigerung von Adjektiven:
  bus**y** – bus**ier** – bus**iest**

Buchstabenverbindungen

Merke dir häufige Buchstabenverbindungen bei der Schreibung englischer Wörter:

-ee-	(to) see, deep, (to) meet, street
-ea-	beach, meat, pea
-igh-	sight, fight, right, night
-oo-	book, good, look
-ous-	dangerous, nervous, famously

Kleine Unterschiede Deutsch–Englisch

- **k** wird zu **c**: Musik – *music*
- **f** wird zu **ph**: Foto – *photo*
- **isch** wird zu **ic**: elektrisch – *electric*
- **el** wird zu **le**: Titel – *title*, Artikel – *article*
- **sch** wird zu **sh**: britisch – *British*
- deutsches **-e** am Wortende entfällt: Lampe – *lamp*, Ende – *end*

🔊 The English alphabet

a	[eɪ]	**h**	[eɪtʃ]	**o**	[əʊ]	**v**	[viː]
b	[biː]	**i**	[aɪ]	**p**	[piː]	**w**	[ˈdʌbljuː]
c	[siː]	**j**	[dʒeɪ]	**q**	[kjuː]	**x**	[eks]
d	[diː]	**k**	[keɪ]	**r**	[ɑː]	**y**	[waɪ]
e	[iː]	**l**	[el]	**s**	[es]	**z**	[zed]
f	[ef]	**m**	[em]	**t**	[tiː]		
g	[dʒiː]	**n**	[en]	**u**	[juː]		

🔊 English sounds

💡 Die Lautschrift zeigt dir die Aussprache von Wörtern und Lauten *(sounds)*.

💡 Einige dieser Laute kommen im Deutschen nicht vor oder werden anders geschrieben. Sie sind hier mit einem Ausrufezeichen gekennzeichnet: . Übe sie mit Hilfe der App.

	[iː]	green, he, sea		[d]	day, window, good
	[ɑː]	ask, class, car, park		[t]	ten, letter, at
❗	[ɔː]	or, ball, door, four, morning		[g]	go, again, bag
	[uː]	ruler, blue, too, two, you		[k]	kitchen, car, back
	[ɜː]	early, her, girl, work, T-shirt		[m]	man, remember, mum
	[ɪ]	in, big, expensive		[n]	no, one, ten
	[e]	yes, bed, again, breakfast	❗	[ŋ]	wrong, young, uncle, thanks
	[æ]	animal, apple, black, cat		[l]	like, old, small
	[ʌ]	mum, bus, colour		[r]	ruler, friend, sorry
	[ɒ]	song, on, dog, what	❗	[w]	we, where, one
	[ʊ]	book, good, put, bully		[j]	yes, you, uniform
	[ə]	again, today, a sister		[f]	family, after, laugh
	[i]	happy, monkey	❗	[v]	very, seven, have
	[eɪ]	name, eight, play, great		[s]	six, poster, yes
	[aɪ]	I, time, right, my	❗	[z]	zoo, quiz, his, music, please
	[ɔɪ]	boy, toilet, noise		[ʃ]	she, station, English
	[əʊ]	old, no, road, yellow	❗	[ʒ]	usually, revision, garage
	[aʊ]	now, house		[tʃ]	chain, teacher, watch
	[ɪə]	here, material, really, year	❗	[dʒ]	job, German, project, orange
	[eə]	where, pair, share, their	❗	[θ]	thing, three, bathroom, north
	[ʊə]	tour	❗	[ð]	the, weather, with
	[b]	bike, table, verb		[h]	house, who, behind
	[p]	pen, paper, shop		[x]	loch

Wordbank 1: Being polite

▶ Unit 1 | pp. 27, 44

Asking for help & information

Excuse me ...
Sorry to bother you, but ...
Could you help me/us, please?
Could you tell me/us ...?

Asking for permission (Erlaubnis)

May I ...
Could I ...
Do you mind if I ...?
Can I sit here? Is this seat free?

Saying yes & no

Yes, of course.
Sure.
Sorry, but ...
I'm afraid I can't help you.

Offering food & drink

Would you like ...?
Can I give you ...?
Can I offer you ...?
Can I get you ...?
How about ...?

Asking for food & drink

Can / Could I have ..., please?
I'd like ...
I'll have ..., please.
Can I get ...?
Do you have ...?

Accepting & refusing
(etwas annehmen & ablehnen)

Yes, please.
No, thanks. (I'm afraid I don't eat ... /
I'm completely full.)

Saying thank you

Thanks. / Thank you.
Thanks for your help.
Thanks a lot for ...
I'm thankful for ...

Saying sorry

I'm (so/very) sorry.
It was my fault.
Sorry about that.

Accepting thanks
(Dank annehmen)

You're welcome.
No problem.
Any time!
Don't mention it.
I'm happy I could help.
Sure thing!

Accepting an apology
(eine Entschuldigung annehmen)

It's fine.
Don't worry about it.
No worries.
We're good.
Thank you for your apology.

Wordbank 2: Music

▶ Unit 2 | pp. 56, 57   ▶ Unit 3 | p. 83   ▶ Unit 4 | p. 116

The song has an energetic rhythm.	*Das Lied hat einen dynamischen Rhythmus.*
The tempo is very fast / slow.	*Das Tempo ist sehr schnell / langsam.*
The melody is very catchy.	*Die Melodie ist sehr eingängig.*
The music makes me feel happy / sad.	*Die Musik macht mich glücklich / traurig.*
The lyrics are easy / not easy to understand.	*Der Text ist einfach / nicht einfach zu verstehen.*
The lyrics are catchy / easy to sing along.	*Der Text ist eingängig / leicht zum Mitsingen.*
The song is inspiring / passionate / relaxing / uplifting / ...	*Das Lied ist begeisternd / leidenschaftlich / entspannend / aufmunternd / ...*
The song is annoying / depressing / horrible / weird / ...	*Das Lied ist nervig / deprimierend / schrecklich / seltsam ...*
The singer has a smooth / strong / ... voice.	*Der Sänger / Die Sängerin hat eine sanfte / kräftige / ... Stimme.*
The song is about ... / makes me think of ...	*Das Lied handelt von ... / erinnert mich an ...*
The main message of the song is ...	*Die Hauptaussage des Liedes ist ...*

styles of music					
jazz	rock	indie	classical	pop	hip-hop
rap	electronic	country	blues	funk	metal

I play the ...
bagpipes, trumpet, violin

drums

recorder

piano

electric guitar

saxophone

trombone

Wordbank 3: Extreme weather

► Unit 2 | p. 58

There was ...

a flood, a hurricane, a lot of snow, a storm, a tornado, hail, thunder and lightning

Water
There was a tsunami /
a storm flood / a flood / ...
Big waves and strong
winds hit the coast.
Many towns were flooded.

wave

storm flood

tsunami

Land
There was a landslide /
a volcanic eruption / ...
Heavy rain caused a
landslide.
A volcano erupted and
caused wildfires.

landslide

volcanic eruption

Heat
The temperature went up
to 40° Celsius.
There was a drought.
The hot weather lasted for
over a month.
A wildfire burned for two
weeks.

drought

wildfire

Cold
The temperature fell to
minus 15° Celsius.
There was a blizzard /
snowstorm / freezing
rain / ...
There was ice on the roads. /
The roads were icy.

blizzard

freezing rain

Wordbank 4: Job training

▶ Unit 3 | p. 87

I could do an apprenticeship in …

catering

childcare

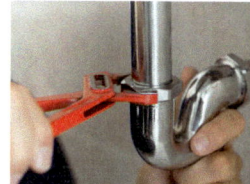
plumbing

agriculture

construction

motor service

I could do a qualification in …

I'd like to work in …
Maybe I'll study …

computing

hairdressing

hospitality

I would / wouldn't want to work …

at night, at a harbour, at a zoo, at home, in a hotel, in a hospital, in an office, in a shop, in a restaurant, on a farm, outdoors

in a retirement home

in a laboratory

in a factory

in a call centre

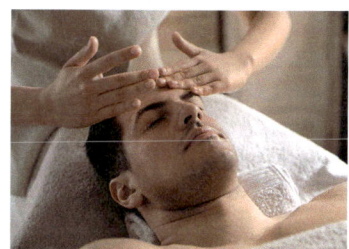
in a beauty salon

as an influencer

Wordbank 5: Charts

▶ Unit 1 | p. 20   ▶ Unit 4 | pp. 124, 134, 139

In this chart you can see …   This diagram shows …   This chart is about …

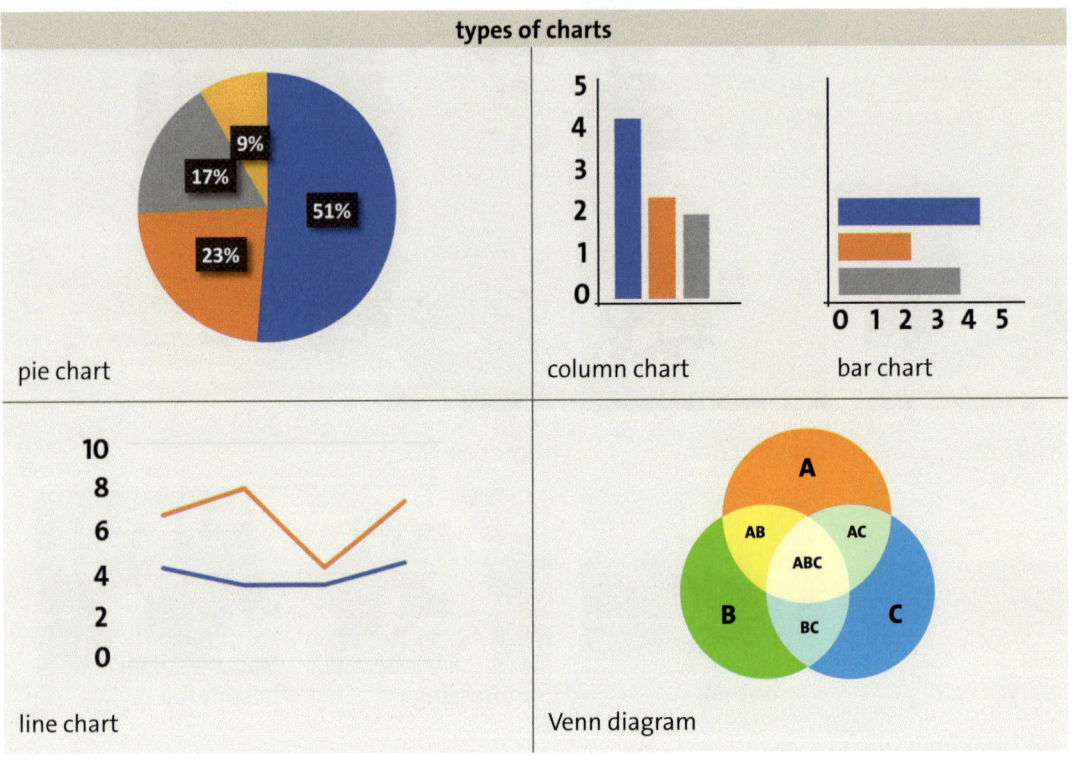

pie chart	column chart	bar chart
line chart	Venn diagram	

Talking about charts and diagrams	
In presentations Let me show you this bar chart. I'd like you to look at this diagram. In this chart you can see the development of … The source of the data / numbers / statistics is … The data was collected … The numbers / statistics are from the year …	**Describing charts** This chart / diagram presents / compares … The number of … increases / grows. The number of … decreases / falls / drops. The line shows an increase / a drop. The x-axis / y-axis shows …
Comparing charts These two charts show … These diagrams are very similar / different. This chart shows …, but this one … The pie chart shows how …, whereas the Venn diagram focuses on … These two charts show very different results.	**How to explain numbers** 98 out of 100 → almost 100 51 % = fifty-one per cent → more than half 45 % = forty-five per cent → less than half 23 % → almost one quarter A low / high number … Only 5% … ▶ English numbers, p. 253

Hier findest du englische Sätze mit ihrer deutschen Übersetzung. Da jede Sprache anders funktioniert, ist eine wortwörtliche Übersetzung oft nicht möglich. Achte daher auf die kleinen Unterschiede.

1   Über Interessen und Dinge sprechen, die einem wichtig sind

What's your favourite book / sport / …?	Was ist dein Lieblingsbuch / -sport / …?
My favourite sport / … is … because …	Mein Lieblingssport / … ist …, weil …
What do you like to do in your free time?	Was machst du gerne in deiner Freizeit?
Are / Is … important to you?	Sind / Ist dir … wichtig?
(My family) is really important to me because …	(Meine Familie) ist mir sehr wichtig, weil …
Do you like … or do you like … (better)?	Magst du … oder magst du … (ieber)?
Have you ever …?	Hast du schonmal …?

2   Sich verabreden und etwas planen

What are we / you going to do this weekend / on Sunday / …?	Was machen wir / machst du am Wochenende / Sonntag / …?
Are you doing anything (today)?	Machst du (heute) irgendetwas?
Let's go to …	Lass uns zu … gehen.
Are you free?	Hast du Zeit?
(Saturday) would be best.	(Samstag) wäre am besten.
Let's meet at the station / in the park / … at 7.30 p.m.	Lass uns um 19.30 Uhr am Bahnhof / im Park / … treffen.
Sorry, I can't. I'm really busy.	Tut mir leid, da kann ich nicht. Ich bin sehr beschäftigt.
See you on (Saturday).	Wir sehen uns am (Samstag).
What about …?	Wie wäre es mit …?

3   Leben in der Stadt

Öffentliche Verkehrsmittel nutzen

How much does (a bus ticket) cost?	Wie viel kostet (eine Busfahrkarte)?
I have to buy a ticket.	Ich muss eine Fahrkarte kaufen.
We have to / don't have to change lines.	Wir müssen / müssen nicht umsteigen.
Let's take the train / the subway / … to …	Lass(t) uns den Zug / die U-Bahn nach / zu … nehmen.
We can take the bus / tram / … from here.	Von hier können wir den Bus / die Straßenbahn / … nehmen.
How long does it take by taxi / bike / …?	Wie lange dauert es mit dem Taxi / Fahrrad / …?

Unit 1	In my area, we (don't) have buses /...	Wo ich wohne, haben wir (keine) Busse /...
	The underground /... runs 24 hours every day.	Die U-Bahn /... fährt 24 Stunden am Tag.
	You need to take the (4 or 5) train to ...	Du musst / Sie müssen die Linie (4 oder 5) zu / nach ... nehmen.
	It's four stops.	Es sind vier Haltestellen.
	You need to get off at the next stop.	Du musst / Sie müssen an der nächsten Haltestelle aussteigen.
	Take the exit for ... street.	Nimm den Ausgang zur ... Straße.
	You're on the right / wrong line.	Das ist die richtige / falsche U-Bahn-Linie.

Nach dem Weg fragen und Wege beschreiben

	Go straight on / across / along / past /...	Geh geradeaus / über / entlang / an ... vorbei /...
	Turn left / right.	Biege links / rechts ab.
	Take the first / second /... road on the right / left.	Nimm die erste / zweite /... Straße auf der rechten / linken Seite.
	Just follow (the river) that way until you come to ...	Folge einfach (dem Fluss) bis du bei / an ... ankommst.
	South / North / East / West from ...	Südlich / Nördlich / Östlich / Westlich von ...
Unit 1	I don't understand which way to go to ...	Ich verstehe nicht, wie man zum / zur ... kommt.
	Could you tell us how to get to ...?	Könnten Sie uns bitte sagen, wie wir nach ... kommen?

Essen gehen und in einem Restaurant bestellen

	Would you like some more (water)?	Möchtest du / Möchten Sie noch etwas mehr (Wasser)?
	Enjoy your meal!	Guten Appetit!
	Everything looks wonderful.	Das sieht alles sehr lecker aus.
	I'm allergic to ...	Ich bin gegen ... allergisch.
	Could I have (some tea), please?	Könnte ich bitte (einen Tee) bekommen?
	I'd like (a cola), please.	Ich hätte gerne (eine Cola).
	I'll have (the falafel), please.	Ich bekomme (die Falafel), bitte.
	Can you tell me what ... is?	Was ist ...?

4   Global goals

Über Umwelt, Natur(schutz) und Nachhaltigkeit sprechen

	I think ... is very / not very green.	Ich finde ... sehr / nicht besonders nachhaltig.
	We live in a green city.	Wir leben in einer nachhaltigen Stadt.
	Fast fashion is a big problem.	Fast fashion ist ein großes Problem.
	There's a lot of rubbish.	Es gibt viel Müll.
	Make your city / area greener.	Mach deine Stadt / Gegend grüner.

| Unit 4 | Turn off the tap when you ... | Dreh den Wasserhahn ab, wenn du ... |
| | Only use (the dishwasher) when ... | Verwende (den Geschirrspüler) nur, wenn ... |

Über Gerechtigkeit und gesellschaftliche Probleme sprechen

Unit 1	People need water / food / ...	Menschen brauchen (Trink)Wasser, Lebensmittel / ...
	It's nice to have a phone / a pet / ...	Es ist schön, ein Smartphone / ein Haustier / ... zu haben.
Unit 2	We should treat each other with respect.	Wir sollten einander respektvoll behandeln.
Unit 3	In our dream school, everyone is equal.	An unserer Traumschule werden alle gleichbehandelt.
	There is no bullying.	Es gibt kein Mobbing.

5   Miteinander reden

Über Probleme sprechen und Ratschläge erteilen

	Could you help me, please?	Könntest du / Könnten Sie mir bitte helfen?
	Should I ...? / What (else) should I do?	Sollte ich ...? / Was könnte / sollte ich (noch) tun?
	I think you have to talk to someone.	Ich denke, du solltest mit jemandem (darüber) sprechen.
	I understand that you're (feeling) unhappy / sad / disappointed / ...	Ich verstehe, dass du unglücklich / traurig / enttäuscht / ... bist.
	I really like that idea.	Das ist eine gute Idee.

Komplimente machen

	I think you're funny / brave / ...	Ich finde dich witzig / mutig / ...
	You're amazing at ...	Du kannst hervorragend ...
	I want to tell you that you're great at football / an amazing friend / ...	Ich wollte dir sagen, dass du sehr gut Fußball spielst / ein/e tolle/r Freund/in bist / ...
	Thank you, that's nice of you.	Danke, das ist lieb / nett von dir.
	You're welcome!	Gern geschehen!

Einen Konflikt lösen und sich entschuldigen

	I'm sorry, it was a bad idea to ...	Es tut mir leid, es war eine schlechte Idee ...
	I don't know why I thought that was (a good idea).	Ich weiß nicht, warum ich dachte, dass das (eine gute Idee) wäre.
	I feel better now.	Jetzt fühle ich mich besser.
	Thank you for saying sorry.	Danke für deine Entschuldigung.
	Next time, you should ...	Beim nächsten Mal solltest du ...

Hilfe anbieten, erbitten und annehmen, sich bedanken

| | I'd like to ... But I don't know where to start. | Ich möchte gerne ... Aber ich weiß gar nicht, wo ich anfangen soll. |

	I can help you if you like.	Ich kann dir helfen, wenn du magst.
	Yes, please.	Ja, bitte.
	Could you / Can you help me …?	Könntest / Kannst du mir helfen …?
	No problem.	Kein Problem.
	Would you like me to …?	Möchtest du, dass ich …?
	Shall I help you with …?	Soll ich dir mit … helfen?
	No, thanks, I'm OK.	Alles gut, danke. / Nein, danke.
Unit 1	Excuse me, could you …, please?	Entschuldigung, könntest du / könnten Sie bitte …?
	Thanks for your help.	Danke für deine / Ihre Hilfe.
Unit 3	Thank you for helping / asking / …	Vielen Dank fürs Helfen / (Nach)fragen / …

6   Über Technologie im Alltag sprechen

	I believe that (social media) is a positive / negative thing for teens because …	Ich denke, dass (soziale Medien) einen positiven / negativen Einfluss auf Jugendliche haben, weil …
	I often / sometimes / never / … use …	Ich nutze … oft / manchmal / nie / …
	Do you use …? Why (not)?	Nutzt du …? Warum (nicht)?
	I think one of the problems with … is that …	Ich denke, ein Problem von … ist, dass …
Unit 4	I think that picture A/B is real because …	Ich glaube, dass Bild A/B echt ist, weil …
	The colours / … look strange / ….	Die Farben sehen seltsam / … aus.
	The background / light / … (doesn't) look …	Der Hintergrund / Das Licht sieht (nicht) … aus.

7   Über Berufe und die Zukunft sprechen

Unit 3	I want to go to college / go travelling / get a job / do an apprenticeship …	Ich möchte studieren / reisen / arbeiten / eine Ausbildung machen …
	I'd like to live in another country / …	Ich möchte gerne in einem anderen Land / … leben.
	I hope I'll have lots of friends / learn how to drive / …	Ich hoffe ich werde viele Freunde haben / lernen Auto zu fahren / …
	Maybe I'll learn to speak other languages / …	Vielleicht werde ich eine andere Sprache lernen / …
	I probably won't live with my parents / have a car / …	Ich werde wahrscheinlich nicht bei meinen Eltern leben / kein Auto haben / …
	I'd like to work outside / …	Ich möchte gerne draußen / … arbeiten.
	I don't mind working (with) …	Es macht mir nichts aus, (mit) … zu arbeiten.
	I need regular hours.	Ich brauche regelmäßige Arbeitszeiten.
	I'd like a flexible job.	Ich hätte gerne einen flexiblen Arbeitsplatz.

8 Seine Meinung äußern, diskutieren und Verständnis zeigen

	I'm not really a fan of ...	Ich bin nicht wirklich ein Fan von ...
	For me that isn't true.	Für mich trifft das nicht zu.
	In my opinion, ...	Meiner Meinung nach, ...
	If you ask me, I'd say that ...	Wenn du mich fragst, würde ich sagen, dass ...
	I (completely) agree.	Ich stimme dir (voll und ganz) zu.
	Maybe, you're right.	Vielleicht hast du recht.
	That's a good point.	Das ist ein gutes Argument.
	I see it a bit differently.	Ich sehe das etwas anders.
	Just a minute, please.	Einen Moment, bitte.
Unit 3	I'm not sure I understood / got that.	Ich bin nicht sicher, ob ich das (richtig) verstanden habe.
	Right.	Stimmt.
	Really? That's interesting.	Wirklich? Das ist interessant.
	Uh-huh. Go on.	Erzähl mir mehr.
	So / Do you mean ...?	(Also) meinst du, dass ...?
	Tell me more about that.	Erzähl mir mehr darüber.
Unit 4	You have a point that ...	Du hast ein gutes Argument dafür, dass ... Da hast du recht, dass ...
	But can't you see that ...?	Aber erkennst du nicht, dass ...?
	The reason why I think that ...	Ich denke so, weil ...
	I hear what you're saying, but I still don't think ...	Ich verstehe, was du meinst, aber ich finde trotzdem nicht, dass ...

9 Ein Thema (und/oder ein Argument) präsentieren

Unit 1	Hi, everyone! Today I'd like to talk about ...	Hallo zusammen! Heute möchte ich über ... sprechen.
	First, I'd like to tell you ...	Zuerst möchte ich euch / Ihnen etwas über ... erzählen.
	Next, I'd like to talk about ...	Dann möchte ich über ... sprechen.
	Finally, I think that ...	Zuletzt / Abschließend finde ich, dass ...
	Thanks for listening.	Vielen Dank für eure / Ihre Aufmerksamkeit.
	Are there any questions?	Habt ihr / haben Sie noch Fragen?
	We should ... because ...	Wir sollten ..., weil ...
	... is a good idea because ...	... ist eine gute Idee, weil ...
	So you see, there are many reasons why ...	Wie du siehst, / Wie Sie sehen können, gibt es viele gute Gründe, warum ...
	Now you know lots of good reasons for ...	Jetzt kennst du / kennen Sie viele gute Gründe, die für ... sprechen.

Classroom English

You and your teacher	Du und deine Lehrerin / dein Lehrer
Good morning, Mr / Mrs / Ms … (bis 12 Uhr)	Guten Morgen, Herr / Frau …
Good afternoon, Mr / Mrs / Ms … (ab 12 Uhr)	Guten Tag / Nachmittag, Herr / Frau …
Sorry, I'm late.	Entschuldigung, dass ich zu spät komme.
Can I open / close the window, please?	Kann ich bitte das Fenster öffnen / zumachen?
Can I go to the toilet, please?	Kann ich bitte zur Toilette gehen?

Homework and exercises	Hausaufgaben und Übungen
Sorry, I don't have my exercise book.	Es tut mir leid, ich habe mein Heft nicht dabei.
I don't understand this exercise.	Ich verstehe die Übung nicht.
I can't do number 3.	Ich kann Nummer 3 nicht lösen.
Sorry, I haven't finished.	Entschuldigung, ich bin noch nicht fertig.
I have … Is that right too?	Ich habe … Ist das auch richtig?
Sorry, I don't know.	Es tut mir leid, das weiß ich nicht.
What's for homework?	Was haben wir (als Hausaufgabe) auf?

You need help	Du brauchst Hilfe
Can you help me, please?	Können Sie / Kannst du mir bitte helfen?
What page is it, please?	Auf welcher Seite sind wir / steht das?
What's … in English / German?	Was heißt … auf Englisch / Deutsch?
Can you speak more loudly, please?	Können Sie / Kannst du bitte lauter sprechen?
Can I say it in German, please?	Kann ich das auf Deutsch sagen, bitte?
Can you write it on the board, please?	Können Sie das bitte an die Tafel schreiben?
Can you say / play that again, please?	Können Sie das bitte noch einmal sagen / abspielen?

Work with a partner	Partnerarbeit
Can I work with Julian?	Kann ich mit Julian arbeiten?
Can I use your (pen), please?	Kann ich bitte deinen (Stift) benutzen?
Yes, here you are.	Hier, bitte.
It's my / your turn.	Ich bin dran. / Du bist dran.
Let's make / draw a / an …	Lass uns ein / eine / einen … machen / zeichnen.
Let's act out the story / the dialogue.	Lass uns die Geschichte / den Dialog spielen.

What your teacher says	Was deine Lehrerin / dein Lehrer sagt
Let's start.	Lasst uns anfangen. / Los geht's.
Listen, please. / Quiet, please.	Hört bitte zu. / Ruhe bitte.
Open your books at page 24, please.	Schlagt bitte Seite 24 auf.
Do exercise 5 for homework, please.	Macht bitte Übung 5 als Hausaufgabe.
Write the correct words.	Schreibt die richtigen Wörter (auf).
Correct the false sentences.	Korrigiert die falschen Sätze.
Where's your book, Dana?	Wo ist dein Buch, Dana?
Try again!	Versuche es noch einmal.
That's all for today. You can go now.	Das ist alles für heute. Ihr könnt jetzt gehen.

Content ☆☆☆

I enjoyed reading your article / blog / ...	
I enjoyed listening to your presentation / talk / ...	
The most interesting part was about ...	Try to make the introduction / the first part / ... more interesting by ...
You included all the points in the instructions.	Next time, remember to include the point about ...
You gave great reasons for your opinions.	Try to give reasons for your opinions.
You used charts to support your ideas.	Don't forget to use charts to support your ideas.

Structure ☆☆☆

Your article / presentation / ... was the right length.	Next time, you could write more / less.
Your title was interesting / made me want to read it.	Maybe you could find a more interesting title.
Your introduction presented the topic well.	Your introduction could present the topic better.
You structured your article / presentation / ... well.	Try to make the structure clearer.
Your conclusion summed up your article / blog / ... well.	Next time, remember to include a title / introduction / conclusion.
You remembered a greeting at the beginning / end of your letter / email.	Next time, remember to include a greeting at the beginning / end of your letter / email.

Media ☆☆☆

Your slides were clear and easy to read.	Next time, make the writing on your slides bigger.
I could see the pictures / charts very well.	You could make the pictures / charts bigger.
Your recording was easy to understand.	Maybe you could speak more clearly on your recording.
You included your sources.	Don't forget to include your sources.
You used Creative Commons photos – great!	Maybe you could use Creative Commons photos.
You used good audio-visual effects / music.	Next time, add audio-visual effects / music.
You pointed to your slides / poster / pictures.	Try and point to your slides while you are speaking.

Speaking and presentations ☆☆☆

You looked at the audience / your group.	Remember to look at the audience / your group.
You made eye contact.	Next time, don't forget to make eye contact.
You smiled and looked friendly.	Maybe you could smile more next time.
You spoke clearly.	Try and speak more clearly / more slowly.
You used phrases to buy time when you didn't know a word — well done!	Try and use phrases to buy time when you don't know a word.

Language ☆☆☆

You used lots of different phrases.	Next time, you could use more adverbs.
I understood most of what you wrote / said.	Remember to explain new words.
I didn't notice any / many mistakes.	Next time, use the present tense / the past tense. / Don't forget to use a spellchecker.
Your pronunciation sounded good.	You could check the pronunciation of words in the app / in an online dictionary.

Im *Vocabulary* findest du neue Wörter und Wendungen. Sie stehen in der Reihenfolge, in der sie im Buch vorkommen. Höre dir in der App jedes Wort genau an und sprich es nach.

Symbole und Abkürzungen

▶ p. 10 ▶ pp. 12/13	Die Seitenzahl in der linken Spalte zeigt dir, wo das Wort zum ersten Mal in diesem Buch vorkommt. *(p. = page, Seite; pp. = pages, Seiten)*
▶▶ **liberty**	Die doppelten Pfeile weisen auf ein Wort mit gleicher Bedeutung hin, das du bereits kennst.
certain ◀▶ uncertain	Das „Gegenteil"-Zeichen bedeutet: *certain* ist das Gegenteil von *uncertain*.
❗ *German:* ein **Symbol für** die Liebe – *English:* a **symbol of** love	Das ❗ bedeutet: Vorsicht, hier keinen Fehler machen!
separate – separately – (to) separate	In den Merkboxen findest du wichtige Hinweise zu den neuen Wörtern und Wendungen.

sb.	*= somebody / sth. = something*	*adj*	*= adjective* (Adjektiv)
infml.	*= informal* (informell, umgangssprachlich)	*adv*	*= adverb* (Adverb)
pl	*= plural* (Plural, Mehrzahlform)	*conj*	*= conjunction* (Konjunktion)
AE	= American English	*prep*	*= preposition* (Präposition)

Hinweise

- Tipps zum Vokabellernen findest du im **Skills file** auf den Seiten 144–145.
- Seite 179 enthält eine Übersicht über die **Lautschriftzeichen**, Seite 253 über die **Zahlen**.
- Die **Wordbanks** (S. 180–184) bieten dir nach wichtigen Themen gesammelte Stichwörter.
- **Let's talk** (S. 185–190) enthält Wendungen für wichtige Situationen, gefolgt von einer Seite **Feedback phrases** (S. 191).
- Im **Dictionary** (S. 226–252) kannst du englische und deutsche Wörter nachschlagen.
- Eine **Liste mit unregelmäßigen Verben** findest du auf den Seiten 254–256, und eine Übersicht über **Continents, countries and regions** auf den Seiten 256–257.
- Englische Wörter, die Wörtern im Deutschen ähnlich sind, findest du auf S. 258.

🔊 Welcome to the USA

▶ pp. 10/11	**alligator** ['ælɪɡeɪtə]	der Alligator	

an **alligator**

❗ Betonung auf der 1. Silbe:
alligator ['ælɪɡeɪtə]

state [steɪt]	der (Bundes-)Staat

❗ state =
1. der (Bundes-)Staat – How many **states** does the USA have?
2. der Zustand – The old house was in a terrible **state**.

(to) **connect (to / with)** [kəˈnekt]	(sich) verbinden (mit)

- The bridge **connects** the two parts of the city. (verbinden)
- My smartwatch can **connect** to my phone. (sich verbinden)
- Your computer **isn't connected to** the internet. = ... ist nicht mit ... verbunden.

verb: (to) **connect** –
noun: **connection** [kəˈnekʃn] (die Verbindung) Something is wrong with our internet **connection** this morning. The train **connections** to the city centre are good.

▶ pp. 12/13	(to) **lead** [liːd], **led, led** [led]	führen, leiten

verb: (to) **lead, led, led** –
noun: (person) **leader** (der/die Leiter/in; der/die (Staats-)Chef/in; der/die (An-)Führer/in)

president ['prezɪdənt]	der Präsident, die Präsidentin

❗ Betonung auf der 1. Silbe:
president ['prezɪdənt]

dollar ($) ['dɒlə]	der Dollar

In the USA you pay with **dollars** and cents.
❗ German: **zehn Dollar** –
English: **ten dollars**

times [taɪmz]	mal

Six **times** three is eighteen.

symbol ['sɪmbl]	das Symbol

❗ German: Die Farbe Rot ist ein **Symbol für** die Liebe.
English: The colour red is a **symbol of** love.
❗ Betonung auf der 1. Silbe: **symbol** ['sɪmbl]

candy (AE) ['kændi]	die Süßigkeiten

▶▶ BE **sweets**

▶ pp. 14/15	**camp** [kæmp]	das (Zelt-)Lager

summer camp = das Ferienlager (im Sommer)

age [eɪdʒ]	das Alter; das Zeitalter

people of all ages = Menschen aller Altersgruppen
❗ German: **im Alter von 12 Jahren** –
English: **at the age of 12**

counsellor ['kaʊnsələ]	der Berater, die Beraterin; der Betreuer, die Betreuerin

The school **counsellor** will help you if you have problems.
❗ AE spelling: **counselor**

🔊 Unit 1 NYC: The world in a city

▶ pp. 16/17	**liberty** [ˈlɪbəti]	die Freiheit	the state of being free to live as you choose
	union [ˈjuːniən]	die Union; die Vereinigung, der Verband; die Gewerkschaft	When I became a teacher I joined the teachers' **union**.
	(to) **prefer** sth. **to** sth. [prɪˈfɜː]	etwas einer Sache vorziehen, etwas lieber tun / haben als etwas	• I **prefer** juice **to** cola. (= I like juice better than cola.) • What about a nice sandwich? – Well, I'**d prefer** (= I **would prefer**) a fruit salad. (Ich würde ... vorziehen.) ❗ *Simple past* und *-ing form* mit **-rr-**: **prefer̲red, prefer̲ring**

Topic 1

▶ p. 18	**out and about** [aʊt ənd əˈbaʊt]	unterwegs	When I'm in London, I'm **out and about** all the time. There's so much to do!
	accent [ˈæksent]	der Akzent	❗ Betonung auf der 1. Silbe: **a̲ccent** [ˈæksent]
	(to) **be / feel homesick (for)** [ˈhəʊmsɪk]	Heimweh haben (nach)	When I'm away from home, I **feel homesick for** my family and my friends.
	trade (in) [treɪd]	der Handel (mit)	nouns: **trade**; *(person)* **trader** verb: (to) **trade (in)** (handeln, Handel treiben (mit)) • She has her own business and **trades in** e-bikes. • Her **trade in** e-bikes is going well.
	ferry	die Fähre	

the Staten Island Ferry

Mit bestimmtem Artikel *the*:		Ohne bestimmten Artikel:	

the 9/11 Memorial
the Bronx
the Brooklyn Bridge
  (❗ *aber:* **Brooklyn**)
the Empire State Building
the High Line
	the Staten Island Ferry
	  (❗ *aber:* **Staten Island**)
	the Statue of Liberty
	  (❗ *aber:* **Liberty Island**)
	the West Village
		Brooklyn
		Central Park
		Koreatown
		Manhattan
		New York City
		One World Trade Center
			Queens
			Staten Island
			Times Square
			Union Square
			Washington Square Park
			Yankee Stadium

▶ p. 19	**local** [ˈləʊkl]	der/die Einheimische, der Einwohner, die Einwohnerin *(eines Ortes)*	**a local of New York** *or* **a New York local** = ein/e Einwohner/in von New York noun: **local** – The best restaurants in this town? Let's ask the **locals**. adj: **local** (einheimisch, am/vom Ort) – Do your friends go to the **local** school? (Gehen ... hier im Ort zur Schule?)
	awesome *(AE infml)* [ˈɔːsəm]	klasse, stark, großartig	▶▶ super, great
	immigrant [ˈɪmɪgrənt]	der Einwanderer, die Einwanderin	❗ Betonung auf der 1. Silbe: **i̲mmigrant** [ˈɪmɪgrənt]

immigration – emigration

- (to) **immigrate** [ˈɪmɪgreɪt] einwandern
  immigration [ɪmɪˈgreɪʃn] die Einwanderung
  immigrant [ˈɪmɪgrənt] der Einwanderer, die Einwanderin

- (to) **emigrate** [ˈemɪgreɪt] auswandern
  emigration [emɪˈgreɪʃn] die Auswanderung
  emigrant [ˈemɪgrənt] der Auswanderer, die Auswanderin

freedom [ˈfriːdəm]	die Freiheit	▶▶ **liberty** noun: **freedom** – adj: **free**
ride [raɪd]	die Fahrt; das Fahrgeschäft *(auf Volksfesten, in Vergnügungsparks)*	I don't want to go on that **ride**. It'll make me feel sick. noun: **ride** – verb: (to) **ride, rode, ridden**

Topic 2

▶ p. 20 **diverse** [daɪˈvɜːs] unterschiedlich, vielfältig adj: **diverse** – noun: **diversity** (die Vielfalt) Many people from different countries live in London. The community is very **diverse**. I love the **diversity** of the community there.

chart [tʃɑːt] das Diagramm; die Tabelle

charts

separate [ˈseprət] getrennt, separat

separate – separately – (to) separate

adj: **separate** [ˈseprət]	The library has a **separate** room for children's books.	getrennt, separat
adv: **separately** [ˈseprətli]	They didn't drive there together (= in the same car), they drove there **separately** (= in different cars).	getrennt
verb: (to) **separate** [ˈsepəreɪt]	It's not right to **separate** children from their parents.	trennen

comma [ˈkɒmə] das Komma

1.6 (one point six) 1,6 (eins Komma sechs) ❗ Im Englischen steht bei Zahlen ein **Punkt**, im Deutschen ein **Komma**: *English:* 1.6 = one **point** six – *German:* 1,6 = eins **Komma** sechs ❗ **point** = 1. der Punkt; 2. das Komma *(Dezimalzeichen)*

▶ p. 21 **certain** [ˈsɜːtn] bestimmt; gewiss; sicher adj: **certain** –
- Try to learn a **certain** number of new words each week. (bestimmte)
- A **certain** Mr Fox phoned. (gewisser)
- Are you **certain**? (= Are you sure?) (sicher)

adv: **certainly** – **Certainly** this is a good idea. **certain** ◀▶ **uncertain** (unsicher) If you're **uncertain**, don't do it.

(back) then [ðen] damals My grandma was born in 1952. Life was a lot slower **(back) then**, she says. ❗ **then** = 1. dann, danach; 2. damals

You know what, ...	Weißt du was, ...	**You know what?** Let's do it this way. (to) **know, knew, known**
equal [ˈiːkwəl]	gleich(berechtigt)	**equal** ◄ ► **unequal** [ʌnˈiːkwəl] (ungleich)
opportunity [ɒpəˈtjuːnəti]	die Gelegenheit, die Möglichkeit, die Chance	► ► **chance** If you get the **opportunity** to see this band live, you must go to their concert!
grandchild [ˈɡræntʃaɪld], *pl* **grandchildren** [ˈɡræntʃɪldrən]	der Enkel, die Enkelin	Donna is my grandma. I'm her **grandchild**.
university [juːnɪˈvɜːsəti]	die Universität	She studied medicine at **university** and became a doctor. ❗ Betonung auf der 3. Silbe: **university** [juːnɪˈvɜːsəti]
challenge [ˈtʃælɪndʒ]	die Herausforderung	

challenge – challenging – (to) challenge

- noun: **challenge** – It is a **challenge** to learn a new language.
  (to) **take on a challenge** = eine Herausforderung annehmen, sich einer Herausforderung stellen
- adj: **challenging** – Learning a new language can be **challenging**.   anspruchsvoll, (heraus)fordernd
- verb: (to) **challenge sb. (to)** – They **challenged** us **to** a football match.   jn. herausfordern

mouth [maʊθ]	der Mund; *(bei Tieren)* das Maul	a **mouth**
► p. 22 **restroom** *(AE)* [ˈrestruːm]	die Toilette *(in öffentlichen Gebäuden)*	❗ In *American English* wird die Toilette in öffentlichen Gebäuden (Restaurants, Theatern, ...) als **restroom** bezeichnet. In privaten Häusern/Wohnungen heißt es **bathroom**.

American English: andere Wörter

British English	American English	
rucksack	backpack	der Rucksack
biscuit	cookie	der Keks, das Plätzchen
chips	French fries	die Pommes frites
mum	mom	die Mama, die Mutti
film	movie	der Film
cinema	movie theater	das Kino
trousers	pants	die Hose
trainers	sneakers	die Sportschuhe
shop	store	der Laden, das Geschäft
underground	subway	die U-Bahn
rubbish	trash	der Müll
holiday(s)	vacation	der Urlaub

► p. 23 **professional** [prəˈfeʃənl]	professionell, Profi-	adj: **professional** – noun: **professional**, *infml auch:* **pro** (der Fachmann, die Fachfrau, der Profi)
(to) speak: **I've spoken** [ˈspəʊkən]	sprechen: ich habe gesprochen	I **have**n't **spoken** to Lee for a long time.

(to) **perform** [pəˈfɔːm]	auftreten *(Künstler/in)*; aufführen	The band first **performed** in the USA in 2014. **Perform** the scene / dialogue for your class.
war [wɔː]	der Krieg	**the First World War** (*or:* **World War I**) = der Erste Weltkrieg **the Second World War** (*or:* **World War II**) = der Zweite Weltkrieg
... as well as ... [əz ˈwel əz]	sowohl ... als auch ...	**!** **as well** = auch **as well as** = sowohl ... als auch I have a bike **as well as** a car. = I have a bike, and I have a car **as well**.
association [əsəʊʃiˈeɪʃn]	der Verband, die Vereinigung	an official group of people who have joined together for special reasons, for example teams who play a sport (football, basketball)
sexist [ˈseksɪst]	sexistisch *(diskriminierend aufgrund des Geschlechts)*	adj: **sexist** – nouns: *(person)* **sexist** (der/die Sexist/in); **sexism** (der Sexismus) • What he said about women was **sexist**. • I didn't know he was a **sexist**, actually! • We must try to stop **sexism**.
male [meɪl]	männlich; der Mann	**male** ◄ ► **female**
female [ˈfiːmeɪl]	weiblich; die Frau	*(nouns)* Our team has **males** and **females**. *(adj)* Our team has **male** and **female** players.

Topic 3

► p. 24	**probably** [ˈprɒbəbli]	wahrscheinlich	You're **probably** right. = I'm sure you're right.
	soccer [ˈsɒkə]	der Fußball	► ► *BE* **football** **!** In den USA ist mit **football** immer **American football** gemeint. Wenn man über Fußball spricht, verwendet man **soccer**.
	court [kɔːt]	der Platz, der Court *(Tennis, Basketball)*	 a tennis **court**
	marathon [ˈmærəθən]	der Marathon(lauf)	a competition where you run about 42 km
	one day	eines Tages	► ► **some day** I hope **one day / some day** all wars will stop.
► p. 25	(to) **recommend** sth. **(to sb.)** [rekəˈmend]	*(jm.)* etwas empfehlen	verb: (to) **recommend** – Can you **recommend** a good bike shop? noun: **recommendation** [rekəmənˈdeɪʃn] – I'm looking for a good bike shop. Can you make a **recommendation**? (die Empfehlung)
	commercial [kəˈmɜːʃl]	der Werbespot	an advert on TV, on the radio or on a website noun: **commercial** – adj: **commercial** (kommerziell *(auf Gewinn ausgerichtet)*)

wing [wɪŋ]	der Flügel	

chicken wings

(potato) chips *(pl) (AE)* [tʃɪps]	die (Kartoffel-)Chips	= *BE* **(potato) crisps** *(pl)* [krɪsps]

> **'Pommes frites' and 'Kartoffelchips'**
>
> ❗ Nicht verwechseln: *German:* **Pommes frites** = *British English:* **chips**
> *American English:* **French fries**
>
> *German:* **(Kartoffel-)Chips** = *British English:* **crisps**
> *American English:* **chips**

▶ p. 26 (to) **run, ran, run**	fahren, verkehren *(Bus, Bahn)*	The New York subway **runs** all day. ❗ (to) **run** = **1.** rennen, laufen; **2.** fahren, verkehren *(Bus, Bahn)*
(to) **refer to** [rɪˈfɜː]	sich beziehen auf, Bezug nehmen auf	The following question **refers to** line 25. ❗ **-rr-** bei *simple past* und *-ing-form*: **referred, referring** (to) **refer to** sth. **by** its name / number = etwas mit seinem Namen / seiner Nummer bezeichnen
▶ p. 27 **exit** [ˈeksɪt]	der Ausgang; die Ausfahrt	noun: **exit** – Where are the fire **exits**? **fire exit** = der Notausgang verb: (to) **exit** – Where can we **exit** this hall? (aussteigen; hinausgehen, (einen Ort) verlassen)
situation [sɪtʃuˈeɪʃn]	die Situation	❗ Betonung auf der 3. Silbe: **situation** [sɪtʃuˈeɪʃn]
seat [siːt]	der (Sitz-)Platz	noun: **seat** – verbs: (to) **sit** / (to) **sit down** ❗ False friends: (to) **take a seat** = Platz nehmen (to) **take place** = stattfinden

Story

▶ p. 28 (to) **fall asleep**: **he has fallen asleep** [ˈfɔːlən]	einschlafen: er ist eingeschlafen	Quiet please! The baby **has** finally **fallen asleep**!
(to) **sigh** [saɪ]	seufzen	verb: (to) **sigh** – 'OK,' she **sighed**. noun: **sigh** (der Seufzer) – 'OK,' she said with a **sigh**.
(to) **shrug** [ʃrʌg]	mit den Achseln / Schultern zucken	She **shrugged** and said, 'I don't know.'
(to) **mean**: **I meant** [ment], **I've meant**	meinen: ich meinte, ich habe gemeint	• What I **meant** was: don't be so shy! • I've never **meant** to hurt you. (Es ist nie meine Absicht gewesen, …)

(shopping) mall [mɔːl]	das Einkaufszentrum	►► *BE* **shopping centre**
part-time [paːt ˈtaɪm]	Teilzeit-, Halbtags-	**part-time ◄ ► full-time** [fʊl ˈtaɪm] He has a **part-time** job. = He works **part-time**. She has a **full-time** job. = She works **full-time**.
(to) skip [skɪp]	überspringen, auslassen	I **skipped** the first pages. They were not very interesting. (= I didn't read the first pages.)
rent [rɛnt]	die Miete	noun: **rent** – The **rent** for the flat is very high. verb: (to) **rent** – I can't **rent** this flat, it's too expensive. (mieten, leihen)
I think so.	Ich glaube/denke ja.	

I think so. / I hope so. / ...
- **Are they at home? – I think so. / I hope so.**   Ich glaube/denke ja. / Das hoffe ich.
- **Is that correct? – I don't think so.**   Ich glaube nicht. / Das glaube/denke ich nicht.
- **Is she going to be at home? – She said so.**   Das hat sie (jedenfalls) gesagt.
- **Do you like the story? If so, say why.**   Wenn ja, ...

jewelry *(AE)* [ˈdʒuːəlri]	der Schmuck	**❗** *BE* spelling: **jewellery** I have a little box for my rings and other **jewellery** *(BE)* / **jewelry** *(AE)*.

American English: Schreibweise und Aussprache

Schreibweise

BE: -tre	**AE: -ter**
cen**tre**	cen**ter**
(kilo)me**tre**	(kilo)me**ter**
thea**tre**	thea**ter**

BE: -our	**AE: -or**
col**our**	col**or**
favo**ur**ite	favo**r**ite
neighb**our**(hood)	neighb**or**(hood)

BE: -ll-	**AE: -l-**
counse**ll**or	counse**l**or
jewe**ll**ery	jewe**l**ry
trave**ll**ed, trave**ll**ing	trave**l**ed, trave**l**ing

Aussprache

	BE: [ɑː]	**AE:** [æ]
ask	[ɑːsk]	[æsk]
can't	[kɑːnt]	[kænt]
plant	[plɑːnt]	[plænt]

	BE: [juː]	**AE:** [uː]
new	[njuː]	[nuː]
student	[ˈstjuːdnt]	[ˈstuːdnt]
Tuesday	[ˈtjuːzdeɪ]	[ˈtuːzdeɪ]

	BE: [ɒ]	**AE:** [ɑː]
body	[ˈbɒdi]	[ˈbɑːdi]
clock	[klɒk]	[klɑːk]
hot	[hɒt]	[hɑːt]

- In *American English* wird das **r** in Wörtern wie **here, more, sure, shirt, farm, hard, better** meist hörbar ausgesprochen.

- In *American English* klingt das **t** zwischen zwei Vokalen oft wie ein **d**: **city** [ˈsɪdi], **better** [ˈbedər], **writer** [ˈraɪdər].

►p. 29 **brochure** [ˈbrəʊʃə]	die Broschüre, der Prospekt	

 a **brochure**

❗ Betonung auf der 1. Silbe: **bro**chure [ˈbrəʊʃə]

insecure [ɪnsɪˈkjʊə]	ungesichert, unsicher	**insecure ◄ ► 1. secure** (gesichert, sicher); **2. confident** • The stairs looked very **insecure**. (= not safe, not secure) • He often felt nervous and **insecure** in class. (= not confident) **a food-insecure family** = eine Familie, die von Nahrungsmittelunsicherheit betroffen ist *(die zeitweise nicht genug zu essen hat)*

diaper [ˈdaɪəpə]	die Windel	

a baby with **diapers**

I used to come here ... [ˈjuːst tə]	Ich kam (früher) immer ... hierher.	I **used to do** a lot of sport when I was young. (= In the past, I always did a lot of sport ...)
shoulder [ˈʃəʊldə]	die Schulter	

child sitting on dad's **shoulders**

grateful (to sb.) [ˈgreɪtfl]	(jm.) dankbar	Thanks for helping me! I'm so **grateful to** you.

Viewing

▶ p. 31	creator [kriˈeɪtə]	der Autor / Zeichner, die Autorin/ Zeichnerin; der Schöpfer, die Schöpferin	verb: (to) **create** noun: (person) **creator** adj: **creative**

Study skills

▶ p. 32	(to) **brainstorm** (ideas / reasons) [ˈbreɪnstɔːm]	(Ideen / Gründe) (ungeordnet) sammeln	(to) collect ideas / reasons in a group Let's **brainstorm** ideas for our presentation.
	(to) **focus (on)** [ˈfəʊkəs]	sich konzentrieren (auf)	verb: (to) **focus** – The article **focuses on** how young people become victims of racism. noun: **focus (on)** – Its **focus** is **on** students' experiences with racism in schools. (der Mittelpunkt, der Hauptpunkt, der Schwerpunkt)
	harbour [ˈhɑːbə]	der Hafen	! AE spelling: **harbor**

The linking r
Normalerweise sprichst du den 'r'-Sound am Ende eines Wortes im BE nicht aus, z. B. *harbour*. Du solltest das 'r' jedoch aussprechen, wenn das darauf folgende Wort mit einem Vokal beginnt, damit die Wörter besser fließen, z. B.: *This harbour is very big.* Im AE sprichst Du das 'r' am Wortende immer mit aus: *harbor* [ˈhɑːrbər]; ebenso z. B. bei: *center, color, theater, ...*

(to) enter [ˈentə]	eintreten, betreten; einreisen (in ein Land)	

DO NOT ENTER

the public [ˈpʌblɪk]	die Öffentlichkeit	**in public** = in der / in aller Öffentlichkeit noun: **the public** – adj: **public**

Unit task

▶ p. 33	**introduction** [ɪntrəˈdʌkʃn]	die Einführung, die Einleitung	the first part of a presentation, a text or a book where you tell people what you want to talk / write about
	conclusion [kɒnˈkluːʒn]	der Schluss; die Schlussfolgerung	Your text should have an introduction, a middle part and a **conclusion**. Which **conclusions** do you come to when you see these facts?
	..., you see.	..., weißt du. / ... nämlich ...	So this problem is more difficult to solve than you would think, **you see**.

Irregular verbs

Infinitive	Simple past	Past participle		Infinitive	Simple past	Past participle	
(to) **become**	became	become	werden	(to) **know**	knew	known	kennen, wissen
(to) **begin**	began	begun	anfangen, beginnen	(to) **lead** [iː]	led [e]	led [e]	führen, leiten
				(to) **mean** [iː]	meant [e]	meant [e]	bedeuten; meinen
(to) **bring**	brought	brought	(mit)bringen	(to) **pay**	paid	paid	(be)zahlen
(to) **catch**	caught	caught	fangen; erwischen; nehmen (Zug, Bus)	(to) **put**	put	put	(etwas wohin) tun, legen, stellen
(to) **cost**	cost	cost	kosten	(to) **run**	ran	run	rennen
(to) **cut**	cut	cut	schneiden	(to) **say**	said	said	sagen
(to) **draw**	drew	drawn	zeichnen	(to) **set**	set	set	stellen, legen, setzen
(to) **drink**	drank	drunk	trinken				
(to) **fall**	fell	fallen	(hin)fallen	(to) **show**	showed	shown	zeigen
(to) **fight**	fought	fought	(be)kämpfen	(to) **speak**	spoke	spoken	sprechen
(to) **fly**	flew	flown	fliegen	(to) **tell**	told	told	erzählen, sagen

Unit 2 The South-East: Changing times

| ▶ pp. 46/47 | **theme** [θiːm] | das Thema | **theme park** = der Themenpark (Freizeitpark mit Attraktionen zu einem bestimmten Thema) |
| | **tram** [træm] | die Straßenbahn |
a tram |
	slavery [ˈsleɪvəri]	die Sklaverei	Many Black people in the US lived in **slavery** in the 1800s.
	drummer [ˈdrʌmə]	der Trommler/Schlagzeuger, die Trommlerin/Schlagzeugerin	a **drum** = eine Trommel **drums** (pl) = das Schlagzeug
	(to) **abandon** sb./sth. [əˈbændən]	jn. verlassen (im Stich lassen); etwas verlassen, etwas aufgeben (zurücklassen; leer stehen lassen)	(to) **abandon** a child / a dog (to) **abandon** a car / a building **an abandoned building** = ein verlassenes Gebäude

Topic 1

▶ p. 48	**everyday** [ˈevrɪdeɪ]	alltäglich, Alltags-	**everyday life** = der Alltag
	security [sɪˈkjʊərəti]	die Sicherheit	This is a **security** check. Would you please open your bags? **security guard** = der/die Sicherheits-bedienstete
	another [əˈnʌðə]	ein/e andere/r/s; noch ein/e	• I don't like this game. Can't we play **another** game? (= a different game?) • Do you really want to buy **another** bag? You have so many! (= a new, an extra bag)
▶ p. 49	**you needn't do it** [ˈniːdnt]	du musst es nicht tun; du brauchst es nicht zu tun	I can do the exercise. You **needn't** help me. (= You don't have to help me.) **!** Nicht verwechseln: You **needn't** help him. = … musst nicht … You **mustn't** help him. = … darfst nicht …
	(to) be able to do sth. [ˈeɪbl]	etwas tun können, in der Lage sein, etwas zu tun	We **weren't able to** get tickets. = We couldn't get tickets.
	(to) treat sb. [triːt]	jn. behandeln	Don't fight! We should **treat** each other with respect.
	they **may** treat … [meɪ]	sie behandeln … vielleicht …; sie können … behandeln …	This **may** not be a good idea. (… ist vielleicht keine gute Idee.)
	receipt [rɪˈsiːt]	der (Kauf-)Beleg, die Quittung, der Kassenzettel	**!** False friends: **receipt** = Beleg, Quittung, Kassenzettel **recipe** = (Koch-)Rezept
	(to) steal [stiːl], **stole** [stəʊl], **stolen** [ˈstəʊlən]	stehlen, rauben	I didn't lose my phone. I'm sure someone **stole** it **from** me. (… hat es **mir** gestohlen.)
	you **might** feel … [maɪt]	du könntest dich … fühlen, vielleicht fühlst du dich …	That **might** be true, but I'm not sure. You **might** hate school, but you learn useful things there.

Topic 2

▶ p. 50	**slave** [sleɪv]	der Sklave, die Sklavin	• Many people from Africa had to work for American farmers. The farmers had bought them as **slaves**. • They lived in **slavery**. = They were **slaves**.
	(to) enslave sb. [ɪnˈsleɪv]	jn. versklaven	**(to)** make sb. a slave **enslaved Africans** = die versklavten Afrikaner/innen
	the 1600s (the sixteen hundreds) [ˈhʌndrədz]	das 17. Jahrhundert	**the 90s (nineties)** = die Neunzigerjahre
	injustice [ɪnˈdʒʌstɪs]	die Ungerechtigkeit; das Unrecht	**injustice** ◀ ▶ **justice** [ˈdʒʌstɪs] (die Gerechtigkeit)

(to) **escape (from)** [ɪˈskeɪp]	entkommen (aus), fliehen (vor/aus)	verb: (to) **escape (from)** – She **escaped from** slavery. noun: **escape (from)** – After her **escape from** slavery, she tried to help other slaves. (die Flucht (aus/vor))
law [lɔː]	das Gesetz; Jura *(Studium)*	• The **law** says that you have to be 17 or older to drive a car in this country. • After school he started studying **law**.
(to) **vote (on** sth.**)** [vəʊt]	wählen; abstimmen (über etwas)	verb: (to) **vote (on** sth.**)** – noun: **vote** (die Abstimmung, das Votum) • (to) **vote for** sb./sth. = für jn./etwas stimmen • (to) **have a vote (on** sth.**)** = abstimmen (über etwas)
segregation [segrɪˈgeɪʃn]	die Trennung *(nach Hautfarbe/ Religion/Geschlecht)*	Until the 1960s there was **segregation** in schools. Black and white children couldn't learn together.
(to) **continue** [kənˈtɪnjuː]	fortfahren, weitermachen; (sich) fortsetzen, weitergehen	• Let's stop now and **continue** later. / … and **continue to write** our presentation later. • (to) **continue to do** sth. = etwas weiterhin tun, (mit) etwas weitermachen, fortfahren
speech [spiːtʃ]	die Rede, die Ansprache; die Sprache	• nouns: **speech**; *(person)* **speaker** (der/die Sprecher/in) • verb: (to) **speak** **She's giving a speech.**
peaceful [ˈpiːsfl]	friedlich; friedfertig	adj: **peaceful** noun: **peace** (der Friede(n)) – Will there ever be **peace** in the world?
violent [ˈvaɪələnt]	gewalttätig; gewaltsam	adj: **violent** noun: **violence** [ˈvaɪələns] (die Gewalt; die Gewalttätigkeit) **Violence** or **violent** protests won't save the world.
▶ p. 51 **army** [ˈɑːmi]	die Armee	(to) **join the army** = zur Armee gehen ❗ Betonung auf der 1. Silbe: **army** [ˈɑːmi]
▶ p. 52 **athlete** [ˈæθliːt]	der (Leicht-)Athlet, die (Leicht-) Athletin; der Sportler, die Sportlerin	❗ Betonung auf der 1. Silbe: **athlete** [ˈæθliːt]
behaviour [bɪˈheɪvjə]	das Verhalten; das Benehmen	These animals show a strange **behaviour**. ❗ *AE* spelling: **behavior**
(to) **speak out** [spiːk ˈaʊt]	(deutlich) seine Meinung sagen, seine Stimme erheben	If you think this is wrong, **speak out** against it!
league [liːg]	die Liga *(Sport)*	a group of sports teams who all play against each other to find out which team is best
(to) **kneel** [niːl], **knelt, knelt** [nelt]	knien	❗ Wie bei **knife, knock, know** wird das „k" von **kneel** nicht gesprochen. Die Aussprache beginnt mit dem Laut [n].

national anthem [ˈnæʃnəl ˈænθəm]	die Nationalhymne	Football players sing the **national anthem** before their games.
award [əˈwɔːd]	der Preis *(Auszeichnung)*	**award-winning** = preisgekrönt **award-winner** = der Preisträger, die Preisträgerin
▶ p. 53 (to) **matter** [ˈmætə]	von Bedeutung sein, wichtig sein	Does it really **matter** which team wins? – No, **it doesn't matter.** (Es/Das ist egal.)
shocked [ʃɒkt]	schockiert	adj: **shocked** (schockiert); **shocking** (schockierend) – verb: (to) **shock** sb. (jn. schockieren) – noun: **shock** (der Schock)
since 2013 [sɪns]	seit 2013	It has been very cold **since** January. (seit)
(to) **sign** sth. [saɪn]	etwas unterschreiben	If you're against something, one way to show your opinion is to **sign** a **petition**.
petition [pəˈtɪʃn]	der Antrag, die Petition *(Unterschriftensammlung)*	❗ **sign** = 1. *(noun)* das Schild, das Zeichen; 2. *(verb)* unterschreiben
discrimination (against) [dɪskrɪmɪˈneɪʃn]	die Diskriminierung (von)	noun: **discrimination (against)** – verb: (to) **discriminate against** sb. [dɪˈskrɪmɪneɪt] (jn. diskriminieren) ❗ *German:* **Diskriminierung von** Frauen/ Schwarzen *English:* **discrimination against** women/Black people

---

Verbs and nouns: *-tion, -ation*

Die Endungen **-tion** bzw. **-ation** werden verwendet, um Nomen aus Verben zu bilden. Beispiele:

(to) **celebrate**	**celebration** (die Feier, das Fest)	(to) **immigrate**	**immigration** (die Einwanderung)
(to) **collect**	**collection** (die Sammlung)		
(to) **connect**	**connection** (die Verbindung)	(to) **organize**	**organization** (die Organisation)
(to) **decorate** sth.	**decoration** (die Dekoration, der Schmuck, die Verzierung)	(to) **prepare (for)**	**preparation** (die Vorbereitung; die Zubereitung)
(to) **discriminate against** sb.	**discrimination (against)** (die Diskriminierung)	(to) **present** sth. **to** sb.	**presentation** (die Präsentation, das Referat)
(to) **explain** sth. **to** sb.	**explanation** (die Erklärung)	(to) **recommend**	**recommendation** (die Empfehlung)

Topic 3

▶ p. 54 (to) **roll** [rəʊl]	rollen	verb: (to) **roll** – noun: **roll** = **1.** die Rolle; **2.** das Brötchen **rolls** **Let the good times roll.** = Genieß(t) das Leben! / Lass(t) es krachen!
Mardi Gras [mɑːdi ˈɡrɑː]	der Faschingsdienstag *(auch: die Karnevalsfeiern in New Orleans)*	
(to) **build** [bɪld], **built, built** [bɪlt]	bauen	verb: (to) **build, built, built** – noun: **building**

float [fləʊt]	der Festwagen (*z. B. beim Karnevalsumzug*)	 a **float**
cup [kʌp]	die Tasse	a **cup of** tea
extreme [ɪkˈstriːm]	extrem	adj: **extreme** – We had **extreme** weather last summer. adv: **extremely** – It was **extremely** hot. noun: **extreme** (das Extrem) – The weather went from one **extreme** to the other: first it was sunny and hot, then it was cold and rainy.
▶ p. 55 **hole** [həʊl]	das Loch	There's a **hole** in this T-shirt.
(to) **be made of** [ˈmeɪd əv]	bestehen aus, (hergestellt) sein aus	I try not to use bags which **are made of** plastic.
corn [kɔːn]	(BE) das Korn, das Getreide; (AE) der Mais	**cornbread** = das Maisbrot
spoon [spuːn]	der Löffel	 **knife**, *pl* **knives** = das Messer **fork** = die Gabel **tablespoon** = der Esslöffel **teaspoon** = der Teelöffel
▶ p. 56 **instrument** [ˈɪnstrəmənt]	das Instrument	**musical instrument** = das Musikinstrument ❗ Betonung auf der 1. Silbe: **instrument** [ˈɪnstrəmənt]
trumpet [ˈtrʌmpɪt]	die Trompete	 a **trumpet**
culture [ˈkʌltʃə]	die Kultur	❗ Betonung auf der 1. Silbe: **culture** [ˈkʌltʃə] noun: **culture** – adj: **cultural** [ˈkʌltʃərəl] (kulturell, Kultur-)
funeral [ˈfjuːnərəl]	die Beerdigung, das Begräbnis	Mr Miller died last week. The **funeral** will be tomorrow.
the only music [ˈəʊnli]	die einzige Musik	❗ **only** = **1.** nur, bloß; erst – Don't be scared, it's **only** a little mouse! **2.** (der/die/das) einzige – Betty is **the only** British student at our school.

mostly [ˈməʊstli]	hauptsächlich	▶▶ **mainly** Our band plays lots of different music, but **mostly/mainly** old pop songs.
▶ p. 57 **violin** [vaɪəˈlɪn]	die Geige, die Violine	 a **violin**
electric [ɪˈlektrɪk]	elektrisch, Elektro-	I play the **electric** guitar in our band.
rhythm [ˈrɪðəm]	der Rhythmus	The band was super, and everyone danced to the **rhythm** of their music.

Story

▶ p. 58 **hurricane** [ˈhʌrɪkən]	der Hurrikan, der Orkan	a bad storm with very strong winds
flood [flʌd]	die Überschwemmung, das Hochwasser; die Flut	noun: **flood** – There was a **flood** in our town. verb: (to) **flood** (überfluten, überschwemmen) – Many streets **were flooded**. (… standen unter Wasser)
hail [heɪl]	der Hagel	We ran inside when a bad **hail** shower started.
storm [stɔːm]	der Sturm; das Gewitter	noun: **storm** – adj: **stormy** (stürmisch)
thunder [ˈθʌndə]	der Donner	 **lightning** **thunderstorm** (das Gewitter)
lightning *(no pl)* [ˈlaɪtnɪŋ]	der Blitz / die Blitze *(bei Gewitter)*	
tornado [tɔːˈneɪdəʊ]	der Tornado *(Wirbelsturm)*	❗ Aussprache: **tornado** [tɔːˈneɪdəʊ]
sky [skaɪ]	der Himmel	❗ *German:* **am** Himmel – *English:* **in** the sky
strange [streɪndʒ]	seltsam, sonderbar	adj: **strange** – What a **strange** question! I don't know what to say. noun: **stranger** (der/die Fremde) – I don't like to talk to **strangers**.
(to) **gather** [ˈgæðə]	sammeln; (sich) versammeln; *(Sturm)* aufziehen, sich zusammenbrauen	• When you do research, you **gather** information. (sammeln) • Lots of people **gathered** when the film stars arrived. (sich versammeln) • We went inside when dark clouds started to **gather**. (aufziehen)

warning (about/against/of) ['wɔːnɪŋ]	die Warnung (vor)	noun: **warning (about/against/of)** – We got a **warning of/about** strong winds. verb: (to) **warn** sb. **(about/of** sth.**)** – They **warned** us **of/about** strong winds. **❗** *German:* Sie **warnten mich davor, dort hinzugehen**. *English:* They **warned me not** to go **there**.
(to) **be over** ['əʊvə]	vorbei sein, zu Ende sein	School **is over**. The kids are going home.

over

• **Can you climb over that wall there?**	über *(räumlich)*
• **Come over here, please. / Your bike is over here.**	hier herüber / hier drüben
• Can you see that man **over there**?	da drüben, dort drüben
• Would you like to **come over** and play cards tonight?	herüberkommen/rüberkommen *(Besuch)*
• I'm going **over** to the shopping centre now.	hinübergehen/rübergehen
• **We met people from all over the world / from all over Europe**.	aus der ganzen Welt / aus ganz Europa
• *(more than)* **There were over 200 people** in the room.	über / mehr als 200 Menschen
• **The party was over** and everybody went home.	war vorbei

▶ p. 59	(to) **grow up** [grəʊ ˈʌp], **grew up** [gruː ˈʌp], **grown up** [grəʊn ˈʌp]	aufwachsen; erwachsen werden	• My grandfather **grew up** on a small farm. Jo wants to be a teacher when she **grows up**. • (to) **grow, grew, grown** = wachsen – If you give this plant more water, it'll **grow** better. • (to) **grow** sth., **grew, grown** = etwas anbauen – We don't have animals on our farm. We **grow** corn.

(to) **kiss** [kɪs]	(sich) küssen	verb: (to) **kiss** – noun: **kiss** (der Kuss)
(to) **blow** [bləʊ], **blew** [bluː], **blown** [bləʊn]	wehen; pusten, blasen	• A cold wind was **blowing**. (wehen) • **Blow** on your tea if it's too hot! (pusten) • Can you **blow up** the balloons? (aufblasen)
close (to) [kləʊs]	knapp; nahe (bei, an)	That was **close**! They almost had an accident. The vote was very **close**. I don't like it when people stand too **close** to me. **❗** Aussprache: verb: (to) **close** (schließen) [kləʊz] – adj: **close** (knapp; nahe) [kləʊs]
roof [ruːf]	das Dach	a **roof**
(to) **destroy** [dɪˈstrɔɪ]	zerstören, vernichten	Fire completely **destroyed** this house. = The house **was** completely **destroyed**. (... wurde total zerstört.)
nothing ['nʌθɪŋ]	nichts	▶▶ **not anything** **nothing** ◀ ▶ **everything**
(to) **check on** sb./sth. ['tʃek ɒn]	nach jm./etwas schauen, sich um jn./etwas kümmern	(to) make sure that sb./sth. is OK

▶ p. 60	**reaction** (to) [riˈækʃn]	die Reaktion (auf)	noun: **reaction (to)** – What's your **reaction to** sad films? Do you cry? verb: (to) **react (to)** – How do you react **to** sad films?
	silent [ˈsaɪlənt]	still, lautlos	(to) **fall/go silent** = still werden, verstummen

Viewing

▶ p. 61	(to) **chase** [tʃeɪs]	verfolgen, jagen	The cat is **chasing** the mouse. verb: (to) **chase** – noun: **chase** (die Verfolgung, die Verfolgungs-jagd) **storm chaser** = der Sturmjäger / die Sturmjägerin
	(to) **live-stream** sth. [laɪv]	etwas live streamen	❗ Aussprache: a **live** show [laɪv] – (to) **live** [lɪv] (leben, wohnen)
	risk [rɪsk]	das Risiko	

risk – risky – (to) risk			
noun:	**risk**	I wouldn't **take** that **risk**. Careful with strange emails! You're more **at risk** than you think. If you do a lot of sport, you're less **at risk of** getting ill.	das Risiko eingehen in Gefahr, gefährdet
adj:	**risky**	Don't do anything **risky** like that!	riskant
verb:	(to) **risk**	Don't ride your bike without a helmet! You're **risking** your life!	riskieren, wagen; aufs Spiel setzen

Study skills

▶ p. 62	**summary** [ˈsʌməri]	die Zusammenfassung	For the **summary** of a text you only need the most important points, no details.
	caption [ˈkæpʃn]	die Bildunterschrift	the words under a picture that describe the picture
	(to) **include** [ɪnˈkluːd]	(mit) einschließen	£80 – does that **include** breakfast? Yes, it's for everything, **including** breakfast. **including** = einschließlich, inklusive
	phrase [freɪz]	der Ausdruck, die (Rede-)Wendung	A **phrase** is a group of words with a special meaning, for example 'for seven seconds'.

Irregular verbs								
Infinitive	Simple past	Past participle		Infinitive	Simple past	Past participle	
(to) **blow**	blew	blown	pusten, blasen; wehen	(to) **hold**	held	held	halten
(to) **build**	built	built	bauen	(to) **kneel**	knelt	knelt	knien
(to) **grow**	grew	grown	wachsen; anbauen	(to) **leave**	left	left	lassen; verlassen; zurücklassen

🔊 Unit 3 Texas: Teen life

▶ pp. 76/77	**downtown** *(AE)* [daʊnˈtaʊn]	im/ins Stadtzentrum	▶▶ *BE* **(in or into) the town/city centre**
	location [ləʊˈkeɪʃn]	der Ort *(Standort; Einsatzort, Drehort)*	• Don't worry, my phone will help us to find the **location** of the building. • This church is famous as a film **location**.
	rural [ˈrʊərəl]	ländlich, Land-	We live in a **rural** area. (= in the country)
	indoor [ˈɪndɔː]	Hallen-, Innen-; im Haus/Gebäude stattfindend	adj: **indoor** – an **indoor** pool; an **indoor** market; **indoor** sports adv: **indoors** – The house had an indoor pool, so we could swim **indoors**. (drinnen; im Haus)

Topic 1

▶ p. 78	**system** [ˈsɪstəm]	das System	❗ Betonung auf der 1. Silbe: **system** [ˈsɪstəm]
▶ p. 79	(to) **get around**	sich fortbewegen (in) *(mobil sein)*	You don't have a car? How do you **get around**? – By bike or by train.
	driver's license *(AE)* [ˈlaɪsns]	der Führerschein	▶▶ *BE* **driving licence** **licence** *(BE)* / **license** *(AE)* = die Genehmigung, die Lizenz
	letter to the editor [ˈedɪtə]	der Leserbrief	**editor** = **1.** der/die Redakteur/in; **2.** der/die Herausgeber/in ❗ *German:* **der Leserbrief** – *English:* **letter to the editor**
	somewhere [ˈsʌmweə]	irgendwo(hin)	**everywhere** – **somewhere** – **nowhere** (nirgendwo, nirgendwohin)
	(to) **run** sth. [rʌn]	etwas betreiben, leiten	She started working in a small hotel, but today she **runs** her own hotel. **family-run business** = der Familienbetrieb
	lottery [ˈlɒtəri]	die Lotterie	(to) **win the lottery** = im Lotto / in der Lotterie gewinnen ❗ Betonung auf der 1. Silbe: **lottery** [ˈlɒtəri]
	Yours faithfully [ˈfeɪθfəli]	Mit freundlichen Grüßen *(Briefschluss)*	I hope to hear from you soon. **Yours faithfully** Joe Smith
▶ p. 81	**electricity** [ɪlekˈtrɪsəti]	der Strom, die Elektrizität	▶▶ **electric power**
	politician [pɒləˈtɪʃn]	der Politiker, die Politikerin	**Politicians** should make more laws to protect our planet!

Topic 2

▶ p. 82	**freshman** [ˈfreʃmən], *pl* **freshmen** *(AE)*	der Studienanfänger, die Studienanfängerin; der Anfänger / die Anfängerin in der Highschool	

Students at American high schools (four years)

freshman ['freʃmən], *pl* **freshmen**	der Studienanfänger, die Studienanfängerin; der Anfänger, die Anfängerin in der amerikanischen Highschool (9. Klasse)
sophomore ['sɒfəmɔ:]	der Schüler, die Schülerin im zweiten Schuljahr (10. Klasse)
junior ['dʒu:niə]	der Schüler, die Schülerin im dritten (vorletzten) Schuljahr (11. Klasse)
senior ['si:niə]	der Schüler, die Schülerin im vierten (letzten) Schuljahr (12. Klasse)

grade *(AE)* [greɪd]	die Klasse, das Schuljahr; die (Schul-)Note, die Zensur	My sister is now in third **grade**. She always gets good **grades** in her tests.

! • German **die Klasse, das Schuljahr** = *BE* **(school) year** / *AE* **grade**
   • German **die (Schul-)Note, die Zensur** = *BE* **mark** [mɑ:k] / *AE* **grade**

American English: different words

British English	**American English**	
canteen	**cafeteria**	die Cafeteria; die Mensa *(an Schule, College, Universität)*
driving licence	**driver's license**	der Führerschein
mark	**grade**	die (Schul-)Note, die Zensur
(school) year	**grade**	die Klasse, das Schuljahr
licence	**license**	die Genehmigung, die Lizenz
transport	**transportation**	das Fortbewegungsmittel; die Beförderung

You are ..., aren't you?	Du bist ..., nicht wahr? / Du bist ..., oder?	• It **is** hot today, **isn't it?** = Heute ist es heiß, nicht wahr? / ..., oder? • It **looks** great, **doesn't it?** = Es sieht gut aus, nicht wahr? / ..., oder? • You **don't know** the answer, **do you?** = Du weißt die Antwort nicht, oder?

Question tags (Frageanhängsel)

Aussagesatz bejaht ▶ Frageanhängsel verneint:

You <u>are</u> going to go ..., **<u>aren't</u> you?**	Du wirst / ihr werdet ... gehen, nicht wahr? / oder?
It <u>is</u> scary, **<u>isn't</u> it?**	Es ist beängstigend, nicht wahr? / oder?
Yes, it **<u>does</u>, <u>doesn't</u> it?**	Ja, das tut es, nicht wahr? / oder?

Aussagesatz verneint ▶ Frageanhängsel bejaht:

We <u>don't</u> want to ..., **<u>do</u> we?**	Wir wollen (doch) nicht ..., oder?

! Bei Frageanhängseln geht es weniger um Informationen, als darum, ein Gespräch in Gang zu halten.

gun [gʌn]	die Schusswaffe, die Pistole	 guns

shooting ['ʃu:tɪŋ]	die Schießerei	noun: **shooting** – verb: (to) **shoot** [ʃu:t], **shot, shot** [ʃɒt] (schießen, erschießen) Someone **shot** three people during a **shooting** at a restaurant. **!** *German:* **auf** jn. **schießen** *English:* (to) **shoot at** sb.
elective *(AE)* [ɪ'lektɪv]	das Wahlfach	a school subject which you can choose
(to) **depend on** sth. [dɪ'pend]	von etwas abhängen	Do you like running? – **It depends.** Not when it's raining! (Es kommt drauf an.)

prom *(AE)* [prɒm]	der Schul(abschluss)ball	They're wearing **fancy** clothes for the **prom.**	
fancy [ˈfænsi]	ausgefallen, extravagant, schick		

▶ p. 83 **swift** [swɪft] — schnell, rasch — ▶▶ **fast, quick**

high school *(AE)* [ˈhaɪ skuːl] — die Schule für 14- bis 18-Jährige — (in the USA) a school for young people between the ages of 14 and 18

forever [fərˈevə], **for ever** — für immer, ewig (lange) —
- The accident changed her life **forever / for ever**.
- I hope Simon arrives soon. We can't wait **forever / for ever**.

(to) **be friends with** sb. — mit jm. befreundet sein —
- (to) **be best friends with** sb. = js. bester Freund / beste Freundin sein
- (to) **stay friends with** sb. = mit jm. befreundet bleiben

(to) **date** sb. [deɪt] — mit jm. gehen, eine Beziehung haben — verb: (to) **date** sb. – noun: **date** = 1. das Datum; 2. die Verabredung, das Date *(auch die Person, mit der man ausgeht)*

guy *(infml)* [gaɪ] — der Typ, der Kerl — **❗ guy** = 1. der Typ, der Kerl – a nice **guy**; 2. **guys** *(pl)* – Hello, **guys**! (Hallo, Leute!)

▶ p. 84 **formal** [ˈfɔːml] — förmlich, formell — **formal ◀ ▶ informal** (informell, locker; umgangssprachlich) When you write to your bank, your letter should be **formal**, but your emails to your friends can be **informal**.

▶ p. 85 **yearbook** [ˈjɪəbʊk] — das Jahrbuch *(auch eine Art Poesiealbum)* — This year's school **yearbook** is great. There are lots of very funny photos in it.

(to) **pass** sth. **(to** sb.**)** [pɑːs] — (jm.) etwas (an)geben, (an)reichen —
- Can you **pass** me the milk, please? (anreichen)
- (to) **pass** sth. **around** = etwas herumreichen – **Pass around** the crisps, please, so we all can take some.

whose [huːz] — wessen — **❗ whose** = 1. *(question word)* wessen – **Whose** bike is that? 2. *(relative pronoun)* dessen, deren – I know the boy **whose** brother took my bike.

(to) **hang out** [hæŋ ˈaʊt], **hung, hung** [hʌŋ] — rumhängen, abhängen — I often **hang out** in the park with my friends.

Topic 3

▶ p. 86 **exactly** [ɪgˈzæktli] — genau — adv: **exactly** – **exactly** the same colour / What **exactly** do you mean? adj: **exact** (genau, exakt) – **exact** information / the **exact** opposite

college [ˈkɒlɪdʒ]	die Hochschule	When I finish school, I want to go to **college** and study art.
vocational [vəʊˈkeɪʃənl]	beruflich, Berufs-	**vocational school** = die Berufsschule
apprenticeship [əˈprentɪʃɪp]	die Ausbildung, die Lehre	My brother is doing an **apprenticeship** as a hairdresser. **apprentice** [əˈprentɪs] = der Lehrling, der/die Auszubildende
▶ p. 87 **reliable** [rɪˈlaɪəbl]	verlässlich, zuverlässig	My best friend is very **reliable**. She's always there for me.
stable [ˈsteɪbl]	der Stall	a **stable** (to) **clean out the stables** = ausmisten
(to) **offer** [ˈɒfə]	bieten, anbieten	verb: (to) **offer** – noun: **offer** (das Angebot)
pay [peɪ]	die Bezahlung *(Lohn)*	noun: **pay** – verb: (to) **pay, paid, paid**
flexible [ˈfleksəbl]	flexibel	❗ Betonung auf der 1. Silbe: **flexible** [ˈfleksəbl]
responsible (for) [rɪˈspɒnsəbl]	verantwortlich (für); verantwortungsbewusst	• When my parents are out, I'm **responsible for** my little sister. (verantwortlich (für)) • He always cleans his room and gets up on time. He's a very **responsible** boy. (verantwortungsbewusst)
five-year-old son	der fünf Jahre alte Sohn	**a five-year-old kid** (ein fünf Jahre altes Kind) = **a five-year-old** (ein/e Fünfjährige/r)
twice [twaɪs]	zweimal	**once** = one time **twice** = two times
punctual [ˈpʌŋktʃuəl]	pünktlich	▶▶ (arriving or doing sth.) **on time**
regular [ˈreɡjələ]	regelmäßig; gewohnt, normal	adj: **regular** – Is 'arrive' a **regular** verb? (regelmäßig) Mr Brown is not our **regular** maths teacher. (gewohnt, normal) adv: **regularly** – I do sport **regularly**. (regelmäßig)
working hours *(pl)* [ˈwɜːkɪŋ aʊəz]	die Arbeitszeit(en)	• I need a job with regular **(working) hours**. (... mit regelmäßigen Arbeitszeiten.) • (to) **work long hours** = lange arbeiten, Überstunden machen • **opening hours** *(pl)* / **opening times** *(pl)* = die Öffnungszeiten
I don't mind ... [maɪnd]	Es macht mir nichts aus ...	**I don't mind** helping you. (Ich helfe dir gern.) **I don't mind** the rain, but I hate the cold.

Story

▶ p. 88 **sweatpants** *(pl, AE)* [ˈswetpænts]	die Trainingshose, die Jogginghose	

preppy [ˈprepi]	für eine/n Schüler/in auf einer prep school typisch	a **preppy** outfit, **preppy** clothes **prep school (= preparatory school)** *(AE)* = *die (meist teure, private) Schule, die Lernende auf die Universität vorbereitet*
not … either [ˈaɪðə]	auch nicht	**!** **either** = 1. **not … either** (auch nicht) – I hate coffee and I do**n't** like tea **either**. 2. **either … or** (entweder … oder) – Dr Cox could see you **either** at 10.30 **or** at 4 pm on Friday.
stressful [ˈstresfl]	stressig	• verb: (to) **stress** sb. – My job really **stresses** me. (jn. stressen, (über)belasten) • noun: **stress** – I have a lot of **stress** in my job. (der Stress) • adj: **stressful** – My job is really **stressful**. Too much work and not enough time! (stressig) **stressed** (*infml auch:* **stressed out**) – I'm tired and **stressed (out)**. I need a holiday! (gestresst)
line *(AE)* [laɪn]	die (Warte-)Schlange	▶▶ *BE* **queue** [kjuː] (to) **stand in line** = Schlange stehen, sich anstellen noun: **queue** – verb: (to) **queue** (Schlange stehen, sich anstellen) a **line** / a **queue**
(to) **bump into/against** sb./sth. [bʌmp]	jn./etwas (an)stoßen, gegen etwas stoßen	(to) **bump into** sb. *(infml)* = 1. mit jm. zusammenstoßen – A man **bumped into** me and I fell down. 2. jn. zufällig treffen, jm. zufällig begegnen – In a small town you often **bump into** people that you know.
although [ɔːlˈðəʊ], **though** [ðəʊ]	obwohl	**Although** / **Though** I don't usually like Indian food, I think these curries are delicious. **!** **though** = 1. *(conj)* obwohl (= **although**); 2. *(adv)* allerdings – She was born in France. She isn't French **though**. (= But she isn't French.)
▶ p.89 **fishing** [ˈfɪʃɪŋ]	das Fischen, das Angeln; die Fischerei	nouns: **fish**; **fishing** – verbs: (to) **fish** (fischen, angeln); (to) **go fishing** (fischen/angeln gehen)

(to) **wish (for** sth.) [wɪʃ]	(sich etwas) wünschen	verb: (to) **wish** – noun: **wish** (der Wunsch) • If you had three **wishes**, what would you **wish for**? • (to) **make a wish** = sich etwas wünschen • **Best wishes** = Viele Grüße *(Briefschluss)*
(to) **disappear** [dɪsəˈpɪə]	verschwinden	The message was on my phone yesterday! Now it has **disappeared**. (to) **appear** ◀ ▶ (to) **disappear**
(to) **keep going** [kiːp ˈɡəʊɪŋ]	(immer) weiter machen; (immer) weiter gehen	You're doing well! **Keep going!** (Mach (so) weiter!)
Shut up! *(infml)* [ʃʌt ˈʌp]	Halt den Mund!	▶▶ **Be quiet!** ❗ Vorsicht! Viele Menschen finden Shut up! sehr unhöflich. (to) **shut, shut, shut** = schließen, zumachen
(to) **hold** [həʊld], **held, held** [held]	halten	Can you **hold** my bag for a minute, please?
upset [ʌpˈset]	bestürzt; aufgebracht, verärgert	Don't be **upset**. She's just a bully. I was very **upset** when my sister had an accident. adj: **upset** = bestürzt; aufgebracht, verärgert – verb: (to) **upset** sb., **upset, upset** (jn. erschüttern; jn. aufregen, ärgern)
(to) **ignore** [ɪɡˈnɔː]	nicht beachten, ignorieren	I try to **ignore** all the bullies at school.
(to) **nod (your head)** [nɒd]	(mit dem Kopf) nicken	verb: (to) **nod (your head)** – noun: **nod (of your head)** (das Kopfnicken) • 'You're right', he said and **nodded (his head)**. = 'You're right', he said with a **nod**. • (to) **nod to** sb. = jm. zunicken
(to) **deal with** sth. [diːl], **dealt, dealt** [delt]	mit etwas klarkommen, mit etwas fertigwerden; mit etwas umgehen	• Let's try and **deal with** this problem first and think about everything else later. • When people at school bully you, you'll find it hard to **deal with** your school work.

Viewing

▶ p. 91 **examination** [ɪɡzæmɪˈneɪʃn], *auch:* **exam** [ɪɡˈzæm]	die Prüfung	I really need to study for my maths **exam** next week. ❗ *German:* eine **Prüfung** machen/ablegen *English:* (to) **take/do** an **exam**

Short forms of nouns

Short form:	Long form:	German:
bio	**biography**	die Biografie
exam	**examination**	die Prüfung
intro	**introduction**	die Einführung, die Einleitung
mag	**magazine**	die Zeitschrift
pro	**professional**	der Fachmann, die Fachfrau, der Profi
sci-fi	**science fiction**	die Science-Fiction
tech	**technology**	die Technik, die Technologie
veg, *pl* **veg** [vedʒ]	**vegetable(s)**	das Gemüse
veggie	**vegetarian**	der Vegetarier, die Vegetarierin
vocab	**vocabulary**	der Wortschatz, das Vokabular; das Vokabelverzeichnis

textbook [ˈtekstbʊk]	das Schulbuch, das Lehrbuch	This is the **textbook** for your English lessons at school.
quality [ˈkwɒləti]	die Qualität; die Eigenschaft	noun: **quality** – • These clothes are of high **quality**. (… von hoher Qualität.) • For me, kindness is an important **quality** in people. (die Eigenschaft) adj: **quality** (hochwertig, von hoher Qualität) – **quality** clothes/bikes/…
education [edʒuˈkeɪʃn]	die Erziehung, die (Schul-)Bildung	I got a very good **education** at our local school.
latest [ˈleɪtɪst]	neueste(r, s), aktuelle(r, s)	The band's **latest** album is their best, I think.

Study skills

▶ p. 92 (to) **communicate** [kəˈmjuːnɪkeɪt]	kommunizieren, sich verständigen	verb: (to) **communicate** – It's important to **communicate** well in a team. noun: **communication** [kəmjuːnɪˈkeɪʃn] – Good **communication** is important in a team. (die Kommunikation, die Verständigung)
(to) **encourage** [ɪnˈkʌrɪdʒ]	ermutigen, ermuntern; unterstützen	verb: (to) **encourage** – My friends supported and **encouraged** me before my exams. adj: **encouraging** – They were very **encouraging**. (ermutigend)
(to) **go on**	weitermachen, weiterreden; (sich) fortsetzen	▶▶ (to) **continue** • Let's have a break and **go on** with this job later. • 'There's another problem, too …', she **went on**. • How long will this cold weather **go on** for?
patient [ˈpeɪʃnt]	geduldig	**patient** ◀▶ **impatient** (ungeduldig)
strategy [ˈstrætədʒi]	die Strategie	❗ Betonung auf der 1. Silbe: **stra**tegy [ˈstrætədʒi]

Unit task

▶ p. 93 (to) **introduce** sb. **to** sb./sth. [ɪntrəˈdjuːs]	jm. jn. / etwas vorstellen, jn. mit jm. / etwas bekanntmachen	Teacher: 'May I **introduce** our new student to you? This is Cara.' 'We haven't met. Let me **introduce** myself,' said Cara. verb: (to) **introduce** – noun: **introduction**
(to) **sum** sth. **up** [sʌm ˈʌp]	etwas zusammenfassen	**To sum up, …** = Um (es) zusammenzufassen, … / Zusammenfassend kann man sagen, … verb: (to) **sum** sth. **up** – noun: **summary**

Irregular verbs

Infinitive	Simple past	Past participle		Infinitive	Simple past	Past participle	
(to) **deal with**	dealt	dealt	fertigwerden mit; umgehen mit	(to) **shoot**	shot	shot	(er)schießen
				(to) **shut**	shut	shut	schließen, zumachen
(to) **hang out**	hung	hung	rumhängen, abhängen	(to) **upset**	upset	upset	erschüttern; aufregen, ärgern
(to) **hold**	held	held	halten				

◀) Unit 4 California: State of contrasts

▶ pp. 108/109

contrast [ˈkɒntrɑːst]	der Kontrast, der Gegensatz	noun: **contrast** [ˈkɒntrɑːst] – Coming home to London from Peru … what a **contrast**! verb: (to) **contrast** [kənˈtrɑːst] – **Contrast** schools in Japan with your own school. (vergleichen, (einander) gegenüberstellen)
death [deθ]	der Tod	noun: **death** – adj: **dead** – verb: (to) **die (of)**
desert [ˈdezət]	die Wüste	**desert island** = die einsame Insel ❗ Nicht verwechseln: **desert** [ˈdezət] = die Wüste **dessert** [dɪˈzɜːt] = die Nachspeise
giant [ˈdʒaɪənt]	riesig	adj: **giant** – These **giant** trees are very old. noun: **giant** – She's a basketball star and a real **giant**. (= a very tall woman) (der Riese, die Riesin)
celebrity [səˈlebrəti]	der Prominente, die Prominente, der/die Promi	a famous person
dry [draɪ]	trocken	adj: **dry** – verb: (to) **dry** ((ab)trocknen)
flat [flæt]	flach, eben; (Reifen) platt	• The landscape is very **flat** here. • My bike has a **flat** tyre.
ocean [ˈəʊʃn]	der Ozean	▶▶ sea
few [fjuː]	wenige	❗ • **a few** = einige, ein paar – I talked to **a few** people at the party. • **few** = (nur) wenige – Very **few** people came to the party. **few** ◀ ▶ many, a lot of

German 'wenig, weniger, am wenigsten'

1. mit dem Plural von zählbaren Nomen:	**few** cars/coins wenige Autos/Münzen	**fewer** cars/coins weniger Autos/Münzen	the **fewest** cars/coins die wenigsten Autos/Münzen
2. mit nicht zählbaren Nomen:	**little** traffic/money wenig Verkehr/Geld	**less** traffic/money weniger Verkehr/Geld	the **least** traffic/money der wenigste Verkehr/das wenigste Geld

none (of) [nʌn]	keine(r, s) (von)	**None of** my friends has ever tried German Pumpernickel bread.

Topic 1

▶ p. 110 **company** [ˈkʌmpəni]	die Firma, die Gesellschaft	This **company** makes and sells special bikes. ❗ Betonung auf der 1. Silbe: **company** [ˈkʌmpəni]
▶ p. 111 **artificial** [ɑːtɪˈfɪʃl]	künstlich; unecht	Those are not real flowers. They're made of plastic. They're **artificial** flowers.

intelligence [ɪnˈtelɪdʒəns]	die Intelligenz	**artificial intelligence (AI)** = die künstliche Intelligenz (KI) noun: **intelligence** – adj: **intelligent** ❗ Betonung auf der 2. Silbe: in**tel**ligence [ɪnˈtelɪdʒəns] – in**tel**ligent [ɪnˈtelɪdʒənt]
data [ˈdeɪtə]	die Daten	❗ Auf **data** kann ein Verb im Singular oder Plural folgen: **Data** is/are collected ... (Daten werden gesammelt ...)
device [dɪˈvaɪs]	das Gerät, der Apparat	A clock is a **device** that tells you the time.
service [ˈsɜːvɪs]	der Service; der Dienst; die Bedienung	The food and the **service** were super, so we gave the waiter a good tip. There's a good bus **service** into the town centre. **bus/train service** = die Bus-/Zug-Verbindung
personal digital assistant (PDA) [pɜːsənl dɪdʒɪtl əˈsɪstənt]	der elektronische Organizer *(wörtlich: persönlicher digitaler Assistent)*	**personal assistant (PA)** = der persönliche Assistent, die persönliche Assistentin
expert [ˈekspɜːt]	der Experte, die Expertin	❗ Betonung auf der 1. Silbe: **ex**pert [ˈekspɜːt]
(to) **copy** [ˈkɒpi]	kopieren, abschreiben	verb: (to) **copy** – **Copy** these sentences and write the correct words in the gaps. noun: **copy** (die Kopie; das Exemplar) – I'll give you all **copies** of the text.
dialogue [ˈdaɪəlɒg]	der Dialog	a conversation between people, for example in a book or film ❗ Betonung auf der 1. Silbe: **dia**logue [ˈdaɪəlɒg]
feature [ˈfiːtʃə]	das Merkmal, die Eigenschaft	noun: **feature** – What are the **features** of this new device? verb: (to) **feature** – Does the device **feature** important new things? (bieten, haben) Do my wishes **feature** in your plans at all? (vorkommen, eine Rolle spielen)
▶ p.112 **detention** [dɪˈtenʃn]	das Nachsitzen *(in der Schule)*	I was late three times this week, so I had **detention** on Friday.
(to) **cheat (at/on** sth.**)** [tʃiːt]	betrügen, mogeln, schummeln (bei etwas)	verb: (to) **cheat** – nouns: **cheat** (der Betrug, der Schwindel, die Mogelei); *(person)* **cheater** (der Betrüger, die Betrügerin)
essay (on/about) [ˈeseɪ]	der Aufsatz (über)	What do you think about electric cars? Collect arguments and write a short **essay**.
(to) **change your mind** [maɪnd]	seine Meinung ändern	Daniel had wanted to go out, but then he **changed his mind** and stayed at home.
deer [dɪə], *pl* **deer**	das Reh; der Hirsch	This is a big forest with lots of wild **deer**.

image [ˈɪmɪdʒ]	das Bild, die Abbildung	►► a picture or a photo
(to) train sb. [treɪn]	jn. trainieren; jn. ausbilden	verb: (to) **train** – nouns: *(what you do)* **training**; *(person)* **trainer**
photographer [fəˈtɒɡrəfə]	der Fotograf, die Fotografin	

photo(graph) – photography – photographer – (to) photograph

nouns:	**photo / photograph** [ˈfəʊtəɡrɑːf] **photography** [fəˈtɒɡrəfi] **photographer** [fəˈtɒɡrəfə]	das Foto, die Fotografie die Fotografie *(Hobby)*, das Fotografieren der Fotograf, die Fotografin	**!** *False friends:* *German* **der Fotograf,** **die Fotografin =** *English* **the photographer**
verb:	(to) **photograph** = (to) **take photos /** (to) **take a photo**	fotografieren	

►p.113 **(to) ban** [bæn]	verbieten	verb: (to) **ban** – Phones **are banned** during lessons. (... sind verboten) noun: **ban (on)** – There's a **ban on** phones during lessons. (das Verbot (von))
task [tɑːsk]	die Aufgabe	Most students did the **task** / completed the **task** in less than 30 minutes.
(to) predict [prɪˈdɪkt]	vorhersagen, voraussagen	It's hard to **predict** how this story will end. verb: (to) **predict** – noun: **prediction**
disaster [dɪˈzɑːstə]	die Katastrophe, das Unglück	The test was a complete **disaster**. I only got three points!

Topic 2

►p.114 **people** [ˈpiːpl], *pl* **peoples**	das Volk	**!** **people =** **1.** *(pl)* die Menschen – A lot of **people** are afraid of dogs. **2.** das Volk – the Zulu **people** (das Volk der Zulu) the native **peoples** of Africa (die indigenen Völker Afrikas)
Native American [neɪtɪv əˈmerɪkən]	der/die amerikanische Indigene	noun: **Native American** adj: **Native (American)** *(zur indigenen Bevölkerung Amerikas gehörend oder sie betreffend)* – • a **Native American** dish • **Native** land • **native birds/plants** = einheimische Vögel/Pflanzen • **native language** = die Muttersprache
by ...	von ... *(in Passivsätzen)*	Did you write this essay? Or was it written **by** AI?
tens of thousands of years	zehntausende Jahre	**Tens of thousands of** people came to Brighton's Pride Parade this year.

(to) **force** sb. **to do** sth. [fɔːs]	jn. zwingen, etwas zu tun	verbs: (to) **force** (zwingen) (to) **force** sth. – We'll have to **force** a decision now. (erzwingen) noun: **force** – People don't react well to **force**. (der Zwang; die Gewalt; die Kraft)
boarding school [ˈbɔːdɪŋ skuːl]	das Internat; das Internat für Indigene, in das Kinder zwangsweise gebracht wurden, um sie kulturell anzupassen	We became friends when we went to the same **boarding school**. Many Native American children were **forced** to go to **boarding schools**.
(to) **survive** [səˈvaɪv]	überleben	verb: (to) **survive** – noun: *(person)* **survivor** (der/die Überlebende)
tribe [traɪb]	die Volksgruppe	
government [ˈgʌvənmənt]	die Regierung	We'll vote for a new **government** soon. nouns: **government**; *(person)* **governor** (der Gouverneur, die Gouverneurin) verb: (to) **govern** [ˈgʌvn] (regieren)
direction [dəˈrekʃn]	die Richtung	No, don't turn left. That's the wrong **direction**. Turn right! ❗ **direction** = die Richtung **directions** *(pl)* = die Wegbeschreibung(en)
▶ p.115 **condor** [ˈkɒndɔː]	der Kondor	 a **condor**
zoo [zuː]	der Zoo	Do you like looking at the animals in a **zoo**?
▶ p.116 **salmon** [ˈsæmən], *pl* **salmon**	der Lachs	 a **salmon** ❗ Aussprache: [ˈsæmən] – das **l** wird nicht gesprochen.
permission [pəˈmɪʃn]	die Erlaubnis	• I asked for **permission** to use the photo. (= I asked to be allowed to use the photo.) • I got **permission** to use the photo. (= I was allowed to use the photo.)
wolf [wʊlf], *pl* **wolves** [wʊlvz]	der Wolf	 a **wolf**
▶ p.117 **stereotype** [ˈsteriətaɪp]	der Stereotyp, das Klischee, die Klischeevorstellung	The main characters in this book seem to be just the **stereotype** of teenagers in love.

Topic 3

▶ p.118 **nearly** ['nɪəli]	fast	▶▶ **almost** It's **nearly / almost** 8 o'clock! We're late!
bear [beə]	der Bär	 a **bear**
cabin ['kæbɪn]	die Hütte; die Kabine	 a **cabin**

(to) **taste** [teɪst]	schmecken; kosten, probieren	• **Taste** these burgers! (kosten, probieren)
		  They **taste** wonderful. (schmecken)
		• verb: (to) **taste** –
		  noun: **taste** (der Geschmack) –
		  adj: **tasty** (schmackhaft, lecker)

unless [ən'les]	es sei denn; außer (wenn)	You'll have problems at school **unless** you work harder. (= ... if you don't work harder) ▶▶ **if ... not**
▶ p.119 **pepper** ['pepə]	der Pfeffer; die Paprika, die Peperoni	 **pepper** three **peppers**

Story

▶ p.120 **wildfire** ['waɪldfaɪə]	der Waldbrand; der Großbrand, der Flächenbrand	a very big fire, e.g. in a forest

(to) **burn** [bɜːn]	brennen	• What's that smell? Is something **burning**?
		  (= Is there a fire?)
		• (to) **burn** sth. = etwas verbrennen
		• (to) **burn** sth. **down** = etwas abbrennen,
		                   etwas niederbrennen

wood [wʊd]	das Holz; der Wald	noun: **wood** (**1.** das Holz; **2.** der Wald)
		adj: **wooden** ['wʊdn] (Holz-, hölzern)
		• I love floors which are made of **wood**.
		  (= I love **wooden** floors.)
		• I like walking through the **woods**
		  and listening to the birds.

(to) **wake up** [weɪk 'ʌp],
woke up [wəʊk],
woken up ['wəʊkən]
	aufwachen	• I **wake up** early every morning.
		• (to) **wake** sb. (**up**) = jn. (auf)wecken
		  My phone alarm **wakes me** (**up**) at 6.30
		  in the morning.

smoke [sməʊk]	der Rauch	

smoke

noun: **smoke** – verb: (to) **smoke** (rauchen)

▶ p. 121 **(to) block** [blɒk] — blockieren, versperren; verstopfen

verb: (to) **block** – A tree had fallen over and was **blocking** the road.
noun: **block** (der Block; der Klotz; der Häuserblock)
We don't have a house, we live in a **block of flats**. (der Wohnblock)

heavy ['hevi] — schwer (Gewicht)

! German **schwer** =
1. (von Gewicht) **heavy** – a heavy box
2. (schwierig) **hard, difficult** – a **hard** exercise, a **difficult** question

thick [θɪk] — dick; dicht

thick – a **thick** book; **thick** dark hair
◀ ▶ **thin** (dünn; schlank) – a **thin** magazine; **thin** hair
My sister is tall and **thin**.

rope [rəʊp] — das Seil

a **rope**

(to) tie [taɪ] — binden, schnüren

• When it's hot, I always **tie** my hair back.
• (to) **tie** sb./sth. **to** sth. = jn./etwas an etwas festbinden
! (to) **tie** (verb) = binden, schnüren
tie (noun) = die Krawatte
Can you **tie** a **tie**?

▶ p. 122 **OMG (Oh my God!)** [əʊ em 'dʒiː] — Oh mein Gott!

Chat abbreviations

ASAP	as soon as possible	so bald wie möglich	LMK	Let me know.	Lass es mich wissen.
ATM	at the moment	im Moment / zur Zeit	NGL	not going to lie	Um ehrlich zu sein, … / Ehrlich gesagt, …
BTW	by the way	übrigens			
CYA	See you! (See ya!)	Bis dann. / Tschüs.	NVM	Never mind.	(Das) macht nichts. / Nicht (so) schlimm.
IDK	I don't know.	Ich weiß nicht. / Das weiß ich nicht.	TTYL	Talk to you later.	Wir sprechen uns später.

crowdfunding ['kraʊdfʌndɪŋ] — das Crowdfunding (Schwarmfinanzierung)

noun: **crowdfunding** – Could **crowdfunding** be a way to get enough money for our project?
verb: (to) **crowdfund** sth. – Could we **crowdfund** our project? (etwas durch Crowdfunding finanzieren)

exhibition [eksɪˈbɪʃn]	die Ausstellung; die Messe	• I want to see the Van Gogh **exhibition** at the museum. (die Ausstellung) • This new machine was presented at last year's technology **exhibition**. (die Messe)

(robot) builder [ˈbɪldə]	der (Roboter-)Konstrukteur, die (Roboter-)Konstrukteurin	**builder** = der/die Konstrukteur/in;
		        der/die Bauarbeiter/in;
		        der/die Bauunternehmer/in
		verb: (to) **build** – noun: **builder**

Viewing

▶ p. 123	**centimetre** (= cm) [ˈsentɪmiːtə]	der Zentimeter	One hundred **centimetres** are one metre.
	narrator [nəˈreɪtə]	der Erzähler, die Erzählerin	someone who tells a story
	(to) **pick** sb. **up**	jn. abholen	• (to) **pick** = (aus)wählen, aussuchen • (to) **pick** sth. **up** = etwas aufheben (vom Boden), etwas hochheben; etwas abholen • (to) **pick** sb. **up** = jn. abholen
	(to) **realize** sth. [ˈrɪəlaɪz]	etwas erkennen, sich einer Sache bewusst werden	verb: (to) **realize** – When I got home, I **realized** that I had left my bag on the train. noun: **realization** [riːəlaɪˈzeɪʃn] – Suddenly the **realization** that my bag was still on the train hit me. (die Erkenntnis)

Verbs ending in -ize or -ise

British English: *-ize* or *-ise*	American English: <u>always</u> *-ize*
(to) **organize** or (to) **organise**	(to) **organize**
(to) **realize** or (to) **realise**	(to) **realize**
(to) **recognize** or (to) **recognise**	(to) **recognize**

(to) **turn** sth. **on/off** [tɜːn ˈɒn], [tɜːn ˈɒf]	etwas ein-/ausschalten; hier: (den Wasserhahn) auf-/abdrehen	• The light is still on. Please **turn** it **off**. (ausschalten) • It's too dark when the lights are off. Please **turn** them **on**. (einschalten)
tap [tæp]	der Wasserhahn	• Save water: please **turn off** the **tap**.  a **tap** **tap water** = das Leitungswasser

Study skills

▶ p. 124	**landscape** [ˈlændskeɪp]	die Landschaft; das Landschaftsbild

What a great **landscape**!

wildlife *(no pl)* ['waɪldlaɪf]	die Tiere *(in freier Wildbahn)*, die Tierwelt	The **wildlife** of Africa is very different from the **wildlife** in Europe.
e.g. *(aus dem Lateinischen)* [iː 'dʒiː]	z.B. (zum Beispiel)	❗ **e.g.** wird in geschriebenem Englisch benutzt. Wenn man spricht, sagt man **for example**.
chart [tʃɑːt]	das Diagramm; die Tabelle	**bar chart** = das Balkendiagramm **column chart** = das Säulendiagramm **line chart** = das Liniendiagramm **pie chart** = das Tortendiagramm, das Kreisdiagramm
source [sɔːs]	die Quelle *(z.B. Website, Text)*	Where did you find this information? You always have to give your **source** or **sources**.
(to) measure ['meʒə]	(aus)messen	• We have to **measure** this room. (ausmessen) • It **measures** 3 x 2 metres. (Er misst ... = Er ist ... groß.)
square [skweə]	das Quadrat	**square kilometre** = der Quadratkilometer ❗ **square** = **1.** *(adj)* rechteckig; quadratisch, Quadrat- **2.** *(noun)* das Quadrat; der Platz *(in der Stadt)*
acre ['eɪkə]	*britisches/amerikanisches Flächenmaß, entspricht 0,405 Hektar*	
by state / **by** name / **by** population / ...	(sortiert) nach (Bundes-)Staat / nach dem Namen / nach der Bevölkerungszahl / ...	

by a text **by** Tina / a text written **by** Tina a campsite **by** the river (to) go **by** bus / **by** bike (to) pay **by** card (to) send sth. **by** email	ein Text / eine SMS von Tina *(von Tina geschrieben)* ein Campingplatz am Fluss mit dem Bus / dem Rad fahren mit Karte bezahlen etwas per E-Mail schicken

Unit task

▶ p.125 **use** [juːs]	der Gebrauch, die Verwendung	noun: **use** – This church is no longer **in use**. (in Gebrauch) verb: (to) **use** – They **use** it as a cafe now. ❗ Aussprache: **use** *(noun)* [juːs] – (to) **use** *(verb)* [juːz]
the pros and cons *(pl)* [prəʊz ənd 'kɒnz]	das Pro und Kontra; das Für und Wider	What are **the pros and cons** of buying a new car now?
(to) touch [tʌtʃ]	anfassen, berühren	verb: (to) **touch** – You mustn't **touch** the photos. noun: **touch** – The cat didn't like the touch of my cold hands and ran away. (die Berührung)

🔊 °Unit 5 Canada: The northern neighbour

> Die Unit 5 ist keine Pflicht-Unit, daher sind die neuen Wörter alle mit einem Kringel (°) markiert. Wenn ihr die Unit bearbeitet, kannst du die neuen Wörter lernen, aber sie werden nicht in Band 5 vorausgesetzt.

▶ pp. 140/141	°**population** [pɒpjuˈleɪʃn]	die Bevölkerung, die Einwohner(zahl)	Twenty per cent of this country's **population** are over 50.
	°**ocean** [ˈəʊʃn]	der Ozean	• the **Pacific** [pəˈsɪfɪk] = the **Pacific Ocean** (der Pazifik, der Pazifische Ozean) • the **Atlantic** [ətˈlæntɪk] = the **Atlantic Ocean** (der Atlantik, der Atlantische Ozean) • the **Arctic Ocean** (der Arktische Ozean, das Nordpolarmeer) • the **Arctic** [ˈɑːktɪk] (die Arktis)
	°**First Nations (people)** [fɜːst ˈneɪʃnz]	die indigenen Völker Kanadas	The **First Nations people** are native people in Canada, but they're not Inuit or Metis.
	°**Metis** [meɪˈtiː], *pl* **Metis**	die Metis *(Nachfahren europäischer Einwanderer/Einwanderinnen in Kanada und kanadischer Indigener)*	The **Metis** are native people in Canada who have both European and First Nations backgrounds.
	°**Inuit** *or* **Inuits** *(pl)* [ˈɪnjuɪt], [ˈɪnuɪt]	die Inuit, die Indigenen im Norden Kanadas, in Grönland und Alaska	The **Inuit** are native peoples from Northern Canada, Greenland or Alaska.
	°**(to) welcome** sb. **(to)** [ˈwelkʌm]	jn. begrüßen (in), jn. willkommen heißen (in)	I'd like to **welcome** you to our new book club. **welcoming** = (gast)freundlich, einladend
	°**waterfall** [ˈwɔːtəfɔːl]	der Wasserfall	 a **waterfall**
	°**maple leaf** [ˈmeɪpl liːf], *pl* **maple leaves** [ˈmeɪpl liːvz]	das Ahornblatt	**maple** = der Ahorn **leaf**, *pl* **leaves** = das Blatt *(Pflanze)* a **maple leaf**
	°**moose** [muːs], *pl* **moose**	der Elch	a **moose** 
	°**orca** [ˈɔːkə]	der Schwertwal	**Orcas** are black and white whales which eat meat and fish.

°**whale** [weɪl]	der Wal	

a **whale**

°**lacrosse** [ləˈkrɒs]	das Lacrosse *(Ballspiel, ähnlich wie Hockey)*	**Lacrosse** is a ball game for two teams of ten players. It's a bit like hockey.

Topic 1

▶ p. 142	°**unique** [juˈniːk]	einzigartig, einmalig	Your user name has to be **unique**. (= no one else can have the same name)
	°**independent (of/from)** [ɪndɪˈpendənt]	unabhängig (von)	I'd like to earn my own money and be **independent of/from** my parents.
▶ p. 143	°**common** [ˈkɒmən]	häufig, weit verbreitet, gewöhnlich	One of the most **common** names for girls in Britain today is Olivia.
	°**mounted** [ˈmaʊntɪd]	beritten	**mounted police** = die berittene Polizei
	°**loon** [luːn]	der Seetaucher *(Wasservogel)*	a bird that eats fish and makes a noise like a laugh
	°**pond** [pɒnd]	der Teich	
	°(to) **skate** [skeɪt]	Schlittschuh laufen, eislaufen	

They're **skating** on a frozen **pond**.

°(to) **lift** [lɪft]	heben, hochheben	I can't **lift** this box. It's too heavy.

Im *English-German Dictionary* kannst du nachschlagen, was ein Wort bedeutet oder wie es ausgesprochen wird.

Es werden folgende **Abkürzungen und Symbole** verwendet:

AE = American English
infml = informal (umgangssprachlich)
sb. = somebody (jemand)
jd. = jemand   jm. = jemandem

BE = British English
pl = plural (Mehrzahl)
sth. = something (etwas)
                              jn. = jemanden

° Mit diesem Kringel sind Wörter markiert, die nicht zum Lernwortschatz gehören.

Die **Fundstellenangaben** zeigen, wo ein Wort zum ersten Mal vorkommt.
Die Ziffern in Klammern bezeichnen Seitenzahlen.

1 = Lighthouse 1   2 = Lighthouse 2   3 = Lighthouse   4: 1 (18) = Lighthouse 4, Unit 1, Seite 18

A

a [ə] ein, eine 1 **one hour a day** eine Stunde pro Tag 2
abandon sb./sth. [əˈbændən] jn. verlassen *(im Stich lassen)*; etwas verlassen *(leer stehen lassen)* 4: 2 (46/47)
able [ˈeɪbl]: **be able to do sth.** etwas tun können, in der Lage sein etwas zu tun 4: 2 (49)
about [əˈbaʊt]:
1. ungefähr 2
2. **out and about** unterwegs 4: 1 (18)
3. **about me/you/...** über mich/dich/... 1
What about ... ? Wie wäre es mit ... ? 1 **What about you?** Und du? / Was ist mit dir? 1
above [əˈbʌv] über, oberhalb (von); oben 2
accent [ˈæksent] der Akzent 4: 1 (18)
accident [ˈæksɪdənt]:
1. der Unfall 2
2. der Zufall 2
by accident zufällig 2
account [əˈkaʊnt] das (Bank-)Konto; der Account 2
acoustic [əˈkuːstɪk] akustisch 2
acre [ˈeɪkə] *britisches/amerikanisches Flächenmaß, entspricht 0,405 Hektar* 4: 4 (124)
across [əˈkrɒs] über *(quer über)* 2
act [ækt] Theater spielen, schauspielern; aufführen 2 **act out** aufführen, vorspielen 2
action [ˈækʃn] die Aktion, die (spannende) Handlung 1
°**active** [ˈæktɪv] aktiv 2
activist [ˈæktɪvɪst] der Aktivist, die Aktivistin 2
activity [ækˈtɪvəti] die Aktivität, die Tätigkeit 1
actor [ˈæktə] der Schauspieler, die Schauspielerin 2
actually [ˈæktʃuəli] eigentlich; tatsächlich 3
ad [æd] *(infml) siehe* **advert**
add [æd] hinzufügen; addieren 1
additional [əˈdɪʃənl] zusätzliche(r, s) 3
additional time [əˈdɪʃənl taɪm] die Nachspielzeit *(Fußball)* 3
address [əˈdres] die Adresse 1
adult [ˈædʌlt] der/die Erwachsene 3

adventure [ədˈventʃə] das Abenteuer 2
advert [ˈædvɜːt] *infml auch* **ad** die Anzeige, das Inserat; der Werbespot 2
advice *(no pl)* [ədˈvaɪs] der Rat(schlag), Ratschläge 3 **give sb. advice** jm. Rat geben 3 **take sb.'s advice** auf js. Rat hören 3
after [ˈɑːftə]:
1. **after (school)** nach (der Schule) 1
2. **after (you read)** nachdem (du liest) 1
afternoon [ɑːftəˈnuːn] der Nachmittag 1 **in the afternoon** nachmittags, am Nachmittag 1
again [əˈɡen] wieder, noch einmal 1
against [əˈɡenst] gegen 2
age [eɪdʒ] das Alter, die Altersgruppe 4: (14/15) **at the age of 12** im Alter von 12 (Jahren) 4: (14/15) **people of all ages** Menschen aller Altersgruppen 4: (14/15)
agent [ˈeɪdʒənt] der/die Agent/in 2
ago [əˈɡəʊ]: **two years ago** vor zwei Jahren 3
agree [əˈɡriː]: **agree (with sb./sth.)** jm. zustimmen; mit etwas einverstanden sein 2 **agree on** sich einigen auf 2
°**agreement** [əˈɡriːmənt] die Zustimmung, die Übereinstimmung 3
ahead [əˈhed] voran, voraus 3
air [eə] die Luft 3
album [ˈælbəm] das Album 2
all [ɔːl] alle(s) 1 **all day** der ganze Tag, den ganzen Tag (lang) 2 **all over** total, ganz und gar 2 **all over the world** überall auf der Welt, auf der ganzen Welt, weltweit 2 **all the family** die ganze Familie 2 **all the time** die ganze Zeit, ständig 2 **not ... at all** überhaupt nicht(s), gar nicht(s); überhaupt kein/e, gar kein/e 2
allergic (to) [əˈlɜːdʒɪk] allergisch (gegen) 1
alligator [ˈælɪɡeɪtə] der Alligator 4: (10/11)
allowed [əˈlaʊd] erlaubt 3 **be allowed to do sth.** etwas tun dürfen 3
almost [ˈɔːlməʊst] fast, beinahe 2
alone [əˈləʊn] allein 1

along the river [əˈlɒŋ] den Fluss entlang, am Fluss entlang 2
alphabet [ˈælfəbet] das Alphabet 1
already [ɔːlˈredi] schon 1
also [ˈɔːlsəʊ] auch 1
although [ɔːlˈðəʊ] obwohl 4: 3 (88)
always [ˈɔːlweɪz] immer 1
am [æm]: **I'm (= I am)** ich bin 1
a.m. [eɪˈem]: **4 a.m.** 4 Uhr (früh)morgens 1 **9 a.m.** 9 Uhr vormittags 1
amazing [əˈmeɪzɪŋ] erstaunlich; großartig 1
ambulance [ˈæmbjələns] der Krankenwagen 2
American football [əmerɪkən ˈfʊtbɔːl] der American Football 4: 1 (24)
an [ən] ein/e *(vor Vokalen)* 1
and [ænd], [ənd] und 1
angry [ˈæŋɡri] wütend 1
animal [ˈænɪml] das Tier 1
animal charity [ˈænɪml tʃærəti] die wohltätige Organisation, die Tiere unterstützt 2
ankle [ˈæŋkl] der Knöchel, das Fußgelenk 2
°**announcement** [əˈnaʊnsmənt] die Durchsage, die Ansage, die Ankündigung 2
annoy sb. [əˈnɔɪ] jn. ärgern 3
annoyed [əˈnɔɪd] verärgert, ärgerlich 3
annoying [əˈnɔɪɪŋ] ärgerlich *(unangenehm)* 3
another [əˈnʌðə] ein/e andere/r/s; noch ein/e 4: 2 (48)
answer [ˈɑːnsə]:
1. die Antwort 1
2. (be)antworten 1
answer the door aufmachen, zur/an die Tür gehen 3 **answer the phone** ans Telefon gehen 3
°**antonym** [ˈæntənɪm] das Antonym *(Gegenteil)*
any [ˈeni] jede(r/s) (beliebige), jegliche(r/s) 2 **(at) any time** zu jeder Zeit, jederzeit 2 **Do you have any questions?** Habt ihr / Hast du (irgendwelche) Fragen? 1 **not (...) any more** nicht mehr 2 **there aren't any ...** es gibt keine ... 1
anybody [ˈenibɒdi] irgendjemand; jede/r (beliebige) 2 **not (...) anybody** niemand 2

anyone [ˈeniwʌn] irgendjemand; jede/r (beliebige) 2 **not (...) anyone** niemand 2

anything [ˈeniθɪŋ] (irgend)etwas; alles; egal, was 2 **not ... anything** nichts 2

apartment [əˈpɑːtmənt] die Wohnung 2

app [æp] die App 1

appear [əˈpɪə] auftauchen, erscheinen 3 **appear to be/do** zu sein/zu tun scheinen 3

apple [ˈæpl] der Apfel 1

apprentice [əˈprentɪs] der Lehrling, der/die Auszubildende 4: 3 (86)

apprenticeship [əˈprentɪʃɪp] die Ausbildung, die Lehre 4: 3 (86)

°**approach** [əˈprəʊtʃ] sich nähern, näher kommen

April [ˈeɪprəl] der April 1

°**aquarium** [əˈkweərɪəm] das Aquarium

°**Arabic** [ˈærəbɪk] arabisch; Arabisch

architect [ˈɑːkɪtekt] der Architekt, die Architektin 2

°**Arctic** [ˈɑːktɪk] die Arktis **Arctic Ocean** der Arktische Ozean, das Nordpolarmeer

are [ɑː]: **The books are £2.** Die Bücher kosten 2 Pfund. 2 **they are** sie sind 1 **they aren't** sie sind nicht 1 **you are** du bist / ihr seid 1

area [ˈeərɪə] der Bereich, die Gegend, die Fläche 1

argue [ˈɑːgjuː]:
1. argumentieren 3
argue an opinion eine Meinung vertreten 3 **argue for/against sth.** sich für/gegen etwas aussprechen 3
2. **argue (about)** (sich) streiten (über/wegen) 3

argument [ˈɑːgjumənt]:
1. das Argument 3
2. der Streit 3

arm [ɑːm] der Arm 2

army [ˈɑːmi] die Armee 4: 2 (51) **join the army** zur Armee gehen 4: 2 (51)

around [əˈraʊnd]:
1. around ... um (... herum), in ... umher 2
all around the globe auf der ganzen Welt 3
2. **get around** sich fortbewegen (mobil sein) 4: 3 (79)
°**I haven't seen you around.** Ich habe dich hier noch nie gesehen.

arrival [əˈraɪvl] die Ankunft 2

arrive [əˈraɪv] ankommen 2

art [ɑːt] die Kunst 1

°**article** [ˈɑːtɪkl] der Artikel

artificial [ɑːtɪˈfɪʃl] künstlich; unecht 4: 4 (111)

artificial intelligence (AI) [ɑːtɪfɪʃl ɪnˈtelɪdʒəns] die künstliche Intelligenz (KI) 4: 4 (111)

artist [ˈɑːtɪst] der/die Künstler/in 2

as [æz], [əz]:
1. als, während (Konjunktion) 2
as they walk während sie gehen 2

2. als (Präposition) 2
as a teacher als als Lehrer/in 2
3. wie (Präposition) 2
as well auch 4: 1 (23) **(not) as bad as** (nicht) so schlecht/schlimm wie 2 **... as well as ...** sowohl ... als auch ... 4: 1 (23)

ASAP (as soon as possible) [eɪ es eɪ ˈpiː] so bald wie möglich 4: 4 (122)

ask [ɑːsk]:
1. fragen 1
ask a question eine Frage stellen 1
2. **ask sb. for sth.** jn. um etwas bitten 1
ask sb. to do sth. jn. bitten, etwas zu tun 1

asleep [əˈsliːp]: **be asleep** schlafen 2 **fall asleep** einschlafen 2

assembly [əˈsembli] die Schulversammlung 2

assistant [əˈsɪstənt]:
1. der/die Assistent/in 2
2. (= shop assistant) der/die Verkäufer/in 2

association [əsəʊʃiˈeɪʃn] der Verband, die Vereinigung 4: 1 (23)

at [æt], [ət] an; in; bei; auf 1 **at 8 o'clock** um 8 Uhr 1 **at a good price** zu einem guten Preis 3 **at least** wenigstens, zumindest 2 **at night** nachts, in der Nacht 2 **at the cinema** im Kino 1 **at the top (of)** oben, am oberen Ende (von); an der Spitze (von) 1 **at work** bei der Arbeit, am Arbeitsplatz 1 **be good at sth. / at doing sth.** etwas gut können; gut in etwas sein 1 **Open your books at page 10.** Schlagt eure Bücher auf Seite 10 auf. 1

ate [eɪt], [et] siehe eat

athlete [ˈæθliːt] der/die (Leicht-) Athlet/in, der/die Sportler/in 4: 2 (52)

°**Atlantic** [əˈtlæntɪk]:
1. atlantisch
2. the Atlantic (Ocean) der Atlantik, der atlantische Ozean

ATM (at the moment) [eɪ tiː ˈem] im Moment, zurzeit 4: 4 (122)

audio [ˈɔːdɪəʊ] Audio-, Ton- 3

August [ˈɔːgəst] der August 1

aunt [ɑːnt] die Tante 1

award [əˈwɔːd] der Preis (Auszeichnung) 4: 2 (52)

award-winner [əˈwɔːd wɪnə] der/die Preisträger/in 4: 2 (52)

award-winning [əˈwɔːd wɪnɪŋ] preisgekrönt 4: 2 (52)

away [əˈweɪ] weg, fort 1

awesome [ˈɔːsəm] (AE, infml) klasse, stark, großartig 4: 1 (19)

baby [ˈbeɪbi] das Baby 2

babysat [ˈbeɪbisæt] siehe babysit

babysit [ˈbeɪbisɪt], babysat, babysat babysitten 2

babysitter [ˈbeɪbisɪtə] der/die Babysitter/in 2

babysitting [ˈbeɪbisɪtɪŋ] das Babysitten 2

back [bæk]:
1. zurück 2
back at home wieder zu Hause 2 **like/love sb. back** js. Liebe erwidern, jn. auch mögen/lieben 3
2. **at the back (of the bus/cinema)** hinten (im Bus/im Kino) 2
at the back of the book hinten im Buch 2 **on the back of the card** auf der Rückseite der Karte 2

background [ˈbækgraʊnd] der Hintergrund 3

backpack [ˈbækpæk] der Rucksack 4: 1 (22)

bad [bæd] schlecht; schlimm 1

badly [ˈbædli]: **do badly** schlecht abschneiden, keinen Erfolg haben 3

bag [bæg] die Tasche 1

bagpipes (pl) [ˈbægpaɪps] der Dudelsack 3

bake [beɪk] backen 2

baker [ˈbeɪkə] der/die Bäcker/in 2

bakery [ˈbeɪkəri] die Bäckerei 2

ball [bɔːl] der Ball 1

balloon [bəˈluːn] der Ballon 1

ban [bæn]:
1. verbieten 4: 4 (113)
be banned verboten sein/werden 4: 4 (113)
2. **ban (on)** das Verbot (von) 4: 4 (113)

banana [bəˈnɑːnə] die Banane 1

band [bænd] die Band, die Musikgruppe 1

bank [bæŋk] die Bank (Geldinstitut) 2

bank account [ˈbæŋk əkaʊnt] das Bankkonto 2

bar chart [ˈbɑː tʃɑːt] das Balkendiagramm 4: 4 (124)

barbecue [ˈbɑːbɪkjuː] das Grillfest, das Grillen 3

bark (at sb.) [bɑːk] (jn. an)bellen 1

baseball [ˈbeɪsbɔːl] der Baseball 4: 1 (24)

basketball [ˈbɑːskɪtbɔːl] der Basketball 1

bathroom [ˈbɑːθruːm]:
1. das Bad(ezimmer) 1
2. (AE) die Toilette (in privaten Häusern/Wohnungen) 4: 1 (22)

be [biː], was/were, been sein 1
I want to be a firefighter. Ich möchte Feuerwehrmann/-frau werden. 2
It is hot today, isn't it? Heute ist es heiß, nicht wahr? /..., oder? 4: 3 (82)
You are ..., aren't you? Du bist ..., nicht wahr? /..., oder? 4: 3 (82)

beach [biːtʃ] der Strand 1 **on the beach** am Strand 1 **to the beach** zum Strand, an den Strand 1

bear [beə] der Bär 4: 4 (118)

beautiful [ˈbjuːtɪfl] wunderschön 2

beauty [ˈbjuːti] die Schönheit 2

became [bɪˈkeɪm] siehe become

because [bɪˈkɒz] weil 1

because of [bɪˈkɒz əv] wegen 3

become [bɪˈkʌm], became, become werden 2

bed [bed] das Bett 1 **go to bed** ins Bett gehen 1

bedroom ['bedru:m] das Schlafzimmer 1

been [bi:n] *siehe* be

before [bɪˈfɔ:]:
1. vorher; zuvor; schon einmal 3
2. **before (you read)** bevor (du liest) 1
3. **before (school / the lesson)** vor (der Schule / der Unterrichtsstunde) 1

began [bɪˈgæn] *siehe* begin

begin [bɪˈgɪn], began, begun anfangen, beginnen 3

beginning [bɪˈgɪnɪŋ] der Anfang 3

begun [bɪˈgʌn] *siehe* begin

behaviour [bɪˈheɪvjə] das Verhalten; das Benehmen 4: 2 (52)

behind [bɪˈhaɪnd] hinter 1

°**beignet** ['benjeɪ] der Beignet *(gefüllter Krapfen)*

believe (in) [bɪˈli:v] glauben (an) 2

below [bɪˈləʊ] unter(halb von); unten 2

°**beneath** [bɪˈni:θ] unter(halb von), unten

best [best] beste(r, s); am besten 1 **Best wishes** Viele Grüße *(Briefschluss)* 4: 3 (89) **like sth. best** etwas am liebsten mögen 2

better ['betə] besser 2 **like sth. better** etwas lieber mögen 2

between [bɪˈtwi:n] zwischen 2

big [bɪg]:
1. groß 1
2. schwer, dick *(Person)* 2

big wheel [bɪg ˈwi:l] das Riesenrad 3

bike [baɪk] das Fahrrad 1

bike lane ['baɪk leɪn] der Radweg 3

bio ['baɪəʊ] *siehe* biography

biography [baɪˈɒgrəfi] *kurz auch* bio die Biografie 3

bird [bɜ:d] der Vogel 2

birthday ['bɜ:θdeɪ] der Geburtstag 1 **Happy birthday!** Herzlichen Glückwunsch zum Geburtstag! 1 **My birthday is in April.** Ich habe im April Geburtstag. 1 **on my birthday** an meinem Geburtstag 1 **When's your birthday?** Wann hast du Geburtstag? 1

biscuit ['bɪskɪt] der Keks, das Plätzchen 2

bit [bɪt]: **a bit** ein bisschen, ein wenig 2

black [blæk] schwarz 1

blame sb. (for sth.) [bleɪm] jm. die Schuld geben (an etwas), es jm. übelnehmen 3

blanket ['blæŋkɪt] die Decke *(zum Zudecken u. Ä.)* 1

blew [blu:] *siehe* blow

block [blɒk]:
1. blockieren, versperren; verstopfen 4: 4 (121)
2. der Block; der Klotz; der Häuserblock 4: 4 (121)

blog [blɒg]:
1. bloggen 3
2. der/das Blog *(Internet-Tagebuch)* 3

blond [blɒnd] blond 2

blow [bləʊ], blew, blown wehen; pusten, blasen 4: 2 (59) **blow sth. up** etwas aufblasen *(z. B Ballon)* 4: 2 (59)

blown [bləʊn] *siehe* blow

blue [blu:] blau 1

bluegrass ['blu:grɑ:s] der Bluegrass *(Musikrichtung innerhalb der Countrymusic)* 4: 2 (57)

board [bɔ:d] die Tafel 1

boarding school ['bɔ:dɪŋ sku:l]:
1. das Internat 4: 4 (114)
°2. *das Internat für Indigene, in das Kinder zwangsweise gebracht wurden, um sie kulturell anzupassen*

boat [bəʊt] das Boot; das Schiff 1

body ['bɒdi] der Körper 2

book [bʊk] das Buch 1

boot [bu:t] der Stiefel 2

bored [bɔ:d] gelangweilt 2 **be bored / get bored** sich langweilen 2 **I'm bored** mir ist langweilig 2

boring ['bɔ:rɪŋ] langweilig 2

born [bɔ:n]: **he was born** er wurde geboren 2

°**borough** ['bʌrə] *(AE)* der (Stadt-)Bezirk

borrow ['bɒrəʊ] (aus)leihen, sich borgen 3

boss [bɒs] der Boss, der/die Chef/in 2

both [bəʊθ] beide 3 **both ... and ...** sowohl ... als auch ... 3

bottle ['bɒtl] die Flasche 2

bottom ['bɒtəm] das untere Ende 2

bottomless ['bɒtəmləs] bodenlos, unerschöpflich; mit kostenlosem Nachschank *(bei Getränken z. B. in Cafés)* 3

bought [bɔ:t] *siehe* buy

bowling ['bəʊlɪŋ] das Bowling, das Kegeln 1

box [bɒks] die Box, der Kasten 2

boy [bɔɪ] der Junge 1

boyfriend ['bɔɪfrend] der (feste) Freund 2

braces (pl) ['breɪsɪz] die Zahnspange, die Zahnklammer 2

°**bracket** ['brækɪt] die *(runde)* Klammer *(in Texten)*

brainstorm (ideas/reasons) ['breɪnstɔ:m] (Ideen/Gründe) (ungeordnet) sammeln 4: 1 (32)

brand [brænd] die (Produkt-)Marke 3

brave [breɪv] mutig 3

bread [bred] das Brot 1

break [breɪk] die Pause 1

break [breɪk], broke, broken (zer)brechen 2 **break the fast** das Fasten brechen 2

breakfast ['brekfəst] das Frühstück 1

breath [breθ] der Atem(zug) 3 **take a deep breath** tief durchatmen 3

breathe (in/out) [bri:ð] (ein-/aus-) atmen 2

°**breeze** [bri:z] die Brise

bridge [brɪdʒ] die Brücke 2

bring [brɪŋ], brought, brought bringen, mitbringen 1

Britain ['brɪtn] Großbritannien 1

British ['brɪtɪʃ] britisch 1

British Isles (pl) [brɪtɪʃ ˈaɪlz] die Britischen Inseln 3

brochure ['brəʊʃə] die Broschüre, der Prospekt 4: 1 (29)

broke [brəʊk] *siehe* break

broken ['brəʊkən]: **be broken** zerbrochen, kaputt, sein 2

brother ['brʌðə] der Bruder 1

brought [brɔ:t] *siehe* bring

brown [braʊn] braun 1

brunch [brʌntʃ] das Brunch 2

brush [brʌʃ]:
1. die Bürste 1
2. bürsten 1
brush your teeth (sich) die Zähne putzen 1

°**bubble** ['bʌbl]: **speech bubble** die Sprechblase

build [bɪld], built, built bauen 4: 2 (54)

builder ['bɪldə]:
1. der/die Bauarbeiter/in; der/die Bauunternehmer/in 4: 4 (122)
2. der/die Konstrukteur/in 4: 4 (122) **robot builder** der/die Roboter-Konstrukteur/in 4: 4 (122)

building ['bɪldɪŋ] das Gebäude 1

built [bɪlt] *siehe* build

bully ['bʊli]:
1. der/die Mobber/in; der Tyrann, die Tyrannin 1
2. tyrannisieren, mobben 1

bump [bʌmp]: **bump into/against sb./ sth.** jn./etwas (an)stoßen, gegen etwas stoßen 4: 3 (88) **bump into sb.** *(infml)* mit jm. zusammenstoßen; jn. zufällig treffen, jm. zufällig begegnen 4: 3 (88)

°**bureau** ['bjʊərəʊ] das Büro; *(AE:)* die Behörde

burger ['bɜ:gə] der Hamburger *(Frikadelle)* 3

burn [bɜ:n] brennen 4: 4 (120) **burn sth.** etwas verbrennen 4: 4 (120) **burn sth. down** etwas abbrennen, niederbrennen 4: 4 (120)

bus [bʌs] der Bus 1 **by bus** mit dem Bus 1 **on the bus** im Bus 1

business ['bɪznəs] das Geschäft, der Betrieb 2 **start a business** ein Geschäft aufmachen, einen Betrieb gründen/eröffnen 2 **study business** Business studieren *(Betriebswirtschaft, Management)* 4: 3 (86)

business card ['bɪznəs kɑ:d] die Visitenkarte, die Geschäftskarte 2

business owner ['bɪznəs əʊnə] der/die Geschäftsinhaber/in 2

busy ['bɪzi] (viel)beschäftigt 1 **be busy** beschäftigt sein, (viel) zu tun haben 1

but [bʌt], [bət] aber 1

butter ['bʌtə] die Butter 1

buy [baɪ], bought, bought kaufen 1

by [baɪ]:
1. **by ...** von ... (in Passivsätzen) 4: 4 (114)
2. **by bus** mit dem Bus 1
pay by card mit Karte (be)zahlen (z. B Bankkarte) 2
3. **by the sea** am Meer, an der See 1
4. **by state/name/population/...** nach (Bundes-)Staat / dem Namen / der Bevölkerungszahl / ... (sortiert) 4: 4 (124)
refer to sth. by its name/number etwas mit seinem Namen / seiner Nummer bezeichnen 4: 1 (26)
5. **by the way (BTW)** übrigens 4: 4 (122)
Bye. [baɪ] Tschüs. 1

C

cabin [ˈkæbɪn] die Hütte; die Kabine 4: 4 (118)
cafe [ˈkæfeɪ] das Café 1
cafeteria [kæfəˈtɪəriə] (AE) die Kantine; die Cafeteria 4: 3 (88)
°**cage** [keɪdʒ] der Käfig
cake [keɪk] der Kuchen, die Torte 1
calendar [ˈkælɪndə] der Kalender 2
call [kɔːl]:
1. nennen; rufen; anrufen 2
call sb. names jn. beschimpfen 3
2. der Ruf 2
3. (kurz für: **phone call**) der (Telefon-)Anruf 2
called [kɔːld]: **be called** heißen 1
calm [kɑːm] ruhig, besonnen 2
came [keɪm] siehe **come**
camera [ˈkæmərə] die Kamera 2
camp [kæmp] das (Zelt-)Lager 4: (14/15)
camper [ˈkæmpə] der Camper, die Camperin 4: (14/15)
camping [ˈkæmpɪŋ] das Camping 3
campsite [ˈkæmpsaɪt] der Campingplatz 2
can [kæn], [kən] können 1
canal [kəˈnæl] der Kanal 3
candle [ˈkændl] die Kerze 2
candy [ˈkændi] (AE) die Süßigkeiten 4: (12/13)
can't [kɑːnt]: **I can't (= cannot)** ich kann nicht 1
canteen [kænˈtiːn] die Kantine, die (Schul-)Mensa 1
°**Canuck** [kəˈnʌk] (AE, infml) der/die Kanadier/in
cap [kæp] die (Schirm-)Mütze, die Kappe 1
cape [keɪp] das Cape (Umhang) 2
capital [ˈkæpɪtl]:
1. **capital (city)** die Hauptstadt 3
2. **capital (letter)** der Großbuchstabe 3
capsule [ˈkæpsjuːl] die Kapsel; die Raumkapsel; die Kabine (auf einem Riesenrad) 3
caption [ˈkæpʃn] die Bildunterschrift 4: 2 (62)
car [kɑː] das Auto 1

card [kɑːd] die Karte 1 **business card** die Visitenkarte, die Geschäftskarte 2 **pay by card** mit Karte (be)zahlen (z. B Bankkarte) 2 **playing card** die Spielkarte 1
care [keə]:
1. die Sorgfalt, die Vorsicht 2 **take care** vorsichtig sein, aufpassen 2
2. die Versorgung, die Betreuung; die Pflege 3 **take care of sb./sth.** sich um jn./etwas kümmern 3
3. **care about sth.** etwas wichtig nehmen 3 **care for** betreuen, pflegen; sich kümmern um; aufpassen auf 3 **I care about animals.** Tiere liegen mir am Herzen. 3
careful [ˈkeəfl] vorsichtig 1
careless [ˈkeələs] unvorsichtig, leichtsinnig 3
carer [ˈkeərə] die Pflegekraft; der/die Betreuer/in 3
carnival [ˈkɑːnɪvl] der Karneval 2
carrot [ˈkærət] die Möhre, die Karotte 1
carry [ˈkæri] tragen; bei sich haben; befördern 3
°**cart** [kɑːt] der Wagen (Einkaufswagen, Golfwagen etc.)
cartoon [kɑːˈtuːn] der Zeichentrickfilm; der Comic, der Cartoon 2
case [keɪs] das Etui, der Behälter, der Kasten 1
cash [kæʃ] das Cash, das Bargeld 2 **pay (in) cash** bar bezahlen 2
cash machine [ˈkæʃ məʃiːn] der Geldautomat 2
castle [ˈkɑːsl] die Burg 2
cat [kæt] die Katze 1
catch [kætʃ], **caught, caught** fangen; erwischen; nehmen (z. B Zug, Bus) 3
caught [kɔːt] siehe **catch**
°**Caution!** [ˈkɔːʃn] Vorsicht!, Warnung!
cave [keɪv] die Höhle 3
celebrate [ˈselɪbreɪt] feiern 2
celebration [selɪˈbreɪʃn] die Feier, das Fest 2
celebrity [səˈlebrəti] der/die Prominente, der/die Promi 4: 4 (108/109)
°**census** [ˈsensəs], pl **censuses** die (Daten-)Erhebung, die (Volks-)Zählung
cent [sent] der Cent 2
centimetre (= cm) [ˈsentimiːtə] der Zentimeter 4: 4 (123)
central [ˈsentrəl] zentral 3
centre [ˈsentə] das Zentrum; die Mitte 2
certain [ˈsɜːtn] gewiss, bestimmt; sicher 4: 1 (21)
certainly [ˈsɜːtnli] sicher(lich), gewiss 4: 1 (21)
chair [tʃeə] der Stuhl 1
challenge [ˈtʃælɪndʒ]:
1. die Herausforderung 4: 1 (21) **take on a challenge** eine Herausforderung annehmen, sich einer Herausforderung stellen 4: 1 (21)

2. **challenge sb. (to sth.)** jn. (zu etwas) herausfordern 4: 1 (21)
challenging [ˈtʃælɪndʒɪŋ] anspruchsvoll, (heraus)fordernd 4: 1 (21)
champion [ˈtʃæmpiən] der/die Meister/in (in einer Sportart), der Champion 3
chance [tʃɑːns]:
1. die Chance, die Gelegenheit 3
2. das Risiko 3
Don't take any chances! Geh auf Nummer sicher! / Geh keine Risiken ein! 3
change [tʃeɪndʒ]:
1. **change (into)** (sich) (ver)ändern (zu/in); wechseln; (sich) verwandeln (in), werden (zu) 2
change your mind seine Meinung ändern 4: 4 (112) **Changing of the Guards** die Wachablösung 3
change (clothes) sich umziehen (frische Kleidung anziehen) 2 **change (trains)** umsteigen 2
2. die Veränderung, der Wechsel, die Verwandlung 2
a change of clothes die (frische) Kleidung zum Wechseln 2
3. das Wechselgeld 2
channel [ˈtʃænl] der Sender, der (TV-)Kanal 3 **the (English) Channel** der Ärmelkanal 3
character [ˈkærəktə] der Charakter; die Figur (aus einer Geschichte) 2
charge [tʃɑːdʒ] aufladen (Smartphone, Batterie, ...) 3
charger [ˈtʃɑːdʒə] das Ladegerät 3
charity [ˈtʃærəti] die wohltätige Organisation 2 **animal charity** die wohltätige Organisation, die Tiere unterstützt 2
charity shop [ˈtʃærəti ʃɒp] das Geschäft, das gespendete Waren für wohltätige Zwecke verkauft 2
chart [tʃɑːt] das Diagramm; die Tabelle 4: 1 (20) **bar chart** das Balkendiagramm 4: 4 (124) **column chart** das Säulendiagramm 4: 4 (124) **line chart** das Liniendiagramm 4: 4 (124) **pie chart** das Tortendiagramm, das Kreisdiagramm 4: 4 (124)
chase [tʃeɪs]:
1. verfolgen, jagen 4: 2 (61)
2. die Verfolgung(sjagd) 4: 2 (61)
chat [tʃæt]:
1. die Unterhaltung; der Chat 2 **have a chat** eine Unterhaltung führen, sich unterhalten 2
2. **chat (with)** chatten (mit); sich unterhalten (mit) 2
chatbot [ˈtʃætbɒt] der Chatbot (Computerprogramm, mit dem man chatten kann) 4: 4 (111)
cheap [tʃiːp] billig, preiswert 3
cheat [tʃiːt]:
1. der Betrug, der Schwindel, die Mogelei 4: 4 (112)
2. **cheat (at/on sth.)** betrügen, mogeln, schummeln (bei etwas) 4: 4 (112)

cheater [ˈtʃiːtə] der/die Betrüger/in, der/die Schwindler/in, der/die Falschspieler/in 4: 4 (112)

check [tʃek]:
1. die (Über-)Prüfung, die Kontrolle 1
2. (über)prüfen, kontrollieren 1
check on sb./sth. nach jm./etwas schauen, sich um jn./etwas kümmern 4: 2 (59)   check sb./sth. out (infml) sich jn./etwas anschauen, anhören; etwas ausprobieren 2

checklist [ˈtʃeklɪst] die Checkliste 2

°checkpoint [ˈtʃekpɔɪnt] der Kontrollpunkt

cheer [tʃɪə] jubeln, (Sportler/innen) anfeuern 3

cheese [tʃiːz] der Käse 1

chemical [ˈkemɪkl]:
1. Chemikalie 2
2. chemisch 2

chicken [ˈtʃɪkɪn] das Huhn; das (Brat-)Hähnchen 1

chicken wing [ˈtʃɪkɪn wɪŋ] der Hähnchenflügel 4: 1 (25)

chickpea [ˈtʃɪkpiː] die Kichererbse 3

child [tʃaɪld], pl children das Kind 2

children [tʃɪldrən] Plural von child

chips (pl) [tʃɪps]:
1. die Pommes frites 1
fish and chips der Fisch mit Pommes Frites 1
2. (AE) die (Kartoffel-)Chips 4: 1 (25)

chocolate [ˈtʃɒklət] die Schokolade 1
hot chocolate der Kakao, die heiße (Trink-)Schokolade 1

choice [tʃɔɪs] die (Aus-)Wahl; die Entscheidung 3

choir [ˈkwaɪə] der Chor 3

choose [tʃuːz], chose, chosen (aus)wählen 2   choose to do sth. sich entscheiden, beschließen etwas zu tun 3

chore [tʃɔː] die (Haus-)Arbeit, die (lästige) Pflicht 2   do chores (Haus-)Arbeiten erledigen 2

°chorus [ˈkɔːrəs] der Refrain (Lied)

chose [tʃəʊz] siehe choose

chosen [ˈtʃəʊzn] siehe choose

Christmas [ˈkrɪsməs] (das) Weihnachten 2

Christmas Day [krɪsməs ˈdeɪ] der 1. Weihnachtstag (25. 12.) 2

church [tʃɜːtʃ] die Kirche 2

cinema [ˈsɪnəmə] das Kino 1
at the cinema im Kino 1

circle [ˈsɜːkl] der Kreis 1

circus [ˈsɜːkəs] der Zirkus 1

city [ˈsɪti] die (Groß-)Stadt 1

clap (your hands) [klæp] (in die Hände) klatschen 3

class [klɑːs] die Klasse; der Unterricht; der Kurs 1   in class im Unterricht 1

class teacher [ˈklɑːs tiːtʃə] der/die Klassenlehrer/in 1

classic [ˈklæsɪk]:
1. der Klassiker 3
2. klassisch 3

classical [ˈklæsɪkl] klassisch 2

classical music [klæsɪkl ˈmjuːzɪk] klassische Musik 2

classmate [ˈklɑːsmeɪt] der/die Mitschüler/in 3

classroom [ˈklɑːsruːm] das Klassenzimmer 1

clean [kliːn]:
1. sauber 1
2. sauber machen, putzen 1
clean out the stables ausmisten 4: 3 (87)   clean sth. up etwas aufräumen, sauber machen 1

clean-up [ˈkliːn ʌp] das Säubern, das Saubermachen 1

clean-up day [ˈkliːn ʌp deɪ] der Dreckweg-Tag (Aktionstag zum Müllsammeln) 1

cleaner [ˈkliːnə] die Reinigungskraft 1

clear [klɪə] klar, deutlich 2

clever [ˈklevə] schlau, klug 1

click [klɪk]:
1. der Klick, das Klicken 2
2. click (on) klicken (auf), anklicken 2

cliff [klɪf] die Klippe 3

cliff jumping [ˈklɪf dʒʌmpɪŋ] das Klippenspringen 3

climate [ˈklaɪmət] das Klima 3

climate change [ˈklaɪmət tʃeɪndʒ] der Klimawandel 3

climb [klaɪm]:
1. der Aufstieg, die Klettertour; der Anstieg 2
2. klettern (auf) 2

climber [ˈklaɪmə] der Kletterer, die Kletterin 2

clip [klɪp] der (Video-)Clip 4: 2 (56)

clock [klɒk] die (Wand-, Stand-, Turm-)Uhr 1

close [kləʊz] schließen, zumachen 1

close (to) [kləʊs] knapp; nahe (bei, an) 4: 2 (59)

closed [kləʊzd] geschlossen 1

clothes (pl) [kləʊðz] die Kleidung, die Kleidungsstücke 1   a change of clothes (frische) Kleidung zum Wechseln 2

clothes swap [ˈkləʊðz swɒp] der Kleidertausch, die Kleidertauschparty 1

cloud [klaʊd] die Wolke 1

cloudy [ˈklaʊdi] wolkig, bewölkt 1

clown [klaʊn] der Clown 1

club [klʌb] der Klub, der Verein 1
school club die AG (in der Schule) 1

clue [kluː] der (Lösungs-)Hinweis; der Anhaltspunkt 3   I don't have a clue. / I have no clue. (infml) Ich habe keine Ahnung. / Keine Ahnung. 3

coach [kəʊtʃ] der (Reise-)Bus 3

coast [kəʊst] die Küste 3

cocoa [ˈkəʊkəʊ] der Kakao 1

code [kəʊd] programmieren (Computer); kodieren 1

coding [ˈkəʊdɪŋ] das Programmieren (Computer) 1

coffee [ˈkɒfi] der Kaffee 1

coin [kɔɪn] die Münze 2

cola [ˈkəʊlə] die Cola 1

cold [kəʊld]:
1. kalt 1
be cold frieren 1
2. die Kälte 1
3. die Erkältung 1
have a cold erkältet sein 1

collect [kəˈlekt] (ein)sammeln 1

collection [kəˈlekʃn] die Sammlung 4: 3 (92)

college [ˈkɒlɪdʒ] die Hochschule 4: 3 (86)

colour [ˈkʌlə] die Farbe 1   What colour is ...? Welche Farbe hat ...? 1

colourful [ˈkʌləfl] farbig, bunt 3

colourless [ˈkʌlələs] farblos 3

column [ˈkɒləm] die Säule; die Spalte (in Texten) 3

column chart [ˈkɒləm tʃɑːt] das Säulendiagramm 4: 4 (124)

come [kʌm], came, come (mit)kommen 1   come after sb. hinter jm. herkommen 3   come off (sth.) abgehen (von etwas), (herunter)fallen (von etwas), sich lösen (von etwas) 2   come over hinüberkommen, rüberkommen 2

comfortable [ˈkʌmftəbl] bequem, gemütlich 3

comic [ˈkɒmɪk] der Comic 1

comma [ˈkɒmə] das Komma 4: 1 (20)

command [kəˈmɑːnd] der Befehl, das Kommando 3

comment (about/on sth.) [ˈkɒment]:
1. (etwas) kommentieren 3
2. der Kommentar (über/zu etwas) 3

commercial [kəˈmɜːʃl]:
1. der Werbespot 4: 1 (25)
2. kommerziell (auf Gewinn ausgerichtet) 4: 1 (25)

°common [ˈkɒmən] häufig, weit verbreitet, gewöhnlich

communicate [kəˈmjuːnɪkeɪt] kommunizieren, sich verständigen 4: 3 (92)

communication [kəmjuːnɪˈkeɪʃn] die Kommunikation, die Verständigung 4: 3 (92)

community [kəˈmjuːnəti] die Gemeinschaft, die Gemeinde 3

company [ˈkʌmpəni] die Firma, die Gesellschaft 4: 4 (110)

compare (to/with) [kəmˈpeə] vergleichen (mit) 3

competition [kɒmpəˈtɪʃn] der Wettbewerb 1   hold a competition einen Wettbewerb veranstalten, abhalten 4: 4 (122)

complete [kəmˈpliːt]:
1. vervollständigen 3
2. vollständig, komplett 3

completely [kəmˈpliːtli] völlig, absolut (Adv.) 3

compliment [ˈkɒmplɪmənt] das Kompliment 3   pay sb. a compliment jm. ein Kompliment machen 3

computer [kəmˈpjuːtə] der Computer 1

computing [kəmˈpjuːtɪŋ] die Informatik 1

concert [ˈkɒnsət] das Konzert 2

conclusion [kənˈkluːʒn] der Schluss; die Schlussfolgerung 4: 1 (33)

condor [ˈkɒndɔː] der Kondor (Vogel) 4: 4 (115)

°conference [ˈkɒnfərəns] die Konferenz, die Besprechung

confidence [ˈkɒnfɪdəns] das (Selbst-) Vertrauen, die Zuversicht 3

confident [ˈkɒnfɪdənt] (selbst)sicher; zuversichtlich 2

conflict [ˈkɒnflɪkt] der Konflikt, die Auseinandersetzung, der Streit 3

confused [kənˈfjuːzd] verwirrt 3

connect (to/with) [kəˈnekt] (sich) verbinden (mit) 4: (10/11)

connection [kəˈnekʃn] die Verbindung 4: (10/11)

cons (pl) [kɒnz]: the pros and cons das Pro und Kontra; das Für und Wider 4: 4 (125)

console [kənˈsəʊl] die Konsole 1

contact [ˈkɒntækt]:
1. der Kontakt 2
2. contact sb. Kontakt aufnehmen mit jm., sich in Verbindung setzen mit jm. 2

continue [kənˈtɪnjuː] fortfahren, weitermachen; (sich) fortsetzen, weitergehen 4: 2 (50) continue to do sth. etwas weiterhin tun, (mit) etwas weitermachen, fortfahren 4: 2 (50)

contrast [kənˈtrɑːst] vergleichen, (einander) gegenüberstellen 4: 4 (108/109)

contrast [ˈkɒntrɑːst] der Kontrast, der Gegensatz 4: 4 (108/109)

°conversation [kɒnvəˈseɪʃn] das Gespräch

°convince sb. of sth. [kənˈvɪns] jn. von etwas überzeugen

cook [kʊk]:
1. der Koch, die Köchin 1
2. kochen 1

cookie [ˈkʊki] (AE) der Keks, das Plätzchen 4: 1 (21)

cooking [ˈkʊkɪŋ] das Kochen 1

cool [kuːl] cool 1

copy [ˈkɒpi]:
1. die Kopie; das Exemplar 4: 4 (111)
2. kopieren, abschreiben 4: 4 (111)

corn [kɔːn]:
1. das Korn, das Getreide 4: 2 (55)
2. (AE) der Mais 4: 2 (55)

cornbread [ˈkɔːnbred] das Maisbrot 4: 2 (55)

correct [kəˈrekt]:
1. korrekt 3
2. korrigieren 3

cosplay [ˈkɒspleɪ] das Cosplay (Sichverkleiden als eine Figur z. B aus einem Manga) 3

cost [kɒst]:
1. die Kosten; der Preis 1
2. cost, cost, cost kosten 1

costume [ˈkɒstjuːm] das Kostüm, die Verkleidung 3

cough [kɒf]:
1. husten 2
2. der Husten 2

could [kʊd]:
1. I could ich konnte 2
2. he could er könnte 2

counsellor [ˈkaʊnsələ] der/die Berater/in; der/die Betreuer/in 4: (14/15)

°count (to ten) [kaʊnt] (bis zehn) zählen

country [ˈkʌntri]:
1. das Land, (auch:) die ländliche Gegend 1
2. country (music) die Countrymusic (Musikstil) 4: 2 (46/47)

course [kɔːs]:
1. der Kurs 2
2. main course das Hauptgericht 1

court [kɔːt] der Platz, der Court (Tennis, Basketball) 4: 1 (24)

cousin [ˈkʌzn] der Cousin, die Cousine 1

cowboy [ˈkaʊbɔɪ] der Cowboy 4: (10/11)

cowgirl [kaʊgɜːl] das Cowgirl 4: (10/11)

crafts (pl) [krɑːfts] das Kunsthandwerk, das Basteln 1

crazy [ˈkreɪzi] verrückt 2 be crazy about sth. wild auf etwas sein, versessen auf etwas sein 2

cream [kriːm] die Sahne 1

°creamy [ˈkriːmi] cremig; sahnig

create [kriˈeɪt] (er)schaffen, erstellen 2

creative [kriˈeɪtɪv] kreativ 2

°creative commons [krieɪtɪv ˈkɒmənz] „das schöpferische Gemeingut" (gemeinnützige Organisation, die das einfache Verbreiten von Nutzungsrechten zum Ziel hat)

creator [kriˈeɪtə] der/die Autor/in, der/die Zeichner/in, der/die Schöpfer/in 4: 1 (25)

cricket [ˈkrɪkɪt] das Kricket (Mannschaftssportart) 1

crisps (pl) [krɪsps] die (Kartoffel-) Chips 4: 1 (25)

°criticize [ˈkrɪtɪsaɪz] kritisieren

cross [krɒs]:
1. das Kreuz 3
2. kreuzen, überqueren 3
cross your fingers die Daumen drücken/halten (jm. Glück / gutes Gelingen wünschen) 3
°3. mit einem Kreuz versehen

crowdfund sth. [ˈkraʊdfʌnd] etwas durch Crowdfunding finanzieren 4: 4 (122)

crowdfunding [ˈkraʊdfʌndɪŋ] das Crowdfunding (Schwarmfinanzierung) 4: 4 (122)

crush [krʌʃ]:
1. die Schwärmerei, das Verliebtsein 3
have a crush (on sb.) in jn. verliebt sein 3
2. der Schwarm (jd., in den/die man verliebt ist) 3

cry [kraɪ]:
1. der Schrei, der Ruf 3
2. weinen; rufen, schreien 3

cucumber [ˈkjuːkʌmbə] die Gurke (Salatgurke) 3

cultural [ˈkʌltʃərəl] kulturell, Kultur- 4: 2 (56)

culture [ˈkʌltʃə] die Kultur 4: 2 (56)

cup [kʌp]:
1. die Tasse 4: 2 (54)
°2. der Cup (Pokalwettbewerb; Siegespokal)

cupcake [ˈkʌpkeɪk] der Cupcake (kleiner Muffin-ähnlicher Kuchen) 2

°curious (about) [ˈkjʊəriəs] neugierig (auf)

curl [kɜːl] die Locke 2

curly [ˈkɜːli] lockig 2

curry [ˈkʌri] das Curry (Gewürz und auch Gericht) 2

cushion [ˈkʊʃn] das Kissen 1

custard [ˈkʌstəd] der Custard (Vanillesoße) 1

customer [ˈkʌstəmə] der Kunde, die Kundin 2

cut [kʌt]:
1. der Schnitt 1
2. cut, cut, cut schneiden 1

cute [kjuːt] niedlich, süß 1

CYA (See you!) [ˈsiː juː] Bis dann. / Tschüs. 4: 4 (122)

cyberbullying [ˈsaɪbəbʊliŋ] das Cybermobbing 3

cycle [ˈsaɪkl] Rad fahren 1

cycle lane [ˈsaɪkl leɪn] der Radweg 3

cycling [ˈsaɪklɪŋ] das Radfahren 1

D

dad [dæd] der Papa, der Vati 1

dance [dɑːns]:
1. tanzen 1
2. der Tanz 1
3. die Tanzveranstaltung, der Ball 4: 3 (82)

dancer [ˈdɑːnsə] der/die Tänzer/in 1

dancing [ˈdɑːnsɪŋ] das Tanzen 1

danger [ˈdeɪndʒə] die Gefahr 2

dangerous [ˈdeɪndʒərəs] gefährlich 2

dark [dɑːk]:
1. dunkel 2
2. das Dunkel, die Dunkelheit 3

data [ˈdeɪtə] die Daten 4: 4 (111)

date [deɪt]:
1. das Datum 1
birthday date das Datum des Geburtstags 1
2. die Verabredung, das Date (auch die Person, mit der man ausgeht) 4: 3 (83)
3. date sb. mit jm. gehen, eine Beziehung haben 4: 3 (83)

daughter [ˈdɔːtə] die Tochter 2

day [deɪ] der Tag 1 one day / some day eines Tages 4: 1 (24) the days of the week (pl) die Wochentage 1 work long days lange arbeiten, lange Arbeitstage haben 1

dead [ded] tot 1 **My phone is dead.** Mein Telefon-Akku ist leer. 3

deal with [ˈdiːl wɪð], **dealt, dealt** klarkommen mit, fertigwerden mit, umgehen mit 4: 3 (89)

dealt [delt] *siehe* **deal with**

Dear ... [dɪə] Liebe/r ... 2

death [deθ] der Tod 4: 4 (108/109)

debate [dɪˈbeɪt]:
1. debattieren 3
2. die Debatte 3
hold/have a debate eine Debatte führen 3

December [dɪˈsembə] der Dezember 1

decide [dɪˈsaɪd] beschließen, sich entscheiden 3 **decide on sth.** etwas beschließen, sich für etwas entscheiden 3 **decide to do sth.** beschließen, sich entscheiden etwas zu tun 3

decorate [ˈdekəreɪt] dekorieren, schmücken 2

decoration [dekəˈreɪʃn] der Dekoration, der Schmuck, die Verzierung 2

deep [diːp] tief 3

deer [dɪə], *pl* **deer** das Reh; der Hirsch 4: 4 (112)

°**definition** [defɪˈnɪʃn] die Definition

delete [dɪˈliːt] löschen 3

delicious [dɪˈlɪʃəs] köstlich, lecker 2

department store [dɪˈpɑːtmənt stɔː] das Kaufhaus 2

depend on sth. [dɪˈpend] von etwas abhängen 4: 3 (82) **It depends.** Es kommt drauf an. 4: 3 (82)

describe [dɪˈskraɪb] beschreiben 2

description [dɪˈskrɪpʃn] die Beschreibung 2

desert [ˈdezət] die Wüste 4: 4 (108/109)

desert island [dezət ˈaɪlənd] die einsame Insel 4: 4 (108/109)

design [dɪˈzaɪn]:
1. die Gestaltung, das Design 1
2. entwerfen, gestalten 2

design and technology [dɪzaɪn ən tekˈnɒlədʒi] das Werken, der Werkunterricht 1

designer [dɪˈzaɪnə] der Designer, die Designerin 2

desk [desk]:
1. der Schreibtisch 1
2. der Schalter (*z. B Verkaufs-, Postschalter*) 3

dessert [dɪˈzɜːt] die Nachspeise, das Dessert 1 **for dessert** zum/als Nachtisch 1

destroy [dɪˈstrɔɪ] zerstören, vernichten 4: 2 (59)

°**detail** [ˈdiːteɪl] das Detail, die Einzelheit

detention [dɪˈtenʃn] das Nachsitzen (*in der Schule*) 4: 4 (112)

device [dɪˈvaɪs] das Gerät, der Apparat 4: 4 (111)

dialogue [ˈdaɪəlɒɡ] der Dialog 4: 4 (111)

diaper [ˈdaɪəpə] die Windel 4: 1 (29)

dictionary [ˈdɪkʃənri] das Wörterbuch, das (*alphabetische*) Wörterverzeichnis 2

did [dɪd] *siehe* **do I didn't buy ...** (= **did not**) ich kaufte nicht; ich habe nicht gekauft 2

die (of) [daɪ] sterben (an) 2

difference [ˈdɪfrəns] der Unterschied 1 **make a difference** etwas bewirken, etwas ausmachen 3

different (to) [ˈdɪfrənt] verschieden; anders (als) 1

difficult [ˈdɪfɪkəlt] schwierig, schwer 3

dig [dɪɡ] graben 1

digital [ˈdɪdʒɪtl] digital 3

dining area [ˈdaɪnɪŋ eəriə] der Essbereich, die Essecke 1

dining room [ˈdaɪnɪŋ ruːm] das Esszimmer 1

dinner [ˈdɪnə] das Abendessen 1 **for dinner** zum Abendessen 1

dip [dɪp] der Dip 3

direction [dəˈrekʃn] die Richtung 4: 4 (114)

directions (*pl*) [dəˈrekʃnz] die Wegbeschreibung(en) 3 **ask for directions** nach dem Weg fragen 3 **give directions** den Weg beschreiben 3

dirty [ˈdɜːti] schmutzig 1

disability [dɪsəˈbɪləti] die Behinderung 3

disabled [dɪsˈeɪbld] (körper)behindert 3

disagree [dɪsəˈɡriː] nicht zustimmen, widersprechen 3

disappear [dɪsəˈpɪə] verschwinden 4: 3 (89)

disaster [dɪˈzɑːstə] die Katastrophe, das Unglück 4: 4 (113)

disco [ˈdɪskəʊ] die Disco 2

discover [dɪsˈkʌvə] entdecken 2

discriminate against sb. [dɪˈskrɪmɪneɪt] jn. diskriminieren 4: 2 (53)

discrimination (against sb.) [dɪskrɪmɪˈneɪʃn] die Diskriminierung (eines Menschen) 4: 2 (53)

discuss [dɪˈskʌs] diskutieren 3

discussion [dɪˈskʌʃn] die Diskussion 3

dish [dɪʃ]:
1. die Schüssel, die Schale 1
2. das Gericht (*Mahlzeit*) 1
main dish das Hauptgericht 1

dishwasher [ˈdɪʃwɒʃə] die Geschirrspülmaschine 2

diverse [daɪˈvɜːs] unterschiedlich, vielfältig 4: 1 (20)

diversity [daɪˈvɜːsəti] die Vielfalt 4: 1 (20)

do [duː], **did, done** machen, tun 1 **do badly** schlecht abschneiden, keinen Erfolg haben 3 **do well** gut abschneiden, erfolgreich sein 3 **do your homework** Hausaufgaben machen 1 **It looks great, doesn't it?** Es sieht toll aus, nicht wahr? / ..., oder? 4: 3 (82) **You don't know ..., do you?** Du weißt nicht ..., oder? 4: 3 (82)

doctor (Dr) [ˈdɒktə] der Arzt, die Ärztin; der/die Doktor/in (Dr.) 2

dog [dɒɡ] der Hund 1

dollar ($) [ˈdɒlə] der Dollar 4: (12/13)

dolphin [ˈdɒlfɪn] der Delfin 2

done [dʌn] *siehe* **do Well done.** Gut gemacht! 2

donkey [ˈdɒŋki] der Esel 3

donut [ˈdəʊnʌt] der Donut (*ringförmiges Gebäck aus Hefeteig*) 2

door [dɔː] die Tür 1 **answer the door** aufmachen, zur/an die Tür gehen 3

doorkeeper [ˈdɔːkiːpə] der/die Pförtner/in 2

down [daʊn] hinunter, herunter 2

download [ˈdaʊnləʊd]:
1. der/das Download 3
2. herunterladen 3

downtown [daʊnˈtaʊn] (*AE*) im/ins Stadtzentrum 4: 3 (75/76)

dragon [ˈdræɡən] der Drache 3

drank [dræŋk] *siehe* **drink**

draw [drɔː], **drew, drawn** zeichnen 1

drawing [ˈdrɔːɪŋ]:
1. die Zeichnung 1
2. das Zeichnen 1

drawn [drɔːn] *siehe* **draw**

dream [driːm]:
1. der Traum 1
2. **dream (of/about sth.)** träumen (von etwas) 1

dress [dres]:
1. das Kleid 2
2. sich kleiden, sich anziehen 2

dress code [ˈdres kəʊd] der Dresscode (*Kleiderordnung*) 4: 3 (84)

dressed [drest]: **get dressed** sich anziehen 1

drew [druː] *siehe* **draw**

drink [drɪŋk]:
1. das Getränk 1
2. **drink, drank, drunk** trinken 1

drive [draɪv], **drove, driven** (*mit dem Auto*) fahren 1

driven [ˈdrɪvn] *siehe* **drive**

°**driver's license** [ˈdraɪvəz laɪsns] (*AE*) der Führerschein

driving licence [ˈdraɪvɪŋ laɪsns] der Führerschein 4: 3 (79)

drone [drəʊn] die Drohne 1

drove [drəʊv] *siehe* **drive**

drum [drʌm] die Trommel 4: 2 (46/47) **drums** (*pl*) das Schlagzeug 4: 2 (46/47)

drummer [ˈdrʌmə] der Trommler, die Trommlerin 4: 2 (46/47)

drunk [drʌŋk] *siehe* **drink**

dry [draɪ]:
1. (ab)trocknen 4: 4 (108/109)
2. trocken 4: 4 (108/109)

during [ˈdjʊərɪŋ] während 2

E

each [iːtʃ] jede(r, s) (einzelne), jeweils 2

each other [iːtʃ ˈʌðə] einander, sich (gegenseitig) 3

earlier [ˈɜːliə] vorhin; vorher, früher 3

early [ˈɜːli] früh 2

earn [ɜːn] verdienen (*Geld*) 2

earth [ɜːθ] die Erde 2

east [iːst] der Osten; östlich; Ost- 3

Easter [ˈiːstə] (das) Ostern 2

eastern [ˈiːstən] östlich(r,s), Ost- 3
easy [ˈiːzi] einfach, leicht 1
eat [iːt], **ate, eaten** essen; fressen 1
eaten [ˈiːtn] *siehe* eat
°**echo** [ˈekəʊ] (wider)hallen
edit [ˈedɪt] bearbeiten, editieren 3
editor [ˈedɪtə]:
  1. der/die Herausgeber/in 4: 3 (79)
  2. der/die Redakteur/in 4: 3 (79)
  letter to the editor der Leserbrief
  4: 3 (79)
education [edʒuˈkeɪʃn] die Erziehung,
  die (Schul-)Bildung 4: 3 (91)
eel [iːl] der Aal 3
effect [ɪˈfekt]: **special effects** *(pl)* die
  Special Effects *(in Filmen)* 2
e.g. [iː ˈdʒiː] *(aus dem Lateinischen)*
  z.B (zum Beispiel) 4: 4 (124)
egg [eg] das Ei 1
eight [eɪt] acht 1
eighteen [eɪˈtiːn] achtzehn 1
eighty [ˈeɪti] achtzig 1
either [ˈaɪðə]:
  1. either … or … entweder …
  oder … 4: 3 (88)
  2. not … either auch nicht 4: 3 (88)
elective [ɪˈlektɪv] *(AE)* das Wahl-
  fach 4: 3 (82)
electric [ɪˈlektrɪk] elektrisch, Elektro-
  4: 2 (57)
electricity [ɪlekˈtrɪsəti] der Strom,
  die Elektrizität 4: 3 (81)
electro [ɪˈlektrəʊ] der Electro, die
  Elektromusik 2
electronic [ɪlekˈtrɒnɪk] elektronisch 2
electronics *(pl)* [ɪlekˈtrɒnɪks] die Elekt-
  ronik; die elektronischen Geräte 2
elephant [ˈelɪfənt] der Elefant 1
eleven [ɪˈlevən] elf 1
else [els]: **What else?** Was sonst
  noch? 2 **Would you like anything**
  else? Möchten Sie sonst noch
  etwas? 2
email [ˈiːmeɪl]:
  1. die E-Mail 2
  2. email sb. jm. mailen, eine E-Mail
  schicken 2
embarrass sb. [ɪmˈbærəs] jn. in Verle-
  genheit bringen, jm. peinlich sein 3
embarrassed [ɪmˈbærəst] verlegen,
  peinlich berührt 3 **be/feel embar-**
  rassed peinlich berührt sein 3
embarrassing [ɪmˈbærəsɪŋ] peinlich 3
emigrant [ˈemɪgrənt] der Auswanderer, die Auswanderin 4: 1 (19)
emigrate [ˈemɪgreɪt] auswandern,
  emigrieren 4: 1 (19)
emigration [emɪˈgreɪʃn] die Auswanderung 4: 1 (19)
emoji [ɪˈməʊdʒi] das Emoji 3
emotion [ɪˈməʊʃn] die Emotion, das
  Gefühl 3
emotional [ɪˈməʊʃənl] emotional 3
empty [ˈempti]:
  1. leer 2
  2. leeren 2
encourage [ɪnˈkʌrɪdʒ] ermutigen, er-
  muntern; unterstützen 4: 3 (92)

encouraging [ɪnˈkʌrɪdʒɪŋ] ermuti-
  gend 4: 3 (92)
end [end]:
  1. enden; beenden 1
  2. das Ende, der Schluss 1
  at the end (of) am Ende (von) 1 **in**
  the end schließlich; zum Schluss 1
ending [ˈendɪŋ] die Endung; das Ende
  (Text, Geschichte) 3
endless [ˈendləs] endlos 3
energetic [enəˈdʒetɪk] aktiv, tatkräftig,
  energiegeladen 2
energy [ˈenədʒi] Energie 2
England [ˈɪŋglənd] England 1
English [ˈɪŋglɪʃ] Englisch; englisch 1
enjoy [ɪnˈdʒɔɪ] genießen 1 **enjoy**
  doing sth. es genießen, etwas zu
  tun 1 **Enjoy your meal.** Guten
  Appetit! 2 **Enjoy yourselves.** Viel
  Spaß! Amüsiert euch gut! 3 **Enjoy!**
  Viel Vergnügen! / Guten Appetit! 1
enough [ɪˈnʌf] genug 1
enslave sb. [ɪnˈsleɪv] jn. versklaven
  4: 2 (50)
enter [ˈentə] eintreten, betreten;
  einreisen *(in ein Land)* 4: 1 (32)
equal [ˈiːkwəl] gleich(berechtigt)
  4: 1 (21)
°**equipment** *(no pl)* [ɪˈkwɪpmənt]
  die Ausrüstung
escape (from) [ɪˈskeɪp]:
  1. entkommen (aus), fliehen (vor/
  aus) 4: 2 (50)
  2. die Flucht (aus/vor) 4: 2 (50)
especially [ɪˈspeʃəli] insbesondere 2
essay (on/about) [ˈeseɪ] der Aufsatz
  (über) 4: 4 (112)
estate [ɪˈsteɪt] die Wohnsiedlung; das
  Gewerbegebiet 1
euro [ˈjʊərəʊ], *pl* **euros** Euro 1
even [ˈiːvn] sogar, selbst 3 **even if**
  selbst wenn, sogar wenn 3 **not even**
  nicht einmal 3
evening [ˈiːvnɪŋ] der Abend 1 **in the**
  evening abends, am Abend 1
event [ɪˈvent] das Ereignis 3
ever [ˈevə] jemals, schon einmal 2
  for ever für immer, ewig
  (lange) 4: 3 (83) **the best party ever**
  die beste Party überhaupt / die beste
  Party, die man sich wünschen kann 1
every [ˈevri] jede(r, s) 2 **every 30**
  minutes alle 30 Minuten 2
everybody [ˈevribɒdi] jeder; alle 1
  Hello everybody! Hallo allerseits! 1
everyday [ˈevrideɪ] alltäglich, All-
  tags- 4: 2 (48)
everyday life [evrideɪ ˈlaɪf] der All-
  tag 4: 2 (48)
everyone [ˈevriwʌn] jeder, alle 1
everything [ˈevriθɪŋ] alles 2
everywhere [ˈevriweə] überall 1
exact [ɪgˈzækt] genau, exakt 4: 3 (86)
exactly [ɪgˈzæktli] genau *(Adv.)*
  4: 3 (86)
exam [ɪgˈzæm] *siehe* examination
examination [ɪgzæmɪˈneɪʃn] *infml*
  auch **exam** die Prüfung 4: 3 (91)

take/do an exam(ination) eine Prüfung machen 4: 3 (91)
example [ɪgˈzɑːmpl] das Beispiel 3
  for example zum Beispiel 3
except (for) [ɪkˈsept] außer, bis auf 3
exchange [ɪksˈtʃeɪndʒ]:
  1. der Schüleraustausch; der Aus-
  tausch, der Wechsel 3
  2. exchange sth. for sth. austauschen, etwas in/gegen etwas um-
  tauschen 3
exchange class [ɪksˈtʃeɪndʒ klɑːs] *die*
  Schulklasse, die am Schüleraustausch
  teilnimmt 3
exchange partner [ɪksˈtʃeɪndʒ pɑːtnə]
  der/die Austauschpartner/in 3
exchange student [ɪksˈtʃeɪndʒ stjuːdnt]
  der/die Austauschschüler/in 3
excited [ɪkˈsaɪtɪd] aufgeregt, ge-
  spannt 2
exciting [ɪkˈsaɪtɪŋ] aufregend 2
Excuse me, … [ɪksˈkjuːz miː] Entschuldigung, … / Entschuldigen Sie, … 1
exercise [ˈeksəsaɪz] die Übung, die
  Aufgabe 1
exercise book [ˈeksəsaɪz bʊk] das
  Schulheft, das Übungsheft 1
exhibition [eksɪˈbɪʃn] die Ausstellung;
  die Messe 4: 4 (122)
exit [ˈeksɪt]:
  1. aussteigen; hinausgehen, *(einen*
  Ort) verlassen 4: 1 (27)
  2. der Ausgang; die Ausfahrt 4: 1 (27)
  fire exit der Notausgang 4: 1 (27)
expensive [ɪkˈspensɪv] teuer 1
experience [ɪkˈspɪəriəns]:
  1. die Erfahrung; das Erlebnis 2
  2. experience sth. etwas erfahren;
  erleben 2
expert [ˈekspɜːt] der Experte, die
  Expertin 4: 4 (111)
explain sth. to sb. [ɪkˈspleɪn] jm.
  etwas erklären 1
explanation [ekspləˈneɪʃn] die
  Erklärung 1
explore [ɪkˈsplɔː] erforschen, erkun-
  den 3
extra [ˈekstrə] Extra-, zusätz-
  liche(r, s) 3
extreme [ɪkˈstriːm]:
  1. das Extrem 4: 2 (54)
  2. extrem 4: 2 (54)
eye [aɪ] das Auge 2

F

face [feɪs] das Gesicht 2
fact [fækt] die Tatsache 3 **in fact**
  tatsächlich, in Wirklichkeit, genau
  genommen 3
fair [feə] fair 2
faithfully [ˈfeɪθfəli]: **Yours faithfully**
  Mit freundlichen Grüßen *(Brief-*
  schluss) 4: 3 (79)
fake [feɪk]:
  1. falsch, gefälscht 3
  2. der/das Fake, die Fälschung 3
  3. fake sth. etwas faken, fälschen,
  vortäuschen 3

falafel [fəˈlæfl] die/das Falafel 3
fall [fɔːl], **fell, fallen** fallen; hinfallen 2
fallen [ˈfɔːlən] *siehe* **fall**
°**falls** *(pl)* [fɔːlz] der Wasserfall *(besonders in Namen)*
false [fɔːls] falsch, unrichtig 2
false friend [fɔːls ˈfrend] der „falsche Freund" *(Übersetzungsfalle)* 2
fame [feɪm] Ruhm 2
family [ˈfæməli] die Familie 1
famous (for) [ˈfeɪməs] berühmt (für, wegen) 2
fan [fæn] der Fan 1
fancy [ˈfænsi] ausgefallen, extravagant, schick 4: 3 (82)
°**fantastic** [fænˈtæstɪk] fantastisch
far [fɑː] weit (entfernt) 3 **so far** bis jetzt, bis hierher 3
farm [fɑːm] der Bauernhof, die Farm 2
farmer [ˈfɑːmə] der Bauer, die Bäuerin; der/die Landwirt/in 4: 1 (16/17)
fashion [ˈfæʃn] die Mode, die Fashion 3
fast [fɑːst] schnell 1
fast [fɑːst]:
 1. fasten 2
 2. das Fasten, die Fastenzeit 2
 break the fast das Fasten brechen 2
father [ˈfɑːðə] der Vater 2
favourite [ˈfeɪvərɪt]:
 1. der Liebling, der/die Favorit/in 1
 2. Lieblings- 1
feature [ˈfiːtʃə]:
 1. bieten, haben; vorkommen, eine Rolle spielen 4: 4 (111)
 2. das Merkmal, die Eigenschaft 4: 4 (111)
February [ˈfebruəri] der Februar 1
feedback *(no pl)* [ˈfiːdbæk] das Feedback *(Rückmeldung)* 4: 1 (33)
feel [fiːl], **felt, felt** sich fühlen; fühlen 1 **feel sorry for sb.** Mitleid haben mit jm. 1
feeling [ˈfiːlɪŋ] das Gefühl 1
feet [fiːt] *Plural von* **foot**
fell [fel] *siehe* **fall**
felt [felt] *siehe* **feel**
female [ˈfiːmeɪl]:
 1. die Frau 4: 1 (23)
 2. weiblich 4: 1 (23)
ferry [ˈferi] die Fähre 4: 1 (18)
festival [ˈfestɪvl] das Fest(ival) 2
few [fjuː] wenige 4: 4 (108/109) **a few** ein paar, einige 2
fifteen [fɪfˈtiːn] fünfzehn 1
fifty [ˈfɪfti] fünfzig 1
fight [faɪt]:
 1. der Kampf 2
 2. **fight, fought, fought** kämpfen, bekämpfen 2
 fight (with sb. about/over sth.) sich (mit jm. um etwas) streiten 2
fighter [ˈfaɪtə] der Kämpfer die Kämpferin 2
°**figure sth. out** [fɪɡər ˈaʊt] etwas (heraus)finden, durchschauen, aus etwas schlau werden
file [faɪl] die Datei; der Ordner, die Liste 1

film [fɪlm]:
 1. der Film 1
 2. **film sth.** etwas filmen 3
filter [ˈfɪltə]:
 1. der Filter 3
 2. filtern 3
finally [ˈfaɪnəli] schließlich, endlich 1
find [faɪnd], **found, found** finden 1
 find out (about) herausfinden; sich informieren (über) 1
fine [faɪn] gut, in Ordnung; schön 2
 He feels fine. Er fühlt sich gut. / Es geht ihm gut. 2
finger [ˈfɪŋɡə] der Finger 3 **cross your fingers** die Daumen drücken/ halten *(jm. Glück / gutes Gelingen wünschen)* 3 **tap your fingers** mit den Fingern klopfen 3
finish [ˈfɪnɪʃ]:
 1. das Ende, das Ziel *(z. B beim Sport)* 2
 2. enden; beenden, zu Ende machen 2
 be finished fertig(gestellt) sein 3
fire [ˈfaɪə] das Feuer 2 **stop a fire** ein Feuer löschen 2
fire exit [ˈfaɪər eksɪt] der Notausgang 4: 1 (27)
firefighter [ˈfaɪəfaɪtə] der Feuerwehrmann, die Feuerwehrfrau 2
fireworks *(pl)* [ˈfaɪəwɜːks] das Feuerwerk 2
first [fɜːst]:
 1. erste(r, s) 1
 2. zuerst, als Erstes 1
 at first zuerst, am Anfang 1
°**First Nations (people)** *(pl)* [fɜːst ˈneɪʃnz] *die indigenen Völker Kanadas*
fish [fɪʃ]:
 1. der Fisch 1
 2. fischen, angeln 4: 3 (89)
fish and chips [fɪʃ ən ˈtʃɪps] der Fisch mit Pommes Frites 1
fishing [ˈfɪʃɪŋ] das Fischen, das Angeln; die Fischerei 4: 3 (89)
 go fishing angeln/fischen gehen 4: 3 (89)
fit [fɪt] fit 4: 4 (111)
fitness [ˈfɪtnəs] die Fitness 4: 4 (111)
five [faɪv] fünf 1
fix sth. [fɪks] *(infml)* etwas in Ordnung bringen; etwas reparieren 2
flag [flæɡ] die Fahne, die Flagge 2
flat [flæt] die Wohnung 1
flat [flæt] flach, eben; *(Reifen)* platt 4: 4 (108/109)
flew [fluː] *siehe* **fly**
flexible [ˈfleksəbl] flexibel 4: 3 (87)
float [fləʊt] der Festwagen *(z. B beim Karnevalsumzug)* 4: 2 (54)
flood [flʌd]:
 1. die Überschwemmung, das Hochwasser; die Flut 4: 2 (58)
 2. überschwemmen, überfluten 4: 2 (58)
 be flooded unter Wasser stehen 4: 2 (58)
floor [flɔː]:
 1. der Fußboden 1

 2. die Etage, der Stock, das Stockwerk 1
 top floor die oberste Etage, der oberste Stock, das oberste Stockwerk 1
flour [ˈflaʊə] das Mehl 1
flow [fləʊ]:
 1. der Fluss; der Strom 3
 2. fließen; strömen 3
flower [ˈflaʊə] die Blume; die Blüte 3
flown [fləʊn] *siehe* **fly**
fly [flaɪ], **flew, flown** fliegen 2
focus (on) [ˈfəʊkəs]:
 1. sich konzentrieren (auf) 4: 1 (32)
 2. der Mittelpunkt, der Hauptpunkt, der Schwerpunkt (auf) 4: 1 (32)
 focus of attention das Zentrum der Aufmerksamkeit 4: 1 (32)
fold [fəʊld] falten 2
follow [ˈfɒləʊ] (be)folgen; verfolgen 3
follower [ˈfɒləʊə] der Follower 3
food [fuːd] das Essen, das Lebensmittel; das Futter 1
food-insecure family [fuːd ɪnsɪˈkjʊə] die Familie, die von Nahrungsmittelunsicherheit betroffen ist *(die zeitweise nicht genug Nahrung hat)* 4: 1 (29)
foot [fʊt], *pl* **feet**:
 1. der Fuß *(Körperteil)* 2
 2. der Fuß *(Längenmaß; ca. 30 cm)* 2
football [ˈfʊtbɔːl] der Fußball 1
footballer [ˈfʊtbɔːlə] der/die Fußballspieler/in 2
for [fɔː] für 1 **for light** als Licht(quelle) 3 **change for the better** sich verbessern, zum Bessern verändern 3 **to change sth. for the better** etwas verbessern, zum Bessern verändern 3 **What's for homework?** Was haben wir als Hausaufgabe(n) auf? 1
force [fɔːs]:
 1. der Zwang; die Gewalt; die Kraft 4: 4 (114)
 2. **force sth.** etwas erzwingen 4: 4 (114)
 force sb. to do sth. jn. zwingen, etwas zu tun 4: 4 (114)
foreground [ˈfɔːɡraʊnd] der Vordergrund 3
forest [ˈfɒrɪst] der Wald 2
forever, for ever [fərˈevə] für immer, ewig (lange) 4: 3 (83)
forget [fəˈɡet], **forgot, forgotten** vergessen 3
forgot [fəˈɡɒt] *siehe* **forget**
forgotten [fəˈɡɒtn] *siehe* **forget**
fork [fɔːk] die Gabel 4: 2 (55)
formal [ˈfɔːml] förmlich, formell 4: 3 (84)
forty [ˈfɔːti] vierzig 1
forward [ˈfɔːwəd]: **look forward to doing sth.** sich darauf freuen, etwas zu tun 2 **look forward to sth.** sich auf etwas freuen 2
fought [fɔːt] *siehe* **fight**
found [faʊnd]:
 1. *siehe* **find**
 °2. gründen

fountain [ˈfaʊntən] der (Spring-/Trink-)Brunnen 3 **memorial fountain** der Gedenkbrunnen 3

four [fɔː] vier 1

fourteen [fɔːˈtiːn] vierzehn 1

free [friː]:
1. frei 1
free time die Freizeit, die freie Zeit 1 **Are you free after school?** Hast du nach der Schule Zeit? 1
2. kostenlos 1
for free kostenlos, umsonst 2

freedom [ˈfriːdəm] die Freiheit 4: 1 (19)

freeze [friːz], **froze, frozen** erstarren; (ge)frieren 3

°**freeze-frame** [ˈfriːz freɪm] das Standbild *(Film)*

French [frentʃ] Französisch; französisch 1

French fries [frentʃ ˈfraɪz] *(pl, AE)* die Pommes frites 4: 1 (22)

freshman [ˈfreʃmən], *pl* **freshmen** der/die Studienanfänger/in; der/die Anfänger/in in der Highschool 4: 3 (82)

Friday [ˈfraɪdeɪ], [ˈfraɪdi] der Freitag 1

fried [fraɪd] frittiert, gebraten 1

friend [frend] der/die Freund/in 1 **be friends with sb.** mit jm. befreundet sein 4: 3 (83)

friendly [ˈfrendli] freundlich, nett 1

friendship [ˈfrendʃɪp] die Freundschaft 3

fries *(pl)* [fraɪz]: **French fries** *(AE)* die Pommes frites 4: 1 (22)

from [frɒm] von, aus 1 **from now on** von nun an 4: 3 (89)

front [frʌnt]: **a house with trees in front** ein Haus mit Bäumen davor 1 **in front of** vor 1

front door [frʌnt ˈdɔː] die Haustür, die Eingangstür 2

froze [frəʊz] *siehe* **freeze**

°**frozen** [ˈfrəʊzn] *siehe* **freeze**

fruit [fruːt] das Obst 1

frustrate sb. [frʌˈstreɪt] jn. frustrieren 3

frustrated [frʌˈstreɪtɪd] frustriert 3

frustrating [frʌˈstreɪtɪŋ] frustrierend 3

fry [fraɪ] braten; frittieren 1

frying pan [ˈfraɪɪŋ pæn] die Bratpfanne 1

full [fʊl]:
1. voll 2
full of ... voller ... 2
2. satt 2

full-time [fʊl ˈtaɪm] Vollzeit-, Ganztags- 4: 1 (28)

fun [fʌn]: **be fun** Spaß machen; lustig sein 1 **have fun** Spaß haben 1

funeral [ˈfjuːnərəl] die Beerdigung, das Begräbnis 4: 2 (56)

funk [fʌŋk] der Funk *(Musikstil)* 4: 2 (56)

funny [ˈfʌni] witzig, komisch 1

future [ˈfjuːtʃə]:
1. die Zukunft 2
2. zukünftige(r, s) 2

G

°**gallery** [ˈgæləri] die Galerie

game [geɪm]:
1. das Spiel 1
2. Computerspiele spielen 2

gamer [ˈgeɪmə] der/die Gamer/in *(Computerspieler/in)* 2

gaming [ˈgeɪmɪŋ] das Gaming *(Spielen am Computer)* 2

garden [ˈgɑːdn] der Garten 1

gate [geɪt] das Tor 3

gather [ˈgæðə] sammeln; (sich) versammeln; *(Sturm)* sich zusammenbrauen 4: 2 (58)

gave [geɪv] *siehe* **give**

°**gay** [geɪ] schwul, gay

geography [dʒiˈɒgrəfi] die Geografie, die Erdkunde 1

German [ˈdʒɜːmən] deutsch; Deutsch; der/die Deutsche 1

Germany [ˈdʒɜːməni] Deutschland 1

get [get], **got, got:**
1. bekommen 1
get sth. sich etwas holen/besorgen 1
2. werden 1
get ready (for) sich fertig machen (für), sich vorbereiten (auf) 2 **get wet** nass werden 1
3. **get (to)** gelangen, (hin)kommen (nach) 2
get around sich fortbewegen (in) *(mobil sein)* 4: 3 (79) **Get down!** Komm (da) runter! 2 **get off your bike/your horse** vom Fahrrad / vom Pferd absteigen 3 **get up** aufstehen 1 **get on a train/bus** in einen Zug/Bus einsteigen 2 **get off a train/bus** aus einem Zug/Bus aussteigen 2

ghost [gəʊst] der Geist, das Gespenst 3

ghost tour [ˈgəʊst tʊə] die Geistertour *(Stadtführung mit gruseligen Themen/Elementen)* 3

giant [ˈdʒaɪənt]:
1. der Riese, die Riesin 4: 4 (108/109)
2. riesig 4: 4 (108/109)

gift [gɪft] das Geschenk, die Gabe; das Talent 2

gift shop [ˈgɪft ʃɒp] der Geschenk(artikel)laden, der Souvenirladen 2

girl [gɜːl] das Mädchen 1 **a girls' group** eine Mädchengruppe, eine Gruppe für Mädchen 1

girlfriend [ˈgɜːlfrend] die (feste) Freundin 2

give [gɪv], **gave, given** geben 1 **give up** aufgeben 3

given [ˈgɪvn] *siehe* **give**

glasses *(pl)* [ˈglɑːsɪz] die Brille 2

global [ˈgləʊbl] global, weltweit 3

globe [gləʊb] der Globus; die Kugel 3 **across the globe** auf der ganzen Welt 3 **all (a)round the globe** auf der ganzen Welt 3

glove [glʌv] der Handschuh 2

glue [gluː] der Kleber, der Klebstoff 1

glue stick [ˈgluː stɪk] der Klebestift 1

go [gəʊ], **went, gone:**
1. gehen, fahren 1
go down fallen, sinken; *(Sonne)* untergehen 4: 4 (115) **go on** weitermachen, weiterreden; (sich) fortsetzen 4: 3 (92) **go out** rausgehen, weggehen; ausgehen 2 **go up** hochgehen; (an)steigen; aufgehen *(Sonne)* 4: 4 (115) **How's it going?** *(infml)* Wie geht's? / Wie läuft's? 2 **There you go.** Hier, bitte schön.; *(auch:)* Da hast du's! / Na siehst du! 3 °**go (well/great) with** (gut) passen zu
2. werden 1
go green grün/umweltbewusst werden 1 **go red** erröten, rot werden 1
3. **I'm going to ...** ich werde ... *(Plan, Vorhaben)* 2

go-kart [ˈgəʊ kɑːt] der/das Gokart 3

goal [gəʊl] das Ziel *(Absicht, Lebensziel)*; das Tor *(im Sport)* 3

goalkeeper [ˈgəʊlkiːpə] der Torwart, die Torhüterin 3

goat [gəʊt] die Ziege 2

god [gɒd] der Gott 2

gold [gəʊld]:
1. das Gold 1
2. goldfarben 2

°**golden** [ˈgəʊldn] golden, aus Gold

gone [gɒn] *siehe* **go be gone** weg sein 3

good [gʊd]:
1. gut 1
be good at sth. etwas gut können; gut in etwas sein 1 **be good with ...** gut umgehen können mit ... 1
2. brav 2

Goodbye. [gʊdˈbaɪ] Auf Wiedersehen! 1

got [gɒt] *siehe* **get** °**have got** haben

govern [ˈgʌvn] regieren 4: 4 (114)

government [ˈgʌvənmənt] die Regierung 4: 4 (114)

governor [ˈgʌvənə] der/die Gouverneur/in 4: 4 (114)

grade [greɪd] *(AE)* die Klasse, das Schuljahr; die (Schul-)Note 4: 3 (82)

grandchild [ˈgræntʃaɪld], *pl* **grandchildren** der/die Enkel/in 4: 1 (21)

grandchildren [ˈgræntʃɪldrən] *Plural von* **grandchild**

grandfather [ˈgrænfɑːðə] der Großvater 4: 3 (87)

grandma [ˈgrænmɑː] die Oma 1

grandmother [ˈgrænmʌðə] die Großmutter 4: 3 (87)

grandpa [ˈgrænpɑː] der Opa 1

grandparents *(pl)* [ˈgrænpeərənts] die Großeltern 2

grass [grɑːs] das Gras; der Rasen 3

grateful (to sb.) [ˈgreɪtfl] (jm.) dankbar 4: 1 (29)

great [greɪt]:
1. großartig, toll 1
2. groß *(bedeutend, angesehen)* 2

Great Britain [greɪt ˈbrɪtn] Großbritannien 1

green [griːn]:
1. grün 1

2. umweltbewusst 1
go green grün/umweltbewusst werden 1
grew [gru:] *siehe* **grow**
grey [greɪ] grau 1
ground [graʊnd] der (Erd-)Boden 1
ground floor [graʊnd ˈflɔː] das Erdgeschoss 1
group [gru:p] die Gruppe 1
grow [grəʊ], **grew, grown** wachsen; anbauen 4: 2 (59) **grow up** aufwachsen; erwachsen werden 4: 2 (59)
grown [grəʊn] *siehe* **grow**
guard [ɡɑːd]:
  1. schützen, bewachen 3
  2. der/die Wärter/in; die Wache; der/die Sicherheitsbedienstete 3
  Changing of the Guards die Wachablösung 3 **security guard** der/die Sicherheitsbedienstete 4: 2 (48)
guess [ges]:
  1. die Vermutung 1
  2. (er)raten 1
  guessing game das Ratespiel 1
  3. glauben, annehmen 1
  I guess ich glaube, ich nehme an 1
guide [ɡaɪd]:
  1. führen, leiten 1
  2. (= *tour guide*) der/die Reiseleiter/in; der/die Fremdenführer/in 1
guide dog [ˈɡaɪd dɒɡ] der Blindenhund 1
guitar [ɡɪˈtɑː] die Gitarre 1
°**gumbo** [ˈɡʌmbəʊ] *der Eintopf mit Huhn bzw. Meeresfrüchten und Okra*
gun [ɡʌn] die Schusswaffe, die Pistole 4: 3 (82)
guy [ɡaɪ] (*infml*) der Typ, der Kerl 4: 3 (83)
guys [ɡaɪz] (*pl, infml*) Leute (*als Anrede verwendet*) 4: 3 (83)

H

habit [ˈhæbɪt] die (An-)Gewohnheit 3
had [hæd] *siehe* **have**
hail [heɪl] der Hagel 4: 2 (58)
hair [heə] das Haar, die Haare 2
haircut [ˈheəkʌt] der Haarschnitt 3
  give sb. a haircut jm. die Haare schneiden 3
hairdresser [ˈheədresə] der/die Friseur/in 2
hairdresser's [ˈheədresəz] der Friseursalon 2
half [hɑːf]:
  1. halbe(r, s) 3
  half an hour eine halbe Stunde 3
  half full halb voll 3 **half past 6** halb 7 2 **half the time / half the money** die Hälfte der Zeit / des Geldes 3
  2. *pl* **halves** die Hälfte; (*Fußball*) die Halbzeit 3
half-time [hɑːf ˈtaɪm] die Halbzeit(pause) 3
hall [hɔːl]:
  1. der Flur, die Diele 1
  2. die Halle, der Saal 1
  sports hall die Sporthalle 1

halloumi [həˈluːmi] der Halloumi (*Käse*) 3
Halloween [hæləʊˈiːn] das Halloween (*Abend des 31. Oktober*) 2
halves [hɑːvz] *Plural von* **half**
ham [hæm] der Schinken 1
hamster [ˈhæmstə] der Hamster 1
hand [hænd] die Hand 1 **put your hand up** sich melden, aufzeigen 1
handball [ˈhændbɔːl] der Handball 2
handy [ˈhændi] praktisch, nützlich; handlich; griffbereit, zur Hand 2
hang out [hæŋ ˈaʊt], **hung, hung** rumhängen, abhängen 4: 3 (85)
happen (to sb.) [ˈhæpən] (jm.) geschehen, passieren 2
happy [ˈhæpi] glücklich, froh 1
  Happy birthday! Herzlichen Glückwunsch zum Geburtstag! 1
harbour [ˈhɑːbə] der Hafen 4: 1 (32)
hard [hɑːd] schwer, schwierig; hart 1
hard-working [hɑːd ˈwɜːkɪŋ] fleißig 2
has [hæz], [həz]: **he/she/it has** er/sie/es hat 1
hashtag [ˈhæʃtæɡ] das/der Hashtag (*Rautezeichen in einem elektronischen Text*) 3
hat [hæt] der Hut, die Mütze 1
hate [heɪt]:
  1. hassen 2
  2. der Hass 2
have [hæv], **had, had** haben 1 **have to do sth.** etwas tun müssen 2 **I have to go.** Ich muss Schluss machen. (*am Telefon/Briefschluss*) 2 **I'll have ...** Ich nehme ... (*beim Essen, z. B. im Restaurant*) 3 °**have got** haben
he [hiː] er 1 **he's (= he is)** er ist 1
head [hed] der Kopf 1
headache [ˈhedeɪk] Kopfschmerzen 2 **have a headache** Kopfschmerzen haben 2
headphones (*pl*) [ˈhedfəʊnz] der Kopfhörer 1
headpiece [ˈhedpiːs] der Kopfschmuck 3
health [helθ] die Gesundheit 3
healthy [ˈhelθi] gesund 3
hear [hɪə], **heard, heard** hören 1
heard [hɜːd] *siehe* **hear**
heavy [ˈhevi] schwer (*Gewicht*) 4: 4 (121)
held [held] *siehe* **hold**
helicopter [ˈhelɪkɒptə] der Hubschrauber 3
Hello. [həˈləʊ] Hallo. 1 **Hello everybody!** Hallo allerseits! 1
helmet [ˈhelmɪt] der Helm 2
help [help]:
  1. helfen 1
  2. die Hilfe 1
  3. die Hilfskraft 4: 3 (87)
helpful [ˈhelpfl] hilfsbereit; hilfreich, nützlich 1
helpless [ˈhelpləs] hilflos 3
her [hɜː], [hə]:
  1. sie; ihr 1

  2. her friends ihre Freunde/ Freundinnen 1
here [hɪə] hier; hierher 1 **Here you are.** Bitte schön. / Hier, bitte. 1
hero [ˈhɪərəʊ], *pl* **heroes** der Held, die Heldin 2
hers [hɜːz] ihrer, ihre, ihres (*zu "she"*) 3
herself [hɜˈself] sich (selbst) (*zu "she"*) 3
Hi. [haɪ] Hallo. 1
high [haɪ] hoch 3
high school [ˈhaɪ skuːl] (*AE*) die Schule für 14- bis 18-Jährige 4: 3 (83)
Highlands [ˈhaɪləndz]: **the Highlands** (*pl*) das schottische Hochland 3
highlight [ˈhaɪlaɪt]:
  1. der Höhepunkt, das Schlaglicht 1
  2. hervorheben, markieren, unterstreichen 1
hike [haɪk]:
  1. die Wanderung 3
  2. wandern 3
hiker [ˈhaɪkə] der Wanderer, die Wanderin 3
hiking [ˈhaɪkɪŋ] das Wandern 3
°**hill** [hɪl] der Hügel
him [hɪm] ihm, ihn 1
himself [hɪmˈself] sich (selbst) (*zu "he"*) 3
hip-hop [ˈhɪp hɒp] der Hip-Hop 4: 2 (56)
hire [ˈhaɪə]:
  1. der Verleih, die Vermietung 3
  2. mieten, leihen; (*Person:*) einstellen 3
his [hɪz]:
  1. seiner, seine, seins (*zu "he"*) 3
  2. his room sein Zimmer 1
history [ˈhɪstri] die Geschichte (*vergangene Zeiten*) 1
hit [hɪt], **hit, hit**:
  1. schlagen 3
  2. stoßen gegen, zusammenstoßen mit; treffen auf 3
hobby [ˈhɒbi] das Hobby 1
hockey [ˈhɒki] das Hockey 1
hold [həʊld], **held, held** halten 4: 3 (89) **hold a competition** einen Wettbewerb veranstalten, abhalten 4: 4 (122)
hole [həʊl] das Loch 4: 2 (55)
holiday [ˈhɒlədeɪ] der Urlaub 1 **holidays** die Ferien 1 **on holiday** im/in den Urlaub 1
home [həʊm]:
  1. das Heim, das Zuhause 1
  at home zu Hause 1
  2. nach Hause 1
  go home nach Hause gehen 1
homeless [ˈhəʊmləs] obdachlos 3
homesick [ˈhəʊmsɪk]: **be/feel homesick (for)** Heimweh haben (nach) 4: 1 (18)
°**hometown** [həʊmˈtaʊn] die Heimatstadt
homework [ˈhəʊmwɜːk] die Hausaufgabe(n) 1 **do your homework**

Hausaufgaben machen 1 **What's for homework?** Was haben wir als Hausaufgabe(n) auf? 1

honest [ˈɒnɪst] ehrlich 2

hope [həʊp]:
1. hoffen 2
2. die Hoffnung 2

horoscope [ˈhɒrəskəʊp] das Horoskop 2

horrible [ˈhɒrəbl] schrecklich 1

horse [hɔːs] das Pferd 1

hospital [ˈhɒspɪtl] das Krankenhaus 1

hot [hɒt] heiß, warm 1

hot chocolate [hɒt ˈtʃɒklət] der Kakao, die heiße (Trink-)Schokolade 1

hot dog [ˈhɒt dɒg] das Hot Dog *(heißes Würstchen in einem Brötchen)* 2

hot meal [hɒt ˈmiːl] die warme Mahlzeit 1

°**hot seat** [hɒt ˈsiːt] der heiße Stuhl *(Platz im Zentrum der Aufmerksamkeit)*

hotel [həʊˈtel] das Hotel 2

hour [ˈaʊə] die Stunde 1 **opening hours** *(pl)* die Öffnungszeiten 4: 3 (87) **per hour** pro Stunde 3 **work long hours** lange arbeiten, Überstunden machen 2 **working hours** *(pl)* die Arbeitszeit(en) 4: 3 (87)

house [haʊs] das Haus 1

how [haʊ] wie 1 **How are you?** Wie geht's? / Wie geht es dir/euch/Ihnen? 2 **How much is/are ...?** Was (Wie viel) kostet/kosten ...? 2 **how to do sth.** wie man etwas tut / tun kann / tun soll 1

however [haʊˈevə] allerdings, jedoch 3

hug [hʌg]:
1. die Umarmung 2
2. **hug (sb.)** (jn.) umarmen; einander umarmen 2

hummus [ˈhʊməs] der/das Hummus 3

hundred [ˈhʌndrəd]: a/one hundred (ein)hundert 1 **the 1600s (the sixteen hundreds)** das 17. Jahrhundert 4: 2 (50)

hung [hʌŋ] *siehe* hang out

hungry [ˈhʌŋgri] hungrig 1 **I'm hungry.** Ich habe Hunger. 1

hurricane [ˈhʌrɪkən] der Hurrikan, der Orkan 4: 2 (58)

hurry [ˈhʌri]:
1. sich beeilen; eilen 3 **Hurry up!** Beeil dich! / Beeilt euch! 3
2. die Eile 3
in a hurry in Eile 3

hurt [hɜːt], hurt, hurt verletzen; wehtun 2 **be hurt** verletzt sein 2 **get hurt** sich verletzen 2

husband [ˈhʌzbənd] der Ehemann 1

I

I [aɪ] ich 1 **I'm (= I am)** ich bin 1

°**ice** [aɪs] das Eis *(gefrorenes Wasser)*

ice cream [aɪs ˈkriːm] das (Speise-)Eis 1

ice rink [ˈaɪs rɪŋk] die Schlittschuhbahn 1

icing [ˈaɪsɪŋ] die Glasur, der Zuckerguss 1

icing sugar [ˈaɪsɪŋ ˈʃʊgə] der Puderzucker 1

idea [aɪˈdɪə] die Idee 1

IDK (I don't know) [aɪ diː ˈkeɪ] Ich weiß nicht. / Das weiß ich nicht. 4: 4 (122)

if [ɪf]:
1. wenn, falls 1 **even if** selbst wenn, sogar wenn 3 **What if ...?** Was wäre, wenn ...? 1
2. ob 1

ignore [ɪgˈnɔː] nicht beachten, ignorieren 4: 3 (89)

ill [ɪl] krank 2

illness [ˈɪlnəs] die Krankheit 2

image [ˈɪmɪdʒ] das Bild, die Abbildung 4: 4 (112)

°**imagine sth.** [ɪˈmædʒɪn] sich etwas vorstellen

immigrant [ˈɪmɪgrənt] der Einwanderer, die Einwanderin 4: 1 (19)

immigrate [ˈɪmɪgreɪt] einwandern, immigrieren 4: 1 (19)

immigration [ɪmɪˈgreɪʃn] die Einwanderung 4: 1 (19)

impatient [ɪmˈpeɪʃnt] ungeduldig 4: 3 (92)

important (for/to sb.) [ɪmˈpɔːtnt] wichtig (für jn.) 2

in [ɪn] in; auf 1 **in English** auf Englisch 1 **in the afternoon** nachmittags, am Nachmittag 1 **in the country** auf dem Land 1 **in the evening** abends, am Abend 1 **in the morning** morgens, am Morgen 1 **in the photo** auf dem Foto 1 **in the picture** auf dem Bild 1 **in the sky** am Himmel 4: 2 (58) **in town** in der Stadt 1 **one in five** eine/r von fünf(en), jede/r fünfte 3

include [ɪnˈkluːd] (mit) einschließen 4: 2 (62)

including [ɪnˈkluːdɪŋ] einschließlich, inklusive 4: 2 (62)

°**independent (of/from)** [ɪndɪˈpendənt] unabhängig (von)

indoor [ˈɪndɔː] im Haus/Gebäude, drinnen stattfindend 4: 3 (75/76)

indoors [ɪnˈdɔːz] drinnen; in einem Haus/Gebäude 4: 3 (75/76)

influencer [ˈɪnfluənsə] der/die Influencer/in 3

info [ˈɪnfəʊ] *(infml)* die Info *(kurz für „Information")* 4: 1 (19)

informal [ɪnˈfɔːml] informell, locker; umgangssprachlich 4: 3 (84)

information [ɪnfəˈmeɪʃn] die Information(en) 1 **visitor information centre** die Touristeninformation, das Fremdenverkehrsbüro 1

injustice [ɪnˈdʒʌstɪs] die Ungerechtigkeit; das Unrecht 4: 2 (50)

insect [ˈɪnsekt] Insekt 2

insecure [ɪnsɪˈkjʊə] unsicher, ungesichert 4: 1 (29) **food-insecure family**

die Familie, die von Nahrungsmittelunsicherheit betroffen ist *(die zeitweise nicht genug Nahrung hat)* 4: 1 (29)

inside [ɪnˈsaɪd] innerhalb (von) 1 **inside the house** im Haus 1

°**install** [ɪnˈstɔːl] installieren; einbauen

°**instead** [ɪnˈsted] stattdessen

instruction [ɪnˈstrʌkʃn] die Anweisung 3

instructor [ɪnˈstrʌktə] der/die Lehrerin, der/die Ausbilder/in 3

instrument [ˈɪnstrəmənt] das Instrument 4: 2 (56)

intelligence [ɪnˈtelɪdʒəns] die Intelligenz 4: 4 (111) **artificial intelligence (AI)** die künstliche Intelligenz (KI) 4: 4 (111)

intelligent [ɪnˈtelɪdʒənt] intelligent 4: 4 (111)

interest [ˈɪntrəst]:
1. **interest (in)** das Interesse (an) 3
2. **interest sb. (in sth.)** jn. (für etwas) interessieren 3

interested (in) [ˈɪntrəstɪd] interessiert (an) 3

interesting [ˈɪntrəstɪŋ] interessant 1

international [ɪntəˈnæʃnəl] international 3

internet [ˈɪntənet] das Internet 1

interrupt [ɪntəˈrʌpt] unterbrechen 3

interview [ˈɪntəvjuː]:
1. das Interview 2
°**2.** befragen, interviewen

interviewer [ˈɪntəvjuːə] der/die Interviewer/in 4: 3 (93)

into [ˈɪntu], [ˈɪntə] in (... hinein) 2

intro [ˈɪntrəʊ] *(kurz für* **introduction***)* die Einführung, die Einleitung 3

introduce sb. to sb./sth. [ɪntrəˈdjuːs] jm. jn./etwas vorstellen, jn. mit jm./etwas bekanntmachen 4: 3 (93)

introduction [ɪntrəˈdʌkʃn] die Einführung, die Einleitung 4: 1 (33)

°**Inuit or Inuits** *(pl)* [ˈɪnjuɪt], [ˈɪnuɪt] die Inuit *(die Indigenen im Norden Kanadas, in Grönland und Alaska)*

invitation (to) [ɪnvɪˈteɪʃn] die Einladung (zu, nach) 1

invite (to) [ɪnˈvaɪt] einladen (zu, nach) 1

involved [ɪnˈvɒlvd]: **get involved (in)** sich engagieren (für, bei); sich beteiligen (an) 3 **Try not to get involved.** Versuche, dich da rauszuhalten 3

Ireland [ˈaɪələnd] Irland 3

is [ɪz] *(er/sie/es)* ist 1 **he isn't (= is not)** er ist nicht 1 **The football is £3.** Der Fußball kostet 3 Pfund. 2

island [ˈaɪlənd] die Insel 3

isle [aɪl] *(kurz für* **island***)* die Insel 3 **British Isles** *(pl)* die Britischen Inseln 3

it [ɪt] es *(bei Sachen und Tieren auch:* er; sie) 1

its [ɪts]:
1. sein/seine, ihr/ihre *(besitzanzeigend: Dinge und Tiere)* 1
2. seiner, seine, seins; ihrer, ihre, ihres *(zu „it")* 3

itself [ɪtˈself] sich (selbst) (zu „*it*") 3

J

jacket [ˈdʒækɪt] die Jacke, das Jackett 2 **rain jacket** die Regenjacke 2

January [ˈdʒænjuəri] der Januar 1

jazz [dʒæz] der Jazz 2

jealous (of) [ˈdʒeləs] neidisch (auf); eifersüchtig 3

jeans *(pl)* [dʒiːnz] die Jeans(hose) 2

jewellery [ˈdʒuːəlri] der Schmuck 4: 1 (28)

jewelry [ˈdʒuːəlri] *(AE)* der Schmuck 4: 1 (28)

jigsaw (puzzle) [ˈdʒɪgsɔː] das Puzzle 1

job [dʒɒb] der Job, die (Arbeits-)Stelle; die Aufgabe 2

join sb./sth. [dʒɔɪn] sich jm. anschließen; bei etwas mitmachen 3 **join a club** in einen Klub eintreten 3 **join a group** sich einer Gruppe anschließen 3 **join the army** zur Armee gehen 4: 2 (51)

joke [dʒəʊk] der Witz, der Scherz 2

journey [ˈdʒɜːni] die Reise, die Fahrt; der Weg 1

Jr. [ˈdʒuːniə] *siehe* **junior**

judo [ˈdʒuːdəʊ] das Judo 2 **do judo** Judo machen 2

juggle [ˈdʒʌgl] jonglieren 1

juice [dʒuːs] der Saft 3

July [dʒuˈlaɪ] der Juli 1

jump [dʒʌmp] springen; (vor Schreck) zusammenzucken 2

June [dʒuːn] der Juni 1

junior [ˈdʒuːniə]:
1. (Jr.) der/die Junior/in; Junior (als Namensteil) 4: 2 (50)
2. (AE) der/die Schüler/in im vorletzten Schuljahr 4: 3 (82)

just [dʒʌst]:
1. nur, bloß; einfach 1
It's just us. Es sind nur wir. 1
2. gerade (eben) 2
3. **just then / just there** genau dann / genau dort 2

justice [ˈdʒʌstɪs] die Gerechtigkeit 4: 2 (50)

K

karaoke [kæriˈəʊki] das Karaoke 2

karate [kəˈrɑːti] Karate 2

kayak [ˈkaɪæk] das Kajak 3

kayaker [ˈkaɪækə] der/die Kajakfahrer/in 3

kayaking [ˈkaɪækɪŋ] das Kajakfahren 3

kebab [kɪˈbæb] der Kebab 2

keep [kiːp], **kept, kept**:
1. halten; behalten; aufbewahren 3
2. **keep doing sth.** etwas dauernd / immer wieder tun 3
keep going (immer) weiter gehen 3
keep going (immer) weiter machen 4: 3 (89)

kept [kept] *siehe* **keep**

ketchup [ˈketʃəp] Ketchup 3

key [kiː] der Schlüssel; Schlüssel- 2

keyword [ˈkiːwɜːd] das Stichwort, das Schlagwort 3

kid [kɪd] das Kind, der/die Jugendliche 1

kill [kɪl] töten 2

killer [ˈkɪlə] der/die Mörder/in 2

kilometre (km) [ˈkɪləmiːtə] der Kilometer 2

kind [kaɪnd] nett, freundlich 1

kind (of) [kaɪnd] die Art (von), die Sorte (von) 1

king [kɪŋ] der König 3

Kingdom [ˈkɪŋdəm]: **the United Kingdom (= the UK)** das Vereinigte Königreich 2

kiss [kɪs]:
1. (sich) küssen 4: 2 (59)
2. der Kuss 4: 2 (59)

kitchen [ˈkɪtʃɪn] die Küche 1

kneel [niːl], **knelt, knelt** knien 4: 2 (52)

knelt [nelt] *siehe* **kneel**

knew [njuː] *siehe* **know**

knife [naɪf], *pl* **knives** das Messer 4: 2 (55)

knit [nɪt] stricken 2

knives [naɪvz] *Plural von* **knife**

knock [nɒk] stoßen, klopfen 2 **knock at (sth.)** (an)klopfen an (etwas, z. B Tür) 2 **knock sth. over** etwas umstoßen 2

know [nəʊ], **knew, known** wissen; kennen 1 **you know** nämlich, weißt du 3 **You know what, …** Weißt du was, … 4: 1 (21)

known [nəʊn] *siehe* **know**

L

°label [ˈleɪbl] das Etikett, die Beschriftung

°lacrosse [ləˈkrɒs] das Lacrosse (Ballspiel, ähnlich wie Hockey)

lake [leɪk] der (Binnen-)See 3

lamb [læm] das Lamm(fleisch) 2

lamp [læmp] die Lampe 1

land [lænd]:
1. das Land (Grund und Boden) 2
2. landen 2

landscape [ˈlændskeɪp] die Landschaft; das Landschaftsbild 4: 4 (124)

lane [leɪn] die Gasse 3 **bike lane** der Radweg 3 **cycle lane** der Radweg 3

language [ˈlæŋgwɪdʒ] die Sprache 2

large [lɑːdʒ] groß 2

last [lɑːst] letzte(r, s); als letztes 2 **last week/month/year** die letzte/vorige Woche, der letzte/vorige Monat, das letzte/vorige Jahr 2

late [leɪt] (zu) spät 1 **I'm late.** Ich habe mich verspätet. 1

later [ˈleɪtə] später 1 **Speak later.** Tschüs. / Bis später. 1

latest [ˈleɪtɪst] neueste(r, s), aktuelle(r, s) 4: 3 (91)

laugh [lɑːf]:
1. das Lachen 2
2. **laugh (at)** lachen (über) 2
laugh out loud laut auf-/loslachen 2

law [lɔː] das Gesetz; Jura (Studium) 4: 2 (50)

lead [liːd], **led, led** führen, leiten 4: (12/13)

leader [ˈliːdə] der/die Leiter/in; der/die (Staats-)Chef/in; der/die (An-)Führer/in 4: (12/13)

°leaf [liːf], *pl* **leaves** das Blatt (Pflanze)

league [liːg] die Liga (Sport) 4: 2 (52)

learn [lɜːn] lernen 1

least [liːst] am wenigsten 2 **at least** wenigstens, zumindest 2 **the least favourite chores** die Arbeiten (im Haus), die man am wenigsten gerne macht 2

leave [liːv], **left, left** lassen; verlassen; zurücklassen 2 **leave sb. alone** jn. allein lassen; jn. in Ruhe lassen 2

°leaves [liːvz] *Plural von* **leaf**

led [led] *siehe* **lead**

left [left] *siehe* **leave**

left [left] links; nach links 2 **on the left** links, auf der linken Seite 2 **to the left of …** links von … 2

leg [leg] das Bein 2

legend [ˈledʒənd] die Legende, die Sage 3

lemon [ˈlemən] die Zitrone 1

lemonade [leməˈneɪd] die Limonade 1

less [les] weniger 3

lesson [ˈlesn] die (Unterrichts-)Stunde 1

let's (= let us) [lets] lass(t) uns 1

letter [ˈletə]:
1. der Brief 3
2. der Buchstabe 3

level [ˈlevl]:
1. der Grad, die Stufe; das Niveau, die Ebene 2
2. das Stockwerk, die Etage, die Ebene 4: 1 (27)

°LGBTQ [el dʒi bi ti ˈkjuː] LGBTQ

liberty [ˈlɪbəti] die Freiheit 4: 1 (16/17)

library [ˈlaɪbrəri] die Bücherei, die Bibliothek 1

licence [ˈlaɪsns] die Genehmigung, die Lizenz 4: 3 (79) **driving licence** der Führerschein 4: 3 (79)

°license [ˈlaɪsns] *(AE)* die Genehmigung, Lizenz **driver's license** *(AE)* der Führerschein

lie [laɪ]:
1. die Lüge 3
tell a lie / lies lügen 3
2. **lie (to sb.)** (jn. an)lügen 3

life [laɪf], *pl* **lives** das Leben 3

°life skills *(pl)* [ˈlaɪf skɪlz] die Alltagskompetenzen, die lebenswichtigen Fertigkeiten

°lift [lɪft] heben, hochheben

light [laɪt] das Licht; die Lampe 1

lighting [ˈlaɪtɪŋ] die Beleuchtung 3

lightning [ˈlaɪtnɪŋ] der Blitz / die Blitze (bei Gewitter) 4: 2 (58)

like [laɪk]:
1. mögen 1
I like singing. Ich singe gerne. 1
I'd (= I would) like … Ich hätte gern … / Ich möchte … 1

I'd (= I would) like to meet .... Ich würde mich gerne mit ... treffen. 1 **Would you like me to ...?** Möchtest du, dass ich ...? 3
2. liken *(in sozialen Netzwerken: positiv bewerten)* 3
3. der Like *(positive Rückmeldung / „Gefällt mir" in sozialen Netzwerken)* 3
like [laɪk] wie; wie zum Beispiel 2 **like a vampire** wie ein Vampir 2 **like this** so, auf diese Art 1 **a story like this** so/solch eine Geschichte 1 **What's ... like?** Wie ist ...? / Wie sieht ... aus? 1
line [laɪn]:
1. die Reihe 1
2. die Linie 3
3. die Zeile 1
4. die (U-Bahn-)Linie, die (Zug-)Strecke 3
5. *(AE)* die (Warte-)Schlange 4: 3 (88) **stand in line** Schlange stehen, sich anstellen 4: 3 (88)
line chart [ˈlaɪn tʃɑːt] das Liniendiagramm 4: 4 (124)
link [lɪŋk]:
1. die Verbindung; der Link 3
2. **link (to/with)** verbinden (mit) 3
lion [ˈlaɪən] der Löwe 1
list [lɪst]:
1. die Liste 1
2. (auf)listen 1
listen (to) [ˈlɪsn] (sich etwas) anhören; zuhören 3 **listening to music** Musik (an)hören 1
listener [ˈlɪsənə] der/die Zuhörer/in 3
little [ˈlɪtl]:
1. klein 2
2. **a little** ein wenig, ein bisschen 2
live [lɪv] leben, wohnen 1
live [laɪv] live *(z. B Show)* 4: 2 (61)
live-stream sth. [laɪv ˈstriːm] etwas live streamen 4: 2 (61)
lives [laɪvz] *Plural von* life
living room [ˈlɪvɪŋ ruːm] das Wohnzimmer 1
lizard [ˈlɪzəd] die Eidechse 1
LMK (Let me know.) [el em ˈkeɪ] Lass es mich wissen. 4: 4 (122)
local [ˈləʊkl]:
1. der/die Einheimische, der/die Einwohner/in *(eines Ortes)* 4: 1 (19)
2. einheimisch, am/vom Ort 4: 1 (19)
loch [lɒx] der See *(schottisches Wort für „lake")* 3
lonely [ˈləʊnli] einsam 2
long [lɒŋ] lang 1 **work long days** lange arbeiten, lange Arbeitstage haben 1 **work long hours** lange arbeiten, Überstunden machen 2
look [lʊk]:
1. aussehen 1
2. sehen, schauen 1
look after sb./sth. sich um jn./etwas kümmern; auf jn./etwas aufpassen 2
look at sth. sich etwas anschauen 1

look for suchen; Ausschau halten nach 2 **look forward to doing sth.** sich darauf freuen , etwas zu tun 2 **look forward to sth.** sich auf etwas freuen 2 **look sth. up** etwas nachschlagen 1
°**loon** [luːn] der Seetaucher *(Wasservogel)*
°**loonie** [ˈluːni] *(AE, infml)* die kanadische Ein-Dollar-Münze
lose [luːz], lost, lost verlieren 3
loser [ˈluːzə] der Verlierer, die Verliererin 4: 3 (89)
lost [lɒst] *siehe* lose **be lost** sich verlaufen/verirrt haben 3 **get lost** sich verlaufen, sich verirren 3
lot [lɒt]:
1. **a lot (of) / lots (of)** viel/e 1
2. **a lot** sehr 1
lottery [ˈlɒtəri] die Lotterie 4: 3 (79) **win the lottery** im Lotto / in der Lotterie gewinnen 4: 3 (79)
loud [laʊd] laut 1 **laugh out loud** laut auf-/loslachen 2
love [lʌv]:
1. die Liebe 1
be in love (with sb.) verliebt sein (in jn.) 3 **fall in love (with sb.)** sich verlieben (in jn.) 3
2. lieben, sehr mögen 1
I'd (= I would) love ... Ich hätte liebend gern ... / Ich möchte liebend gern... 1 **I'd (= I would) love to meet ...** Ich würde mich liebend gerne mit ... treffen. 1
°**low** [ləʊ] niedrig, tief
°**luck** [lʌk]: **bad luck (on sb.)** das Pech, das Unglück (für jn.) **good luck** das Glück *(glückliche Fügung)*
lucky [ˈlʌki]: **be lucky** Glück haben 1
lunch [lʌntʃ] das Mittagessen 1 **What's for lunch?** Was gibt es zum Mittagessen? 1
lunchtime [ˈlʌntʃtaɪm] die Mittagszeit 2 **at lunchtime** zur Mittagszeit 2
°**lyrics** *(pl)* [ˈlɪrɪks] der Liedtext

M

machine [məˈʃiːn] der Automat, die Maschine 2 **ticket machine** der Fahrkartenautomat 2
made [meɪd] *siehe* make **be made of** bestehen aus, (hergestellt) sein aus 4: 2 (55)
mag [mæg] *siehe* magazine
magazine [mægəˈziːn], *infml auch* mag die Zeitschrift 2
magic [ˈmædʒɪk]:
1. magisch 2
2. die Zauberei 2
do magic zaubern 2
magic show [mædʒɪk ˈʃəʊ] die Zaubershow 2
magic trick [mædʒɪk ˈtrɪk] der Zaubertrick 2
°**magical** [ˈmædʒɪkl] magisch
main [meɪn] Haupt-, wichtigste(r, s) 1

main course [meɪn ˈkɔːs] das Hauptgericht 1
main dish [meɪn ˈdɪʃ] das Hauptgericht 1
mainly [ˈmeɪnli] hauptsächlich, vorwiegend *(Adv.)* 4: 2 (56)
make [meɪk], made, made machen, herstellen 1 **make (money)** (Geld) verdienen 2 **make sb. do sth.** jn. dazu bringen, etwas zu tun 3 **make sb. sth.** jn. zu etwas machen 3 **make sure (that) ...** sicherstellen, dass ...; dafür sorgen, dass ... 3
make-up [ˈmeɪk ʌp] das Make-up 2
male [meɪl]:
1. der Mann 4: 1 (23)
2. männlich 4: 1 (23)
mall [mɔːl] das Einkaufszentrum 4: 1 (28)
man [mæn], *pl* men der Mann 2
mango [ˈmæŋgəʊ], *pl* mangoes die Mango 2
many [ˈmæni] viele 1 **how many?** wie viele? 1
map [mæp] die Landkarte, der Stadtplan 1
°**maple** [ˈmeɪpl] der Ahorn
°**maple leaf** [ˈmeɪpl liːf], *pl* maple leaves das Ahornblatt
°**maple leaves** [ˈmeɪpl liːvz] *Plural von* maple leaf
marathon [ˈmærəθən] der Marathon(lauf) 4: 1 (24)
March [mɑːtʃ] der März 1
Mardi Gras [mɑːdi ˈgrɑː] der Faschingsdienstag *(auch: die Karnevalsfeiern in New Orleans)* 4: 2 (54)
marina [məˈriːnə] der Jachthafen 1
mark [mɑːk] die (Schul-)Note, die Zensur 4: 3 (82)
market [ˈmɑːkɪt] der Markt 1
married (to) [ˈmærid] verheiratet (mit) 1 **get married (to sb.)** jn. heiraten 1
marry [ˈmæri] heiraten 2
marshmallow [mɑːˈʃmæləʊ] das Marshmallow *(weiche Süßigkeit, ähnlich wie Mäusespeck)* 4: 4 (118)
mask [mɑːsk] die Maske 2
°**match** [mætʃ] (passend) zusammenfügen **match to/with** zuordnen
match [mætʃ] das Spiel, der Wettkampf 1
maths [mæθs] die Mathe(matik) 1
matter [ˈmætə] von Bedeutung sein, wichtig sein 4: 2 (53) **It doesn't matter.** Es/Das ist egal. 4: 2 (53)
May [meɪ] der Mai 1
may [meɪ]:
1. dürfen 2
May I ...? Darf ich ...? 2
2. they may treat ... sie behandeln ... vielleicht; sie können ... behandeln 4: 2 (49)
maybe [ˈmeɪbi] vielleicht 1
me [miː]:
1. mich; mir 1
2. *(in bestimmten Wendungen)* ich 1 **It's me.** Ich bin's. 1

Not me! Ich nicht! *(= Ich bin / war / habe / ... es / das nicht!)* 1

meal [miːl] die Mahlzeit, das Essen 1 **Enjoy your meal.** Guten Appetit! 2 **hot meal** die warme Mahlzeit 1

mean [miːn] gemein, fies 1

mean [miːn], **meant, meant** bedeuten; sagen wollen 1

meaning [ˈmiːnɪŋ] die Bedeutung 1

meant [ment] *siehe* **mean**

measure [ˈmeʒə] (aus)messen 4: 4 (124)

meat [miːt] das Fleisch 1

mechanic [mɪˈkænɪk] der/die Mechaniker/in 2

media [ˈmiːdiə] die Medien 3

°**mediate** [ˈmiːdieɪt] vermitteln *(inhaltlich wiedergeben)*

°**mediation** [miːdiˈeɪʃn] die Vermittlung, die Sprachmittlung

medicine [ˈmedsn], [ˈmedɪsn] die Medizin, die Arznei, das Medikament 3

medium [ˈmiːdiəm] medium *(Kleidergröße: mittelgroß/M)* 2

meet [miːt], **met, met** kennenlernen; (sich) treffen 1 **Nice to meet you.** Freut mich, dich/euch/Sie kennenzulernen. 1

meeting [ˈmiːtɪŋ] das Meeting *(Treffen, Zusammenkunft)* 2

melon [ˈmelən] die Melone 1

member [ˈmembə] das Mitglied 2

memorial (to sb./sth.) [məˈmɔːriəl] das Denkmal (für jn./etwas), die Gedenkstätte 3

memorial fountain [məˈmɔːriə faʊntnl] der Gedenkbrunnen 3

men [men] *Plural von* **man**

°**mention** [ˈmenʃn] erwähnen 2

menu [ˈmenjuː] die Speisekarte 3

mess [mes] das Chaos, die Unordnung 1

message [ˈmesɪdʒ] die Nachricht, die Mitteilung 1

messy [ˈmesi] unordentlich 1

met [met] *siehe* **meet**

metal [ˈmetl]:
1. das Metall 4: 2 (57)
2. Metall-, aus Metall 4: 2 (57)

°**Metis** [meɪˈtiː] die Metis *(Nachfahren europäischer Einwanderer/Einwanderinnen in Kanada und kanadischer Indigener)*

metre [ˈmiːtə] der Meter 2

mice [maɪs] *Plural von* **mouse**

middle [ˈmɪdl] die Mitte 3 **in the middle (of)** in der Mitte (von) 3

might [maɪt]: **you might feel ...** du könntest dich ... fühlen, vielleicht fühlst du dich ... 4: 2 (49)

mile [maɪl] die Meile *(ca. 1,6 km)* 3

miles per hour (mph) [maɪlz pər ˈaʊə] Meilen pro Stunde 3 **at 30 miles per hour** mit 30 Meilen pro Stunde 3

milk [mɪlk] die Milch 1

million [ˈmɪljən] die Million 3

mind [maɪnd] der Geist, der Verstand; die Gedanken; der Kopf *(im übertragenen Sinn)* 2 **change your mind**

seine Meinung ändern 4: 4 (112) **make up your mind / make your mind up** sich entscheiden, sich entschließen 2

mind map [ˈmaɪnd mæp] Gedankenkarte, Wörternetz, Mindmap 2

mind sth. [maɪnd]: **I don't mind doing sth.** Es macht mir nichts aus, etwas zu tun. 4: 3 (87) **Never mind! (NVM)** (Das) macht nichts. / Nicht (so) schlimm. 4: 4 (122)

mine [maɪn] meine, meiner, meins 3

mini [ˈmɪni] Mini- 1

mini-drone [ˈmɪni drəʊn] die Minidrohne 1

minigolf [ˈmɪnigɒlf] das Minigolf 2

minute [ˈmɪnɪt] die Minute 1

mirror [ˈmɪrə] der Spiegel 2

miss [mɪs]:
1. vermissen 2
2. verpassen 3
miss a penalty einen Elfmeter verschießen *(= nicht treffen)* 3
3. versäumen, auslassen 3

mistake [mɪˈsteɪk] der Fehler 3 **by mistake** aus Versehen; versehentlich 3

mix [mɪks] (ver)mischen 1

mixture [ˈmɪkstʃə] die Mischung 1

modern [ˈmɒdn] modern 2

mom [mɒm] *(AE)* die Mama, die Mutti 4: 1 (28)

moment [ˈməʊmənt] der Moment 1 **at the moment** im Moment, zurzeit 1

Monday [ˈmʌndeɪ], [ˈmʌndi] der Montag 1

money [ˈmʌni] das Geld 1 **pocket money** das Taschengeld 2

monkey [ˈmʌŋki] der Affe 1

monster [ˈmɒnstə] das Monster 3

month [mʌnθ] der Monat 1

°**moose** [muːs], *pl* **moose** der Elch 1

more [mɔː] mehr, weitere 1 **three more** noch drei, drei weitere 1

morning [ˈmɔːnɪŋ] der Morgen 1 **in the morning** morgens, am Morgen 1

mosque [mɒsk] die Moschee 2

most schools [məʊst] die meisten Schulen 1

mostly [ˈməʊstli] hauptsächlich 4: 2 (56)

mother [ˈmʌðə] die Mutter 2

motto [ˈmɒtəʊ] das Motto 3

mountain [ˈmaʊntən] der Berg 2

mountain biking [ˈmaʊntən baɪkɪŋ] das Mountainbiking 2

°**mounted** [ˈmaʊntɪd] beritten *(auf Pferden)*

°**Mountie** [ˈmaʊnti] *(AE, infml)* das Mitglied der berittenen kanadischen Polizei

mouse [maʊs], *pl* **mice** die Maus 1

mouth [maʊθ] der Mund; *(bei Tieren)* das Maul 4: 1 (21)

move [muːv]:
1. (sich) bewegen 2
move (sth.) *(etwas)* verschieben; aus dem Weg räumen 4: 4 (121)

2. **move (to)** (um)ziehen (nach) 2

movie [ˈmuːvi] *(AE)* der Film, der Spielfilm 4: 1 (16/17)

movie theater [ˈmuːvi θɪətə] *(AE)* das Kino 4: 1 (22)

Mr Lee [ˈmɪstə] Herr Lee 1

Mrs Lee [ˈmɪsɪz] Frau Lee *(Anrede für verheiratete Frauen)* 1

Ms Lee [mɪz] Frau Lee *(allgemeine Anrede f. Frauen)* 1

much [mʌtʃ] viel; sehr 1 **How much is/are ...?** Was (Wie viel) kostet/kosten ...? 2 **Thank you very much.** Vielen Dank. / Danke vielmals. 1

multicultural [mʌltiˈkʌltʃərəl] multikulturell 2

mum [mʌm] die Mama, die Mutti 1

mural [ˈmjʊərəl] das Wandgemälde 3

museum [mjuˈziːəm] das Museum 1

music [ˈmjuːzɪk] die Musik 1 **classical music** klassische Musik 2

music clip [ˈmjuːzɪk klɪp] der Musikclip 4: 2 (56)

musical [ˈmjuːzɪkl] das Musical 2

musical instrument [mjuːzɪkl ˈɪnstrəmənt] das Musikinstrument 4: 2 (56)

musician [mjuˈzɪʃn] der Musiker, die Musikerin 2

must [mʌst] müssen 1 °**a must-see** *(infml)* etwas, was man unbedingt sehen muss

°**mustard** [ˈmʌstəd] der Senf 1

mustn't do [ˈmʌsnt] nicht tun dürfen 1

my [maɪ] mein/e 1

myself [maɪˈself] mich/mir (selbst) 3

N

name [neɪm]:
1. der Name 1
call sb. names jn. beschimpfen 3
What's your name? Wie heißt du? 1
°2. (be)nennen
°**a girl named Sharon** ein Mädchen mit dem Namen Sharon; ein Mädchen, das Sharon heißt/hieß

narrator [nəˈreɪtə] der Erzähler, die Erzählerin 4: 4 (123)

nation [ˈneɪʃn] die Nation 3

national [ˈnæʃnəl] national 3

national anthem [næʃnəl ˈænθəm] die Nationalhymne 4: 2 (52)

national park [næʃnəl ˈpɑːk] der Nationalpark 4: 4 (108/109)

native [ˈneɪtɪv] einheimisch 4: 4 (114)

Native American [neɪtɪv əˈmerɪkən]:
1. der/die amerikanische Indigene 4: 4 (114)
2. zur indigenen Bevölkerung Amerikas gehörend oder sie betreffend 4: 4 (114)

native language [neɪtɪv ˈlæŋgwɪdʒ] die Muttersprache 4: 4 (114)

natural [ˈnætʃrəl] natürlich, Natur- 3

natural history [nætʃrəl ˈhɪstri] die Naturkunde 3

nature [ˈneɪtʃə] die Natur 3

near [nɪə] nahe (bei), in der Nähe von 1

nearly [ˈnɪəli] fast 4: 4 (118)

neck [nɛk] der Hals, der Nacken 3

need [niːd] brauchen 1 **need to do sth.** etwas tun müssen 1 **you needn't do it** du musst es nicht tun; du brauchst es nicht zu tun 4: 2 (49)

negative [ˈnegətɪv]:
1. negativ 3
°2. das Negative, die negative Seite

neighbour [ˈneɪbə] der Nachbar, die Nachbarin 1

neighbourhood [ˈneɪbəhʊd] die Nachbarschaft, die Gegend, das Viertel 1

nervous [ˈnɜːvəs] nervös, aufgeregt 2

nest [nɛst] das Nest 2

never [ˈnevə] nie, niemals 1

new [njuː] neu 1

news [njuːz] die Nachrichten 1

newsagent [ˈnjuːzeɪdʒənt] der/die Zeitungshändler/in 2

newsagent's [ˈnjuːzeɪdʒənts] der Zeitschriftenladen, der Zeitungskiosk 2

newspaper [ˈnjuːspeɪpə] die (Tages-)Zeitung 1

next [nɛkst]:
1. nächste(r, s) 1
the next day am nächsten Tag 1
2. **Next ...** Als Nächstes ... 1

next to [ˈnɛkst tə] neben 1

NGL (not going to lie) [en dʒi ˈel] Um ehrlich zu sein, ... / Ehrlich gesagt, ... 4: 4 (122)

nice [naɪs] nett, schön 1

night [naɪt] die Nacht 2 **at night** nachts, in der Nacht 2

nine [naɪn] neun 1

nineteen [naɪnˈtiːn] neunzehn 1

nineties [ˈnaɪntiz]: **the 90s** die Neunzigerjahre 4: 2 (50)

ninety [ˈnaɪnti] neunzig 1

no [nəʊ]:
1. nein 1
2. kein/e; verboten 1
No dogs! Hunde verboten! 1

no one [ˈnəʊ wʌn] niemand 3

nobody [ˈnəʊbədi] niemand 3

nod [nɒd]:
1. **nod (of your head)** das (Kopf-)Nicken 4: 3 (89)
2. **nod (your head)** (mit dem Kopf) nicken 4: 3 (89)
nod to sb. jm. zunicken 4: 3 (89)

noise [nɔɪz] das Geräusch; der Lärm 1

noisy [ˈnɔɪzi] laut, voller Lärm; lärmend 1

none (of) [nʌn] keine(r, s) (von) 4: 4 (108/109)

normal [ˈnɔːml] normal 3

north [nɔːθ] der Norden; nördlich; Nord- 3

north-east [nɔːθˈiːst] der Nordosten, nordöstlich; Nordost- 3

north-west [nɔːθˈwest] der Nordwesten, nordwestlich; Nordwest- 3

northern [ˈnɔːðən] nördliche(r,s), Nord- 3

nose [nəʊz] die Nase 2

not [nɒt] nicht 1 **I'm not a boy.** Ich bin kein Junge. 1

note [nəʊt] die Notiz; der kurze Brief 1 **make notes** (sich) Notizen machen *(zur Vorbereitung)* 1 **take notes** (sich) Notizen machen *(beim Lesen oder Zuhören)* 3 °**sticky note** die Haftnotiz, der Klebezettel

nothing [ˈnʌθɪŋ] nichts 4: 2 (59)

notice [ˈnəʊtɪs]:
1. (be)merken 2
2. der Anschlag, die Bekanntmachung *(an einem Schwarzen Brett)* 2

November [nəʊˈvembə] der November 1

now [naʊ] nun, jetzt 1 **from now on** von nun an 4: 3 (89)

nowhere [ˈnəʊweə] nirgendwo(hin) 4: 3 (79)

number [ˈnʌmbə]:
1. die Zahl, die Ziffer, die Nummer 1
2. **number (of)** die Anzahl (an) 4: (12/13)

nurse [nɜːs] der Krankenpfleger, die Krankenpflegerin 2

NVM (Never mind!) [en vi ˈem] (Das) macht nichts. / Nicht (so) schlimm. 4: 4 (122)

O

ocean [ˈəʊʃn] der Ozean 4: 4 (108/109)

o'clock [əˈklɒk]: **at 8 o'clock** um 8 Uhr 1

October [ɒkˈtəʊbə] der Oktober 1

of [ɒv], [əv] von 1 **bags of rubbish** Tüten/Säcke mit/voller Müll 1 **the days of the week** *(pl)* die Wochentage 1 **the first of April (1st April)** der erste April 1

of course [əv ˈkɔːs] natürlich, selbstverständlich 1

off [ɒf]:
1. weg von; hinunter von 3
get off (a train/bus) aussteigen (aus einem Zug/Bus) 2 **get off your bike/your horse** vom Fahrrad / vom Pferd absteigen 3
2. **be off** aus sein *(ausgeschaltet sein)* 2

offer [ˈɒfə]:
1. (an)bieten 4: 3 (87)
2. das Angebot 4: 3 (87)

office [ˈɒfɪs] das Büro 1

official [əˈfɪʃl] offiziell 3

official language [əfɪʃl ˈlæŋgwɪdʒ] die Amtssprache 3

often [ˈɒfn], [ˈɒftən] oft 1

oh [əʊ] Null *(im gesprochenen Englisch)* 1

OK [əʊˈkeɪ] okay, in Ordnung 1 **Are you OK?** Geht es dir gut? / Bist du okay? 1 **I'm OK.** Es geht mir gut. 1

old [əʊld] alt 1

OMG (Oh my God!) [əʊ em ˈdʒiː] Oh mein Gott! 4: 4 (122)

on [ɒn]:
1. auf 1

on holiday im/in den Urlaub 1 **on Monday** am Montag 1 **on Mondays** an jedem Montag, montags 1 **on my birthday** an meinem Geburtstag 1 **on the beach** am Strand 1 **on the bus** im Bus 1 **get on (a train/bus)** einsteigen (in einen Zug/Bus) 2
2. **be on** gezeigt werden *(Kino, Fernsehen)*, stattfinden, „laufen"; an sein *(eingeschaltet sein)* 2

once [wʌns]:
1. einst 3
2. einmal 3
at once auf einmal 3

one [wʌn]:
1. eins 1
one way eine Strecke (= *ohne Rückfahrt/Rückflug*) 2 **one-way ticket** die einfache Fahrkarte *(= ohne Rückfahrt)* 2 **a one-day tour** eine eintägige Tour 2 **a one-hour boat trip** eine einstündige Bootsfahrt 3 **one day** eines Tages 4: 1 (24)
2. **the round one** der/die/das Runde 2

onion [ˈʌnjən] die Zwiebel 2

online [ɒnˈlaɪn] online, Online- 1

only [ˈəʊnli]:
1. nur, bloß; erst 1
2. **the only music** die einzige Musik 4: 2 (56)

onto the table [ˈɒntu], [ˈɒntə] auf den Tisch 2

open [ˈəʊpən]:
1. öffnen; aufschlagen *(Buch)* 1
2. sich öffnen, aufgehen 3
3. offen, geöffnet 1
°**open to** offen für

opening hours *(pl)* [ˈəʊpənɪŋ aʊəz] die Öffnungszeiten 4: 3 (87)

opening times *(pl)* [ˈəʊpənɪŋ taɪmz] die Öffnungszeiten 4: 3 (87)

opinion [əˈpɪnjən] die Meinung 2 **in my opinion** meiner Meinung nach 2

opportunity [ɒpəˈtjuːnəti] die Gelegenheit, die Möglichkeit, die Chance 4: 1 (21)

opposite [ˈɒpəzɪt] das Gegenteil 1

option [ˈɒpʃn] die Wahl(möglichkeit), die Option 3

or [ɔː] oder; sonst 1

orange [ˈɒrɪndʒ]:
1. orange(farben) 1
2. die Orange, die Apfelsine 1

°**orca** [ˈɔːkə] der Schwertwal

order [ˈɔːdə]:
1. ordnen, anordnen 3
2. die Reihenfolge; die Ordnung 3
in order in eine(r) Reihenfolge 3
in the correct order in der richtigen Reihenfolge, in die richtige Reihenfolge 3

order [ˈɔːdə]:
1. die Bestellung 3
2. **order sth.** etwas bestellen 3

organization [ɔːgənaɪˈzeɪʃn] die Organisation 3

organize [ˈɔːgənaɪz] organisieren 3

organizer [ˈɔːɡənaɪzə] der/die Organisator/in 3

other [ˈʌðə] andere(r, s) **each other** einander, sich (gegenseitig) 2 **the others** die anderen 1

our [ˈaʊə] unser/e 1

ours [ɑːz], [ˈaʊəz] unserer, unsere, unseres 3

ourselves [aʊəˈselvz] uns (selbst) 3

out (of ...) [aʊt]:
1. **out** heraus, hinaus, nach draußen 2
out and about unterwegs 4: 1 (18)
go out rausgehen, weggehen; ausgehen 2
2. **out of ...** aus ... (heraus/hinaus) 2

outdoor [ˈaʊtdɔː] Outdoor- 3

outdoor activity [ˈaʊtdɔː] die Outdoor-Aktivität; die Aktivität für draußen / im Freien 3

outdoors [aʊtˈdɔːz] im Freien, draußen 3

outfit [ˈaʊtfɪt] das Outfit 3

outside [aʊtˈsaɪd]:
1. draußen; nach draußen 4: 2 (48)
2. außerhalb (von) *(Präp.)* 1
outside the house außerhalb des Hauses 1

oven [ˈʌvn] der Backofen 1

over [ˈəʊvə]:
1. über; mehr als 1
over 50 über / mehr als 50 1 **over here** hier herüber; hier drüben 1
over there da drüben, dort drüben 1
all over the world überall auf der Welt, auf der ganzen Welt, weltweit 2
2. hinüber, herüber 2
come / walk over hinüberkommen/-gehen, rüberkommen/-gehen 2
3. **be over** vorbei sein, zu Ende sein 4: 2 (58)

own [əʊn]:
1. **my/your own room** mein/dein/ein eigenes Zimmer 1
2. **own sth.** etwas besitzen 2

owner [ˈəʊnə] der/die Besitzer/in 2

P

°Pacific [pəˈsɪfɪk]:
1. pazifisch
2. **the Pacific (Ocean)** der Pazifik, der Pazifische Ozean

pack [pæk] packen, einpacken 3

packet [ˈpækɪt] die Packung, das Päckchen 1

°paddleboarding [ˈpædlbɔːdɪŋ] das Stehpaddeln, das Paddleboardfahren

page (= p.) [peɪdʒ] die (Buch-/Heft-)Seite 1 **Open your books at page 10.** Schlagt eure Bücher auf Seite 10 auf. 1

paid [peɪd] *siehe* **pay**

paint [peɪnt]:
1. die Farbe, der Lack 3
2. (an)malen; lackieren, (an)streichen 3

pair [peə]:
1. das Paar 2
2. **pair sth. (with sth.)** etwas (mit etwas) koppeln *(z. B Geräte)* 3

palace [ˈpæləs] der Palast, das Schloss 3

pan [pæn] die Pfanne 1

pants [pænts] *(pl, AE)* die Hose 4: 1 (22)

paper [ˈpeɪpə]:
1. die (Tages-)Zeitung 1
2. das Papier 1
°piece of paper das Stück Papier, der Zettel

parade [pəˈreɪd] die Parade, der Umzug 2

°paragraph [ˈpærəɡrɑːf] der (Text-)Abschnitt

°parallel [ˈpærəlel] parallel, Parallel-

parents *(pl)* [ˈpeərənts] die Eltern 1

park [pɑːk] der Park 1

parkour [pɑːˈkʊə] der Parkour *(akrobatischer Hindernislauf in der Stadt)* 1

parrot [ˈpærət] der Papagei 1

part (of) [pɑːt] der Teil (von) 1
°take part (in) teilnehmen (an), mitmachen (bei)

part-time [pɑːt ˈtaɪm] Teilzeit-, Halbtags- 4: 1 (28)

partner [ˈpɑːtnə] der/die Partner/in 1

party [ˈpɑːti] die Party 1

pass [pɑːs]: **pass sth. (to sb.)** (jm.) etwas (an)geben, (an)reichen 4: 3 (85)
pass sth. around etwas herumreichen 4: 3 (85)

past [pɑːst]:
1. die Vergangenheit 3
2. vergangene(r, s) 3

past [pɑːst]:
1. nach *(bei Uhrzeitangaben)* 2
half past 6 halb 7 2 **quarter past 7** viertel nach 7 2
2. vorbei an, vorüber an 2

pasta [ˈpæstə] die Pasta *(italienische Bezeichnung für Teigwaren)* 1

path [pɑːθ] der Weg, der Pfad 3

patient [ˈpeɪʃnt] geduldig 4: 3 (92)

pay [peɪ]:
1. die Bezahlung *(Lohn)* 4: 3 (87)
2. **pay (for sth.), paid, paid** (etwas be)zahlen 1
pay by card mit Karte (be)zahlen *(z. B Bankkarte)* 2

PE (= physical education) [piː ˈiː] der (Schul-)Sport 1

pea [piː] die Erbse 1

peace [piːs] der Friede(n) 4: 2 (50)

peaceful [ˈpiːsfl] friedlich; friedfertig 4: 2 (50)

°peer [pɪə] der/die Gleichaltrige, der/die Ebenbürtige, jemand aus derselben sozialen Gruppe

pen [pen] der Kugelschreiber, der Stift; der Füller 1

penalty [ˈpenəlti] der Strafstoß; der Elfmeter *(Fußball)* 3

pence [pens] *Plural von* **penny**

pencil [ˈpensl] der Bleistift 1

pencil case [ˈpensl keɪs] das Federmäppchen 1

pencil sharpener [ˈpensl ʃɑːpnə] der Bleistift(an)spitzer 1

penny (p) [ˈpeni], *pl* **pence** der Penny *(kleinste britische Münze)* 2

people [ˈpiːpl]:
1. *(pl)* die Leute, die Menschen 1
2. *pl* **peoples** das Volk 4: 4 (114)

pepper [ˈpepə]:
1. die Paprika, die Peperoni 4: 4 (119)
2. der Pfeffer 4: 4 (119)
pepper spray das Pfefferspray 4: 4 (119)

per [pɜː], [pə] pro 3 **miles per hour (mph)** Meilen pro Stunde 3

per cent (%) [pə ˈsent] das Prozent 3

perfect [ˈpɜːfɪkt] perfekt 1

perfectly (still) [ˈpɜːfɪktli] ganz/völlig (still) 1

perform [pəˈfɔːm] auftreten *(Künstler/Künstlerin)*; aufführen 4: 1 (23)

performance [pəˈfɔːməns] die Vorstellung, die Aufführung 4: 1 (23)

perhaps [pəˈhæps] vielleicht 2

permission [pəˈmɪʃn] die Erlaubnis 4: 4 (116)

person [ˈpɜːsn] die Person 1

personal [ˈpɜːsənl] persönlich 3

personal assistant (PA) [pɜːsənl əˈsɪstənt] der/die persönliche Assistent/in 4: 4 (111)

personal digital assistant (PDA) [pɜːsənl dɪdʒɪtl əˈsɪstənt] der elektronische Organizer *(wörtlich: persönlicher digitaler Assistent)* 4: 4 (111)

personality [pɜːsəˈnæləti] die Persönlichkeit; der Charakter 3

pet [pet] das (Haus-)Tier 1

petition [pəˈtɪʃn] der Antrag, die Petition *(Unterschriftensammlung)* 4: 2 (53)

phone [fəʊn]:
1. anrufen; telefonieren 1
2. das Telefon 1
answer the phone ans Telefon gehen 3 **on the phone** am Telefon 1

phone call [ˈfəʊn kɔːl] der (Telefon-)Anruf 2

phone number [ˈfəʊn nʌmbə] die Telefonnummer 1

photo [ˈfəʊtəʊ] das Foto 1 **in the photo** auf dem Foto 1 **take photos** Fotos machen 1 **taking photos** das Fotografieren *(Hobby)* 1

photograph [ˈfəʊtəɡrɑːf]:
1. das Foto 4: 4 (112)
2. fotografieren 4: 4 (112)

photographer [fəˈtɒɡrəfə] der/die Fotograf/in 4: 4 (112)

photography [fəˈtɒɡrəfi] die Fotografie *(Hobby)*, das Fotografieren 2

phrase [freɪz] der Ausdruck, die (Rede-)Wendung 4: 2 (62)

physical education (PE) [fɪzɪkl edʒuˈkeɪʃn] der (Schul-)Sport 1

pick [pɪk] (aus)wählen, aussuchen 2
pick sb. up jn. abholen 4: 4 (123)
pick sb./sth. up jn./etwas abholen 2

pick sth. up etwas aufheben *(vom Boden)*, etwas hochheben 2

picnic ['pɪknɪk] das Picknick 1 **have a picnic** ein Picknick machen 1

picture ['pɪktʃə] das Bild 1

pie chart ['paɪ tʃɑːt] das Tortendiagramm, das Kreisdiagramm 4: 4 (124)

°**piece** [piːs] das Stück, der/das Teil **piece of paper** das Stück Papier

pier [pɪə] der Pier, die Seebrücke 1

pig [pɪg] das Schwein 1

piggy bank ['pɪgi bæŋk] das Sparschwein 1

pink [pɪŋk] rosa 1

piper ['paɪpə] der/die Dudelsackspieler/in 3

pitch [pɪtʃ] der Platz *(Sport)*, das Spielfeld 3

pizza ['piːtsə] die Pizza 2

place [pleɪs] der Ort, der Platz 1 **take place** stattfinden 2

°**placemat** ['pleɪsmæt] das Platzdeckchen

plan [plæn]:
1. der Plan 2
2. planen 2
plan to do sth. planen, etwas zu tun 2

plane [pleɪn] das Flugzeug 2

planet ['plænɪt] der Planet 2

plant [plɑːnt]:
1. die Pflanze 3
2. pflanzen 3

°**plantation** [plæn'teɪʃn] die Plantage 3

plastic ['plæstɪk] das Plastik, der Kunststoff 2

platform ['plætfɔːm] der Bahnsteig 2 **at platform 4** auf Gleis 4 2

play [pleɪ] spielen 1

player ['pleɪə] der/die Spieler/in 1

playing card ['pleɪɪŋ kɑːd] die Spielkarte 1

playlist ['pleɪlɪst] die Playlist 1

please [pliːz] bitte 1

°**Pledge of Allegiance** [pledʒ əv ə'liːdʒəns] das Treuegelöbnis

plumber ['plʌmə] der/die (Sanitär-)Installateur/in 2

p.m. [piː'em]: **4 p.m.** 4 Uhr nachmittags, 16 Uhr 1 **9 p.m.** 9 Uhr abends, 21 Uhr 1

°**po'boy** ['pəʊ bɔɪ] das Po'Boy-Sandwich *(reichhaltig gefülltes Stück Baguette)*

pocket ['pɒkɪt] die Tasche *(an Kleidungsstücken)* 2

pocket money ['pɒkɪt mʌni] das Taschengeld 2

podcast ['pɒdkɑːst] der Podcast *(Audiodatei zum Herunterladen aus dem Internet)* 3

poem ['pəʊɪm] das Gedicht 2

point [pɔɪnt]:
1. der Punkt 1
2. das Komma *(Dezimalzeichen)* 4: 1 (20)
1.6 (one point six) 1,6 (eins Komma sechs) 4: 1 (20)
3. das Argument, der Standpunkt 3

I take your point. Ich verstehe, was du sagen willst. 3 **make a/your point** ein Argument vortragen/vorbringen 3 **Make your point.** Leg deinen Standpunkt dar. / Sag, wie du darüber denkst. 3 **take a point** einen Standpunkt verstehen 3 **That's a good point.** Das ist ein gutes Argument. 3

police *(pl)* [pə'liːs] die Polizei 3

polite [pə'laɪt] höflich 1

politician [pɒlə'tɪʃn] der Politiker, die Politikerin 4: 3 (81)

°**pond** [pɒnd] der Teich 1

pool [puːl] *(kurz für* **swimming pool***)* das Schwimmbad 1

poor [pɔː], [pʊə] arm 3 **Poor George!** Der arme George! / Armer George! 3

pop (music) ['pɒp mjuːzɪk] der Pop, die Popmusik 2

popular (with) ['pɒpjələ] beliebt, populär (bei) 1

°**population** [pɒpju'leɪʃn] die Bevölkerung, die Einwohner(zahl)

pork [pɔːk] das Schweinefleisch 1

pose [pəʊz]:
1. posieren 3
2. die Pose, die Haltung 3
power pose die Machtpose 3

°**position** [pə'zɪʃn] die Position, der Standort

positive ['pɒzətɪv]:
1. positiv 3
°2. das Positive, die positive Seite

post [pəʊst]:
1. der Post *(Teil eines Blogs)* 1
2. posten *(im Internet veröffentlichen)* 1

poster ['pəʊstə] das Poster 1

potato [pə'teɪtəʊ], *pl* **potatoes** die Kartoffel 1

pound (£) [paʊnd] das Pfund *(britische Währung)* 1

poverty ['pɒvəti] die Armut 3

powder ['paʊdə] das Pulver 1

power ['paʊə] die Kraft, die Macht, die Energie; der (elektrische) Strom 2

power pose ['paʊə pəʊz] die Machtpose 3

°**powwow** ['paʊwaʊ] die Versammlung *(amerik. Indigener)*, der Kriegsrat

practice ['præktɪs] die Übung(en) 2

practise ['præktɪs] üben 2

pray [preɪ] beten 2

prayer [preə] das Gebet 2

predict [prɪ'dɪkt] vorhersagen, voraussagen 4: 4 (113)

prediction [prɪ'dɪkʃn] die Vorhersage, die Voraussage 2

prefer sth. to sth. [prɪ'fɜː] etwas einer Sache vorziehen, etwas lieber tun/ haben als etwas 4: 1 (16/17) **I'd prefer ....** Ich würde ... vorziehen. 4: 1 (16/17)

prep school ['prep skuːl] *(AE) siehe* **preparatory school**

preparation [prepə'reɪʃn] die Vorbereitung; die Zubereitung 2

preparatory school [prɪ'pærətri skuːl] *(AE) (kurz auch* **prep school***)* die (meist teure, private) Schule, die Schüler/innen auf die Universität vorbereitet 4: 3 (88)

prepare (for) [prɪ'peə] vorbereiten, zubereiten; sich vorbereiten (auf) 2

preppy ['prepi] *für eine/n Schüler/in auf einer prep school typisch* 4: 3 (88)

present ['preznt] das Geschenk 1

present ['preznt]:
1. die Gegenwart 3
2. gegenwärtig 3

present sth. (to sb.) [prɪ'zent] (jm.) etwas präsentieren, vorstellen 1

presentation [prezn'teɪʃn] das Referat, die Präsentation 1

president ['prezɪdənt] der/die Präsident/in 4: (12/13)

pretty ['prɪti] hübsch 3

price [praɪs] der (Kauf-)Preis 2

pride [praɪd] der Stolz 2

prime minister [praɪm 'mɪnɪstə] der/ die Premierminister/in 3

prince [prɪns] der Prinz 3

princess [prɪn'ses] die Prinzessin 3

°**prison** ['prɪzn] das Gefängnis

private ['praɪvət] privat; persönlich 3

prize [praɪz] der Preis, der Gewinn 1

prize show ['praɪz ʃəʊ] die Preisverleihung *(Zeremonie)* 1

pro [prəʊ] *siehe* **professional**

probably ['prɒbəbli] wahrscheinlich 4: 1 (24)

problem ['prɒbləm] das Problem 1

problem-solving ['prɒbləm sɒlvɪŋ] das Lösen von Problemen, die Problemlösung 4: 4 (122)

°**product** ['prɒdʌkt] das Produkt

professional [prə'feʃnl]:
1. professionell, Profi- 4: 1 (23)
2. *(infml auch* **pro***)* der Fachmann, die Fachfrau, der Profi 4: 1 (23)

profile ['prəʊfaɪl] das Profil; die Beschreibung, das Portrait 2

program ['prəʊgræm]:
1. das (Computer-)Programm 2
2. programmieren 2

programme ['prəʊgræm] das (Fernseh-)Programm, die Sendung 2

programmer ['prəʊgræmə] der/die Programmierer/in 2

project ['prɒdʒekt] das Projekt 1

prom [prɒm] *(AE)* der Schul(abschluss)ball 4: 3 (82)

pros *(pl)* [prəʊz]: **the pros and cons** das Pro und Kontra; das Für und Wider 4: 4 (125)

protect (from/against) [prə'tekt] (be)schützen (vor) 3

protest ['prəʊtest] der Protest, die Protestdemonstration 3

protest [prə'test] protestieren 3

protester [prə'testə] der/die Demonstrant/in 3

proud (of) [praʊd] stolz (auf) 2

public ['pʌblɪk]:
1. öffentlich 3

2. the public die Öffentlichkeit 4: 1 (32)

in public in der / in aller Öffentlichkeit 4: 1 (32)

public transport *(no pl)* [ˈpʌblɪk ˈtrænspɔːt] die öffentlichen Verkehrsmittel 3

°**pull** [pʊl] ziehen

°**pumpkin pie** [ˈpʌmpkɪn paɪ] *(AE)* die Kürbistorte *(traditionelle herbstliche Nachspeise in den USA)*

punctual [ˈpʌŋktʃuəl] pünktlich 4: 3 (87)

punk [pʌŋk] der Punk 2

purple [ˈpɜːpl] violett, lila 1

put [pʊt], **put, put** *(etwas wohin)* tun, legen, stellen, stecken 1 **put out a fire** ein Feuer löschen 4: 4 (120) **put sth. on** etwas anziehen *(Kleidung)*, aufsetzen *(z. B Hut, Brille)* 2 **put your hand up** sich melden, aufzeigen 1

puzzle [ˈpʌzl] das Rätsel 1

Q

quality [ˈkwɒləti]:
1. die Qualität, Qualitäts-; die Eigenschaft 4: 3 (91)
2. hochwertig, von hoher Qualität 4: 3 (91)

quarter [ˈkwɔːtə]: **quarter past 7** viertel nach 7 2 **quarter to 7** viertel vor 7 2

queen [kwiːn] die Königin 3

question [ˈkwestʃən] die Frage 1 **ask a question** eine Frage stellen 1

queue [kjuː]:
1. Schlange stehen, sich anstellen *(in einer Warteschlage)* 4: 2 (46/47)
2. die (Warte-)Schlange 4: 3 (88)

quick [kwɪk] schnell 3

quiet [ˈkwaɪət] ruhig, still, leise 1

quiz [kwɪz], *pl* **quizzes** das Quiz, das Ratespiel; der Test 1 **do a quiz** ein Quiz / ein Ratespiel / einen Test machen 1

quizzes [ˈkwɪzɪz] *Plural von* **quiz**

°**quote** [kwəʊt] das Zitat

R

rabbit [ˈræbɪt] das Kaninchen 1

racism [ˈreɪsɪzəm] der Rassismus 3

racist [ˈreɪsɪst]:
1. der/die Rassist/in 3
2. rassistisch 3

radio [ˈreɪdiəʊ] das Radio 3

°**rafting** [ˈrɑːftɪŋ] das Rafting *(Schlauchbootfahren auf Flüssen)*

rain [reɪn]:
1. der Regen 1
2. regnen 1

rain jacket [ˈreɪn dʒækɪt] die Regenjacke 2

rainbow [ˈreɪnbəʊ] der Regenbogen 2

rainy [ˈreɪni] regnerisch 1

ran [ræn] *siehe* **run**

ranch [rɑːntʃ], [ræntʃ] die Ranch *(Viehfarm in den USA)* 4: 3 (75/76)

rap [ræp]:
1. der Rap 2
2. rappen 2

rapper [ˈræpə] der/die Rapper/in 4: 2 (53)

°**rat** [ræt] die Ratte

react (to) [riˈækt] reagieren (auf) 4: 2 (60)

reaction (to) [riˈækʃn] die Reaktion (auf) 4: 2 (60)

read [red] *siehe* **read**

read [riːd], **read, read** lesen 1

reader [ˈriːdə] der/die Leser/in 1

ready [ˈredi] fertig, bereit 1 **get ready (for)** sich fertig machen (für), sich vorbereiten (auf) 2

real [rɪəl] echt, wirklich 2

realistic [riːəˈlɪstɪk] realistisch 2

realization [riːəlaɪˈzeɪʃn] die Erkenntnis 4: 4 (123)

realize sth. [ˈrɪəlaɪz] etwas erkennen, sich einer Sache bewusst werden 4: 4 (123)

really [ˈriːəli], [ˈrɪəli] wirklich 1

reason [ˈriːzn] der Grund, die Begründung 3 **for this reason** aus diesem Grund 3 **the reason why ...** der Grund dafür, dass ... 3

receipt [rɪˈsiːt] der (Kauf-)Beleg, die Quittung, der Kassenzettel 4: 2 (49)

recipe [ˈresəpi] das (Koch-)Rezept 1

recipe book [ˈresəpi bʊk] das Kochbuch 1

recognize [ˈrekəgnaɪz] (wieder)erkennen 3

recommend sth. (to sb.) [rekəˈmend] (jm.) etwas empfehlen 4: 1 (25)

recommendation [rekəmənˈdeɪʃn] die Empfehlung 4: 1 (25)

record [rɪˈkɔːd] aufnehmen, aufzeichnen 1

recording [rɪˈkɔːdɪŋ] die Aufnahme 1

recycle [riːˈsaɪkl] recyceln, wiederverwerten 3

recycling [rɪˈsaɪklɪŋ] das Recycling 3

red [red] rot 1 **go red** erröten, rot werden 1

°**redhead** [ˈredhed] der Rotschopf *(rothaariger Mensch)*

°**redwood (tree)** [ˈredwʊd] der Mammutbaum

refer to [rɪˈfɜː] sich beziehen auf, Bezug nehmen auf 4: 1 (26) **refer to sth. by its name/number** etwas mit seinem Namen / seiner Nummer bezeichnen 4: 1 (26)

regular [ˈregjələ] regelmäßig; gewohnt, normal 4: 3 (87)

relax [rɪˈlæks] sich entspannen 2

relaxed [rɪˈlækst] entspannt 2

relaxing [rɪˈlæksɪŋ] entspannend 2

reliable [rɪˈlaɪəbl] verlässlich, zuverlässig 4: 3 (87)

remember [rɪˈmembə]:
1. daran denken, nicht vergessen 1 **remember to do sth.** daran denken, etwas zu tun 1
2. sich erinnern an 1

remember doing sth. sich daran erinnern, etwas getan zu haben 1

rent [rent]:
1. die Miete 4: 1 (28)
2. mieten; leihen 4: 1 (28)

repeat [rɪˈpiːt] wiederholen 2

reply (to) [rɪˈplaɪ]:
1. antworten (auf) 3
2. die Antwort (auf) 3

republic [rɪˈpʌblɪk] die Republik 3

rescue [ˈreskjuː]:
1. retten 3
2. die Rettung 3

rescuer [ˈreskjuːə] der/die Retter/in 3

research [rɪˈsɜːtʃ]:
1. erforschen, untersuchen, recherchieren 3
2. die Forschung(en), die Recherche(n) 3
do research recherchieren 3

respect [rɪˈspekt]:
1. respektieren, achten 2
2. **respect (for)** der Respekt (vor) 2

responsible (for) [rɪˈspɒnsəbl] verantwortlich (für); verantwortungsbewusst 4: 3 (87)

rest [rest]:
1. ruhen; sich ausruhen 3
2. die Ruhe, die Pause, die Erholung 3 **take a rest** Pause machen 3
3. der Rest 4: (10/11)

restaurant [ˈrestrɒnt] das Restaurant 2

restroom [ˈrestruːm] *(AE)* die Toilette *(in öffentlichen Gebäuden)* 4: 1 (22)

result [rɪˈzʌlt] das Ergebnis 3 **as a result** folglich, demzufolge 3

return [rɪˈtɜːn]:
1. zurückkehren, zurückkommen 2
2. *(kurz für:* **return ticket***)* die (Hin- und) Rückfahrkarte 2

return ticket [rɪˈtɜːn tɪkɪt] die (Hin- und) Rückfahrkarte 2

°**revision** [rɪˈvɪʒn] die Wiederholung *(von Lernstoff)*

rhyme [raɪm]:
1. (sich) reimen 2
2. der Reim 2

rhythm [ˈrɪðəm] der Rhythmus 4: 2 (57)

rice [raɪs] der Reis 1

rich [rɪtʃ] reich 2

ridden [ˈrɪdn] *siehe* **ride**

ride [raɪd]:
1. die Fahrt; das Fahrgeschäft *(auf Volksfesten, in Vergnügungsparks)* 4: 1 (19)
2. **ride, rode, ridden** reiten; fahren *(z. B Fahrrad)* 2
ride a bike mit dem Fahrrad fahren 2
ride a horse reiten 2

right [raɪt]:
1. richtig *(Adj.)* 1 **be right** Recht haben 1
2. das Recht 3
You had no right to do this. Du hattest kein Recht, das zu tun. 3
3. *(adv.)* genau, gerade, direkt 3
right after school gleich/direkt nach

der Schule 3 **right by the sea** direkt am Meer 3 **right from the start** gleich/direkt von Anfang an 3 **right now** gerade jetzt, genau jetzt 3 **right then** genau dann 3

right [raɪt] rechts; nach rechts 2 **on the right** rechts, auf der rechten Seite 2 **to the right of ...** rechts von ... 2

ring [rɪŋ] der Ring 1 **wedding ring** der Ehering 2

rip [rɪp] zerreißen, (ein)reißen 3

ripped [rɪpt] zerrissen, (ein)gerissen 3

risk [rɪsk]:
1. riskieren, wagen 4: 2 (61)
2. das Risiko 4: 2 (61)
at risk in Gefahr 4: 2 (61) **take a risk** ein Risiko eingehen 4: 2 (61)

risky [ˈrɪski] riskant 4: 2 (61)

river [ˈrɪvə] der Fluss 2

°**riverside** [ˈrɪvəsaɪd] das Flussufer

road [rəʊd] die Straße *(in oder zwischen Orten)* 1

road trip [ˈrəʊd trɪp] die Autoreise 3

robot [ˈrəʊbɒt] der Roboter 1

robot builder [ˈrəʊbɒt bɪldə] der/die Roboter-Konstrukteur/in 4: 4 (122)

rock [rɒk]:
1. der Rock *(Rockmusik)* 2
°2. der Stein; der Fels(en)

rode [rəʊd] *siehe* **ride**

role [rəʊl] die Rolle *(Film, Theater)* 2

role model [ˈrəʊl mɒdl] das Vorbild 3

role-play [ˈrəʊlpleɪ]:
1. das Rollenspiel 2
2. **role-play sth.** etwas in einem Rollenspiel darstellen 2

roll [rəʊl]:
1. die Rolle; das Brötchen 4: 2 (54)
2. rollen 4: 2 (54)

roof [ruːf] das Dach 4: 2 (59)

room [ruːm] der Raum, das Zimmer 1

°**root** [ruːt] die Wurzel

rope [rəʊp] das Seil 4: 4 (121)

round [raʊnd]:
1. rund *(Adj.)* 2
2. **round ...** um (... herum), in ... umher 2
all round the globe auf der ganzen Welt 3 **all round the stadium** überall im Stadion, im ganzen Stadion 3

roundabout [ˈraʊndəbaʊt] der Kreisverkehr 3

route [ruːt] die Route, der Weg 3

royal [ˈrɔɪəl] königlich 3

rubber [ˈrʌbə] das Radiergummi 1

rubbish [ˈrʌbɪʃ] der (Haus-)Müll, der Abfall 1

rucksack [ˈrʌksæk] der Rucksack 1

rugby [ˈrʌɡbi] das Rugby *(Ballsportart)* 3

rule [ruːl] die Regel 2

ruler [ˈruːlə] das Lineal 1

run [rʌn], **ran**, **run**:
1. rennen, laufen 1
2. fahren, verkehren *(Bus, Bahn)* 4: 1 (26)
3. **run sth.** etwas betreiben, leiten 4: 3 (79)

family-run business der Familienbetrieb 4: 3 (79)

running [ˈrʌnɪŋ] das Laufen *(Sport)* 1

rural [ˈrʊərəl] ländlich, Land- 4: 3 (75/76)

°**rush** [rʌʃ] (schnell) fließen; eilen; hetzen

S

sad [sæd] traurig 1

safe [seɪf] sicher *(gefahrlos)* 3

safety [ˈseɪfti] die Sicherheit 3

said [sed] *siehe* **say**

salad [ˈsæləd] der Salat *(als Gericht oder Beilage)* 1

salmon [ˈsæmən], *pl* **salmon** der Lachs 4: 4 (116)

same [seɪm]: **the same** gleich; derselbe/dieselbe/dasselbe; dieselben 1

sandwich [ˈsænwɪtʃ], [ˈsænwɪdʒ] das Sandwich 1

sang [sæŋ] *siehe* **sing**

sari [ˈsɑːri] der Sari *(Kleid/Gewand indischer Frauen)* 2

sat [sæt] *siehe* **sit**

Saturday [ˈsætədeɪ], [ˈsætədi] der Samstag 1

sauce [sɔːs] die Soße 1

sausage [ˈsɒsɪdʒ] das (Brat-, Bock-) Würstchen, die Wurst 1

save [seɪv]:
1. retten 2
2. sparen 2

savings *(pl)* [ˈseɪvɪŋz] die Ersparnisse 2

savings account [ˈseɪvɪŋz əkaʊnt] das Sparkonto 2

saw [sɔː] *siehe* **see**

say [seɪ], **said**, **said** sagen 1 **say sorry to sb.** sich bei jm. entschuldigen 3 **it says that ...** es heißt (im Text), dass ... 3

°**scan (a text for sth.)** [skæn] (einen Text) überfliegen, (einen Text) absuchen (nach etwas)

scare sb. [skeə] jn. erschrecken, jm. Angst machen 2

scared [skeəd]: **be scared (of)** Angst haben (vor) 1

scarf [skɑːf], *pl* **scarves** Schal 2

scarves [skɑːvz] *Plural von* **scarf**

scary [ˈskeəri] unheimlich, beängstigend, gruselig 1

scene [siːn] die Szene 1

school [skuːl] die Schule 1 **at school** in der Schule 1

school club [ˈskuːl klʌb] die AG *(in der Schule)* 1

school uniform [skuːl ˈjuːnɪfɔːm] die Schuluniform 1

sci-fi [ˈsaɪ faɪ] *siehe* **science fiction**

science [ˈsaɪəns] die Naturwissenschaft 1

science fiction [saɪəns ˈfɪkʃn] *infml auch* **sci-fi** die Sciencefiction 2

scientist [ˈsaɪəntɪst] der/die (Natur-) Wissenschaftler/in 3

score [skɔː]:
1. der Score *(Spielstand, Spielergebnis)* 2
2. scoren *(einen Punkt / ein Tor / einen Treffer erzielen)* 2

Scotland [ˈskɒtlənd] Schottland 3

screen [skriːn] der Bildschirm; die Leinwand *(Kino)* 2

sea [siː] das Meer, die See 1 **by the sea** am Meer, an der See 1

sea level [ˈsiː levl] der Meeresspiegel 2

seagull [ˈsiːɡʌl] die Möwe 1

seat [siːt] der (Sitz-)Platz 4: 1 (27) **take a seat** Platz nehmen 4: 1 (27)

second (2nd) [ˈsekənd] zweite(r, s) 1

second-hand [sekənd ˈhænd] secondhand *(gebraucht, aus zweiter Hand)* 3

second-hand shop [sekənd hænd ˈʃɒp] der Secondhandladen 3

secondary school [ˈsekəndri skuːl] die weiterführende Schule 3

secret [ˈsiːkrət]:
1. geheim 1
2. das Geheimnis 1

secure [sɪˈkjuə] sicher, gesichert 4: 1 (29)

security [sɪˈkjuərəti] die Sicherheit 4: 2 (48)

security guard [sɪˈkjuərəti ɡɑːd] der/die Sicherheitsbedienstete 4: 2 (48)

see [siː], **saw**, **seen** sehen 1 **See you soon.** Bis bald! 1 **See you.** Bis dann. / Tschüs. 1 **..., you see.** ..., weißt du. / ... nämlich ... 4: 1 (33)

seen [siːn] *siehe* **see**

segregation [seɡrɪˈɡeɪʃn] die Trennung *(nach Hautfarbe/Religion/Geschlecht)* 4: 2 (50)

sell [sel], **sold**, **sold** verkaufen 1

send [send], **sent**, **sent** senden, schicken 1

senior [ˈsiːniə] *(AE)* der/die Schüler/in im letzten Schuljahr der amerikanischen Highschool 4: 3 (82)

sent [sent] *siehe* **send**

°**sentence** [ˈsentəns] der Satz

separate [ˈsepəreɪt] trennen 4: 1 (20)

separate [ˈseprət] getrennt, separat 4: 1 (20)

September [sepˈtembə] der September 1

serious [ˈsɪəriəs] ernst(haft) 3 **Are you serious?** Meinst du das ernst? 3

service [ˈsɜːvɪs] der Service; der Dienst; die Bedienung 4: 4 (111) **bus/train service** die Bus-/Zug-Verbindung 4: 4 (111)

service station [ˈsɜːvɪs steɪʃn] die Tankstelle; die (Autobahn-)Raststätte 3

sesame [ˈsesəmi] der Sesam 3

set [set], **set**, **set** stellen, legen, setzen 2 **set the table** den Tisch decken 2

setting [ˈsetɪŋ] das Setting *(die Einstellung, z. B bei Geräten)* 3

seven [ˈsevn] sieben 1

seventeen [sevnˈtiːn] siebzehn 1

seventy [ˈsevnti] siebzig 1

several [ˈsevrəl] mehrere, einige 3

sew [səʊ], **sewed, sewn** nähen 3

sewing machine [ˈsəʊɪŋ məʃiːn] die Nähmaschine 3

sewn [səʊn] *siehe* **sew**

sexism [ˈseksɪzəm] der Sexismus 4: 1 (23)

sexist [ˈseksɪst]:
1. sexistisch *(diskriminierend aufgrund des Geschlechts)* 4: 1 (23)
2. der/die Sexist/in 4: 1 (23)

Shall I ...? [ʃæl], [ʃəl] Soll ich ...? 3

shame [ʃeɪm]: **a shame** schade; eine Schande 1 **That's / It's a shame!** Das/Es ist schade! 1 **What a shame!** Wie schade! 1

share [ʃeə] teilen 1

sharpener [ˈʃɑːpnə] der Anspitzer 1

she [ʃiː] sie *(weibliche Person)* 1 **she's (= she is)** sie ist 1

sheep [ʃiːp], *pl* **sheep** das Schaf 3

shelf [ʃelf], *pl* **shelves** das Regal(brett) 1

shelves [ʃelvz] *Plural von* **shelf**

shirt [ʃɜːt] das Shirt, das Hemd 2

shock [ʃɒk]:
1. der Schock 4: 2 (53)
2. **shock sb.** jn. schockieren 4: 2 (53)

shocked [ʃɒkt] schockiert 4: 2 (53)

shocking [ˈʃɒkɪŋ] schockierend 4: 2 (53)

shoe [ʃuː] der Schuh 1

shoot [ʃuːt], **shot, shot** (er)schießen 4: 3 (82)

shooting [ˈʃuːtɪŋ] die Schießerei 4: 3 (82)

shop [ʃɒp]:
1. das Geschäft, der Laden 1 **be at the shops** Einkäufe erledigen 1
2. (ein)kaufen, „shoppen" 2 **shop for sth.** etwas kaufen (gehen) 2

shop assistant [ˈʃɒp əsɪstənt] der/die Verkäufer/in 2

shopper [ˈʃɒpə] der Kunde, die Kundin; der/die Einkäufer/in 2

shopping [ˈʃɒpɪŋ] das Einkaufen; die Einkäufe 1 **do the shopping** die Einkäufe erledigen, einkaufen gehen 1 **go shopping** einkaufen gehen 1

shopping centre [ˈʃɒpɪŋ sentə] das Einkaufszentrum 4: 1 (28)

shopping list [ˈʃɒpɪŋ lɪst] die Einkaufsliste 1

shopping mall [ˈʃɒpɪŋ mɔːl] das Einkaufszentrum 4: 1 (28)

short [ʃɔːt]:
1. kurz 1
2. klein *(Person; Körpergröße)* 1

shorts *(pl)* [ʃɔːts] die kurze Hose, die Shorts 2

shot [ʃɒt] *siehe* **shoot**

should [ʃʊd]: **we should ...** wir sollten ... 3

shoulder [ˈʃəʊldə] die Schulter 4: 1 (29)

shout [ʃaʊt]:
1. der Ruf, der Schrei 3
2. rufen, schreien 3 **shout at sb.** jn. anschreien 3

show [ʃəʊ]:
1. die Show, die Aufführung; die Ausstellung 1 **prize show** die Preisverleihung *(Zeremonie)* 1
2. **show, showed, shown** zeigen 2

shower [ˈʃaʊə] die Dusche 1 **have a shower** (sich) duschen 1

shown [ʃəʊn] *siehe* **show**

shrug [ʃrʌg] mit den Achseln/Schultern zucken 4: 1 (28)

shut [ʃʌt], **shut, shut** schließen, zumachen 4: 3 (89) **Shut up!** *(infml)* Halt den Mund! 4: 3 (89)

shy [ʃaɪ] scheu, schüchtern 3

sick [sɪk] krank 2

sickness [ˈsɪknəs] die Krankheit 2

side [saɪd] die Seite *(z. B Straßenseite)* 3

sigh [saɪ]:
1. seufzen 4: 1 (28)
2. der Seufzer 4: 1 (28)

sight [saɪt]:
1. die Sehenswürdigkeit 2
2. der Anblick, das Bild 2

sightseeing [ˈsaɪtsiːɪŋ] das Sightseeing *(Besichtigung von Sehenswürdigkeiten)* 2

sign [saɪn]:
1. das Zeichen; das Schild 2
2. **sign sth.** etwas unterschreiben 4: 2 (53)

sign language [ˈsaɪn læŋgwɪdʒ] die Zeichensprache, die Gebärdensprache 4: 4 (123)

silent [ˈsaɪlənt] still, lautlos 4: 2 (60) **fall/go silent** still werden, verstummen 4: 2 (60)

°silicon [ˈsɪlɪkən] das Silizium

silver [ˈsɪlvə]:
1. Silber 2
2. silberfarben 2

°similar (to sb./sth.) [ˈsɪmələ] (jm./ einer Sache) ähnlich

simple [ˈsɪmpl] einfach 1

since [sɪns]: **since 2013** seit 2013 4: 2 (53)

sing [sɪŋ], **sang, sung** singen 1

singer [ˈsɪŋə] der/die Sänger/in 1

singing [ˈsɪŋɪŋ] das Singen 1

single [ˈsɪŋgl] Einzel-, einzelne(r, s) 2

single ticket [sɪŋgl ˈtɪkɪt] die einfache Fahrkarte (= ohne Rückfahrt) 2

sister [ˈsɪstə] die Schwester 1

sit [sɪt], **sat, sat** sitzen; sich setzen 1 **sit down** sich hinsetzen 1

situation [sɪtʃuˈeɪʃn] die Situation 4: 1 (27)

six [sɪks] sechs 1

sixteen [sɪksˈtiːn] sechzehn 1

sixty [ˈsɪksti] sechzig 1

size [saɪz] die Größe 2 **What size do you take?** Welche Größe hast du? 2

°skate [skeɪt] Schlittschuh laufen, eislaufen

skateboard [ˈskeɪtbɔːd]:
1. das Skateboard 1
2. Skateboard fahren 1

skateboarding [ˈskeɪtbɔːdɪŋ] das Skateboardfahren 1

skatepark [ˈskeɪt pɑːk] der Skatepark 1

ski [skiː]:
1. der Ski 1
2. Ski laufen, Ski fahren 1 **go skiing** (zum) Skilaufen gehen 1

skill [skɪl] die Fähigkeit, die Fertigkeit 2 **°life skills** die Alltagskompetenzen, die lebenswichtigen Fertigkeiten **°study skills** die Lerntechniken

skim a text [skɪm] einen Text überfliegen *(um den Inhalt grob zu erfassen)* 3

skin [skɪn] die Haut; die Schale *(z. B Banane)* 3

skip [skɪp] überspringen, auslassen 4: 1 (28)

skirt [skɜːt] der Rock 3

sky [skaɪ] der Himmel 4: 2 (58) **in the sky** am Himmel 4: 2 (58)

skyscraper [ˈskaɪskreɪpə] der Wolkenkratzer 3

slave [sleɪv] der Sklave, die Sklavin 4: 2 (50)

slavery [ˈsleɪvəri] die Sklaverei 4: 2 (46/47)

sleep [sliːp]:
1. der Schlaf 1
2. **sleep, slept, slept** schlafen 1

slept [slept] *siehe* **sleep**

slide [slaɪd] das Dia; die Folie *(Präsentationssoftware)* 1

slippers *(pl)* [slɪpə] die Hausschuhe 2

slow [sləʊ] langsam 1

small [smɔːl] klein 1

small-town life [smɔːl taʊn ˈlaɪf] das Leben in der Kleinstadt 4: 3 (78)

smart [smɑːt]:
1. schick 1
2. intelligent, clever 1

smartphone [ˈsmɑːtfəʊn] das Smartphone 4: 4 (124)

smartwatch [ˈsmɑːtwɒtʃ] die Smartwatch 3

smell [smel]:
1. der Geruch; der Gestank 3
2. riechen; schlecht riechen 3

smile [smaɪl]:
1. das Lächeln 2
2. lächeln 2 **smile at sb.** jn. anlächeln 2

smiley [ˈsmaɪli] das Smiley 2

smoke [sməʊk]:
1. der Rauch 4: 4 (120)
2. rauchen 4: 4 (120)

°s'more [smɔː] *der Doppelkeks mit Schokolade und Marshmallows, gegrillt*

snack [snæk] der Snack, die kleine Mahlzeit 4: 1 (25)

snake [sneɪk] die Schlange 1

sneaker [ˈsniːkə] *(AE)* der Sportschuh 4: 1 (22)

snow [snəʊ]:
1. der Schnee 1
2. schneien 1

snowboarding [ˈsnəʊbɔːdɪŋ] das Snowboarding 2

snowy [ˈsnəʊi] schneebedeckt; verschneit 1

so [səʊ]:
1. so 1
so weird so seltsam, so komisch 1
2. also, daher 1
3. **so (that)** sodass 2
4. **He said so.** Das hat er gesagt. 4:1 (28)
I don't think so. Das glaube/denke ich nicht. 4:1 (28) **I hope so.** Das hoffe ich. 4:1 (28) **I think so.** Ich glaube/denke ja. 4:1 (28) **If so, ...** Wenn ja, ... 4:1 (28)

so far [səʊ ˈfɑː] bis jetzt, bis hierher 3

soccer [ˈsɒkə] der Fußball 4:1 (24)

social [ˈsəʊʃl] sozial 3

social media [ˌsəʊʃl ˈmiːdiə] die sozialen Medien 3 **on social media** in den sozialen Medien 3

sock [sɒk] die Socke 3

sofa [ˈsəʊfə] das Sofa 1

°**soft** [sɒft] sanft, weich; *(Stimme)* leise

softball [ˈsɒftbɔːl] der Softball 4:3 (82)

software [ˈsɒftweə] die Software 3

sold [səʊld] *siehe* sell

soldier [ˈsəʊldʒə] der/die Soldat/in 3

solve [sɒlv] lösen *(Rätsel, Problem)*, lüften *(Geheimnis)* 2

some [sʌm], [səm] einige, ein paar; etwas, ein wenig 1 **some day** eines Tages 4:1 (24)

somebody [ˈsʌmbədi] jemand 1

someone [ˈsʌmwʌn] jemand 1

something [ˈsʌmθɪŋ] etwas 1

sometimes [ˈsʌmtaɪmz] manchmal 1

somewhere [ˈsʌmweə] irgendwo(hin) 4:3 (79)

son [sʌn] der Sohn 1

song [sɒŋ] das Lied 1

songwriter [ˈsɒŋraɪtə] der/die Songwriter/in *(Liedermacher/in)* 4:2 (53)

soon [suːn] bald 2 °**soon enough** schon bald

sophomore [ˈsɒfəmɔː] *(AE)* der/die Schüler/in im 2. Jahr der amerikanischen Highschool 4:3 (82)

sorry [ˈsɒri]: **Sorry. / I'm sorry.** Tut mir leid. / Entschuldigung. 1 **be/feel sorry for sb.** Mitleid haben mit jm. 1 **I'm / I feel sorry for him.** Ich habe Mitleid mit ihm. / Er tut mir leid. 1 **say sorry to sb.** sich bei jm. entschuldigen 3

sound [saʊnd]:
1. der Laut; das Geräusch; der Klang 2
2. klingen *(sich ... anhören)* 2

source [sɔːs] die Quelle *(z. B Website, Text)* 4:4 (124)

south [saʊθ] der Süden; südlich; Süd- 3

south-east [saʊθˈiːst] der Südosten, südöstlich; Südost- 3

south-west [saʊθˈwest] der Südwesten; südwestlich; Südwest- 3

southern [ˈsʌðən] südlich(r,s), Süd- 3

souvenir [suːvəˈnɪə] das Souvenir 3

space [speɪs] der Weltraum; der Raum, die Fläche; der Platz 2

spaghetti [spəˈɡeti] die Spaghetti 2

speak (to) [spiːk], **spoke, spoken** sprechen (mit) 1 **Speak later.** Tschüs. / Bis später. 1 **speak out** (deutlich) seine Meinung sagen, seine Stimme erheben 4:2 (52)

speaker [ˈspiːkə] der Sprecher, die Sprecherin 4:2 (50)

speaking [ˈspiːkɪŋ] das Sprechen 1

special [ˈspeʃl] besondere(r, s) 1 **... is special** ... ist etwas Besonderes 1 **What's special about this place?** Was ist das Besondere an diesem Ort? 1

special effects *(pl)* [speʃl ɪˈfekts] die Special Effects *(in Filmen)* 2

speech [spiːtʃ] die Rede, die Ansprache; die Sprache 4:2 (50) **give a speech** eine Rede halten 4:2 (50)

°**speech bubble** [ˈspiːtʃ bʌbl] die Sprechblase

spell [spel] buchstabieren 1

spelling [ˈspelɪŋ] die Schreibweise, die Rechtschreibung 1

spend [spend], **spent, spent: spend money (on ...)** Geld ausgeben (für ...) 2 **spend time** Zeit verbringen 2

spent [spent] *siehe* spend

spice [spaɪs] das Gewürz 1

spicy [ˈspaɪsi] würzig 1

°**spin (around)** [spɪn], **spun, spun** (sich) (herum)drehen

spoke [spəʊk] *siehe* speak

spoken [ˈspəʊkən] *siehe* speak

spoon [spuːn] der Löffel 4:2 (55)

sport [spɔːt] der Sport; die Sportart 1 **do/play sport(s)** Sport machen/ treiben 3

sports hall [ˈspɔːts hɔːl] die Sporthalle 1

spray [spreɪ]:
1. (be)sprühen 4:4 (119)
2. das Spray 4:4 (119)
pepper spray das Pfefferspray 4:4 (119)

°**spun** [spʌn] *siehe* spin

square [skweə]:
1. der Platz *(in der Stadt)* 3
2. rechteckig 3
3. das Quadrat 4:4 (124)
4. quadratisch, Quadrat- 4:4 (124)
square kilometre(s) (km²) Quadratkilometer 4:4 (124)

stable [ˈsteɪbl] der Stall 4:3 (87) **clean out the stables** ausmisten 4:3 (87)

stadium [ˈsteɪdiəm] das Stadion 1

stairs *(pl)* [steəz] die Treppe; die (Treppen-)Stufen 2

stall [stɔːl] der (Markt-)Stand, die Bude 3

stand [stænd], **stood, stood** stehen; sich (hin)stellen 2 **stand up** (auf-)stehen 1

star [stɑː]:
1. der Stern 2
2. der (Film-/Pop-)Star 2

star sign [ˈstɑː saɪn] das Sternzeichen 2

start [stɑːt]:
1. der Anfang, der Start 1
2. beginnen, anfangen (mit) 1
start a business ein Geschäft aufmachen, einen Betrieb gründen/ eröffnen 2

state [steɪt]:
1. der (Bundes-)Staat 4: (10/11)
2. der Zustand 4: (10/11)

°**statement** [ˈsteɪtmənt] die Aussage, der Aussagesatz

station [ˈsteɪʃn] der Bahnhof 1

statistic [stəˈtɪstɪk] die statistische Tatsache, die statistische Größe 3 **statistics** *(pl)* die Statistik(en) 3

statue [ˈstætʃuː] die Statue 3

stay [steɪ]:
1. der Aufenthalt 1
2. bleiben; übernachten 1
stay up aufbleiben *(nicht ins Bett gehen)* 2

steal [stiːl], **stole, stolen** stehlen, rauben 4:2 (49)

step [step] die Stufe; der Schritt 1

stepbrother [ˈstepbrʌðə] der Stiefbruder 2

stepdad [ˈstepdæd] der Stiefvater 2

stepdaughter [ˈstepdɔːtə] die Stieftochter 2

stepfather [ˈstepfɑːθə] der Stiefvater 2

stepmother [ˈstepmʌθə] die Stiefmutter 2

stepmum [ˈstepmʌm] die Stiefmutter 2

stepsister [ˈstepsɪstə] die Stiefschwester 2

stepson [ˈstepsʌn] der Stiefsohn 2

stereotype [ˈsteriətaɪp] der Stereotyp, das Klischee, die Klischeevorstellung 4:4 (117)

°**sticky note** [stɪki ˈnəʊt] die Haftnotiz, der Klebezettel

still [stɪl]:
1. (immer) noch 1
2. trotzdem 2

stole [stəʊl] *siehe* steal

stolen [ˈstəʊlən] *siehe* steal

stood [stʊd] *siehe* stand

stop [stɒp]:
1. der Halt, der Haltepunkt; die Unterbrechung 1
2. (an)halten; stoppen; aufhören (mit) 1
stop a fire ein Feuer löschen 2

store [stɔː] *(AE)* das Geschäft 4:1 (27)

storm [stɔːm] der Sturm; das Gewitter 4:2 (58)

storm chaser [ˈstɔːm tʃeɪsə] der/die Sturmjäger/in 4:2 (61)

stormy [ˈstɔːmi] stürmisch 4:2 (58)

story [ˈstɔːri] die Geschichte *(Erzählung)* 1

straight [streɪt]:
1. gerade; (Haare) glatt 2
2. straight on geradeaus (weiter) 2
strange [streɪndʒ] seltsam, sonderbar 4: 2 (58)
stranger [ˈstreɪndʒə] der/die Fremde 4: 2 (58)
strategy [ˈstrætədʒi] die Strategie 4: 3 (92)
strawberry [ˈstrɔːbəri] die Erdbeere 1
stream [striːm] streamen 3
streamer [ˈstriːmə] der/die Streamer/in (Person, die etwas streamt) 3
street [striːt] die Straße (in Ortschaften) 2
street musician [ˈstriːt mjuzɪʃn] der/die Straßenmusiker/in 2
strength [streŋθ] die Stärke, die Kraft 2
stress [stres]:
1. der Stress 4: 3 (88)
2. stress sb. jn. stressen, (über-) belasten 4: 3 (88)
stressful [ˈstresfl] stressig 4: 3 (88)
°**strict** [strɪkt] streng 2
strong [strɒŋ] stark 2
structure [ˈstrʌktʃə]:
1. die Struktur 1
2. strukturieren, aufbauen 1
student [ˈstjuːdnt] der/die Schüler/in; der/die Student/in 1
study [ˈstʌdi] studieren; lernen (z. B für Prüfungen) 2
°**study skills** (pl) [ˈstʌdi skɪlz] die Lerntechniken
stuff [stʌf] (infml) das Zeug, der Kram 2
stupid [ˈstjuːpɪd] dumm, blöd; albern 3
°**style** [staɪl] der Stil ...-**style** im Stil von ..., nach ...-Art, ...-mäßig
subject [ˈsʌbdʒɪkt] das (Schul-)Fach 1
subscribe to sth. [səbˈskraɪb] etwas abonnieren 3
subway [ˈsʌbweɪ] (AE) die U-Bahn 4: 1 (22)
success [səkˈses] der Erfolg 2
successful [səkˈsesfl] erfolgreich 2
sudden [ˈsʌdn] plötzliche(r, s) 3
suddenly [ˈsʌdənli] plötzlich, auf einmal 3
sugar [ˈʃʊgə] der Zucker 1
°**suggestion** [səˈdʒestʃən] der Vorschlag
suit [suːt] der (Herren-)Anzug; das (Damen-)Kostüm 2
sum sth. up [sʌm ˈʌp] etwas zusammenfassen 4: 3 (93) **To sum up, ...** Um (es) zusammenzufassen, ... / Zusammenfassend kann man sagen, ... 4: 3 (93)
°**summarize** [ˈsʌməraɪz] zusammenfassen
summary [ˈsʌməri] die Zusammenfassung 4: 2 (62)
summer [ˈsʌmə] der Sommer 1
summer camp [ˈsʌmə kæmp] das Ferienlager (im Sommer) 4: (14/15)
sun [sʌn] die Sonne 1

Sunday [ˈsʌndeɪ], [ˈsʌndi] der Sonntag 1
°**sung** [sʌŋ] siehe **sing**
sunglasses (pl) [ˈsʌnglɑːsɪz] die Sonnenbrille 1
sunny [ˈsʌni] sonnig 1 **It's sunny.** Die Sonne scheint. 1
super [ˈsuːpə] super 2
superhero [ˈsuːpəhɪərəʊ], pl **superheroes** der/die Superheld/in 2
supermarket [ˈsuːpəmɑːkɪt] der Supermarkt 1
superpower [ˈsuːpəpaʊə] die Superkraft 2
support [səˈpɔːt]:
1. unterstützen 3
2. die Unterstützung 3
supporter [səˈpɔːtə] der/die Anhänger/in, der Fan 3
sure [ʃʊə], [ʃɔː] sicher 1 **make sure (that)** ... sicherstellen, dass ...; dafür sorgen, dass ... 3
surf [sɜːf] surfen 2
surfing [ˈsɜːfɪŋ] das Surfing 1
surprise [səˈpraɪz]:
1. überraschen 2
2. die Überraschung 2
surprised [səˈpraɪzd] überrascht 1
°**survey** [ˈsɜːveɪ] die Umfrage **do a survey** eine Umfrage durchführen
survive [səˈvaɪv] überleben 4: 4 (114)
survivor [səˈvaɪvə] der/die Überlebende 4: 4 (114)
swam [swæm] siehe **swim**
swap [swɒp]:
1. tauschen 1
2. der Tausch 1
clothes swap der Kleidertausch, die Kleidertauschparty 1
sweater [ˈswetə] der Sweater 3
sweatpants [ˈswetpænts] (pl, AE) die Trainingshose, die Jogginghose 4: 3 (88)
sweatshirt [ˈswetʃɜːt] das Sweatshirt 1
sweet [swiːt]:
1. süß 1
2. das Bonbon 1
sweets (pl) die Süßigkeiten 1
swift [swɪft] schnell, rasch 4: 3 (83)
swim [swɪm], **swam, swum** s chwimmen 1
swimmer [ˈswɪmə] der/die Schwimmer/in 1
swimming [ˈswɪmɪŋ] das Schwimmen 1
swimming pool [ˈswɪmɪŋ puːl] das Schwimmbad 1
swimsuit [ˈswɪmsuːt] der Badeanzug 2
swipe [swaɪp] wischen (auf Touchscreen); (z. B Kreditkarte) durchziehen, einlesen 3
switch [swɪtʃ]:
1. der Schalter 3
2. switch sth. on/off etwas einschalten / ausschalten 3
swum [swʌm] siehe **swim**

symbol (of) [ˈsɪmbl] das Symbol (für) 4: (12/13)
°**synonym** [ˈsɪnənɪm] das Synonym (Wort mit gleicher Bedeutung)
system [ˈsɪstəm] das System 4: 3 (78)

T

T-shirt [ˈtiː ʃɜːt] das T-Shirt 1
table [ˈteɪbl]:
1. der Tisch 1
set the table den Tisch decken 2
°**2.** die Tabelle
table tennis [ˈteɪbl tenɪs] das Tischtennis 1
tablespoon [ˈteɪblspuːn] der Esslöffel 4: 2 (55)
take [teɪk], **took, taken:**
1. dauern, (Zeit) brauchen, in Anspruch nehmen 1
2. (mit)nehmen; bringen 1
take notes (sich) Notizen machen (beim Lesen oder Zuhören) 3 **take out the rubbish** den Müll rausbringen 2 **take photos** Fotos machen 1 **take place** stattfinden 2 **take sb.'s advice** auf js. Rat hören 3 **take sth. off** etwas ausziehen (Kleidung), ablegen (z. B Hut, Brille) 2 **taking photos** das Fotografieren (Hobby) 1 °**take part (in)** teilnehmen (an), mitmachen (bei) °**take sth. in** etwas (in sich) aufnehmen, etwas wahrnehmen
taken [ˈteɪkn] siehe **take**
talk [tɔːk]:
1. das Gespräch; die Rede, der Vortrag 1
give a talk einen Vortrag halten 1
2. talk (to) sprechen, reden (mit) 1
talk about sprechen, reden über 1
tall [tɔːl] groß (Person); hoch (Gebäude) 2
tap [tæp]:
1. das (leise) Klopfen 3
2. tap sth. tippen an/auf etwas; (leise) klopfen 3
tap your fingers mit den Fingern klopfen 3
tap [tæp] der Wasserhahn 4: 4 (123)
tap water [ˈtæp wɔːtə] das Leitungswasser 4: 4 (123)
task [tɑːsk] die Aufgabe 4: 4 (113)
taste [teɪst]:
1. der Geschmack 4: 4 (118)
2. schmecken; kosten, probieren 4: 4 (118)
tasty [ˈteɪsti] schmackhaft, lecker 4: 4 (118)
taught [tɔːt] siehe **teach**
taxi [ˈtæksi] das Taxi 3
tea [tiː] der Tee 1
teach [tiːtʃ], **taught, taught** lehren, unterrichten 2
teacher [ˈtiːtʃə] der/die Lehrer/in 1
team [tiːm] das Team, die Mannschaft 1
teamwork [ˈtiːmwɜːk] das Teamwork, die Zusammenarbeit 2

teaspoon [ˈtiːspuːn] der Teelöffel 4: 2 (55)

tech [tek] *(infml) siehe* **technology**

technology [tekˈnɒlədʒi], *infml auch* **tech** die Technik, der Technikunterricht; die Technologie 1

teen [tiːn] der Teenager 3

teenager [ˈtiːneɪdʒə] der Teenager 3

teeth [tiːθ] *Plural von* **tooth** **brush your teeth** (sich) die Zähne putzen 1

tell [tel], **told, told** erzählen, sagen 1 **tell sb. (not) to do sth.** jn. auffordern, etwas (nicht) zu tun; jm. sagen, dass er/sie etwas (nicht) tun soll 3 **I / I'll tell you what, ...** Weißt du was, ... / Ich mache dir einen Vorschlag: ... 4: 1 (21)

ten [ten] zehn 1 **tens of thousands of years** zehntausende Jahre 4: 4 (114)

ten thousand [ten ˈθaʊznd] zehntausend (10000) 2

tennis [ˈtenɪs] das Tennis 1

tent [tent] das Zelt 3

terrarium [teˈreəriəm] das Terrarium 1

terrible [ˈterəbl] schrecklich, fürchterlich 2

test [test]:
1. testen 1
2. der Test; die Klassenarbeit 1

text [tekst]:
1. der Text 1
2. die SMS 1
3. **text sb.** jm. eine SMS schicken 1

textbook [ˈtekstbʊk] das Schulbuch, das Lehrbuch 4: 3 (91)

than [ðən]: **louder than ...** lauter als ... 2

thank sb. [θæŋk] jm. danken, sich bei jm. bedanken 2

thank you [ˈθæŋk juː] danke (schön) 1 **Thank you very much.** Vielen Dank. / Danke vielmals. 1

°**thankful** [ˈθæŋkfl] dankbar

thanks [θæŋks] danke (schön) 1

°**Thanksgiving (Day)** [θæŋksˈɡɪvɪŋ] das Erntedankfest

that [ðæt]:
1. das (dort) 1 **that's (= that is)** das (da) ist 1
2. dass *(leitet einen Nebensatz ein)* 3 **it says that ...** es heißt (im Text), dass ... 3 **so that** sodass 2
3. der, die, das *(Relativpronomen)* 1 **things that people can use** Dinge, die Menschen gebrauchen/benutzen können 1

the [ðə] der, die, das 1

theatre [ˈθɪətə] das Theater 2

their [ðeə] ihr/e *(Plural)* 1

theirs [ðeəz] ihrer, ihre, ihrs *(zu „they")* 1

them [ðem], [ðəm] sie, ihnen 1

theme [θiːm] das Thema 4: 2 (46/47)

theme park [ˈθiːm pɑːk] der Themenpark *(Freizeitpark mit Attraktionen zu einem bestimmten Thema)* 4: 2 (46/47)

themselves [ðəmˈselvz] sich (selbst) *(zu „they")* 3

then [ðen]:
1. dann, danach 1
2. **(back) then** damals 4: 1 (21)

there [ðeə] da, dort; dahin, dorthin 1 **there are** es sind ... / es gibt ... 1 **there's (= there is)** es ist ... / es gibt ... 1

these [ðiːz] diese (hier) 1 **These are my friends.** Das hier sind meine Freunde/Freundinnen. 1

they [ðeɪ]:
1. sie *(Plural)* 1 **they're (= they are)** sie sind 1
2. er/sie *(geschlechtsneutral)* 3

thick [θɪk] dick; dicht 4: 4 (121)

thin [θɪn] dünn; schlank 4: 4 (121)

thing [θɪŋ] das Ding, die Sache 1 **How are things?** Wie geht's (so)? 3

think [θɪŋk], **thought, thought** denken, meinen, glauben 1 **think about** nachdenken über 2 **think of sb./sth.** an jn./etwas denken 2 **think of sth.** sich etwas überlegen, ausdenken 2 **I think ...** Ich denke/meine/glaube/finde, ... 1

third (3rd) [θɜːd] dritte(r, s) 1

thirteen [θɜːˈtiːn] dreizehn 1

thirty [ˈθɜːti] dreißig 1

this [ðɪs] dies; diese(r, s) 1

those [ðəʊz] die dort, jene (dort) 2

though [ðəʊ]:
1. obwohl 4: 3 (88)
2. ... **though.** ... allerdings ... 4: 3 (88)

thought [θɔːt]:
1. *siehe* **think**
2. der Gedanke 3

thousand [ˈθaʊznd] tausend 2 **tens of thousands of years** zehntausende Jahre 4: 4 (114)

three [θriː] drei 1

threw [θruː] *siehe* **throw**

through [θruː] durch 2

throw [θrəʊ], **threw, thrown** werfen 2 **throw away** wegwerfen 2

°**thrown** [θrəʊn] *siehe* **throw**

thunder [ˈθʌndə] der Donner 4: 2 (58)

thunderstorm [ˈθʌndəstɔːm] das Gewitter 2

Thursday [ˈθɜːzdeɪ], [ˈθɜːzdi] der Donnerstag 1

°**tick** [tɪk] ankreuzen, abhaken

ticket [ˈtɪkɪt] die Eintrittskarte, Fahrkarte, das Ticket 1 **one-way ticket** die einfache Fahrkarte *(= ohne Rückfahrt)* **return ticket** die (Hin- und) Rückfahrkarte 2 **single ticket** die einfache Fahrkarte *(= ohne Rückfahrt)* 2

ticket machine [ˈtɪkɪt məʃiːn] der Fahrkartenautomat 2

tidy [ˈtaɪdi]:
1. ordentlich 1
2. aufräumen 1

tie [taɪ]:
1. die Krawatte 1
2. binden, schnüren 4: 4 (121) **tie sb./sth. (to sth.)** jn./etwas (an etwas) festbinden 4: 4 (121)

till [tɪl] bis 2 **not ... till** erst, wenn ... 2

time [taɪm]:
1. die Zeit; die Uhrzeit 1 **have a great/good time** (viel) Spaß haben, sich vergnügen 2 **on time** pünktlich 2 **opening times** *(pl)* die Öffnungszeiten 4: 3 (87) **What's the time?** Wie spät ist es? 1
2. das Mal 2 **for the first time** zum ersten Mal 2 **this time** dieses Mal 2

times [taɪmz] mal 4: (12/13)

timetable [ˈtaɪmteɪbl] der Stundenplan 1

tip [tɪp] der Tipp 2

tired [ˈtaɪəd] müde 1

title [ˈtaɪtl] der Titel, die Überschrift 1

to [tu], [tə]:
1. zu, nach 1 **to sb.** an jn. *(z. B schreiben an jn., eine E-Mail an jn.)* **Have you ever been to London?** Bist du schon mal in London gewesen? 2 **the answer to the question** die Antwort auf die Frage 1
2. bis 2 **(from) 2 o'clock to 5 o'clock** (von) 2 Uhr / 14 Uhr bis 5 Uhr / 17 Uhr 1
3. (um) zu 1 **how to do sth.** wie man etwas tut / tun kann / tun soll 1 **things to eat** Dinge zum Essen 1
4. vor *(bei Uhrzeitangaben)* 2 **quarter to 7** viertel vor 7 2

today [təˈdeɪ] heute 1

together [təˈɡeðə] zusammen 1

toilet [ˈtɔɪlət] die Toilette 1

told [təʊld] *siehe* **tell**

tomato [təˈmɑːtəʊ], *pl* **tomatoes** die Tomate 1

tomato sauce [təˈmɑːtəʊ sɔːs] die Tomatensoße 1

tomorrow [təˈmɒrəʊ] morgen 3

tonight [təˈnaɪt] heute Nacht, heute Abend 3

too [tuː]:
1. auch 1 **from York too** auch aus York 1
2. **too slow** zu langsam 1

took [tʊk] *siehe* **take**

°**toonie** [ˈluːni] *(AE, infml)* die kanadische Zwei-Dollar-Münze

tooth [tuːθ], *pl* **teeth** der Zahn 1

top [tɒp] die Spitze, das obere Ende 1 **top floor** die oberste Etage, der oberste Stock, das oberste Stockwerk 1 **at the top (of)** oben, am oberen Ende (von); an der Spitze (von) 1 **the top five hobbies** die fünf besten/beliebtesten Hobbys 1

topic [ˈtɒpɪk] das Thema 3

tornado [tɔːˈneɪdəʊ] der Tornado *(Wirbelsturm)* 4: 2 (58)

touch [tʌtʃ]:
1. anfassen, berühren 4: 4 (125)
2. die Berührung 4: 4 (125)

tour (of) [tʊə] Tour, Reise, Rundgang/ Rundfahrt 1

tour guide [ˈtʊə gaɪd] der/die Reiseleiter/in; der/die Fremdenführer/in 1
tourist [ˈtʊərɪst] der/die Tourist/in 1
tower [ˈtaʊə] der Turm 3
town [taʊn] die Stadt 1
town centre [taʊn ˈsentə] das Stadtzentrum 1
toy [tɔɪ] das Spielzeug 1
°**track** [træk] das (Bahn-)Gleis
trade [treɪd]:
  1. der Handel 4: 1 (18)
  2. handeln, Handel (be)treiben 4: 1 (18)
trader [ˈtreɪdə] der Händler, die Händlerin 4: 1 (18)
tradition [trəˈdɪʃn] die Tradition 2
traditional [trəˈdɪʃənl] traditionell 2
traffic [ˈtræfɪk] der (Straßen-)Verkehr 3
trailer [ˈtreɪlə] der Trailer (Filmvorschau) 2
train [treɪn] der Zug, die Eisenbahn 1
train sb. [treɪn] jn. trainieren; ausbilden 4: 4 (112)
train station [ˈtreɪn steɪʃn] der Bahnhof 1
trainer [ˈtreɪnə]:
  1. der/die Trainer/in 1
  2. der Sportschuh 3
training [ˈtreɪnɪŋ] das Training, die Ausbildung 4: 4 (112)
tram [træm] die Straßenbahn 4: 2 (46/47)
trampoline [ˈtræmpəliːn] das Trampolin 1
trampolining [ˈtræmpəliːnɪŋ] das Trampolinspringen/-turnen 1
transport (no pl) [ˈtrænspɔːt] das Fortbewegungsmittel; die Beförderung 2
  public transport die öffentlichen Verkehrsmittel 3
transportation [trænspɔːˈteɪʃn] (AE, no pl) das Fortbewegungsmittel; die Beförderung 4: 3 (78)
trash [træʃ] (AE) der Abfall, der Müll 4: 1 (22)
travel [ˈtrævl]:
  1. das Reisen 1
  2. reisen, fahren 1
treat [triːt] der Hochgenuss, das besondere Vergnügen; die (besondere) Leckerei 2
treat sb. [triːt] jn. behandeln 4: 2 (49)
tree [triː] der Baum 1
trend [trend] der Trend 4: 4 (124)
trendy [ˈtrendi] modisch, trendy, „angesagt" 4: 3 (88)
tribe [traɪb] die Volksgruppe 4: 4 (114)
trick [trɪk] der Trick, das Kunststück 1
trip [trɪp] der Ausflug; die Reise 2
  boat trip der Bootsausflug, die Bootsfahrt 2 **go on a trip** eine Reise machen 2 **take a trip** eine Reise machen 2
troll [trəʊl] der Troll (Provokateur/in in Online-Medien) 3
trophy [ˈtrəʊfɪ] die Trophäe; der Pokal 2

trouble [ˈtrʌbl] der Ärger, Schwierigkeiten 1 **be in trouble** Ärger haben, in Schwierigkeiten sein 1
trousers (pl) [ˈtraʊzəz] die Hose 2
true [truː] wahr, richtig 2
trumpet [ˈtrʌmpɪt] die Trompete 4: 2 (56)
truth [truːθ] die Wahrheit 3 **tell the truth** die Wahrheit sagen 3 **To tell the truth, ...** Ehrlich gesagt, ... 3
try [traɪ]:
  1. versuchen, (aus)probieren 2
  try sth. on anprobieren (Kleidung) 2 **try to do sth.** versuchen, etwas zu tun 2
  2. der Versuch 2
  Have a try! / Give it a try! Versuch's/Probier's doch mal! 2
TTYL (talk to you later) [ti: ti: waɪ 'el] Wir sprechen uns später. 4: 4 (122)
Tuesday [ˈtjuːzdeɪ], [ˈtjuːzdi] der Dienstag 1
tunnel [ˈtʌnl] der Tunnel 3
°**turkey** [ˈtɜːki] der Truthahn, die Pute; das Putenfleisch 3
turn [tɜːn]:
  1. (sich) (um)drehen 1
  Turn it upside down. Dreh/Stell es auf den Kopf. 1 **turn right/left** (nach) rechts/links abbiegen 2 **turn sth. (over)** etwas umdrehen 1 **turn sth. off** etwas ausschalten 4: 4 (123) **turn sth. on** etwas einschalten 4: 4 (123) **turn sth. on/off** etwas ein-/ausschalten (123)
  2. it is sb.'s turn (to do sth.) jd. ist dran / an der Reihe (etwas zu tun) 1 **take turns (to do sth.)** sich abwechseln; sich dabei abwechseln, etwas zu tun 1
TV [ti:ˈvi:] der Fernseher; das Fernsehen 1
twelfth (12th) [twelfθ] zwölfte(r, s) 1
twelve [twelv] zwölf 1
twenty [ˈtwenti] zwanzig 1
twice [twaɪs] zweimal 4: 3 (87)
two [tuː] zwei 1
type (of) [taɪp] die Art (von), die Sorte (von) 3

UK [juː ˈkeɪ] das Vereinigte Königreich 2
umbrella [ʌmˈbrelə] der (Regen-)Schirm 3
uncertain [ʌnˈsɜːtn] unsicher 4: 1 (21)
uncle [ˈʌŋkl] der Onkel 1
uncomfortable [ʌnˈkʌmftəbl] unbequem, ungemütlich 3
uncool [ʌnˈkuːl] uncool 2
under [ˈʌndə] unter 1
underground [ˈʌndəɡraʊnd] die U-Bahn 3
understand [ʌndəˈstænd], understood, understood verstehen 2
understood [ʌndəˈstʊd] siehe understand

°**underwear** [ˈʌndəweə] die Unterwäsche
unequal [ʌnˈiːkwəl] ungleich 4: 1 (21)
unfair [ʌnˈfeə] unfair 2
unfriendly [ʌnˈfrendli] unfreundlich 1
unhappy [ʌnˈhæpi] unglücklich, unzufrieden 2
unhelpful [ʌnˈhelpfl] nicht hilfreich; nicht hilfsbereit 2
unhurt [ʌnˈhɜːt] unverletzt 4: 2 (59)
uniform [ˈjuːnɪfɔːm] die Uniform 1
union [ˈjuːnɪən] die Union; die Vereinigung, der Verband; die Gewerkschaft 4: 1 (16/17)
°**unique** [juˈniːk] einzigartig, einmalig
unit [ˈjuːnɪt] die Unit (Lerneinheit) 1
United Kingdom (= the UK) [juːnaɪtɪd ˈkɪŋdəm] das Vereinigte Königreich 2
university [juːnɪˈvɜːsəti] die Universität 4: 1 (21)
unkind [ʌnˈkaɪnd] unfreundlich, herzlos 2
unless [ənˈles] es sei denn; außer (wenn) 4: 4 (119)
unlucky [ʌnˈlʌki] unglücklich 2 **be unlucky** Pech haben 3
unpack [ʌnˈpæk] auspacken 3
untidy [ʌnˈtaɪdi] unordentlich, unaufgeräumt 2
until [ənˈtɪl] bis (zeitlich) 2 **not ... until** erst, wenn ... 2
up [ʌp] hinauf, hoch 2
upload [ʌpˈləʊd]:
  1. der/das Upload 3
  2. uploaden, hochladen 3
upset [ʌpˈset]:
  1. bestürzt; aufgebracht, verärgert 4: 3 (90)
  2. upset sb., upset, upset jn. erschüttern; jn. aufregen, ärgern, 4: 3 (90)
upside down [ʌpsaɪd ˈdaʊn] verkehrt herum, auf dem Kopf 1
us [ʌs], [əs] uns 1 **It's just us.** Es sind nur wir. 1
use [juːz] benutzen, verwenden 1
use [juːs] der Gebrauch, die Verwendung 4: 4 (125)
used to [ˈjuːst tə]: **I used to come here ...** Ich kam (früher) immer ... hierher. 4: 1 (29)
useful [ˈjuːsfl] nützlich, hilfreich 2
useless [ˈjuːsləs] nutzlos, unnütz 3
user [ˈjuːzə] der/die (Be-)Nutzer/in 1
usually [ˈjuːʒuəli] normalerweise, meistens 2

vacation [vəˈkeɪʃn] (AE) der Urlaub 4: 1 (22)
vacuum [ˈvækjuəm] Staub saugen 2
vacuum cleaner [ˈvækjuəm kliːnə] der Staubsauger 2
valley [ˈvæli] das Tal 3
vampire [ˈvæmpaɪə] der Vampir 2
vanilla [vəˈnɪlə] die Vanille 1
veg [vedʒ], pl veg (kurz für vegetables) das Gemüse 4: 3 (91)

vegetables (pl) ['vedʒtəblz] das/die Gemüse 1

vegetarian [vedʒə'teəriən], infml auch veggie:
1. der/die Vegetarier/in 1
2. vegetarisch 1

veggie ['vedʒi] siehe **vegetarian**

°vehicle ['viːəkl] das Fahrzeug

versus (v; vs) ['vɜːsəs] gegen (bei Wettkämpfen); gegenüber 3

very ['veri] sehr 1

vet [vet] der Tierarzt, die Tierärztin 1

victim ['vɪktɪm] das Opfer 3

video ['vɪdiəʊ] das Video; Video- 1

video clip ['vɪdiəʊ klɪp] der Videoclip 4: 2 (56)

video game ['vɪdiəʊ geɪm] das Videospiel 1

view [vjuː]:
1. **view (of)** der (An-)Blick; die (Aus-)Sicht (auf) 1
2. **view sth.** sich etwas anschauen 3

village ['vɪlɪdʒ] das Dorf 1

violence ['vaɪələns] die Gewalt; die Gewalttätigkeit 4: 2 (50)

violent ['vaɪələnt] gewalttätig; gewaltsam 4: 2 (50)

violin [vaɪə'lɪn] die Geige, die Violine 4: 2 (57)

virtual ['vɜːtʃʊəl] virtuell 3

°visible ['vɪzəbl] sichtbar

visit ['vɪzɪt]:
1. der Besuch 1
2. besuchen 1

visitor ['vɪzɪtə] der/die Besucher/in; der Gast 1

visitor information centre [vɪzɪtə ɪnfə'meɪʃn sentə] die Touristeninformation, das Fremdenverkehrsbüro 1

vlog ['vlɒg] der/das Vlog (Video-Blog) 3

vlogger ['vlɒgə] der/die Vlogger/in (Video-Blogger/in) 3

vocab ['vəʊkæb] siehe **vocabulary**

vocabulary [və'kæbjələri], infml auch vocab der Wortschatz, das Vokabular; das Vokabelverzeichnis 1

vocational [vəʊ'keɪʃənl] beruflich, Berufs- 4: 3 (86)

vocational school [vəʊkeɪʃənl 'skuːl] die berufsbildende Schule 4: 3 (86)

voice [vɔɪs] die Stimme 3

voice message ['vɔɪs mesɪdʒ] die Sprachnachricht 3

volunteer [vɒlən'tɪə]:
1. der/die Freiwillige; der/die ehrenamtliche Mitarbeiter/in 3
2. freiwillig/ehrenamtlich arbeiten (unbezahlt) 3

vote [vəʊt]:
1. die Abstimmung, das Votum 4: 2 (50) **have a vote (on)** abstimmen (über) 4: 2 (50)
2. **vote (on)** wählen; abstimmen (über) 4: 2 (50) **vote for sb./sth.** für jn./etwas stimmen 4: 2 (50)

W

wait (for) [weɪt] warten (auf) 2 **Wait a minute.** Warte mal. / Einen Moment. 2 **I can't wait!** Ich kann es kaum erwarten! 2 **°wait up (for)** aufbleiben, wachbleiben (wegen)

waiter ['weɪtə] der Kellner 3

waitress ['weɪtrəs] die Kellnerin 3

wake [weɪk], **woke, woken: wake sb. (up)** jn. (auf)wecken 4: 4 (120) **wake up** aufwachen 4: 4 (120)

Wales [weɪlz] Wales 3

walk [wɔːk]:
1. der Spaziergang 1 **go for a walk** spazieren gehen, einen Spaziergang machen 3
2. (zu Fuß) gehen, wandern 1 **walk over** hinübergehen, rübergehen 2

walking ['wɔːkɪŋ] das Wandern 1

walking boot ['wɔːkɪŋ buːt] der Wanderstiefel 2

wall [wɔːl] die Wand, die Mauer 2 **on the wall** an die Wand; an der Wand 2

want [wɒnt] wollen 1 **want sb. to do sth.** wollen, dass jd. etwas tut 3 **want to do sth.** etwas tun wollen 1

war [wɔː] der Krieg 4: 1 (23)

wardrobe ['wɔːdrəʊb] der Kleiderschrank 1

warm [wɔːm] warm 1

warn sb. (about/against/of) [wɔːn] jn. warnen (vor) 4: 2 (58)

warning (about/against/of) ['wɔːnɪŋ] die Warnung (vor) 4: 2 (58)

was [wɒz], [wəz] siehe **be**

wash [wɒʃ] (sich) waschen 2

washing ['wɒʃɪŋ] die Wäsche 2 **do the washing** die Wäsche erledigen, Wäsche waschen 2

washing machine ['wɒʃɪŋ məʃiːn] die Waschmaschine 4: 4 (123)

watch [wɒtʃ] die Armbanduhr 3

watch (sth.) [wɒtʃ] (sich etwas) anschauen; (etwas) beobachten 1

water ['wɔːtə] das Wasser 1

°waterfall ['wɔːtəfɔːl] der Wasserfall

wave (to sb.) [weɪv] (jm. zu)winken 1

way [weɪ]:
1. die Strecke, der Weg 2 **one way** eine Strecke (= ohne Rückfahrt) 2 **one-way ticket** die einfache Fahrkarte (= ohne Rückfahrt) 2
2. die Art und Weise 3 **(in) this way** auf diese Art/Weise 3 **BTW (by the way)** übrigens 4: 4 (122) **in different ways** unterschiedlich (Adv.), auf unterschiedliche Art/Weise 3
3. die Richtung 3 **both ways** in beide(n) Richtungen 3 **that way** da entlang, in jene(r) Richtung 3 **the wrong way** (in) die falsche Richtung 3 **this way** hier entlang, in diese(r) Richtung 3

we [wiː] wir 1 **we're (= we are)** wir sind 1

wear [weə], **wore, worn** tragen, anhaben (Kleidung) 1

weather ['weðə] das Wetter, die Witterung 1

website ['websaɪt] die Website 2

wedding ['wedɪŋ] die Hochzeit 2

wedding ring ['wedɪŋ rɪŋ] der Ehering 2

Wednesday ['wenzdeɪ], ['wenzdi] der Mittwoch 1

week [wiːk] die Woche 1 **the days of the week** (pl) die Wochentage 1

weekday ['wiːkdeɪ] der Werktag, der Wochentag 1

weekend [wiːk'end] das Wochenende 1 **at the weekend** am Wochenende 1

weird [wɪəd] seltsam, komisch 1

welcome ['welkəm]:
1. **Welcome (to ...)!** Willkommen (in/an ...)! 1
2. **You're welcome.** Bitte, gern geschehen. / Nichts zu danken. 1
°3. welcome sb. (to) jn. begrüßen (in), jn. willkommen heißen (in)

°welcoming ['welkəmɪŋ] (gast)freundlich, einladend

well [wel] gut (Adv.) 1 **Well done.** Gut gemacht! 1 **... as well as ...** sowohl ... als auch ... 4: 1 (23) **as well** auch 4: 1 (23) **do well** gut abschneiden, erfolgreich sein 3

went [went] siehe **go**

were [wɜː], [wə] siehe **be**

west [west] der Westen; westlich; West- 3

western ['westən] westlich(r,s), West- 3

°whale [weɪl] der Wal

what [wɒt]:
1. was 1
2. welche(r, s) 1 **I / I'll tell you what, ...** Weißt du was, ... / Ich mache dir einen Vorschlag: ... 4: 1 (21) **You know what, ...** Weißt du was, ... 4: 1 (21) **What about a ... ?** Wie wäre es mit einer/einem ... ? 1 **What about you?** Und du? / Was ist mit dir? 1 **What's your name?** Wie heißt du? 1

wheel [wiːl] das Rad 3 **big wheel** das Riesenrad 3

wheelchair ['wiːltʃeə] der Rollstuhl 1

when [wen]:
1. wann 1
2. wenn (zeitlich) 1
3. als (zeitlich) 2

whenever [wen'evə] wann (auch) immer 3

where [weə] wo; wohin 1

which [wɪtʃ]:
1. welche(r, s) 1 **Which part ...?** Welcher Teil ...? 1
2. der, die, das; die (Relativpronomen) 4: 2 (54) **... which is what we call ...** ..., was unser Wort ist für ... 4: 2 (54)

while [waɪl] während 3

white [waɪt] weiß 1

who [huː]:
1. wer 1
2. der, die *(Relativpronomen)* 3
somebody who ... jemand, der/die ... 3
whole [həʊl] ganze(r, s) 3
whose [huːz]:
1. wessen 4: 3 (85)
2. dessen, deren *(Relativpronomen)* 4: 3 (85)
why [waɪ] warum 1 **that's why** deshalb, darum 3 **the reason why ...** der Grund dafür, dass ... 3
wife [waɪf], *pl* **wives** die (Ehe-)Frau 3
wild [waɪld] wild 3
wildfire [ˈwaɪldfaɪə] der Waldbrand; der Großbrand, der Flächenbrand 4: 4 (120)
wildlife *(no pl)* [ˈwaɪldlaɪf] die Tiere *(in freier Wildbahn)*, die Tierwelt 4: 4 (124)
will [wɪl]: **I'll (= I will) be ...** Ich werde ... sein. 2
win [wɪn], **won, won** gewinnen 1 **win the lottery** im Lotto / in der Lotterie gewinnen 4: 3 (79)
wind [wɪnd] der Wind 1
window [ˈwɪndəʊ] das Fenster 1
windsurfing [ˈwɪndsɜːfɪŋ] das Windsurfing 1
windy [ˈwɪndi] windig 1
wing [wɪŋ] der Flügel 4: 1 (25) **chicken wing** der Hähnchenflügel 4: 1 (25)
°**wink (at sb.)** [wɪŋk] (jm. zu-)zwinkern
winner [ˈwɪnə] der/die Gewinner/in; der/die Sieger/in 1
winter [ˈwɪntə] der Winter 1
wish [wɪʃ]:
1. der Wunsch 4: 3 (89) **Best wishes** Viele Grüße *(Briefschluss)* 4: 3 (89) **make a wish** sich etwas wünschen 4: 3 (89)
2. **wish (for sth.)** (sich etwas) wünschen 4: 3 (89)
with [wɪð] mit; bei 1 **popular with** beliebt bei 2
without [wɪˈðaʊt] ohne 3
wives [waɪvz] *Plural von* **wife**
woke [wəʊk] *siehe* **wake up**
woken [ˈwəʊkən] *siehe* **wake up**
wolf [wʊlf], *pl* **wolves** Wolf 4: 4 (116)
wolves [wʊlvz] *Plural von* **wolf**

woman [ˈwʊmən], *pl* **women** die Frau 2
women [ˈwɪmɪn] *Plural von* **woman**
won [wʌn] *siehe* **win**
wonderful [ˈwʌndəfl] wunderbar 2
won't [wəʊnt]: **I won't (= I will not) be ...** Ich werde nicht ... sein. 2
wood [wʊd] das Holz; der Wald 4: 4 (120)
wooden [ˈwʊdn] Holz-, hölzern 4: 4 (120)
word [wɜːd] das Wort 1 **words (of a song)** *(pl)* der (Song-)Text 2
°**wordbank** [ˈwɜːdbæŋk] die Wortbank *(Sammlung von Wörtern zu einem Thema)*
wore [wɔː] *siehe* **wear**
work [wɜːk]:
1. die Arbeit 1 **at work** bei der Arbeit, am Arbeitsplatz 1
2. arbeiten; funktionieren 1 **work on sth.** an etwas arbeiten 4: 3 (91) **work sth. out** etwas herausfinden, etwas erarbeiten, etwas verstehen 2
work experience [ˈwɜːk ɪkspɪəriəns] die Arbeitserfahrung(en), die Praxiserfahrung(en); das Praktikum 2
world [wɜːld] die Welt 2 **the best place in the world** der beste Ort der Welt / auf der Welt 2
worn [wɔːn] *siehe* **wear**
worried (about) [ˈwʌrid] beunruhigt, besorgt (wegen) 2
worry [ˈwʌri]:
1. die Sorge 2
2. **worry (about)** sich Sorgen machen (wegen, um) 2
Don't worry. Mach dir keine Sorgen. 2
worse [wɜːs] schlechter, schlimmer 2
worst [wɜːst] der/die/das schlechteste, schlimmste; am schlechtesten, am schlimmsten 2
would [wʊd]: **I'd (= I would) like/love ...** Ich hätte (liebend) gern ... / Ich möchte (liebend gern) ... 1 **I'd love/like to meet ....** Ich würde mich (liebend) gerne mit ... treffen. 1
write [raɪt], **wrote, written** schreiben 1 **write sth. down** etwas aufschreiben 3
writer [ˈraɪtə] der/die Autor/in 2

written [ˈrɪtn] *siehe* **write**
wrong [rɒŋ] falsch 1 **be wrong** Unrecht haben 1 **Something is wrong.** Irgendetwas ist nicht in Ordnung. / Irgendetwas stimmt nicht. 2 **What's wrong?** Was ist los? / Was/Wo ist das Problem? 2
wrote [rəʊt] *siehe* **write**

Y

year [jɪə] das Jahr; der Jahrgang 1 **a five-year-old** ein/e Fünfjährige/r 4: 3 (87) **five-year-old son** der fünf Jahre alte Sohn 4: 3 (87)
yearbook [ˈjɪəbʊk] das Jahrbuch 4: 3 (85)
yellow [ˈjeləʊ] gelb 1
yes [jes] ja 1
yesterday [ˈjestədeɪ] gestern 2
yet [jet]: **... yet?** ... schon ...? 2 **not ... yet** noch nicht ... 2
°**Yiddish** [ˈjɪdɪʃ] jiddisch; Jiddisch
yoga [ˈjəʊgə] das Yoga 1
yoghurt [ˈjɒgət] der/die/das Joghurt 2
you [juː] du; dich; dir; ihr; euch; Sie; Ihnen 1
young [jʌŋ] jung 3
your [jɔː], [jə] dein/e; euer/eure; Ihr/e 1
yours [jɔːz] deine, deiner, deins; eurer, eure, eures; Ihrer, Ihre, Ihres *(zu „you")* 3 **Yours, Jill** Deine/Ihre/Eure Jill *(am Briefschluss)* 3
yourself [jəˈself] dir/dich (selbst) 3
yourselves [jɔːˈselvz] ihr/euch (selbst) 3 **Enjoy yourselves.** Viel Spaß! Amüsiert euch gut! 3
youth [juːθ] die Jugend; der Jugendliche 1
youth centre [ˈjuːθ sentə] das Jugendzentrum 1

Z

zoo [zuː] der Zoo 4: 4 (115)

Cardinal numbers

0 **oh, zero, nil** [əʊ, ˈzɪərəʊ, nɪl]
1 **one** [wʌn]
2 **two** [tuː]
3 **three** [θriː]
4 **four** [fɔː]
5 **five** [faɪv]
6 **six** [sɪks]
7 **seven** [ˈsevn]
8 **eight** [eɪt]
9 **nine** [naɪn]
10 **ten** [ten]

11 **eleven** [ɪˈlevn]
12 **twelve** [twelv]
13 **thirteen** [θɜːˈtiːn]
14 **fourteen** [fɔːˈtiːn]
15 **fifteen** [fɪfˈtiːn]
16 **sixteen** [sɪksˈtiːn]
17 **seventeen** [sevnˈtiːn]
18 **eighteen** [eɪˈtiːn]
19 **nineteen** [naɪnˈtiːn]
20 **twenty** [ˈtwenti]

21 **twenty-one** [twentiˈwʌn]
22 **twenty-two** [twentiˈtuː]
23 **twenty-three** [twentiˈθriː]
…

30 **thirty** [ˈθɜːti]
40 **forty** [ˈfɔːti]
50 **fifty** [ˈfɪfti]
60 **sixty** [ˈsɪksti]
70 **seventy** [ˈsevnti]
80 **eighty** [ˈeɪti]
90 **ninety** [ˈnaɪnti]
100 **a / one hundred** [ə / wʌn ˈhʌndrəd]

101 **one hundred and one**
102 **one hundred and two**
…

Ordinal numbers

1st **first** [fɜːst]
2nd **second** [ˈsekənd]
3rd **third** [θɜːd]
4th **fourth** [fɔːθ]
5th **fifth** [fɪfθ]
6th **sixth** [sɪksθ]
7th **seventh** [ˈsevnθ]
8th **eighth** [eɪtθ]
9th **ninth** [naɪnθ]
10th **tenth** [tenθ]

11th **eleventh** [ɪˈlevnθ]
12th **twelfth** [twelfθ]
13th **thirteenth** [θɜːˈtiːnθ]
14th **fourteenth** [fɔːˈtiːnθ]
15th **fifteenth** [fɪfˈtiːnθ]
16th **sixteenth** [sɪksˈtiːnθ]
17th **seventeenth** [sevnˈtiːnθ]
18th **eighteenth** [eɪˈtiːnθ]
19th **nineteenth** [naɪnˈtiːnθ]
20th **twentieth** [ˈtwentiəθ]

21st **twenty-first** [twentiˈfɜːst]
22nd **twenty-second** [twentiˈsekənd]
23rd **twenty-third** [twentiˈθɜːd]
…

30th **thirtieth** [ˈθɜːtiəθ]
40th **fortieth** [ˈfɔːtiəθ]
50th **fiftieth** [ˈfɪftiəθ]
60th **sixtieth** [ˈsɪkstiəθ]
70th **seventieth** [ˈsevntiəθ]
80th **eightieth** [ˈeɪtiəθ]
90th **ninetieth** [ˈnaɪntiəθ]
100th **hundredth** [ˈhʌndrədθ]

101st **one hundred and first**
102nd **one hundred and second**
…

Large numbers

6,513 six thousand five hundred thirteen
7,500,000 seven million five hundred thousand

In English, you use a comma (not a point) to divide large numbers into groups of three. You don't say the comma.

Percentages (Prozentsätze)

42% forty-two per cent (of New Yorkers)
90% ninety per cent (of the population)

Decimals (Dezimalzahlen)

0.48 zero **point** four eight
null Komma vier acht

9.7 million
nine **point** seven million
neun Komma sieben Millionen

In English, you write and say decimals with a point (not a comma). Say the point and each number after the point separately.

Fractions (Brüche)

½ a/one half   ⅕ a/one fifth   1½ one and a half

⅓ a/one third   ⅔ two thirds   2½ two and a half

¼ a/one quarter   ¾ three quarters   3⅔ three and two thirds

Dates

In most of the world, you write the day first, then the month, then the year (**day/month/year**), e.g.:
You write: 3 April 2025 or **3/4/2025** – **You say:** the third of April, 2025

In the USA, you write the month first, then the day, then the year (**month/day/year**), e.g.:
You write: April 3, 2025 or **4/3/2025** – **You say:** April third, 2025

infinitive	simple past	past participle	
(to) babysit	babysat	babysat	babysitten
(to) be	was / were	been	sein
(to) beat	beat	beaten	schlagen, besiegen
(to) become	became	become	werden
(to) begin	began	begun	anfangen, beginnen
(to) blow	blew [uː]	blown	pusten, blasen; wehen
(to) break	broke	broken	zerbrechen
(to) breed	bred	bred	züchten; brüten, Junge bekommen, sich vermehren
(to) bring	brought	brought	(mit)bringen
(to) build [ɪ]	built [ɪ]	built [ɪ]	bauen
(to) buy	bought	bought	kaufen
(to) catch	caught [ɔː]	caught [ɔː]	(ein)fangen; erwischen
(to) choose	chose	chosen	(aus)wählen
(to) come	came	come	(mit)kommen
(to) cost	cost	cost	kosten
(to) cut	cut	cut	(aus)schneiden
(to) deal with [iː]	dealt [e]	dealt [e]	klarkommen (mit), fertigwerden (mit)
(to) do	did	done [ʌ]	tun, machen
(to) draw	drew	drawn	zeichnen
(to) drink	drank	drunk	trinken
(to) drive [aɪ]	drove [əʊ]	driven [ɪ]	fahren
(to) eat [iː]	ate [et, eɪt]	eaten [iː]	essen; fressen
(to) fall	fell	fallen	(hin)fallen
(to) feed	fed	fed	füttern; ernähren
(to) feel	felt	felt	fühlen, sich fühlen
(to) fight	fought	fought	(be)kämpfen
(to) find	found	found	finden
(to) fly	flew	flown	fliegen
(to) forget	forgot	forgotten	vergessen
(to) freeze	froze	frozen	(ge)frieren; erstarren
(to) get	got	got	bekommen; (sich etwas) holen; werden
(to) give [ɪ]	gave	given [ɪ]	geben
(to) go	went	gone	gehen, fahren
(to) grow	grew	grown	wachsen; anbauen; werden
(to) hang out	hung out [ʌ]	hung out	rumhängen, abhängen
(to) have	had	had	haben; etwas essen
(to) hear [ɪə]	heard [ɜː]	heard	hören
(to) hide	hid	hidden	(sich) verstecken
(to) hit	hit	hit	treffen auf, schlagen, stoßen gegen
(to) hold	held	held	halten
(to) hurt	hurt	hurt	verletzen; wehtun
(to) keep	kept	kept	(be)halten; aufbewahren
(to) kneel	knelt	knelt	knien
(to) know [nəʊ]	knew [njuː]	known [nəʊn]	wissen; kennen

(to) lead [iː]	led [e]	led [e]	führen, leiten
(to) leave	left	left	lassen, zurücklassen, verlassen
(to) let	let	let	lassen
(to) lie	lay	lain	liegen
(to) lose [uː]	lost	lost	verlieren
(to) make	made	made	machen, herstellen
(to) mean	meant	meant	bedeuten, meinen
(to) meet	met	met	treffen; (sich) treffen
(to) pay	paid	paid	(be)zahlen
(to) put	put	put	legen, stellen, stecken
(to) read [iː]	read [e]	read [e]	lesen
(to) rewrite	rewrote	rewritten	neu schreiben, umschreiben
(to) ride [aɪ]	rode	ridden [ɪ]	reiten; (Rad) fahren
(to) ring	rang	rung	läuten, klingeln
(to) rise	rose	risen	(an)steigen; sich erheben
(to) run	ran	run	rennen, laufen
(to) say	said [sed]	said [sed]	sagen
(to) see	saw	seen	sehen
(to) sell	sold	sold	verkaufen
(to) send	sent	sent	senden, schicken
(to) set	set	set	stellen, legen, setzen
(to) sew [əʊ]	sewed [əʊ]	sewn [əʊ]	nähen
(to) shake	shook	shaken	schütteln; zittern
(to) shoot	shot	shot	(er)schießen
(to) show	showed	shown	zeigen
(to) sing	sang	sung	singen
(to) sink	sank	sunk	sinken
(to) sit	sat	sat	sitzen; sich setzen
(to) sleep	slept	slept	schlafen
(to) slide	slid	slid	rutschen; schieben; gleiten (lassen)
(to) speak [iː]	spoke	spoken	sprechen
(to) spend	spent	spent	(Geld) ausgeben, (Zeit) verbringen
(to) spit	spat	spat	(aus)spucken; zischen / fauchen (in gereiztem Ton sagen)
(to) split	split	split	(sich) (auf)teilen, sich (auf)spalten
(to) stand	stood	stood	stehen; sich (hin)stellen
(to) steal	stole	stolen	stehlen, rauben
(to) stick	stuck	stuck	kleben; stecken
(to) swim	swam	swum	schwimmen
(to) take	took	taken	(mit)nehmen; bringen; dauern
(to) teach	taught	taught	lehren, unterrichten
(to) tell	told	told	sagen; erzählen, berichten
(to) think	thought	thought	denken, glauben, meinen
(to) throw	threw [uː]	thrown	werfen
(to) understand	understood	understood	verstehen
(to) upset	upset	upset	jn. erschüttern; jn. aufregen, ärgern

(to) **wake (up)**	**woke**	**woken**	aufwachen; jn. (auf)wecken
(to) **wear** [eə]	**wore** [ɔː]	**worn** [ɔː]	tragen, anhaben (Kleidung)
(to) **win**	**won** [ʌ]	**won** [ʌ]	gewinnen
(to) **write** [aɪ]	**wrote**	**written** [ɪ]	schreiben

Du kannst die unregelmäßigen Verben in Gruppen einteilen, damit das Lernen leichter wird:
- Alle drei Formen sind gleich (chicken verbs): put, put, put – das klingt wie gackernde Hühner
- Zwei Formen sind gleich:
  1 (echo verbs): z. B. bring, brought, brought
  2 (sandwich verbs): become, became, become
- Alle drei Formen sind verschieden: Da gibt es z. B. die cat verbs, bei denen der Klang der drei Formen an das Miau einer Katze erinnert: sing, sang, sung
  Wenn du diese Formen in ähnlichen Zweiergruppen lernst, kannst du sie besser behalten:
  be, was, been – see, saw, seen oder break, broke, broken – speak, spoke, spoken
Finde zu jeder Gruppe weitere Beispiele in der Übersicht auf diesen Seiten 254–256. Lerne am besten immer gleich alle drei Formen der Verben! Du kannst dir dazu einen Chant anhören. 🔊

Continents, countries and regions

continent / country / region	adjective	person	people
Afghanistan [æfˈgænɪstɑːn] Afghanistan	Afghan [ˈæfgæn]	an Afghan	the Afghans
Africa [ˈæfrɪkə] Afrika	African [ˈæfrɪkən]	an African	the Africans
Albania [ælˈbeɪnɪə] Albanien	Albanian [ælˈbeɪnɪən]	an Albanian	the Albanians
America [əˈmerɪkə] Amerika	American [əˈmerɪkən]	an American	the Americans
Asia [ˈeɪʒə] Asien	Asian [ˈeɪʒn]	an Asian	the Asians
Austria [ˈɒstrɪə] Österreich	Austrian [ˈɒstrɪən]	an Austrian	the Austrians
the Bahamas [bəˈhɑːməz] die Bahamas	Bahamian [bəˈheɪmɪən]	a Bahamian	the Bahamians
Bangladesh [bæŋgləˈdeʃ] Bangladesch	Bangladeshi [bæŋgləˈdeʃi]	a Bangladeshi	the Bangladeshis
Bolivia [bəˈlɪvɪə] Bolivien	Bolivian [bəˈlɪvɪən]	a Bolivian	the Bolivians
California [kæləˈfɔːnɪə] Kalifornien	Californian [kæləˈfɔːnɪən]	a Californian	the Californians
Canada [ˈkænədə] Kanada	Canadian [kəˈneɪdɪən]	a Canadian	the Canadians
Caribbean [kærɪˈbiːən] die Karibik	Caribbean [kærɪˈbiːən]	a Carib [ˈkærɪb]	the Caribs
China [ˈtʃaɪnə] China	Chinese [tʃaɪˈniːz]	a Chinese	the Chinese
Cuba [ˈkjuːbə] Kuba	Cuban [ˈkjuːbən]	a Cuban	the Cubans
Czechia, the Czech Republic [tʃek rɪˈpʌblɪk] Tschechien, die Tschechische Republik	Czech [tʃek]	a Czech	the Czechs
Denmark [ˈdenmɑːk] Dänemark	Danish [ˈdeɪnɪʃ]	a Dane [deɪn]	the Danes
England [ˈɪŋglənd] England	English [ˈɪŋglɪʃ]	an Englishman /-woman	the English
Europe [ˈjuərəp] Europa	European [ˌjuərəˈpiːən]	a European	the Europeans
France [frɑːns] Frankreich	French [frentʃ]	a Frenchman /-woman	the French
Germany [ˈdʒɜːmənɪ] Deutschland	German [ˈdʒɜːmən]	a German	the Germans
Great Britain [ˈbrɪtn] Großbritannien	British [ˈbrɪtɪʃ]	a Briton [ˈbrɪtn]	the British

Haiti [ˈheɪti] *Haiti*	Haitian [ˈheɪʃn]	a Haitian	the Haitians
India [ˈɪndiə] *Indien*	Indian [ˈɪndiən]	an Indian	the Indians
Ireland [ˈaɪələnd] *Irland*	Irish [ˈaɪrɪʃ]	an Irishman / -woman	the Irish
Italy [ˈɪtəli] *Italien*	Italian [ɪˈtæliən]	an Italian	the Italians
Jamaica [dʒəˈmeɪkə] *Jamaika*	Jamaican [dʒəˈmeɪkən]	a Jamaican	the Jamaicans
Japan [dʒəˈpæn] *Japan*	Japanese [dʒæpəˈniːz]	a Japanese	the Japanese
Kenya [ˈkenjə] *Kenia*	Kenyan [ˈkenjən]	a Kenyan	the Kenyans
Korea [kəˈriːə] *Korea*	Korean [kəˈriːən]	a Korean	the Koreans
Latin America [latɪn əˈmerɪkə] *Lateinamerika*	Latin American [latɪn əˈmerɪkən]	a Latin American	the Latin Americans
Lebanon [ˈlebənən] *der Libanon*	Lebanese [lebəˈniːz]	a Lebanese	the Lebanese
Lithuania [lɪθjuˈeɪniə] *Litauen*	Lithuanian [lɪθjuˈeɪniən]	a Lithuanian	the Lithuanians
Mexico [ˈmeksɪkəʊ] *Mexiko*	Mexican [ˈmeksɪkən]	a Mexican	the Mexicans
Morocco [məˈrɒkəʊ] *Marokko*	Moroccan [məˈrɒkən]	a Moroccan	the Moroccans
Nepal [nəˈpɔːl] *Nepal*	Nepalese [nepəˈliːz]	a Nepalese	the Nepalese
(the) Netherlands [ˈneðələndz] *die Niederlande, Holland*	Dutch [dʌtʃ]	a Dutchman / -woman	the Dutch
Nigeria [naɪˈdʒɪəriə] *Nigeria*	Nigerian [naɪˈdʒɪəriən]	a Nigerian	the Nigerians
Pakistan [pɑːkɪˈstɑːn] *Pakistan*	Pakistani [pɑːkɪˈstɑːni]	a Pakistani	the Pakistanis
(the) Philippines [ˈfɪlɪpiːnz] *die Philippinen*	Filipino [fɪlɪˈpiːnəʊ]	a Filipino / a Filipina [fɪlɪˈpiːnə]	the Filipinos / Filipinas
Poland [ˈpəʊlənd] *Polen*	Polish [ˈpəʊlɪʃ]	a Pole [pəʊl]	the Poles
Portugal [ˈpɔːtʃʊgl] *Portugal*	Portuguese [pɔːtʃuˈgiːz]	a Portuguese	the Portuguese
Puerto Rico [pwɜːtə ˈriːkəʊ] *Puerto Rico*	Puerto Rican [pwɜːtə ˈriːkən]	a Puerto Rican	the Puerto Ricans
Romania [ruˈmeɪniə] *Rumänien*	Romanian [ruˈmeɪniən]	a Romanian	the Romanians
Russia [ˈrʌʃə] *Russland*	Russian [ˈrʌʃn]	a Russian	the Russians
Scotland [ˈskɒtlənd] *Schottland*	Scottish [ˈskɒtɪʃ]	a Scot [skɒt]	the Scots
South Africa [saʊθ ˈæfrɪkə] *Südafrika*	South African [saʊθ ˈæfrɪkən]	a South African	the South Africans
South America [saʊθ əˈmerɪkə] *Südamerika*	South American [saʊθ əˈmerɪkən]	a South American	the South Americans
Spain [speɪn] *Spanien*	Spanish [ˈspænɪʃ]	Spaniard [ˈspænjəd]	the Spanish / the Spaniards
Turkey [ˈtɜːki]; Türkiye [ˈtʊəkijə] *die Türkei*	Turkish [ˈtɜːkɪʃ]	a Turk [tɜːk]	the Turks
the United Kingdom (the UK) [juˌnaɪtɪd ˈkɪŋdəm, ˌjuːˈkeɪ] *das Vereinigte Königreich (Großbritannien und Nordirland)*	British [ˈbrɪtɪʃ]	a Briton [ˈbrɪtn]	the British
the United States of America (the USA) *die Vereinigten Staaten von Amerika*	American	an American	the Americans
Ukraine [juːˈkreɪn] *die Ukraine*	Ukrainian [juːˈkreɪniən]	a Ukrainian	the Ukrainians
Vietnam [viːetˈnɑːm], [viːetˈnæːm] *Vietnam*	Vietnamese [viːetnəˈmiːz]	a Vietnamese	the Vietnamese
Wales [weɪlz] *Wales*	Welsh [welʃ]	a Welshman / -woman	the Welsh

Ähnliche Wörter im Englischen und Deutschen

Viele englische Wörter ähneln deutschen Wörtern: *a cowboy* = ein Cowboy
Beachte aber die Unterschiede 1–3!

(1) Nomen werden im Deutschen großgeschrieben, aber im Englischen klein.
(2) Manche Wörter haben im Deutschen andere Endungen, aber einen ähnlichen Stamm, z. B. planen – *(to) plan*.
(3) Oft unterscheidet sich die Aussprache. Höre dir die blau markierten Wörter in der App an und sprich sie nach.

active / activity
address
allergic (to)
alphabet
alternative
anonymous
April
article
August
balcony
ball
banana
barbecue
bass
biology
blues
bowling
Brexit
(to) bring
British
browser
bus
butter
cafe
camera
card
character
chocolate
circus
class
classroom
clever
club
coffee
comic
computer
console
cool
corridor
cost / (to) cost
cousin
creative
crown
culture
curry

dance / (to) dance
December
decoration
definition
detail
dialogue
drama
drink / (to) drink
electric
elephant
end / (to) end
England / English
experiment
family
February
film
(to) find
fish
football
friend / friendly
gallery
garage
garden
gold
group
guest
hamster
happy
hello
highlight
horn
house
hungry
idea
information
insect
January
jewels
July
June
karaoke
kebab
kilometre (km)
kiosk
lamp

market
maths
melon
milk
millilitre
minute
modern
moment
museum
music
name
negative
November
number
object
October
online
open
orange
parallel
partner
pasta
pause
perfect
person
photo
picnic
plan / (to) plan
pool
post
poster
problem
project
pronoun
rafting
respect
restaurant
ring
robot
room
rucksack
salad
sandwich
sauce
scene

school
(to) send
September
shopping centre
silver
(to) sink
skateboard
smart
sofa
software
song
sport
star
stop
story
student
summer
supermarket
surfing
sweatshirt
(to) swim
synagogue
test / (to) test
text / (to) text
title
toilet
tomato
top
tourist
tradition
trainer
trick
uniform
vanilla
vegan
vegetarian / veggie
video
warm
website
wind
winner
winter
word
yoghurt
zoo

Typical tasks	Häufige Arbeitsanweisungen
Act out the conversation / song / story.	Führt das Gespräch / das Lied / die Geschichte vor.
Add more ideas / points / …	Füge weitere Ideen / Punkte / … hinzu.
Answer the questions / partner B's questions.	Beantworte die Fragen / Partner Bs Fragen.
Brainstorm ideas.	Sammle spontane Einfälle / Gedanken.
Check the spelling / your answers / ideas (with a partner).	Überprüfe deine Rechtschreibung / Antworten / Ideen (mit einem/r Partner/-in).
Choose the correct answer / word.	Wähle die richtige Antwort / das richtige Wort aus.
Collect ideas / words / phrases / information.	Sammle Ideen / Wörter / Ausdrücke / Informationen.
Compare the pictures / your answers / ideas / …	Vergleiche die Bilder / deine Antworten / Ideen / …
Complete the table / list / sentences / conversation / …	Vervollständige die Tabelle / Liste / Sätze / Unterhaltung / …
Copy the table / list / notes.	Schreibe die Tabelle / die Liste / Notizen ab.
Correct the false / wrong sentences / answers.	Berichtige die falschen Sätze / Antworten.
Describe the picture / your room / …	Beschreibe das Bild / dein Zimmer / …
Discuss with a partner.	Diskutiere mit einem/r Partner/-in.
Explain what … means.	Erkläre was … bedeutet.
Find the answers / the correct / right / wrong words / information / images / …	Finde die Antworten / die richtigen / falschen Wörter / Informationen / Bilder / …
Find reasons for and against …	Finde Gründe, die für und gegen … sprechen.
Finish the sentences.	Vervollständige die Sätze.
Give advice / feedback.	Gib Ratschläge / Rückmeldung.
Give reasons.	Begründe (deine Antwort).
Give your opinion.	Sag / Äußere deine Meinung.
Have a conversation with (two partners).	Unterhalte dich mit (zwei Partner/-innen).
Listen and check / practise / repeat / guess / take notes.	Höre zu und überprüfe / übe / wiederhole / rate / mache Notizen.
Look at the photos / pictures / map / title.	Sieh dir die Fotos / Bilder / Karte / die Überschrift an.
Make groups (of six / … students).	Bildet Gruppen (zu je sechs / … Schüler/-innen).
Make sentences / notes / lists / a mind map.	Fertige Sätze / Notizen / Listen / eine Mindmap an.
Match the sentence parts / the words to/with …	Verbinde die Satzhälften / die Wörter mit …
Put the sentences / dialogue in the correct order.	Bringe die Sätze / den Dialog in die richtige Reihenfolge.
Read the conversation / text / story / article.	Lies den Dialog / Text / die Geschichte / den Artikel.
Swap cards / roles.	Tauscht die Karten / die Rollen.
Take notes (about …).	Mache dir Notizen (zu …).
Take turns.	Wechselt euch ab.
Talk to a partner / in groups.	Sprich mit einem/r Partner/-in / deiner Gruppe.
Tell your partner / the class.	Erzähle es deinem Partner / deiner Partnerin / der Klasse.
Think of (reasons for) …	Überlege dir (Gründe für) …
True, false or not in the text?	Richtig, falsch oder nicht im Text?
Use your notes / the words in a) / keywords / the information (in the table).	Benutze deine Notizen / die Wörter aus Aufgabe a) / Stichworte / die Informationen (aus der Tabelle).
Watch part 1 / scene 1 / all the film / the video.	Sieh dir Teil 1 / Szene 1 / den ganzen Film / das Video an.
Work alone / in pairs / in groups.	Arbeite allein / in Partnerarbeit / in Gruppen.
Work out the meaning of (the words).	Finde die Bedeutung (der Wörter) heraus.
Write the correct answers / sentences / questions.	Schreibe die richtigen Antworten / Sätze / Fragen (auf).
Write a short description / a blog post / an ending to the story …	Schreibe eine kurze Beschreibung / einen Blogeintrag / ein Ende für die Geschichte …

Titelbild
Statue: stock.adobe.com/Oleksandr Dibrova; Kinder: Chocolate Films; Hintergrund: stock.adobe.com/wajan

Illustrationen
Cornelsen / Carlos Borrell Eiköter: S. 140/A, Umschlaginnenseite hinten (U3);
Cornelsen / Harald Ardeias: S. 20, S. 22, S. 26/u., S. 27, S. 28, S. 29, S. 30/o., S. 36, S. 43, S. 48/o. l., S. 53, S. 54/u., S. 80, S. 88/m. l., S. 89/o., S. 95, S. 96/o., S. 98/u., S. 99, S. 100, S. 101/o., S. 106/u., S. 118/o., S. 137/u., S. 139/o.;
Cornelsen / Inhouse/Josephine Bienert-Köhler: S. 154;
Cornelsen / Irina Zinner: S. 163, S. 164, S. 165, S. 169, S. 170, S. 174, S. 175, S. 176, S. 185, S. 186, S. 189, S. 190, S. 191;
Cornelsen / Peter Kast bearbeitet von Carlos Borrell Eiköter: S. 264

Abbildungen
S. 2: PEFC Deutschland e.V.; **S. 4:** stock.adobe.com/f11photo; **S. 5:** stock.adobe.com/SeanPavonePhoto; **S. 6:** Shutterstock.com/Daniel M Ernst; **S. 7:** stock.adobe.com/Aerial Film Studio; **S. 8:** stock.adobe.com/surangaw; **S. 10/Hintergrund:** stock.adobe.com/ii-graphics; **S. 10/m. l.:** stock.adobe.com/KBDESIGNPHOTO; **S. 10/u. l.:** mauritius images/Cavan Images; **S. 10/u. r.:** mauritius images/Maxim Kalitvintsev/Alamy Stock Photos; **S. 11/m.:** Shutterstock.com/Photomika-com; **S. 11/o.:** stock.adobe.com/oscity; **S. 11/u.:** stock.adobe.com/Terri Cage; **S. 12/1:** stock.adobe.com/ii-graphics; **S. 12/2:** Shutterstock/Lucky-photographer; **S. 12/3:** stock.adobe.com/Orhan Çam; **S. 12/4:** stock.adobe.com/rdnzl; **S. 12/u./Emoji:** stock.adobe.com/Cali6ro; **S. 13/10:** stock.adobe.com/Olga Yastremska and Leonid Yastremskiy/New Africa; **S. 13/5:** Cornelsen/Klein & Halm; Deutschland: Shutterstock.com/vectorlight; USA: stock.adobe.com/ii-graphics; **S. 13/6:** stock.adobe.com/alexlmx; **S. 13/7:** Shutterstock.com/Svet foto; **S. 13/8:** Shutterstock.com/Prostock-studio; **S. 13/9:** Shutterstock.com/TeddyandMia; **S. 14/l.:** Cornelsen/Chocolate Films; **S. 14/r.:** Shutterstock.com/Drazen Zigic; **S. 15/l.:** Shutterstock.com/MJTH; **S. 15/r. o.:** Shutterstock.com/SNEHIT PHOTO; **S. 15/r. u.:** Cornelsen/Chocolate Films; **S. 16/A:** Digital Learning Ass. Ltd.; **S. 16/B:** Digital Learning Ass. Ltd.; **S. 16/C:** Digital Learning Ass. Ltd.; **S. 17/D:** Digital Learning Ass. Ltd.; **S. 17/E:** Digital Learning Ass. Ltd.; **S. 17/F:** Digital Learning Ass. Ltd.; **S. 18/l.:** stock.adobe.com/susanne2688; **S. 18/m. m.:** stock.adobe.com/f11photo; **S. 18/m. u.:** stock.adobe.com/magann; **S. 18/r. m.:** stock.adobe.com/dell; **S. 18/r. o.:** Rechts: stock.adobe.com/Krakenimages.com; Links: Cornelsen/Chocolate Films; **S. 19:** stock.adobe.com/Grandbrothers; **S. 19/m./Emoji:** stock.adobe.com/Cali6ro; **S. 21:** stock.adobe.com/twinsterphoto; **S. 23/l.:** dpa Picture-Alliance/CJ Rivera/Invision/AP; **S. 23/r.:** imago sport/@guelbergoes; **S. 24/2. v. o.:** stock.adobe.com/Julianna Olah; **S. 24/3. v. o.:** imago sport; **S. 24/o.:** stock.adobe.com/steven hendricks; **S. 24/u.:** stock.adobe.com/CreativePhotography; **S. 25/l. u.:** stock.adobe.com/Krakenimages.com; **S. 25/r. m.:** stock.adobe.com/Tixel; **S. 25/r. u.:** stock.adobe.com/ninamunha; **S. 26/o.:** mauritius images/Felix Lipov/Alamy Stock Photos; **S. 30/u.:** stock.adobe.com/Seventyfour; **S. 31:** Digital Learning Ass. Ltd.; **S. 32/o.:** stock.adobe.com/Drazen; **S. 32/u.:** stock.adobe.com/littleny; **S. 34/l. o. + m.:** Cornelsen/Chocolate Films; **S. 34/l. u.:** stock.adobe.com/Krakenimages.com; **S. 34/r. u.:** mauritius images/Robertharding/Alamy Stock Photos; **S. 35/o.:** Shutterstock.com/Ground Picture; **S. 35/u.:** stock.adobe.com/Fototocam; **S. 37/A:** Shutterstock.com/Denise Kappa; **S. 37/B:** Shutterstock.com/Pond Saksit; **S. 37/C:** Shutterstock.com/NATNN; **S. 37/D:** Shutterstock.com/Billion Photos; **S. 37/E:** Shutterstock.com/4 PM production; **S. 37/u.:** stock.adobe.com/ManuPadilla; **S. 38/Fahne:** stock.adobe.com/valvectors; **S. 38/United:** Ungermeyer; **S. 38/m.:** mauritius images/alamy stock photo/John Muggenborg; **S. 38/o.:** Cornelsen/Chocolate Films; **S. 39/l. m.:** mauritius images/Richard Levine/Alamy Stock Photos; **S. 39/l. u.:** mauritius images/Sergey Yatunin/Alamy Stock Photos; **S. 39/r. m.:** mauritius images/ZUMA Press, Inc./Alamy Stock Photos; **S. 39/r. u.:** mauritius images/Michael Marquand/Alamy Stock Photos; **S. 40/l. m.:** stock.adobe.com/James; **S. 40/l. u.:** stock.adobe.com/ange1011; **S. 40/r. m.:** stock.adobe.com/Raanan; **S. 40/r. u.:** stock.adobe.com/vectorwin; **S. 41/2. v. o.:** stock.adobe.com/Tierney; **S. 41/3. v. o.:** Imago Stock & People GmbH; **S. 41/4. v. o.:** stock.adobe.com/SeanPavonePhoto; **S. 41/5. v. o.:** Shutterstock.com/heymynameismark; **S. 41/o.:** stock.adobe.com/Sanja; **S. 41/u.:** stock.adobe.com/Charles; **S. 42/m.:** Imago Stock & People GmbH; **S. 42/u.:** stock.adobe.com/Krakenimages.com; **S. 45:** stock.adobe.com/Studio Romantic; **S. 46/A:** Digital Learning Ass. Ltd.; **S. 46/B:** Shutterstock.com/Sean Pavone; **S. 46/C:** stock.adobe.com/Joe O'Neill; **S. 46/D:** Shutterstock.com/Khairil Azhar Junos; **S. 47/E:** stock.adobe.com/SeanPavonePhoto; **S. 47/F:** Digital Learning Ass. Ltd.; **S. 47/l.:** Shutterstock.com/Peter Hermes Furian; **S. 48/o. m.:** Shutterstock.com/fizkes; **S. 48/o. r.:** stock.adobe.com/Valerii Honcharuk; **S. 48/u.:** Shutterstock.com/Drazen Zigic; **S. 49/m.:** stock.adobe.com/digitalskillet1; **S. 49/u.:** stock.adobe.com/StockPhotoPro; **S. 50/l.:** mauritius images/Archive Pics/Alamy Stock Photos; **S. 50/r.:** mauritius images/JT Vintage; **S. 51:** Imago Stock & People GmbH/TT; **S. 52:** Depositphotos/Leonard Zhukovsky; **S. 54/m.:** stock.adobe.com/Lynne Ann Mitchell; **S. 54/o.:** Shutterstock.com/GTS Productions; **S. 55/1:** stock.adobe.com/myviewpoint; **S. 55/2:** stock.adobe.com/myviewpoint; **S. 55/3:** stock.adobe.com/FomaA; **S. 55/4:** Shutterstock.com/Brent Hofacker; **S. 56/l.:** mauritius images/Paul Wood/Alamy Stock Photos; **S. 56/r.:** Imago Stock & People GmbH/imago/ZUMA Press; **S. 56/m./Emoji:** stock.adobe.com/Cali6ro; **S. 57:** mauritius images/Laura Prieto/Alamy Stock Photos; **S. 57/u./Emojis:** stock.adobe.com/Cali6ro; **S. 58/1:** Shutterstock.com/Suzanne Tucker; **S. 58/2:** Shutterstock.com/Rasica; **S. 58/3:** stock.adobe.com/MIKHAIL;

Dean; **S. 119/m.**: stock.adobe.com/duaneups; **S. 119/o.**: stock.adobe.com/elvis901; **S. 120/Amy**: Cornelsen/Chocolate Films; **S. 120/Diego**: Shutterstock.com/MJTH; **S. 120/Tiana**: Cornelsen/Chocolate Films; **S. 120/Troy**: Shutterstock.com/Drazen Zigic; **S. 120/o./Emoji**: stock.adobe.com/Cali6ro; **S. 120/u. l.**: stock.adobe.com/Usmanify; **S. 120/u. r.**: Shutterstock.com/Mariia Boiko; **S. 121/o.**: stock.adobe.com/AkuAku; **S. 121/u. l.**: stock.adobe.com/Maurice; **S. 121/u. r.**: Shutterstock.com/Gorodenkoff; **S. 122/o./Emojis**: stock.adobe.com/Cali6ro; **S. 122/Amy + Tiana u. r.**: Cornelsen/Chocolate Films; **S. 122/Diego**: Shutterstock.com/MJTH; **S. 122/Troy**: Shutterstock.com/Drazen Zigic; **S. 123/l.**: "Swimming in the desert" by Alvaro Ron, USA, 2017, 18 Min/interfilmBerlin Management GmbH; **S. 123/r.**: stock.adobe.com/infadel; **S. 125/l.**: Shutterstock.com/Alliance Images; **S. 125/m.**: mauritius images/Jeffrey Isaac Greenberg 19+/Alamy Stock Photos; **S. 125/r.**: stock.adobe.com/© James Baker 2007/James Baker 2007/James; **S. 126/A**: stock.adobe.com/Aerial Film Studio; **S. 126/B**: stock.adobe.com/Michal; **S. 126/C**: Shutterstock.com/Tint Media; **S. 126/D**: Shutterstock.com/frank_peters; **S. 127/o.**: mauritius images/World Book Inc.; **S. 127/m./Emojis**: stock.adobe.com/Cali6ro; **S. 127/u.**: stock.adobe.com/Zack Frank; **S. 128**: stock.adobe.com/Hanyun; **S. 129**: Shutterstock.com/Gorodenkoff; **S. 130/Fahne**: stock.adobe.com/valvectors; **S. 130/United**: Ungermeyer; **S. 130/m. l.**: imago sport/imago images/ZUMA Wire; **S. 130/m. r.**: mauritius images/Media Punch Inc/Alamy Stock Photos; **S. 130/o. r.**: stock.adobe.com/Krakenimages.com; **S. 130/u.**: Imago Stock & People GmbH; **S. 131/m.**: mauritius images/Lucy Clark/Alamy Stock Photos; **S. 131/o.**: mauritius images/Alamy Stock Photos; **S. 131/u.**: stock.adobe.com/Анна Д; **S. 132/Fahne**: stock.adobe.com/valvectors; **S. 132/United**: Ungermeyer; **S. 132/m. l.**: stock.adobe.com/René Stevens; **S. 132/m. m.**: Shutterstock.com/Richard Thornton; **S. 132/m. r.**: Shutterstock.com/Simone Hogan; **S. 132/o.**: Cornelsen/Chocolate Films; **S. 133/l.**: Shutterstock.com/Ebtikar; **S. 133/r.**: Shutterstock.com/Sudowoodo; **S. 135/A**: Shutterstock.com/kropic1; **S. 135/B**: stock.adobe.com/f11 photo; **S. 135/C**: Shutterstock.com/Image Source Trading Ltd; **S. 135/D**: Imago Stock & People GmbH/imago images/ZUMA Press; **S. 135/E**: stock.adobe.com/JFL Photography; **S. 136**: stock.adobe.com/Krakenimages.com; **S. 137/m.**: stock.adobe.com/LIGHTFIELD STUDIOS; **S. 137/o.**: mauritius images/ZUMA Press, Inc./Alamy Stock Photos; **S. 138/m.**: Shutterstock.com/photomaster; **S. 138/u.**: Imago Stock & People GmbH; **S. 140/B**: stock.adobe.com/R.M. Nunes; **S. 140/C**: stock.adobe.com/Facto Photo; **S. 141/D**: stock.adobe.com/surangaw; **S. 141/E**: stock.adobe.com/peteleclerc; **S. 141/F**: stock.adobe.com/Jim; **S. 141/G**: stock.adobe.com/slowmotiongli; **S. 141/H**: Digital Learning Ass. Ltd.; **S. 142/l.**: stock.adobe.com/surangaw; **S. 142/m. r.**: Imago Stock & People GmbH/ZUMA Press; **S. 142/u. r.**: Shutterstock.com/Gary A Corcoran Arts; **S. 143/m. l.**: stock.adobe.com/Sergey Novikov; **S. 143/m. r.**: stock.adobe.com/Cavan; **S. 143/o.**: mauritius images/nature picture library; **S. 143/u.**: imago sport; **S. 145**: Shutterstock.com/Elsa Nur Afiana; **S. 146**: Shutterstock.com/IIIerlok_xolms; **S. 147**: Shutterstock.com/Red Vector; **S. 148/m./Emojis**: stock.adobe.com/Cali6ro; **S. 149/m./Emojis**: stock.adobe.com/Cali6ro; **S. 150**: CartoonStock/Phil Juliano; **S. 152**: Shutterstock.com/Kateryna Onyshchuk; **S. 153**: "Swimming in the desert" by Alvaro Ron, USA, 2017, 18 Min/interfilmBerlin Management GmbH; **S. 158/o.**: Shutterstock.com/fizkes; **S. 158/u.**: stock.adobe.com/babimu; **S. 159**: Shutterstock.com/Iakov Filimonov; **S. 180/m.**: stock.adobe.com/cherryandbees; **S. 180/o. l.**: Shutterstock.com/Iryna Inshyna; **S. 180/o. r.**: stock.adobe.com/isarawut; **S. 180/u. l.**: stock.adobe.com/Zamrznuti tonovi; **S. 180/u. r.**: stock.adobe.com/Antonioguillem; **S. 181/m. l.**: stock.adobe.com/Athena; **S. 181/m. m.**: stock.adobe.com/ValentinValkov; **S. 181/m. r.**: stock.adobe.com/klikk; **S. 181/u. l.**: stock.adobe.com/PNG Aom.WingWon; **S. 181/u. m.**: stock.adobe.com/AGCuesta; **S. 181/u. r.**: stock.adobe.com/Dimitrius; **S. 182/l. 2. v. o.**: stock.adobe.com/Fotograf; **S. 182/l. 3. v. o.**: stock.adobe.com/Generative AI; **S. 182/l. o.**: stock.adobe.com/Yuliia; **S. 182/l. u.**: stock.adobe.com/ugljesaras; **S. 182/r. 2. v. o.**: stock.adobe.com/oleg525; **S. 182/r. 3. v. o.**: Shutterstock.com/Alaskagirl8821; **S. 182/r. o.**: Shutterstock.com/lax15las; **S. 182/r. u.**: Shutterstock.com/FedBul; **S. 183/2. v. o. l.**: stock.adobe.com/photoschmidt 2017/photoschmidt; **S. 183/2. v. o. m.**: stock.adobe.com/Gorodenkoff; **S. 183/2. v. o. r.**: stock.adobe.com/Minerva Studio; **S. 183/3. v. o. l.**: Shutterstock.com/Gorodenkoff; **S. 183/3. v. o. m.**: stock.adobe.com/Monkey Business; **S. 183/3. v. o. r.**: Shutterstock.com/DC Studio; **S. 183/4. v. o. l.**: Shutterstock.com/belushi; **S. 183/4. v. o. m.**: stock.adobe.com/StockPhotoPro; **S. 183/4. v. o. r.**: stock.adobe.com/Unique Vision; **S. 183/o. l.**: Shutterstock.com/Drazen Zigic; **S. 183/o. m.**: stock.adobe.com/Halfpoint; **S. 183/o. r.**: stock.adobe.com/Rido; **S. 183/u. l.**: stock.adobe.com/Atstock Productions; **S. 183/u. m.**: stock.adobe.com/New Africa; **S. 183/u. r.**: stock.adobe.com/oneinchpunch; **S. 193**: stock.adobe.com/Eastman Arts; **S. 194**: stock.adobe.com/Nicholas J. Klein; **S. 195**: Shutterstock.com/Ico Maker; **S. 196**: stock.adobe.com/moodboard; **S. 197**: stock.adobe.com/dbvirago; **S. 198/m.**: Shutterstock.com/Tobik; **S. 198/o.**: Shutterstock.com/nelea33; **S. 198/u.**: stock.adobe.com/innafoto2017; **S. 199**: stock.adobe.com/FSEID; **S. 200/m.**: stock.adobe.com/fizkes; **S. 200/o.**: stock.adobe.com/Dmytro; **S. 200/u.**: Shutterstock.com/John Arehart; **S. 201**: stock.adobe.com/Leonid Andronov; **S. 202**: Shutterstock.com/Perfect Vectors; **S. 203/o.**: stock.adobe.com/Wattana; **S. 203/u.**: stock.adobe.com/Shotmedia; **S. 204/o.**: stock.adobe.com/GalleryGlider; **S. 204/u.**: stock.adobe.com/MissesJones; **S. 205/2. v. o.**: Shutterstock.com/Ruslan Semichev; **S. 205/3. v. o.**: Shutterstock.com/JADA photos; **S. 205/4. v. o.**: Shutterstock.com/Polina Persikova; **S. 205/5. v. o.**: stock.adobe.com/drummatra; **S. 205/o.**: Imago Stock & People GmbH/depositphotos; **S. 205/u.**: stock.adobe.com/Iryna; **S. 206/m.**: stock.adobe.com/Vladimir Melnikov; **S. 206/o.**: Shutterstock.com/sumire8; **S. 206/u.**: Shutterstock.com/mike_expert; **S. 207**: Shutterstock.com/tatiana80; **S. 208**: Shutterstock.com/Motimo; **S. 209**: Shutterstock.com/rigsbyphoto; **S. 210**: stock.adobe.com/guruXOX; **S. 211**: stock.adobe.com/

digitalskillet1; **S. 212/o.:** stock.adobe.com/Savo Ilic; **S. 212/u.:** stock.adobe.com/shabbir; **S. 213/o.:** stock.adobe.com/Olga Yastremska, New Africa, Africa Studio/New Africa; **S. 213/u.:** Shutterstock.com/Dan Thornberg; **S. 215:** stock.adobe.com/LIGHTFIELD STUDIOS; **S. 217:** stock.adobe.com/Yuval Helfman; **S. 219/m.:** stock.adobe.com/EmmaStock; **S. 219/o.:** stock.adobe.com/blueringmedia; **S. 219/u.:** stock.adobe.com/Renato; **S. 220/o.:** stock.adobe.com/ding; **S. 220/2. v. o.:** Shutterstock.com/a2l; **S. 220/m. l.:** stock.adobe.com/Chaded; **S. 220/m. r.:** stock.adobe.com/Taras Vykhopen; **S. 221/m.:** stock.adobe.com/Rosie; **S. 221/o.:** stock.adobe.com/leszekglasner; **S. 222/m.:** stock.adobe.com/Alex Mit; **S. 222/u.:** stock.adobe.com/photobboy/Pawel Pajor; **S. 224/2. v. u.:** stock.adobe.com/Carlos Caetano; **S. 224/m.:** Shutterstock.com/Apolinariy; **S. 224/u.:** stock.adobe.com/Dan; **S. 225/o.:** stock.adobe.com/Mr image; **S. 225/u.:** stock.adobe.com/FranCortizo; **S. 253/u.:** stock.adobe.com/Hanna

Textquellen
S. 38/u.: *Helaina's story: What the 20 Years Since 9/11 Have Been Like For a Survivor* by Helaina Hovitz in Teen Vogue; https://www.teenvogue.com/story/what-the-20-years-since-911-have-been-like-for-a-survivor, September 10 2021; gekürzt und leicht verändert
S. 98–101: *Hartford moves* (chapter 14) by Marc Proulx, Cornelsen 2022, gekürzt

Liedquellen
S. 102/u.: *Fifteen:* Universal/MCA Music Publishing GmbH, Berlin. Text: Taylor Swift;
S. 116/u.: *Run with the wolves:* Songtrust Blvd./St. Music Europe Ltd. Text: Ben Wylen/Joseph V Pisapia/Zaragoza Raye (Ausschnitt); **S. 138/u.:** *Run with the wolves:* Songtrust Blvd./St. Music Europe Ltd. Text: Ben Wylen/Joseph V Pisapia/Zaragoza Raye

Datenquellen
S. 20: Das Diagramm basiert auf Daten des Unites States Census Bureau, U.S. Department of Commerce: B16001 Language Spoken at Home by Ability to Speak English for the Population 5 Years and Over, https://data.census.gov/table/ACSDT1Y2022.B16001?t=Language%20Spoken%20at%20Home&g=160XX00US3651000 (Zugriff 29.07.2024);
S. 124: Das Diagramm basiert auf Daten des Frontline Wildfire Defense, https://www.frontlinewildfire.com/wildfire-news-and-resources/california-wildfires-history-statistics/ (Zugriff am 10.10.2024);
S. 128: Das Diagramm basiert auf Daten des U.S. Fish and Wildlife Service, https://www.fws.gov/media/condor-population-graph-1980-2022 (Zugriff 06.03.2025);
S. 139: Das Diagramm basiert auf Daten des United States Census Bureau (2020 Census), https://www.census.gov/library/stories/2023/10/2020-census-dhc-a-aian-population.html (Zugriff 22.08.2024);
S. 140: Die Zahlen basieren auf Daten von Statistics Canada: www.statcan.gc.ca:
41 million: Canada's population clock (real-time model) (statcan.gc.ca) (Zugriff 10.09.2024)